MAKE WE MERRY
MORE AND LESS

Make We Merry More and Less

An Anthology of Medieval English Popular Literature

Selected and introduced by Douglas Gray
Edited by Jane Bliss

https://www.openbookpublishers.com

The Faculty of English, University of Oxford, has generously contributed to this publication.

ISBN Paperback: 978-1-78374-710-8
ISBN Hardback: 978-1-78374-711-5
ISBN Digital (PDF): 978-1-78374-712-2
ISBN Digital ebook (epub): 978-1-78374-713-9
ISBN Digital ebook (mobi): 978-1-78374-714-6
ISBN Digital (XML): 978-1-78374-715-3
DOI: 10.11647/OBP.0170

Cover image: Jeanie Dean from John Francis Waller *et al.*, *Pictures From English Literature* (1870), p. 142, https://www.flickr.com/photos/internetarchivebookimages/14801723273/

Cover design: Anna Gatti.

Contents

Acknowledgements[1]

My first thanks must go to Dr Nick Gray, who kindly allowed me access to his father's files. I thank the team at Open Book Publishers, and their readers. I thank the Faculty of English, University of Oxford, who have generously contributed to this publication. In addition I am indebted to the following, for timely advice when consulted on various matters arising in this work:

David Atkinson, Richard Beadle, Ronald Black, Daron Burrows, Vincent Gillespie, Linda Gowans, Heidi Joeken, Don Kennedy, Matthew Kilburn, Kylie Murray, Ad Putter, Samantha Rayner, Gillian Rogers, Frances White, and many helpful librarians. Finally I thank my best friend and partner Quentin Miller for love, support, and technical help.

1   Gray left a heading for acknowledgements, but listed none; I wish I could thank his friends and advisers as he would so generously have done. I have compiled a list of scholars and friends who deserve my own hearty thanks.

Abbreviations

ANTS	Anglo-Norman Text Society
DMH	*Dictionary of Medieval Heroes* (Gerritsen, van Melle, Guest)
EETS	Early English Text Society; ES Extra Series, OS Original Series, SS Supplementary Series
MED	*Middle English Dictionary* https://t.co/etTLCLyAe5
OCCL	*Oxford Concise Companion to Classical Literature* (Howatson, Chilvers)
ODS	*Oxford Dictionary of Saints* (Farmer)
OED	*Oxford English Dictionary*
PFMS	*Percy Folio Manuscript* (eds Hales and Furnivall)
Rymes	[Robyn] *Rymes of Robyn Hood* (Dobson and Taylor)
Whiting	*Proverbs, Sentences, and Proverbial Phrases* (Whiting and Whiting)

Editor's Preface

Douglas Gray was planning this anthology to be a companion volume to his *Simple Forms*, but he left it unfinished at his death: the Introduction, and presentation of selections (including head-notes), were more or less complete but there were no notes or bibliography. The file vouchsafed to posterity was headed 'Master — edited so far'; it has been possible to identify and locate most, if not all, of the references.[1] For example, he does not say where he gets his extracts from Walter Map's *De Nugis Curialium*, and they do not correspond to the well-known translation by M. R. James. However, he says in an earlier anthology that he prefers to make his own new translations (however excellent the existing ones);[2] some stories in this match the ones in the present volume, so it is fair to deduce that he re-used his own translations. Further, he said then that he wished to keep costs down; a reason to believe he made his own transcriptions from manuscripts in some if not all cases as well. There are a number of editions of, for example, the *Paston Letters*; it is not possible to identify which he used. Therefore the word 'editor' in my footnotes will always mean the editor of the text in question (possibly Gray himself; otherwise the editor of any text as detailed in

---

1   In order to keep notes to a helpful minimum I have indicated one or two references for each, to enable readers to explore further if they wish; it has been impossible to ascertain Gray's sources.

2   *From The Norman Conquest* (2011), pp. vii–iii; extracts from *De Nugis* are on pp. 81–94. Compare versions in Walter Map's *De Nugis Curialium*, trans. M. R. James (1923).

the Bibliography); I refer to Gray by name, and to myself as editor of this book as little as possible.

Make We Merry is a long book, and every selection has been included as Gray set them out. It would be possible to shorten it by cutting some of the pieces, but we have decided not to do so: the selection represents the range and depth of Gray's vision, and there will be no more from him now.

The order of chapters, as he left them, corresponded very closely with those in *Simple Forms* although it could not be an exact match. Apart from reversing Ballads and Romances to match the earlier book, I have not conflated or divided any chapters; the chapters have been left in his order, as providing the closest possible 'companion'.

Sources are indicated as briefly as possible in footnotes; the rationale has been to identify an anthology or other source-book for each, because this is how Gray worked, and cite one or perhaps two for each. These anthologies provide a wealth of context and other information that readers may consult; footnotes can thus be kept brief and unobtrusive. Only where a convenient source is not available have *IMEV* numbers been used. But *IMEV* is an index, not an anthology; putting these numbers for every selection would duplicate information and make for cumbersome notes.

Because it has proved impossible to identify his sources with any certainty, footnotes indicate where the texts may easily be found (in most cases).[3] Having no access to Gray's library, I would naturally search my own shelves, libraries, and the internet; then choose among what is available for readers to follow up. I have edited as lightly as possible, so as to preserve the Master's style, but there were naturally a few lapses to correct and ambiguities to smooth out. Where it was impossible to locate what he was thinking of when he marked [nt] for notes to be added, these have been explored as far as practicable or silently omitted. In order to keep notes to a minimum, I have not given references for every single book or work that Gray mentions;[4] I have identified only where the text in question, that is, the passage selected for inclusion, may be found. Online versions of books have been added

---

3   What is easily available for one reader may be more difficult for another, therefore any selection is going to seem arbitrary to some. More than one source is possible for most of the texts.
4   Some of these may be identified in the introductions to cited texts; for example, all known references to Robin Hood in medieval literature.

to the Bibliography where available.[5] Among secondary sources, only the names mentioned in his text have been sought out and listed. It would be possible to replace a number of Gray's references with more recent works, but we prefer to present the book as closely as possible as he left it, and not strive to update it (except in a few special cases, where an up-to-date reference may obviate the need for an over-long footnote).

Given what has been explained above, it will be impossible to ascertain whether the books Gray used (if he did) are still in copyright; some may be, others very probably not. Furthermore, Gray may have made his own transcriptions from manuscripts.

A note about proverbs: Gray has scattered dozens of proverbs throughout his text, many but not all of them identified in Whiting's compendium. I have checked most of these, and he made very few errors (some may simply be copying errors). Therefore, since Whiting is very easy to use, providing clear headwords and an index, I have not attempted to identify every single example of a proverb or what might count as proverbial.

Further, a few of his glosses, which were so copious as to verge on the intrusive, have been deleted on the assumption that most non-specialists likely to use this book can read Middle English words if their spelling approximates to the modern.

Titles of books and so on, and (conventionally) words and phrases in Latin, are printed in italic type.

It may also be useful at this point to identify the famous Percy Folio (*PFMS*), mentioned *passim* below: it is a folio book of English ballads used by Thomas Percy to compile his *Reliques of Ancient Poetry* (see Bibliography). Although compiled in the seventeenth century, some of the material goes back well into the twelfth.

Treatment of texts:[6] to enable modern readers to read without constantly having to consult a glossary or dictionary, glosses are placed on the page with translation of longer passages placed in footnotes. Annotation and bibliographical references are kept to a minimum.

---

5   The online versions supplied cannot always be the same editions as cited in this
     book; they are added for readers' convenience and general interest.
6   This paragraph was written by Gray, his only preface. His 'gentle modernization'
     of spellings makes it even more difficult to know what source he used for any given
     text.

Punctuation is modernized where appropriate, and there is some gentle modernization of spellings: u/v, i/j, and unfamiliar letter forms thorn and yogh.

Using Gray's own unconsciously prophetic words (although my work has been far less extensive than his in that case),[7] I should like to dedicate the volume to the memory of this most humane of medievalists.

7　Preface, to *Middle English Literature* (J. A. W. Bennett, edited and completed by Douglas Gray), p. vi.

Introduction

The nineteenth century saw the appearance of a number of anthologies of medieval English and Scottish popular literature, from Ritson's *Pieces of ancient popular poetry* to Hazlitt's *Remains*.[1] There have not been many modern attempts, which suggests a waning of enthusiasm. There is probably no single simple explanation for this: in part it may be due to academic distrust of areas where the material seems to be uncertain, and its relationships and developments even more so; partly to the increasing specialism of literary studies and a growing separation between literary and folklore studies. Although there have been some very valuable contributions from the later nineteenth and twentieth centuries, modern English departments rarely devote much time to popular literature in their medieval courses. Even ballads, 'rediscovered' in the eighteenth century, rarely appear in lectures on medieval English literature. But possibly an even greater problem has been the real difficulties which are presented by the notion of 'popular literature' and of attempts to define or illustrate it.

In making this anthology I have used, as a general definition, the following (boldly adapted from the suggestion offered in Neuburg's *Popular Literature*, a fine study which runs from the beginning of printing to the year 1897): 'popular literature is what the unsophisticated reader or hearer was given for pleasure and instruction'.[2] Obviously there is much room for questioning or disagreement with such a very general description, and even more in deciding what we might include in

---

1   Ritson, *Pieces of ancient popular poetry* (1791); Hazlitt, *Remains of the popular poetry of England* (4 vols, 1864–6).
2   Victor E. Neuburg, *Popular literature* (1977); and see Gray's *Simple Forms*, p. 240.

    https://doi.org/10.11647/OBP.0170.12

popular literature, and with the criteria we use for inclusion or exclusion. Nor are the related questions — who wrote it? and who read or heard it? — without problems.

It is possible to give a general description of Middle English popular literature, but the details often remain uncertain. It is clear from many references in our surviving texts that there was an extensive oral 'folk' literature. This is now lost, except for what is preserved in scraps and snippets in those texts. Poets and moralists will occasionally give us the title of a popular song or a stanza from it; examples are to be found throughout this anthology. These can give us glimpses into this lost world; and moreover, we can find patterns and plots from oral folktales underlying some of our written narratives. But these 'glimpses of ghosts' are not really numerous or substantial enough to make an anthology from. However, they remind us of a very important point: that though this world is lost to us it was not lost to the literate writers of the period, and it continued for centuries. This world was not a static one: stories and songs were composed, handed on, revised and changed, and this probably had been the case for centuries. The 'simple forms' of this oral literature — folktales, narratives, wisdom literature (proverbs or riddles), and songs, dances and dramatic performances — had already left their mark on the literature of the ancient world: animal fables (from Aesop onwards), merry tales like the Widow of Ephesus,[3] even 'romances' like Apollonius of Tyre (a favourite story in the Middle Ages)[4] and Greek romances. Based on the findings of modern scholarship, on later examples from 'traditional' societies, and on the evidence of written Middle English texts which seem to be close to the oral literature (or perhaps conscious imitations of it), we can make an informed guess as to the stylistic characteristics of this oral literature, such as: a simple and direct vocabulary, an 'anonymous' objective style, the use of repetition and recapitulation for emphasis, with the oral performance rather than literary rhetorical arts controlling the audience's emotions, and tending to produce a dramatic style of narration, 'letting the action unfold itself in event and speech'.[5] An oral poet or storyteller would usually have a

---

3   Known as *Vidua*, this story is usually told against women; it is best known in the collection *Seven Sages of Rome*. See the Midland Version, ed. Whitelock; there are several versions), pp. 70–4.

4   See first *Gesta Romanorum*, Swan and Hooper, pp. 259–99; where it is entitled 'Of Temporal Tribulation'.

5   Gerould, *The Ballad of Tradition*, p. 11.

close relationship with his or her immediate audience, and would be sensitive to local conditions, but not deeply influenced by prevailing 'literary' fashions. However, it existed alongside a growing body of written literature with which it could relate.

We can apply the term 'popular' to a large body of literature occupying an intermediate position between the lost oral literature and the sophisticated literature written by literate 'learned' writers for society's élite readers. This popular literature was for the entertainment and instruction of humble folk, some partly literate, some not at all. Our knowledge of it is dependent on surviving manuscripts and printed books. Perhaps we may sense some general stylistic changes over time, from the Early Middle English Rawlinson songs (which seem very close to their oral antecedents)[6] to the sometimes more literary style of some items in the early sixteenth-century manuscript of Richard Hill,[7] but it is difficult to generalise about 'development'. The spread of literacy during the period seems to have encouraged the development of what was to become the 'reading class' of later times. However, most popular literature was for a long time enjoyed through performance — by reading aloud, reciting, or singing — in streets, halls, and meeting places. It was performed by a large number of 'entertainers': mostly anonymous, like the ballad writers and singers of later centuries, written by some of them, and by others who recorded stories and songs, and retold or recreated works from the literary élite. Some of them were capable of translating works from French; some were probably clerics, but in close touch with their layfolk and with popular culture, parish clerks or preaching friars; some perhaps scribes or others who worked at the edges of manuscript production. Others, no doubt, were would-be authors, professionals or semi-professionals, sometimes hacks (like their successors in modern times), but sometimes writers with genuine literary talent. Many of them were, no doubt, more aware of élite literary trends and fashions than the makers and performers of oral folk literature. This intermediate body of literature is 'popular' by destination, intended for the entertainment and the information of simple folk, and also 'popular' by origin, coming from the 'people', from writers within that group or close to it.

---

6   *The Songs of Rawlinson MS. C 813*, eds Padelford and Benham.
7   *Richard Hill's Commonplace-Book*, ed. Dyboski.

Who read or heard it? The unsophisticated, who were not part of the literary, intellectual, or social élite, were probably a large part of the audience. 'Listneth lordings' is a polite call for attention, but some carols suggest a less deferential view. The audience must have been very varied in composition and behaviour. We need also to remember that medieval society, though stratified, was a class system which allowed contact and communication between the classes. Stories originating in both lower and higher levels could migrate upwards or downwards. So most members of the literary élite were exposed — in various ways, and in some part of their lives — to popular literature, and sometimes remembered or made use of it. Both Geoffrey Chaucer and Robert Henryson must have read (and perhaps heard) popular romances. Literacy was spreading throughout the period; but the categories of 'literate' and 'illiterate' are not straightforward or self-contained groups set in opposition, but were rather a series of gradations. And the illiterate or partly literate could — and did — have books read to them.[8]

When we try to define the parameters of the large and heterogeneous body of writing, further difficulties arise. The literary culture of the Middle Ages is full of overlaps and interactions. Social historians are very aware of this. Peter Burke, for instance, distinguishes a 'great' learned tradition and a 'little' popular tradition.[9] The élite had access to both, but the 'folk' had only the 'little' tradition. We have already had a hint of this when we claimed that alongside an oral folk literature there was a written literature, and that popular literature flourished beside a sophisticated learned or courtly literature. These apparently distinct concepts often have vague or uncertain boundaries. This is the case even with the apparently distinct categories of 'secular' and 'religious' literature. It therefore seems to me unprofitable to think of two clearly marked and opposed divisions of 'popular' and 'learned / courtly / sophisticated' literature. Rather we should think of a spectrum, running from the (lost) oral literature through those popular texts which seem close to it, to those popular texts which are close to the undoubtedly sophisticated courtly poetry, and to that élite writing itself.

It is not, of course, a scientifically exact spectrum. The overlaps and interactions complicate matters enormously. Many literary historians

---

8   See, for example, *Simple Forms*, pp. 8 and 10–14.
9   Burke, *Popular Culture*, cited in *Simple Forms* (p. 4).

would echo the remark of Boklund-Lagopoulou: 'when dealing with material of this sort, the distinction between popular and learned culture breaks down';[10] and we can glimpse some remarkable interactions and transformations. Marie de France apparently based some of her elegant literary lais on Breton stories and folktales, producing a very sophisticated narrative form;[11] the Middle English popular versions of these seem to simplify them, even to bring them back into something not unlike their original form. But the awareness of courtly literature which we may sometimes sense in popular writers can also be problematic. The *Gest of Robyn Hood* begins with a motif apparently similar to that found in Arthurian romances, where the hero will not eat until some wonderful event occurs: 'Than bespake hym gode Robyn, To dyne have I noo lust, Till that I have som bolde baron, Or som uncouth gest' (stanza 6). Is this a hint of gentle parody, or is the author simply using a proven effective narrative device to excite anticipation?[12] Similarly, one could argue over the nature of the relationship of the tale of *Rauf Coilyear* to the Charlemagne romances with which the author was certainly familiar.[13] Sometimes we have popularised versions of courtly narratives.

It seems well-nigh impossible to place our specimens in a fixed place on that spectrum, beyond a general statement that some seem to be closer to the élite, sophisticated work of 'literary' authors, and some closer to the lost oral folk literature. Close to the élite pole, inhabited by French courtly romance but not, presumably, by the Middle English 'popular' versions of them: books of serious theology, written by theologians for other theologians (though these would usually be written in Latin). Some vernacular theological works, written for laymen, like John of Ireland's *Meroure of Wysdom*, or possibly the writings of Bishop Pecock, would probably qualify as 'popular', though close to the élite pole.[14] At this pole we would place

---

10 On texts such as 'Erthe toc of erthe' (in chapter 7, F, xxi, below) see Boklund-Lagopoulou, *I have a yong suster*.
11 Gray does not include any of these 'lais', which are in French, in this anthology. Readers may consult the copious scholarly literature on this writer (or writers), and namely the *Lais*, ed. Ewert.
12 In *Rymes*, Dobson & Taylor. Robin Hood and many others can be found, with narratives and references, in *DMH*.
13 *Rauf Coilyear*, ed. Herrtage.
14 Gray has not included anything by John of Ireland, or Bishop Pecock; their work may be consulted in Johannes de Irlandia, *The Meroure of Wyssdome*; and see Green, *Bishop Reginald Pecock*.

the sophisticated literary writers of England, like Chaucer or Gower, or Lydgate, and James I of Scotland, probable author of the *Kingis Quair* (one of a few works, like Chaucer's *Troilus and Criseyde*, which are remarkable for the paucity or absence of 'popular' elements).[15] The case of Langland is more problematic: he is undoubtedly in touch with popular idiom and concerns, but his theology is perhaps less 'popular' and his work seems to have been transmitted through (numerous) manuscripts. I have not included him, but have included the talented anonymous authors of *Sir Orfeo* and *The Owl and the Nightingale*. I have included the *Tournament of Tottenham*,[16] a fine, hearty burlesque, but not Chaucer's sophisticated pastiche in *Sir Thopas*. However, I would not be surprised or unduly distressed if others disagreed with my decisions. Pieces close to the 'oral' end of the spectrum do not at first sight raise so many questions, but there is one large complicating factor to consider before we start talking about the 'voice of the people': the possibility of imitation. It is certainly possible that learned 'clerkly' writers may have consciously or unconsciously imitated the style of some oral poems, perhaps sometimes in the case of bawdy songs? And sometimes we can see the widespread mixture of popular and learned ideas and style.

What are the criteria for placing any Middle English work in the category of 'popular literature'? I think the honest answer is that they are ultimately subjective, but are based on generally rational (but not absolutely watertight) guidelines. Some are stylistic. The vocabulary is usually simple, plain and direct; there is not usually anything like the 'aureate diction' of Lydgate and others. Sometimes we find rather down-to-earth colloquial speech: 'crack thy crown' in the *Gest of Robyn Hode* (stanza 158), or Margery Kempe's words to Christ.[17] But there are some examples of linguistic 'game', like Paston's doggerel verse,[18] or the apparently meaningless drinking exclamations 'fusty bandias' and 'stryke pantere' in *The King and the Hermit* (in our chapter 5). Sometimes a discourse sounds sententious or semi-proverbial. And some texts (like

---

15 *The Kingis Quair of James Stewart*, ed. McDiarmid. All Chaucer references have been checked with *The Riverside Chaucer*, ed. Benson.

16 *The Owl and the Nightingale*, ed. Stanley; *Sir Orfeo* and *The Tournament of Tottenham* are in *Middle English Verse Romances*, ed. Sands.

17 *The Book of Margery Kempe*, ed. Meech *et al*. In ch. 45 she asks Christ to delay punishing her till after she has got back to England (p. 110, lines 19–22).

18 In *The Paston Letters*.

The Owl and the Nightingale) make extensive use of popular proverbs. Popular texts do not have the elaborate formal rhetoric of some courtly writings; sometimes, as in oral literature, the emphasis seems to be given by the words and the 'performance' of the narrator. Only the simplest figures and devices are used: exclamations from the 'narrator', frequent use of direct speech, and repetition: the ballad of *Saint Stephen and Herod* has a clear hint of the 'incremental repetition' which is characteristic of later ballads (in the repeated phrase 'I forsak the, kyng Herowdes and thi werkes alle').[19] There is much use of emphatic repetition, as in the sad scenes of Orfeo's departure from his kingdom where 'wepeing' is repeated (cf. *Emaré*: 'the lady fleted forth alon … The lady and the lytyll chylde Fleted forth on the water wylde';[20] or *Adam Bell* ' "Set fyre on the house!" saide the sherife … they fyred the house in many a place';[21] or the *Battle of Otterburn*:[22] ' "Awaken, Dowglas!" cryed the knight'). Recapitulation becomes a kind of echoic narrative device. And we should note the way in which old 'formulaic' adjectives can be brought to life and given a new power (like the 'proude sherrif' of Nottingham). There is much use of formulae, not always simple clichés or filler phrases, which seem to derive ultimately from the lost oral works where they could have been useful for improvisation. A sensitive ear can detect these formulae and repetitions even under the elegant stylistic surface of *Sir Orfeo*. Narratives often use common themes ('a recurrent element of narration or description in traditional oral poetry'),[23] such as the arming of the hero, combats, feasts, prayers, and so on. There is a liking for simple metrical forms such as couplets or quatrains, both eminently suitable for recitation, reading aloud, or singing. But the popular writers show that they can cope with alliterative verse and with quite complex stanza forms.

In narrative the figures are strongly differentiated, but are not usually given detailed description (as is sometimes the case in courtly romances) but are presented simply and emphatically, often using repetition of a telling detail. There is a liking for direct speech and

---

19   In the chapter Ballads, below.
20   *Emaré* is in *Six Middle English Romances*, ed. Mills. The previous scene is cited from *Sir Orfeo*.
21   Gray, *Simple Forms*, pp. 79–80 and *passim*. See *Rymes* for Adam and his fellows.
22   In *Two English Border Ballads*, ed. Arngart, but Gray more probably used the five-volume Child Ballads.
23   Baugh, 'Improvisation in the Middle English Romance'.

dialogue. Sometimes a narrative will consist of a series of expressive scenes given emphasis by exclamations from the narrator. A modern reader needs to remember that these texts are meant to be heard. Many are in a kind of 'performative' style. There are many examples to be found in our ballads, romances, and tales like *The Childe of Bristowe*.[24] There is not much interest in psychological elaboration. We find sudden changes of attitude, rather than the self-conscious 'interiority' of courtly French romance, with a character debating within his mind what action he should take. Often there will be only a limited number of characters involved. 'Characterisation' is usually very simple, and usually revealed through a character's speech and deeds. Nor is there much ambiguity: characters tend to be 'black' or 'white'; so, Godard is totally evil in contrast to Havelock or Goldeboru in the romances of Havelock.[25] They range from the highest in society to the humblest (like the fisherman Grim). But the high usually talk and behave like ordinary people, as in later Scottish ballads, like Herod in *Saint Stephen and Herod*, or Orfeo, a 'high lording' and a harper (although his harp has magical power), who shows a simple fidelity and love. But there are some grotesque figures, such as the Turk or the Loathly Lady,[26] and sudden (sometimes violent) changes of emotion or circumstances, or extreme requests, as when the Turk asks Gawain to cut his head off — which produces a typically 'gentil' reaction from Gawain.[27] This is followed by a magic transformation: 'And whan the blod was in the bason light, He stod up a stalworth knight'. In *Sir Gowther* a disguised fiend suddenly reveals himself: 'A felturd [shaggy] fende he start up son And stod and hur beheld'.[28] Here the supernatural and the world of magic is very close at hand — and, interestingly, almost without any immediate reaction from the human figures involved (a technique which suggests the traditional folktale or *Märchen*). More usually, there is some reaction, as in a tale or legend (German *Sage*), as with the entry of the beautiful fairy mistress in *Sir Lambewell*.[29] Magic can be impressively eerie: Thomas of Erceldoune went his way 'whare it was dirke als mydnyght myrke and

24   See our chapter 4, Tales, number xvi.
25   In *Middle English Verse Romances* (Sands gives other references).
26   For the Loathly Lady, see *inter al.* Bliss, *Naming and Namelessness* (index references).
27   *The Turke and Sir Gawain*, in *Sir Gawain: Eleven Romances and Tales*, ed. Hahn.
28   In *Six Middle English Romances*, ed. Mills.
29   In *PFMS*.

ever the water till his knee'.[30] Demons and spirits are close to humans, even in comic tales, like that of the Basin.[31] And animals talk and act like humans.

Medieval English popular literature may not have the subtlety of the best work of the literary élite. But it has its moments of delight, often in touches of comedy: young Enyas being prepared for battle,[32] or the moment when the truth is suddenly revealed to the Sheriff in the *Gest of Robyn Hood*: 'Whan the sheriff sawe his vessel For sorowe he myght not ete.'[33]

The title of this anthology deserves an explanatory note. The phrase 'make we mery, bothe more and lasse' is not meant to evoke or endorse a sentimental view of 'Merry England'.[34] There is plenty of evidence for extreme misery and hardship in this period. The 'folk' suffered continuously: there were wars, rumours of wars, strife and violence, sickness and plague, as well as lesser troubles. And some of the suffering is reflected in popular literature; the texts in our Chapter 1 give more than a hint of this. We find examples of violence, murder or riots, quarrels in the streets, and a lynching in which was shown 'neither mercie nor pite'. The phrase in question comes in fact from the 'burden' of a carol from MS Balliol 354, the early sixteenth-century commonplace book of Richard Hill, grocer of London, the source of several pieces in this anthology: 'Make we mery bothe more and lasse, For now ys the tyme of Crystymas'.[35] Perhaps in performance this burden would have been sung by a group, and the three stanzas by a single singer, who sounds like a master of the festivities: he is dismissive of whoever says he cannot sing, and the man who claims that he can do no other sport is to go to the stocks. It seems to be good evidence for a passionate desire for 'game', which is not limited to this great festive season.

---

30   For Thomas, see first the index and references in Gray's *Simple Forms*. Helen Cooper treats this figure in *The English Romance in Time* (again, see index); for *The Romance and Prophecies*, ed. Murray, see especially the Introduction.

31   *The Tale of the Basyn* is in Hazlitt, and elsewhere (the text is given in our ch. 5, below).

32   In *Chevelere Assigne*, ch. 3 below.

33   Fytte 3, stanza 191.

34   In the verse where it appears (see ch. 9), 'more and lesse' means 'both high and low'. But 'more or less' (depending on your status, the weather, your love affairs, and so on) is a good catch-all for an England that was not always Merry.

35   In *Richard Hill's Commonplace-Book*, p. 15, Carol number 27 (number 6 begins similarly: 'Now let vs syng, both more & lesse').

Sometimes, it seems, these calls to make merry sound like heroic attempts to find merriment in harsh circumstances. One proverb urges: 'Be thou mery, thow thou be hard betid'.[36] Of course sentiments like this are not confined to popular culture; cf. the Green Knight's sententious remark: 'Make we mery while we may and mynne upon joy, For the lur [sorrow] may mon lach [have] whenso mon likes.'[37] But perhaps the harshness of life helped to accentuate one quality in popular merriment: a liking for successful 'tricksterism', as witnessed by the cunning tricks of Reynard or the disguises and deceits of Robin Hood or Little John, or the merry stratagems of the comic tale or fabliau. So some proverbs instruct you to look after yourself rather than be altruistic to others.

Like the sophisticated literature of the time, popular literature enjoys the mingling of 'game' and 'ernest'. This is not usually done with the delicate touch of a Chaucer, although there is perhaps a hint of it in the uneasy jesting relationship between the main figures in *The King and the Hermit* or in *Rauf Coilyear*. Huizinga argued that play is of central importance in culture itself. Indeed his study opens with the statement: 'Play is older than culture, for culture, however inadequately defined, always presupposes human society. And animals have not waited for man to teach them their playing'.[38] But, it might be argued, mankind finally caught up with them in the fiction that animals can not only talk and act like humans, but also instruct them.

'Game' was of great importance in medieval culture, both popular and sophisticated; see the excellent Afterword to *Medieval Comic Tales*:[39] it was deep-seated, going well beyond simple explanations like 'letting off steam'. Parody sometimes seems to have been part of life: the courtly praise of the lady's beauty seems to produce, almost automatically, detailed descriptions of her ugliness. A fine example is the Early Middle English *Land of Cokaygne*,[40] where the world of monasticism and the description of the joys of the Earthly Paradise are turned completely upside down. It has, on the one hand, affinities with the world of 'nonsense' writing and, on the other, it demonstrates how play can create its own order (as Huizinga said, within a playground 'an

---

36   Meaning: although things have turned out badly for you. Whiting M 513.
37   *Sir Gawain and the Green Knight*, ed. Burrow, vv. 1681–2.
38   Johan Huizinga, *Homo Ludens*, p. 1.
39   'Notes towards a Theory of Medieval Comedy', *Medieval Comic Tales*, ed. Brewer (1972).
40   In *Early Middle English Verse and Prose*.

absolute and peculiar order reigns').[41] Play was important in all levels of medieval culture and literature, but in popular literature it has a special intensity, and shows a remarkable variety.

Contests are an important setting for 'play' in early societies, as Huizinga pointed out.[42] And they were still widespread in Middle English popular literature, from the bird debate in the *Owl and the Nightingale* to the Mystery Plays. We have examples of the ancient riddle contest in the ballads of the *Devil and the Maid* and *King John and the Bishop* (and they still contain the ancient forfeit of death).[43] They are found in the outlaw ballads; and in festival games (see one of the earliest fragments in our anthology, 'atte wrastlinge ...').[44] Besides the seasonal folk festival there were flytings and slanging matches in the streets. Contests are important in narratives, in ballads (*Stephen and Herod*), in merry tales, and in romances. There we find contests and confrontations in plenty: violence in earnest, as in the ballads of *Otterburn*, or murder (*Sir Aldingar*), and in game (the Robin Hood ballads, plays and games).

'Variety' and 'intensity' are words very hard to avoid in any discussion of 'mirth' in popular literature. Medieval comedy is often cruel — it will make fun of the old, the malformed, and the unfortunate — but there is much evidence of its joyous involvement in the sheer fun of 'play'. There are examples of what Bernard O'Donoghue has aptly called 'cheerful indecency', which occasionally seems close to Rabelaisian heights of obscenity (as Brewer remarks,[45] 'because there was more faith there was also more blasphemy') although a modern reader is more likely to be shocked by the apparent brutality and callousness to suffering often found in medieval 'humour'.

The folk were certainly very attached to their festivities. In 1545 the reformer Latimer records that his offer to preach a sermon was rejected:

---

41 *Homo Ludens*, p. 10.
42 *Ibid.* chapter 'Play and Contest as Civilizing Functions'.
43 For a full chapter on ballads, see *Simple Forms* (pp. 71–88).
44 Chapter I Section A, Snatches and Snippets (iii) below.
45 It seems clear from *Simple Forms* that Gray probably used the first edition (1972) of *Medieval Comic Tales*; this was substantially rewritten for the next edition (2008) and is now rather hard to find. The later edition has no 'afterword', and neither of the citations above appears in the Introduction. However, this introduction is nevertheless a valuable commentary; and both remarks cited remain pertinent, whoever said them (or where). A further comment, that may be useful when reading what follows, is that 'derision' might be a better word than 'satire' for much of the medieval comic material (2nd edn, p. xix).

'Syr, thys is a busye daye wyth us, we can not heare you, it is Robyn
Hoodes day. The parishe is gone abrode to gather for Robyn Hoode.'[46]
These were probably not quite the Bacchanalian revelry described with
horror by the Puritans: 'their pipes playing, their drummers thund'ring,
their stumps dauncing, their bels jangling, their handkerchiefs swinging
about their heads like madmen, their hobbie horses and other monsters
skirmishing about the rout',[47] but rather festivities intended to collect
money for the parish and to celebrate the parish community, but there
was real merriment, and sometimes abandonment. We find moments
of exhilaration even in hostile satires (cf. Minot's attacks on the Scots);[48]
and other examples in our chapter on Satire. This can rise to an extreme
intensity of emotion: the nonsense poems, the drinking cries in the
King and the Hermit, or the Scottish 'eldritch' poems. And there is even
a parallel to this in popular religion, when enthusiasm leads some
devotees to become 'fools for Christ'.[49]

It is not surprising to find matters of 'ernest' in the midst of
apparently total game. 'Game' was not simply mindless 'misrule' in the
ballads and romances. Among scenes of misery and chaos we can find
positive qualities, such as the simple faithfulness and human goodness
of the fisherman Grim against the wickedness and violent cruelty of
Godard.[50] Characters like Grim or the 'child' of Bristol seem to bring
us close to the ordinary people of this period.[51] And it is arguable that
the pervasive presence of 'game' reinforces the brisk and direct style of
popular narrative.

This leads to a final point: to emphasize the range and the variety of
this popular literature. In some areas we are very conscious of a body
of 'lost literature': we have little direct evidence of popular drama, for
instance. On the other hand, we are fortunate in having texts of a mass
of songs and carols of many kinds, some probably written by clerks
in imitation of the oral songs they could hear. Narrative is an area
particularly well represented in the surviving popular literature. It is
tempting to suppose that the tales and legends found in oral literature

---

46   In *Rymes*, Introduction, p. 39.
47   Cited in Gray's *Later Medieval English Literature*, p. 37.
48   In chapter 8, below.
49   *Later Medieval English Literature*, p. 149.
50   In the romance of *Havelok*.
51   Grim belongs in the Havelock story, the Child is 'of Bristowe'.

carried within them the seeds of the more literary genres which appear in antiquity and the Middle Ages: the romance weaving together the adventures of a hero in a quest (or the simpler shorter 'lais'), ballads or ballad-like poems, sometimes long, sometimes brief, often making the adventures into a series of dramatic moments, and the simpler, shorter tales in verse or prose, moral or merry. The literary achievement of these popular forms certainly varies considerably, but at its best popular literature is a fascinating and delightful area.

This anthology is designed to illustrate its variety and quality as extensively as can be done in limited space, to give the reader some idea of its range, in various genres and kinds, and of the nature of medieval popular literature. My examples in general come from the fourteenth and fifteenth centuries, but occasionally I have gone back to earlier Latin chroniclers, and quite often have come forward to the mid-seventeenth century *PFMS* (which almost certainly contains some late medieval pieces). I have been concerned to make the selection not too long, and not too forbidding; I doubt whether modern readers (let alone publishers!) would be at ease with a collection of texts which extends, as does Hazlitt's, to several volumes. I have attempted to give a fairly wide coverage by mixing many short extracts with some longer or complete texts. I have tried to offer both pleasure and instruction, as does Middle English popular literature itself. The Appendix gives some evidence in support of the view that medieval popular literature did not suddenly disappear but that many of its forms (romances, ballads, including those which pass on 'news' — of battles, executions and wonderful events — tales, and so forth) lived on, sometimes being transformed, and that medieval popular literature is in a real sense the ancestor of the popular literature which flourished in the following centuries.

Chapter 1

Voices from the Past

This introductory chapter consists of extracts from chronicles, and other texts which illustrate medieval English life (and its anxieties and hazards), popular beliefs, magic and popular religion. 'Voices from the past' may seem a somewhat hopeful title, but extracts such as these are probably the nearest we can get to the actual voices. Snatches from songs are quoted by moralists and chroniclers. Chroniclers of course are interested in great events, but although they often sound impersonal they will often reveal their own opinions or record the opinions of humble folk. Letters (now being written in English) survive in some numbers in the fifteenth century. They are not the product of the humblest social class; those of the Pastons, a mercantile family in East Anglia, offer an unrivalled picture of local and family life. We have a precious Valentine letter, an appeal for money, and news and gossip from the area. The remarkable *Book of Margery Kempe*, a kind of spiritual 'personal experience narrative', the full text of which came to light only in the twentieth century, is another gold-mine. Margery was the wife of a merchant of Lynn (now King's Lynn, in Norfolk), and seems to have been illiterate or semi-literate: her 'book' was written by a priest who knew her. It records some vivid accounts of her experiences in England, and in Europe and the Holy Land. She was a religious enthusiast and a determined pilgrim.[1] The rest of this chapter contains examples of pieces provided for the entertainment and instruction of the 'folk'. Prophecies were very common, and seem to have satisfied a fascinated curiosity about the future and a yearning for order

---

1   The Pastons, and Margery, are cited at some length later in this chapter.

   https://doi.org/10.11647/OBP.0170.01

(perhaps their enigmatic quality added to the pleasure); magical charms, and the simple prayers of popular religion.

A. Snatches and Snippets,
which give us a glimpse of the lost oral literature

i) This early fragment of a song is recorded by a twelfth-century chronicler in his Latin 'Book of Ely'.[2] He says that even at the present time these verses are still sung publicly in dances and remembered in the sayings of the wise. Perhaps there was a local legend concerning it, and King Cnut as its supposed author.

Merie sungen the muneches° binnen° Ely	*monks*	*in*
Tha° Cnut ching reu° ther by.	*when*	*rowed*
'Roweth knightes noer the lant		
And here° we thes muneches sang.'	*hear*	

ii) A rare example of a secular lullaby (see the religious examples in ch. 9, esp. xxix),[3] found in a Latin sermon: *Karissimi, bene scitis quod iste mulieres ...* that lulle the child wyth thair fote and singes an hauld [old] song, *sic dicens:*[4]

Wake° wel, Annot	*watch*
Thi mayden boure;°	*bower*
And get the fra° Walterot,	*keep thee from*
For he es lichure.°	*a lecher*

iii) Two fragments of a Dance song[5]

Atte wrastlinge° my lemman I ches°	*wrestling*	*lover I chose;*
And atte ston-kasting I him forles.°	*lost*	

---

2   *Liber Eliensis*, trans. Fairweather, book. II, ch. 85 (p. 182). Ely was then a virtual island surrounded by fens.

3   Gray cites this verse in both *From the Norman Conquest* (p. 420) and *Simple Forms* (p. 221).

4   [Dear brethren, you know well that those women... saying thus].

5   Gray cites this verse in *From the Norman Conquest* (pp. 170–1).

At the ston-castinges my lemman I ches,
And at the wrastlinges sone I him les;
Alas that he so sone fel!
Why nadde he stonde, vile gorel?º   *fat fellow*

iv) One of a number of snippets in a thirteenth-century Worcester Cathedral manuscript;[6]

Ne saltou, levedi,º   *lady*
Tuynklenº wyt thin eyen…   *wink*

v) and from the same Worcester MS;

Ich habbe ydonº al myn youth   *have spent*
Ofte, ofte, and ofte,
Long yloved and yerne ybeden,º   *eagerly entreated*
Ful dere it is aboght!º   *very dearly paid for*

vi) from the same.

Dore,º go thou stille,º   *door*   *silently*
Go thou stille, stille,
That ichil habbeº in the bowre   *until I have*
Ydon al myn wille, wille…

vii) A lament quoted in a lawsuit involving the Neville family and the prior of Durham.[7]

Wel[a]! qwa sal thir hornes blau,º   *alas who shall these blow*
Haly Rod,º thy day?   *Holy Rood*[8]
Now is he dede and lies law
Was wontº to blaw thaim ay.º   *used*   *always*

---

6   These three fragments are printed together, as one piece, in *Early Middle English Verse and Prose*, number VIII R (and note p. 333).

7   This, and the next (from the *Red Book of Ossory*), are both cited by Gray in his *Simple Forms* (pp. 215–16).

8   Holy Rood Day is 14th September.

viii) From the *Red Book of Ossory*.[9]

Alas! How shold y singe?		
Yloren⁰ is my playinge;⁰	*lost*	*delight*
How shold y with that olde man		
To leven and lete⁰ my lemman,	*live and give up*	
Swettist of al thinge.		

ix)[10] Whenne bloweth⁰ the brom⁰	*flowers*	*broom*
Thenne woweth⁰ the grom;⁰	*woos*	*youth*
Whenne bloweth the furs⁰	*gorse*	
Thenne woweth he wurs.		

B. Scenes and Events from Chronicles and Letters

Chronicles

x) [1336][11]

... there arose suche a sprynggynge and welling op of waters and floodes, bothe of the see and also of fresshe ryvers and sprynges, that the see brynke wallaes [sea-walls] and coostes broken up [so that] men, bestes, and houses in meny places, and namely [especially] in lowe cuntres [regions], violently and soddenly were dreynt and driven awey; and the fruyte of the erthe, thorugh continuance and abundaunce of the see waters, evermore after were turned into more saltnes and sournes of savour...

xi) The Plague of 1348, the Black Death[12]

And in the xxiii yere of his [Edward III's] regne, in the este parteys of the world ether aros and bygan a pestilence and deth of Sarasines and

---

9   See Gray's *From the Norman Conquest*, pp. 420–1.
10   This verse is cited in Orme's *Fleas, Flies, and Friars*, chapter-title School Days; it is juxtaposed with a verse in Latin, as part of a lesson on Latin Grammar.
11   In *Brut*, ed. Brie, p. 292.
12   In Brie, ed. p. 301; the second passage is on p. 303.

payngneins [pagans], that so grete a deth was never herde of afore, and that wasted awey so the peple that unnethes the xthe persone was left alive. And in the same yere, aboute the sowth cuntreys and also in the west cuntres, there fell so much reyne and so grete waters that, from Cristemasse unto Midsomer, ther was unnethes day ne nyght but that it rayned sumwhat; thorugh whiche waters the pestilence was sone fectid and so habundant in all cuntres, and namely aboute the court of Rome and other places and s[e]re [various] costes, that unnethes there were left alive folk to bery ham that were ded honestly. But maden grete diches and puttes [pits] that were wunder brood and depe, and therin beried, and made a renge [pile] of the dede bodyes, and another renge of erthe above ham; and thus were they buried, and non other wise, but yf [unless] it were the fewer that were grete men of state.

[A few years later]
In this same yere [1352], and in the yere afore, and also in the yere aftir, was so grete a pestilenc[e] of men fro the est into the west, and namely thorugh bocches [swellings], that he that siked this day, deid on the iii day after. To the wich men that so deaden in this pestilens, that haddyn but litel respite of lyggyng, the pope Clement, of his goodness and grace, yaf ham ful remissioun and foryevyng of all hire synnes that they were shriven of. And this pestilence lasted in London from Michelmasse into Auguste next folowyng almoste an hool yere.[13] And in thes dayes was deth withoute sorwe, weddyng withoute friendship, wilfull penaunce, and derthe without scarste [scarcity], and fleyng withoute refute or socour; for meny fledden fro place to place bycause of the pestilens; but they were enfecte, and might not ascape the dethe, after the prophete Isaye seith: 'ho that fleeth fro the face of drede, he shal fall into the diche; and he that wyndeth himself out of the diche, he shal be holde and teyd with a grenne [snare]',[14] but whan this pestilens was cesid and endid, as God wolde, unnethes the x parte of the peple was left alive, and in the same yere bygan a wonder thing that al that evere were born after that pestilens hadden ii chekteth [molars] in her hed than they had afore.

---

13 The date of Michaelmas is 29th September.
14 Isaiah 24:18.

xii) A Storm ... [1364][15]

About evesong tyme, ther aroos and come such a wynd out of the suoth, with such a fersnes, that he brast and blewe doun to ground hye houses and strong byldynges, toures, churches and steples, and other strong thynges; and al other strong werkes that stoden still, were so yshake therewith that they ben yet, and shol be evermore the feblere and weyker while they stonde; and this wynd lasted withoute eny cesyng vii. dayes.

... and a Great Frost.[16]

... in the yere of grace 1435, the grete, hard, bityng frost bygan the vii day of Decembre, and endured unto the xxii day of Feverere next, which greved the peple wonder sore; and moche pepel deyed in that tyme, for colde and for skarcite of wode and cole. And tender herbes were slayne with this frost, that is to say, rosemary, sauge, tyme, and many other herbes.

xiii) A Lynching [1427][17]

... in the same yere, a fals Breton, between Ester and Witsontyde,[18] mordrede a good wedowe in hir bedde, the whiche hadde found [provided for] hym, for almesse, withoute Algate, in the suburbs of London. And he bar away all that sche hadde, and after toke girth [asylum] of holy churche at Saint Georges in Suthwerk; but at the last he toke the crosse, and forsuore the kyng land. And as he went his way, it happid hym to come by the same place where he did that cursede dede. And women of the same parish come oute to hym with stones and with canell [gutter] dong and there made an ende of hym in the high streit so that he went no ferthere, notwithstondyng the constablis and other men also, which had hym in governaunce to convey hym forth in his way, for there was a grete companye of them, and on hym thei had neither mercie nor pite; and thus this fals thefe endede his life in this worlde for his falsnesse.

---

15   In Brie, ed. p. 315.
16   *Ibid.* p. 467 (in Appendix F, worded slightly differently).
17   *Ibid.* pp. 442–3. Gray cites this story in his *Later Medieval English Literature* (p. 62).
18   Whit Sunday (Pentecost) is the seventh after Easter.

xiv) An Affray against the Lombards [1458?][19]

In this same yere fill [occurred] a gret affray in London ayenst the Lumbardes. The cause began for a yong man toke a dagger fro a Lumbard, and brake it; wherfore the yong man on the morne was sent fore to come before the mair and aldermen, and ther, for the offense, he was committed to warde [custody]. And then the mair departed fro the Guyldhall for to go home to his dyner, but in the Chepe [Cheapside] the yong men of the mercerie, for the moste parte apprentises, held the mair and shyreves stil in Chepe and wold nat suffer him to departe unto the tyme that thare felow, which was committed to warde, wer delyvered; and so by force thei rescued ther felowe fro prisone, and that done, the mair and shyreves departed, and the prisoner was delyvered, which, if he had be put to prisone, had be in jubardie of his lyfe. And than began a rumor in the cite ayenst the Lumbardes, and the same evening the handcrafty peple of the town arose, and come to the Lumbardes houses, and dispoyled and robbed diverse of thame, wherfore the mair and aldermen come with the honest peple of the town, and drofe thame thens, and sent some of thame that had stollen to Newgate. And the yong man that was rescued bi his felowes saw this gret rumor, affray and robbery folowed of his first mevyng to the Lumbard. He departed and went to Westmynster to sanctuary, or els it had cost him his lyfe, for anone after come doun an other determine[d] for to do justice on al thame that so rebelled in the cite ayens the Lumbardes, upon which satt with the mayr that tyme William Marow, the duke of Bokyngham, and many other lordes, for to se execucion done, bot the comons of the cite secretely made thame redy, and did arme thame in ther houses and wer in purpose for to have rongen the common bell which is named Bow Bell; but thei wer let by sad [steady] men. Which come to the knowlege of the duke of Bokyngham and othir lordes. And forthwith thei arose, for thei durst no lenger abide, for thei doubted that the hole cite shold have risen ayenst theme, but yett neverthelesse ii or iii of the cite were juged to deth for this robbery, and wer honged at Tiburn.

---

19 In ed. Brie, pp. 522–3.

xv) Religious Unrest at Evesham[20]

And in this same yere the m[e]n and the erles tenauntes of Warwyk
arisen maliciously ayens the abbot and the covent of Evesham and her
tenauntes, and destroyeden fersly the abbot and the toun, and wounded
and bete her men and slowen of hem meny one, and wenten to her
maners and places, and dede myche harme, and brekyn doun her parkes
and her closes, and brenten and slowen her wild bestes, and chaced
hem, brekyng her fishepond hedis, and lete the water of her pondes,
stewes and ryvers renne out; and token the fish, and bere it with hem,
and deden al the harme that they myghte.

xvi) A Heretic Venerated [1440][21]

The xix yeer of kyng Harri, the Friday before midsomer, a prest called ser
Richard Wyche, that was a vicary in Estsexe, was brend on the Tourhille
for heresie, for whoos deth was gret murmur and troubil among the
peple, for some said he was a good man and an holy, and put to deth be
malice; and some saiden the contrary; and so dyvers men hadde of him
dyvers oppinions. And so fer forth the commune peple was brought
in such errour that meny menne and women wente be nyghte to the
place where he was brend, and offrid there money and ymages of wax,
and made thair praiers knelyng as thay wolde have don to a saynt, and
kiste the ground and baar away with thaym the asshis of his body as
for reliques; and this endured viii daies, til the mair and aldermenne
ordeyned men of armes forto restreyne and lette [prevent] the lewd
peple fro that fals ydolatrie, and meny were therfore take and lad to
prisoun. And among othir was take the vicary of Berkyngchirche beside
the tour of Londoun, in whos parishe alle this was done, that received
the offryng of the simple peple. And for to excite and stire thaym to offre
the more fervently, and to fulfille and satisfie his fals coveitise, he took
asshis and medlid thaym with powder of spices and strowed thaym
in the place where the said heretic was brend; and so the simple peple
was deceived, wenyng that the swete flavour hadde commeof the asshis
of the ded heretic: for this the said vicari of Berkyngchirche confessed
afterward in prisoun …

---

20   *Ibid.* p. 330 [1377].
21   *An English Chronicle*, ed. Davies, pp. 56–7.

The Bishop of Salisbury murdered [1450, just after the murder of the Bishop of Chichester][22] And this … yer … William Ascoghe bishop of Salisbury was slayn of his owen parisshens and peple at Edyngdoun aftir that he hadde said masse, and was drawe fro the auter and lad up to an hille therbeside, in his awbe, and his stole aboute his necke; and there thay slow him horribly, their fader and their bisshoppe, and spoillid him unto the nakid skyn, and rente his blody shirte into pecis and baar thaym away with thaym, and made bost of their wickidnesse; and the day befor his deth his chariot was robbed be men of the same cuntre of an huge god and tresour, to the value of x.ml. marc, as thay saide that knewe it. Thise ii bisshoppis were wonder covetous men, and evil beloved among the commune peple, and holde suspect of meny defautes, and were assentyng and willyng to the deth of the duke of Gloucestre, as it was said.

xvii) A Portent [1440][23]

The xxviii yer of king Harri [Henry VI], on Simon day and Jude,[24] and othir daies before and aftir, the sonne in his risyng and goyng doune apperid as reed as blood, as meny a man saw; wherof the peple hadde gret marvaille, and demed that it sholde betokened sum harm sone afterward. And this same yeer, in the feste of saint Mighelle in Monte Tumba,[25] Roon [Rouen] was lost and yolden [surrendered] to the Frensshemenne … And the next yeer aftir alle Normandy was lost.

xviii) Roger Bolingbroke, Necromancer [July, 1440][26]

… and the Sunday the xxv day of the same moneth, the forsaid maister Roger with all his instrumentis of nygromancie — that is to say a chaier ypeynted, wherynne he was wont to sitte whanne he wrought his craft, and on the iiii corners of the chaier stood iiii swerdis, and ypon every swerd hanggyng an ymage of copir — and with meny othir instrumentis according to his said craft, stood in a high stage above alle

---

22   *Ibid.* p. 64.
23   *An English Chronicle*, ed. Davies p. 63 (the date is here given as 1449).
24   28th October.
25   16th October; the events seem not to be in chronological order.
26   *An English Chronicle*, ed. Davies p. 57 (the date is here given as 1441).

mennes heddis in Powlis chircheyerd befor the cros whiles the sermon endured, holding a suerd in his right hand and a septre in his lift hand, araid in a marvaillous aray whereynne he was wont to sitte whanne he wrought his nygromancie. And aftir the sermon was don, he abjured alle maner articles longing in any wise to the said craft of nigromancie, or mys sownyng [discordant] to the Cristen feith …

Letters[27]

In the fifteenth century, collections of letters in English are increasingly found. These are often written by merchants and others who are literate; in general women still seem to have been content to use the services of family scribes. Of especial importance is the extensive collection of those of the Paston family, a mercantile, landowning family of East Anglia, and its scribes and friends. These give us some vivid glimpses of life in that area.[28]

xix) News from a Wife [1448][29]

Right worshipful husband, I recommend me to you and pray you to weet [know] that on Friday last past before noon, the parson of Oxnead being at mass in our parish church, even at the levation of the sacring, James Gloys had been in the town and came homeward by Wymondhams gate. And Wymondham stood in his gate, and John Norwood his man stood by him, and Thomas Hawes his other man stood in the street by the cannel side [gutter]. And James Gloys came with his hat on his head between both his men, as he was wont of custom to do. And when Gloys was against Wymondham, he said thus: 'Cover thy head!' And Gloys said again, 'So I shall for thee'. And when Gloys was further passed by the space of three or four stride, Wymondham drew out his dagger and said, 'Shalt thou so knave?' And therewith Gloys turned him, and drew out his dagger and defended him, fleeing into my mothers place; and Wymondham and his man Hawes cast stones and drove Gloys into my mothers place, and Hawes followed into my mothers place and cast a

---

27 See *Paston Letters*, ed. Norman Davis, part I, though it is not certain that Gray used this edition. Some are cited in his *Later Medieval English Literature*.
28 See also Bennett, *The Pastons and their England*.
29 *Paston Letters*, 129, from Margaret Paston to her husband John Paston I (pp. 223–5).

stone as much as a farthing loaf into the hall after Gloys, and then ran
out of the place again. And Gloys followed out and stood without the
gate, and then Wymondham called Gloys thief and said he should die,
and Gloys said he lied and called him churl, and bade him come himself
or ell [else] the best man he had, and Gloys would answer him one for
one. And then Hawes ran into Wymondhams place and fetched a spear
and a sword, and took [gave] his master his sword. And with the noise
of this assault and affray my mother and I came out of the church from
the sacring, and I bade Gloys go into my mothers place again, and so he
did. And then Wymondham called my mother and me strong whores ...

xx) Another Dispute [pr. 1451][30]

I greet you well, and let you weet that on the Sunday before Saint
Edmund,[31] after evensong, Agnes Ball came to me to my closet and bade
me good even, and Clement Spicer with her. And I asked him what he
would; and he asked me why I had stopped in the kings way. And I said
to him that I stopped no way but mine own, and asked him why he had
sold my land to John Ball; and he swore he was never accorded with
your father. And I told him if his father had do as he did, he would a be
ashamed to a said as he said. And all that time Warren Harman leaned
over the parckos [partition] and listened what we said, and said that the
change was a ruely [deplorable] change, for the town was undo thereby
and is the worse by £100. And I told him it was no courtesy to meddle
him in a matter but if he were called to counsel ...

xxi) Local News [1453][32]

Son, I greet you well and send you Gods blessing and mine ....[33] And
as for tidings, Philip Berney is passed to God on Monday last past
with the greatest pain that ever I saw man. And on Tuesday Sir John
Heveningham yede [went] to his church and heard three masses, and
came home again never merrier, and said to his wife that he would go

---

30   *Ibid.* 24, from Agnes Paston to her son John Paston I (pp. 36–7).
31   20th November.
32   *Ibid.* 26, from Agnes Paston to John Paston 1 (pp. 39–40).
33   'God's blessing and mine' is a formula conventionally used between adult and
     (their own) child.

say a little devotion in his garden and then he would dine; and forthwith he felt a fainting in his leg, and syed [sank] down. This was at 9 of the clock and he was dead ere noon ...

xxii) A Wife's Suggestions[34]

Right worshipful husband, I recommend me unto you. Please it you to weet that I sent your eldest son to my lady Morley to have knowledge what sports were used in her house in Christmas next following after the decease of my lord her husband. And she said there were none disguisings nor harping nor luting nor singing, not no loud disports, but playing at the tables [backgammon] and chess and cards; such disports she gave her folks leave to play, and none other ...

... I pray you that ye will essay to get some man at Caister to keep your buttery, for the man that ye left with me will not take upon him to breve [make up accounts] daily as ye commanded. He saith he hath not used to give a reckoning neither of bread nor ale till at the weeks end, and he saith he wot well that he should not con [know how to] don it; and therefore I suppose he shall not abide. And I trow ye shall be fain to purvey another man for Simond, for ye are never the nearer a wise man for him.

I am sorry that ye shall not at home be for Christmas. I pray you that you will come as soon as ye may; I shall think myself half a widow because ye shall not be at home. God have you in his keeping. Written on Christmas Eve [pr. 1459], By your M. P.

xxiii) A Husband in playful mood writes a letter in doggerel verse[35]

... Item, I shall tell you a tale:

Pamping and I have picked your mail°	*wallet, or luggage*
And taken out pieces° five,	*coins, or dishes*[36]

---

34   *Ibid.* 153, from Margaret to John Paston I (pp. 257–8).
35   *Ibid.* at the end of 77 [1465], from John Paston I to Margaret (pp. 140–5).
36   It is unclear whether John has taken some coins from his wife, to be exchanged (puzzlingly) for the money Calle will bring, or whether the 'peces' are dishes, also round and perhaps valuable. There may be a family joke going on (he can hardly be serious about nailing Calle's ear to a post) that we shall never be able to fathom.

For upon trust of Calles promise we may soon unthrive.

And if Calle bring us hither twenty pound

Ye shall have your pieces again good and round;

Or else, if he will not pay you the value of the pieces there,

To the post do nail his ear …

… And look you be merry and take no thought,

For this rhyme is cunningly wrought.

My lord Percy and all this house

Recommend them to you, dog, cat, and mouse,

And wish ye had be here still …

For they say ye are a good gill.ᵍ   *woman [familiar]*

No more to you at this time,

But God him save that made this rhyme.

Writ the Vigil of St Matthew,[37] By your true and trusty husband, J. P.

xxiv) A Son's Requests[38]

Aftyr humbyll and most dew recommendacyon, in as humbyll wyse as I can I beseche yow of your blyssyng, preying God to reward yow wyth as myche plesyer and hertys ease as I have latward causyd you to have trowbyll and thowght. And, wyth Godys grace, it shall not be longe to or then [before] my wrongys and othyr menys shall be redressyd, for the world was nevyr so lyek to be owyrs as it is now; werfor I prey yow let Lomnor no[t] be to besy as yet. Modyr, I beseche yow, and ye may spare eny money, that ye wyll do your almesse on me and send me some in as hasty wyse as is possybyll, for by my trowthe my lechecrafte and fesyk, and rewardys to them that have kepyd [cared for] me and condyt me to London, hathe cost me sythe Estern Day more then v li [pounds]. And now I have neythyr met, drynk, clothys, lechecraft, nor money but upon borowyng. And I have assayed my frendys so ferre that they begyn to fayle now in my gretest ned that evyr I was in …

---

37   *ODS* gives 24th (or 25th) February; the vigil would be the day before. But the letter is dated 20th September in the edition.

38   *Ibid.* 346, to Margaret Paston from her son John Paston III (pp. 565–6), dated 1471.

… And if it plese yow to have knowlage of our royall person, I thank God I am hole of my syknesse, and trust to be clene hole of all my hurttys within a sevennyght at the ferthest, by wiche tym I trust to have othyr tydyngys. And those tydyngys onys had, I trust not to be longe owght of Norffolk, wyth Godys grace, whom I beseche preserve you and your for my part.

Wretyn the last day of Apryll. The berer herof can tell you tydyngys syche as be trew for the very serteyn.   Your humbylest servaunt, J. of Gelston

xxv) A Valentine Letter, from Margery Brews to John Paston III
[February 1477][39]

Unto my ryght welbelovyd Voluntyn, John Paston, Squyer, be this bill delivered …
Ryght reverent and wurschypfull and my ryght welebeloved Voluntyne, I reccomande me unto yowe full hertely, desyring to here of yowr welefare, whech I beseche Almyghty God long for to preserve unto hys pleasure and yowr hertys desyre. And if it plese yowe to here of my welefare, I am not in good heele of body ner of herte, nor schall be tyll I here from yowe:

   For ther wottys [knows] no creature what peyn I endure,
   And for to be deede, I dare it not dyscure.
And my lady my moder hath labored the mater to my fadure full delygently, but sche can no more gete then ye knowe of, for the whech God knowyth I am full sory.

   But yf that ye loffe me, as I tryste verely that ye do, ye will not leffe me therfor; for if ye hade not halfe the lyvelode that ye hafe, for to do the grettyst labure that any woman on lyve myght, I wold not forsake yowe.
And yf ye commande me to kepe me true whereever I go,
Iwyse I will do all my might yowe to love and never no mo.
And yf my freendys say that I do amys, thei schal not me let so for to do.
Myn herte me byddys ever more to love yowe
Truly over all erthely thing.

---

39   *Ibid.* 415, from Margery Paston (née Brews) soon before her marriage to John Paston III (pp. 662–3).

And yf thei be never so wroth, I tryst it schall be bettur in tyme commyng.

No more to yowe at this tyme, but the Holy Trinite hafe yowe in kepyng. And I besech yowe that this bill be not seyn of non erthely creature safe only your selfe. And this lettur was indyte at Topcroft wyth full hevy herte.   Be your own M. B.

C. Popular Beliefs

xxvi) The Shipman's Vision [1457][40]

The xxxv yere of kyng Harry, and the yere of Oure Lorde m.cccc.lvii, a pylgryme that alle his dayes had be a shipmanne came fro seynt James in Spayne into Englond abowte Mighelmas and was loged in the toune of Weymouthe, in Dorsetshyre, with a brewer, a Duchemanne, the whiche had be with hym in his seyde pylgremage. And as the sayde pylgryme laye in his bedde waking, he sawe one come into the chamber clothed alle in whyte having a whyte heede, and sate doune on a fourme [bench] nat fer fro hys bed, and alle the chambre was as lyghte of hym as it had be clere day. The pylgryme was agaste and durste not speke, and anone the seyde spirite vanysshed awey. The second nyghte the same spyryte came ayene in lyke wyse, and wythoute eny tareyng vanysshed awey. In the morrow the pylgrym tolde alle this to his oste, and seyde he was sore afeerde, and wolde no more lye in that chambre. Hys oste counseled hym to telle this to the parysshe preeste, and shryve hym of all his synnes, demyng that he hadde be acombred [oppressed] with some grete deadly synne. The pylgrym sayd, 'I was late shryve [shriven] at seynt James, and reseved there my Lord God, and sethe that tyme, as fer as I canne remembre, I have nat offended my conscience.' Natheles he was shryvenne, and tolde alle this to the preest; and the preest seyde, 'Sen [since] thow knowest thy selfe clere in conscience, have a good herte and be nat agast [afraid], and yef the sayde spirite come ayene, conjure hym in the name of the Fader and of the Sone and of the Holy Goste to telle the what he ys.' The iiide nighte the spyryte came ayene into the chambre as he had do before, wyth a grete lyghte; and the pylgrym, as the preest had counselled him, conjured the spyryte, and bade hym

---

40 *An English Chronicle*, ed. Marx; this is an enlarged and revised edition of the *Chronicle* ed. Davies. The rubric reads 1456–7, King Harry is Henry VI.

telle what he was. The spyryte answered and seyde, 'I am thyne eme [uncle], thy faderes brother.' The pylgrym seyde, 'How longe ys it ago sen thow deyde?' The spiryte seyde, 'ix yere.' 'Where ys my fader?' seyde the pylgrime. 'At home in his owne hous,' seyde the spiryte, 'and hath another wyfe.' 'And where ys my moder?' 'In hevene,' seyde the spiryte. Thenne seyde the spiryte to the pylgryme, 'Thou haste be at Seynt James; trowest thou that thow hast welle done thy pylgremage?' 'So I hoope,' seyde the pylgryme. Thanne sayde the spiryte, 'Thou haste do [caused] to be sayde there iii masses, one for thy fader, another for thy moder, and the iiide [third] for thyselve; and yef thou haddest lete say a masse for me, I had be deliviered of the peyne that I suffre. But thou most go ayene to Seynt James, and do say a masse for me, and yeve iii d. [pence] to iii pore men.' 'O,' sayde the pylgrime, 'howe shulde I go ayene to Seynt James? I have no money for myne expenses, for I was robbed in the shyppe of v nobles.' 'I know welle thys,' sayde the spirite, 'for thow shalt fynde thy purce hanging at the ende of the shyp and a stoone therynne; but thow most go ageyne to Seynt James, and begge, and lyve of almesse.' And when the spyryte had thus seyde, the pylgryme saw a develle drawe the same spyryte by the sleve, forto have hym thennys. Thenne saide the spyryte to the pylgryme, 'I have folewed the this ix yere, and myghte never speke with the unto now; but blessed be the hous where a spyryte may speke, and farewell, for I may no lenger abyde with the, and therfore I am sory.' And so he vanysshed awey. The pylgryme went into Portyngale, and so forthe to Seynt James, as the spyryte had hym commanded; wherfore I counseylle every man to worship Seynt James.

xxvii) Ghostly Battles [1365][41]

… and in the same tyme in Fraunce and Engelond … soddenly ther apperid ii castels, of the whiche wenten out ii ostes of armed men; and the to[on] oste was helid and clothed in white, and the tothere in blak; and whan batayl bytuene hem was bygunne, the white overcome the blake, and anone aftter, the blak token hert to hem and overcome the white; and after that, they went ayen into her castellis, and tha[n] the castels and al the oostes vanisshed awey …

---

41   In Brie ed. (as above in chronicles), p. 314.

xxviii) A Wife Rescued from the Fairies,
recorded by the twelfth-century writer Walter Map[42]

... a certain knight of Lesser Britain lost his wife, and lamented for a long time after her death. He found her at night in a great band of women in an enclosed valley in a great wilderness. He wondered, and was filled with fear when he saw her, whom he had buried, alive again. He did not believe his eyes, and was doubtful about what was being done by the fairies. He decided in his mind to carry her off so that he might rejoice in the capture if he saw truly, or might be deceived by the ghost, and should not be censured for timidity in giving up. And so he seized her and found delight in wedlock with her for many years, as pleasantly and as solemnly as the first marriage, and by her he had children, whose descendants are numerous today, and are called 'the sons of the dead woman'. This would be an incredible and monstrous offence against nature if there were not dependable signs of its truth.

xxix) A Fairy Lover, from Walter Map[43]

Similar to this [the story of Gwestin Gwestiniog] is what is related of Edric 'Wild', a 'silvestris' [man of the woods], so called from the agility of his body and the liveliness of his words and deeds, a man of great worth and lord of Lydbury North, who, when he was coming back from hunting through remote country accompanied only by a single boy, until midnight wandered uncertain of his path, happened upon a big building on the edge of a wood, such as the English had as drinking houses, called 'ghildhus' in English, and when he was near it and saw a light in it, looking in he saw a great dance with many noble women. They were most beautiful, in elegant dress, of linen only, bigger and taller than ours. The knight observed among them one outstanding in form and figure, inspiring desire more than all the sweethearts of kings. They went around with light movement and with delightful carriage,

---

42   *De Nugis Curialium*, trans. James, Distinction iv, no. VIII (pp. 187–9); Gray made his own translation: see his *From the Norman Conquest*, p. 84 for the rescued wife.

43   This story is not presented in Gray's previous anthology (cited above), but it is clear he has made his own translation of this too (as well as the other two presented here). It is in Map's Distinction ii, no. XII (pp. 82–5). Gray has added the reference to Gwestin (the previous story in Map) so that readers will not think the Edric story is supposed to resemble the Rescued Wife in this volume.

and with lowered voices in solemn concord a delicate sound was heard, but their speech was incomprehensible. When he saw this the knight was wounded in his heart, and could scarcely bear the fires that were inflicted from the bow of Cupid; his whole being was kindled, his whole being burst into flame, and he took courage from that most beautiful of sicknesses, that golden danger. He had heard the tales of the pagans: the nightly hosts of demons, Dictynna [Diana] and the troops of Dryads and riders;[44] and of the vengefulness of the offended gods, and the manner in which they summarily punish those who suddenly glimpse them, how they keep themselves separate and live secretly and apart, how they hate those who attempt to observe their councils to reveal them, who pry into them and lay them bare, how very carefully they conceal themselves, in case, if they are seen, they should be reviled. He had heard of their acts of vengeance and the examples of their victims, but — as Cupid is rightly depicted as blind — forgetting all this, he does not think it an illusion, is not aware of an avenger and, since his mind is darkened, incautiously he offends. He circles the hall, finds its entrance, and rushes in and takes her by whom he is taken. Immediately he is attacked by the others; although held back for a time by this fierce fight, finally, thanks to his efforts and those of his boy, he was freed, although not altogether unhurt, but wounded in the feet and legs by as much as the nails and teeth of women were capable of. He carried her off with him, and used her as he desired for three days and nights but could not extract a word from her; however she suffered the passion of his desire with gentle agreement. On the fourth day she spoke these words to him, 'Greetings, my beloved: you shall be safe and shall live happily in person and in your affairs until you blame me or my sisters from whom I was taken, or the place or the wood whence I came, or anything around it. From that day in truth your felicity shall end, and after I have departed, you will fail, with a series of mishaps, and by your importunity anticipate your final day.' He promised, with whatever security he could, to be steadfast and faithful in his love. He therefore summoned the nobles from near and far, and in that great gathering joined her to him in marriage. At that time there reigned William the

---

44   Gray has printed ? against the word 'riders'; in his translation James writes 'Naiads?' with a note to the effect that the Latin phrase *et alares* is so far unexplained. For Gray's Dictynna as Diana, see *OCCL*, q.v.

Bastard, the new king of England. Hearing of this wonder, he desired to test it, investigate it, and to know publicly if it were true. He summoned both of them to come to London at once, and many witnesses came with them, and testimonies from many who did not come, and the woman's beauty, of a kind not previously seen or heard of, was a convincing proof that she was of fairy origin. And with general amazement they were sent back to their own dwelling.

Later, after the passing of many years it happened that Edric, returning from hunting at about the third hour of the night, when he did not find her called her and commanded that she be summoned, and when she came slowly said in anger as he looked upon her, 'Was it by your sisters that you were delayed so long?', and uttered further reproaches — but to the air only, for she vanished at the mention of her sisters. The young man repented his great and disastrous outburst, and he searched for the place whence he had seized her, but by no weeping or lamentation could he recover her. He called by day and by night, but only to his own folly, for his life ended there in lasting grief.

xxx) Herla and his Troop, another story from Map[45]

Herla, king of the ancient Britons, is suddenly visited by another king, small, like a pygmy, riding on a goat. With his splendidly dressed retinue, he provides a great feast in Herla's honour, and insists that Herla should attend his wedding a year later.

… And now, after a year, he suddenly appeared before Herla, urgently desiring that the agreement should be observed. He assented and, providing himself with enough to repay the debt, followed whither he was led. So they entered a cave in a very high cliff, and after a time of darkness passed into a light which did not seem that of the sun or the moon, but of very many lamps, to the dwelling of the pygmy, a mansion as noble, in truth, in every way as the palace of the Sun described by Ovid.[46] When the wedding had been celebrated more, the

---

45   In Map, see Distinction i, no. XI (pp. 13–17); and in Gray, *From the Norman Conquest*, pp. 86–8. Here again, the latter translation (his own) corresponds almost exactly with the text presented here.

46   Ovid, *Metamorphoses* book ii, 1 ff.

debt to the pygmy repaid in seemly manner, and permission to leave granted, Herla left, burdened with gifts and presents of horses, hounds, hawks and all manner of excellent things for hunting and hawking. The pygmy led them as far as the darkness, and presented him with a small bloodhound to be carried, strictly forbidding that any of them from his whole company should dismount until that dog leapt out from the grasp of its bearer, then bade them farewell, and went back home. After a short time Herla came back to the light of the sun and to his own kingdom. He spoke to an old shepherd, and asked for news of his queen, by name. The shepherd, looking at him with wonder, said: 'Lord, I scarcely understand your speech, since I am a Saxon, and you a Briton. I have not heard the name of that queen, except that they relate that long ago a queen of that name of the very ancient Britons was the wife of King Herla, who in legend is said to have disappeared with a pygmy at this cliff, and was never afterwards seen on earth. The Saxons conquered that kingdom two hundred years ago and drove out the ancient inhabitants.' The king was astounded, who thought that he had stayed only for three days,[47] and could hardly remain on his horse. And some of his companions, forgetful of the pygmy's orders, dismounted before the dog had descended, and were instantly dissolved into dust. The king, realizing the reason for their dissolution, forbade under threat of a similar death that anyone should touch the earth before the dog had descended. However, the dog has not yet descended. And so the story has it that King Herla with his company continues his frantic rounds in endless wandering without rest or stopping. Many assert that they have often seen this band ...

xxxi) Charms[48]

Whatt manere of ivell thou be,
In Goddes name I coungere° the: *conjure*
I coungere the with the holy crosse
That Jesus was done on with fors;°   *violence*

---

47   There is a long annotation to this story in Map, as a footnote to the title King Herla. It begins: 'One of the most famous of the folk-tales related by Map ...'. Readers will be familiar with legends such as that of Sleepy Hollow or Rip Van Winkle.

48   My footnotes indicate one source for these poems; there are certainly others. Number xxxi is printed in *Medieval English Lyrics*, ed. Silverstein, p. 124.

I conure the with nayles thre
That Jesus was nayled upon the tree;
I coungere the with the crowne of thorne
That on Jesus hede was done with scorne;
I coungere the with the precious blode
That Jesus shewyd upon the rode;
I coungere the with woundes fyve
That Jesus suffred be° his lyve;   *in*
I coungere the with that holy spere
That Longeus° to Jesus hert can bere   *Longinus*
I coungere the never the less
With all the vertues of the masse,
And all the holy prayers of seynt Dorathe.°   *Dorothy*
In nomine patris et filii et spiritus sancti.[49] Amen

xxxii) For the Nightmare[50]

Take a flynt stone that hath an hole thorow of his owen growing, and
hange it over the stabill dore, or ell [else] over horse, and ell writhe
this charme:

In nomine patris &c
Seynt Iorge,° our Lady knyghth,   *George*
He walked day, he walked [ny]ghth,
Till he fownde that fowle wyghth,°   *creature*
And whan that he here fownde,
He here bete and he here bownde,
Till trewly ther here trowthe sche plyghth°   *promised*
That sche sholde not come be nyghthe,
Withinne vii rode° of londe space   *rood (a measure)*
Ther as seynt Ieorge inamyd was.
  St Iorge. St Iorge. St Iorge
& wryte this in a bylle & hange it in the hors mane.

---

49   In the name of the Father, the Son, and the Holy Ghost.
50   Number xxxii is printed in *Oxford Book of Medieval English Verse* (ed. Sisam), no. 154,
     p. 384; Gray refers to it in *Later Medieval English Literature*, p. 55.

xxxii a) A charm for staunching blood[51]

Crist was born in Bethlehem,

And cristend in flom° Jordane;   *river*

And als the flom stode als a stane,°   *as a stone*

Stand thy blode, N. (neven° his name)   *name*

In nomine patris et filii et spiritus sancti.

xxxiii) Prognostications[52]

Giff sanct Paullis day be fair and cleir,[53]

Than sal betyd ane happie yeir;

Gif it chances to snaw or rane,

Than sal be deir° all kynde of grayne;   *expensive*

And giff the wind be hie on loft,

Than weir° sall vex the kingdome oft;   *war*

And gif the cloudis mak darke the skye,

Boith nowte and foull° that year sall dye.   *cattle and fowl*

Prophecies[54]

xxxiv) In the twelfth century Geoffrey of Monmouth describes how the British king Vortigern saw two dragons come out of the pool and begin to fight. Merlin was asked to say what the battle portended …

Bursting into tears, he drank in the spirit of prophecy and spoke: 'Woe to the Red Dragon, for its destruction hastens. The White Dragon will occupy its caverns, which signifies the Saxons whom you have invited. The Red Dragon signifies the people of Britain who are oppressed by

---

51   Gray prints this charm in his *Later Medieval English Literature*, on p. 54; unfortunately he does not give a source for it (however, there is a book-list at the end of each chapter).

52   *Index of Middle English Verse* number 1423; it is cited in Oliver (*Poems Without Names*, p. 114) and elsewhere; see also *Secular Lyrics of the XIVth and XVth Centuries*, ed. Robbins (number 71).

53   29th June (see *ODS*).

54   As is his wont, Gray has re-translated from the original Latin rather than using any published translation; see Geoffrey's *History*, trans. Thorpe, p. 171.

the White Dragon. Its mountains and valleys will be made level, and the rivers of the valleys will flow with blood. The practice of religion will be blotted out and the ruin of the churches will be seen by all. At length the oppressed people will prevail and will resist the savagery of the foreign invaders.'

xxxiv a) from a later English version of one of Geoffrey's prophecies[55]

… Then schal Cadwaladre Conan calle,[56]
    And gadre Scotlonde unto hys flocke;
Thanne in ryveres blode schall falle.
    And thanne schal perysche braunche and stocke.

Thanne schal alyons° folde and falle   *foreigners*
    And be deposyde for ever and aye;
To ben free that nowe ben thralle
    Schall befalle thanne ylke a daye.

Off Lytylle Bretayne° lordes fele°   *Brittany*   *many*
    Schall be joyfulle men of thys;
Than schall Bretaynes crownes dele.
    And ben then lordes where non ys.

Then schall Cambere° joyfulle be,   *Kambria*[57]
The might of Cornewayle quycke° anon;   *revive*
Thys Englonde Bretayne calle may ye,
    When thys tym ys commyn and gon.

---

55 *Historical Poems*, ed. Robbins, section headed Political Prophecies, within no. 43. The 'cocke in the north', below, is *ibid.* no. 43.
56 These are British princes.
57 Britain west of the Severn.

xxxv) *Prophecia Merlini doctoris perfecti*[58]

Whane lordes wol lefe° theire olde laws	*leave*
And preestis been varying in theire sawes,°	*doctrine*
And leccherie is holden solace.	
And oppressyoun for truwe purchace,°	*winnings*
And whan the moon is on David stall,°	*seat*
And the kynge passe Arthures hall,	
Than is the lande of Albyoun	
Nexst° to his confusyoun.	*nearest*

xxxvi) When the cocke in the north hath bilde his nest,
       And buskith° his briddis and becenys° hem to fle,   *prepares*   *beckons*
Then shall Fortune his frend the yatis° up cast,   *gates*
       And right shall have his fre entrée;

Thene shall the mone ris in the northewest,
       In a clowde of blacke as the bill of a crowe.
Then shall the lion louse° the boldest and the best,   *loose*
       That in Brytayne was born syne Arthers day.

And a dredefull dragon shall drawe hym from his denne
       To helpe the lion with all his might.
A bull and a bastard with speris to spen°   *grasp*
       Shall abide with the bore° to reken the right ...   *boar*

---

58   'A prophecy of Merlin the perfect doctor'. See The Prophecy of Merlin (Bodley MS),
     Poems of Political Prophecy, in *Medieval English Political Writings*, ed. Dean. In this
     edition, 'stall' is glossed as 'stable'. See also *The Oxford Book of Late Medieval Verse and
     Prose*, ed. Gray, p. 22.

D. Popular Religion

Prayers[59]

xxxvii) Moder of God, wich did lappe thy swete babe in clothes, and between two beestes in a crybbe layde hym in hey, pray for me that my naked soul be lapped in drede and love of my lorde God and the. Alleluya. *Ave Maria.*

O blessed Jesu, swetenes of hertes and gostely hony of soules, I bisiche the that for that bitternes of the asel [vinegar] and gall that thou suffred for me in thy passion, graunte for to receve worthily, holsomly and devoutely in the houre of my deth thi blessed body in the sacrament of the auter for remedy of my synnes and confort of my soule. Amen. *Pater noster. Ave.*

xxxviii) Prayer to a Guardian Angel[60]

O Angel dere, wher ever I goo,
    Me that am committed to thyn awarde.°   *keeping*
Save, defende, and govern also
    That in hewyn with the be my reward.

Clense my sowle from syn that I have do,
And vertuosly me wise° to Godward;   *direct*
Shyld me from the fende evermo
    And fro the peynes of hell so hard.

O thou cumly angell so gud and clere,
    That ever art abydyng with me,
Thowgh I may nother the se nor here
    Yet devoutely with trust I pray to the.

---

59   The first is cited in Gray's *Later Medieval English Literature*, p. 298 (probably from *The Rosary*, p. 304); for the second, see *Women's Writing in Middle English*, ed. Barratt, among the Fifteen Prayers Revealed to a Recluse. The Lord's Prayer (*Pater Noster*) and Hail Mary (*Ave Maria*), with the Creed, were the best-known prayers of the Middle Ages.

60   In *A Selection of Religious Lyrics*, ed. Gray, no. 70.

My body and sowle thou kepe in fere°   *together*
    With sodden deth departed that they not be,
For that is thyn offes,° both fere° and nere,   *office*   *far*
    In every place wher ever I be.

O blessid angell, to me so dere,
    Messangere of God almyght,
Govern my dedis and thowght in fere,
    To the plesaunce of God, both day and nyght.

xxxix) From Richard de Caistre's prayer (stanzas 1–6)[61]

Richard de Caistre (d. 1420), vicar of St Stephen's Norwich, was a 'good priest' admired by Margery Kempe.[62] This poem, of twelve stanzas in almost all copies, and attributed to Richard in several, seems to be an expanded version of a fourteenth-century poem (perhaps Richard's own early version). Judging by the number of copies, this 'Hymn' seems to have been much used. It is carefully arranged for individual devotional use, with six stanzas devoted to petitions for oneself, and six to petitions for others. The tone is calm and gentle; it ends with a general petition: 'and bring tho soules into blys Of qwom I have had ony goode, And spare [forgive] that thei han done amysse.' It is a good example of the simple style of petitions provided by clerks for their humble layfolk.

Jesu lorde that madest me,
And with thi blyssyd blode has bowght,°   *redeemed*
Foryeve that I have grevyd° the   *grieved*
In worde, werke,° [wille] and thowght.   *deeds*

Jesu, for thi woundys smerte°   *severe*
On fote and handys too,°   *two*
Make me meke and lowe in hert,
And the to love as I schulde doo.

---

61   In Gray's *Later Medieval English Literature*, pp. 370–1; see his *Selection of Religious Lyrics*, no. 51 (and notes) for the long version.
62   See ch. 43 in her *Book* (p. 102), for Richard Castyr.

Jesu [Criste] to the I calle,
As thu art [Fader] full of myght,
Kepe me clene, that I ne falle
In fleshely synn, as I have tyght.º   *resolved*

Jesu, grante me myn askyng,
Perfite pacyonisº in my desesse,º   *patience*   *distress*
And never I mot doo that thyng
That schulde yn onythyng dysplese.

Jesu, that art hevene kyng,
Sothfast God and man also,
Yeve me grace of [gode] ending
And hemº that I am beholdyn to.   *them*

Jesu, for thoo dulful terisº   *those sorrowful tears*
That thu gretystº for my gylt,   *wept*
Here and spedeº my preyorys,   *prosper*
And spare [me] that I be not spylt.º   *damned*

From *The Book of Margery Kempe*[63]

This book is a remarkable work by a remarkable woman of Lynn (or Bishop's Lynn, now King's Lynn), helped by her priest. It is not a self-consciously literary work, but is an account of her spiritual experiences, of her travels and tribulations, and a book of comfort for pious readers. After a severe mental illness she had a long conversion experience, and embarked on a life of religious enthusiasm, going (from 1413) on pilgrimages to the Holy Land, Rome, Compostella, and other shrines. The treatment of the events and adventures of her wandering life and of her visionary experiences are vivid and dramatic. She is frequently moved to tears, and her outbursts frequently embarrass bystanders. Her book is one of the most impressive testimonies to the depth of devotion found in popular religion, and one of the most compelling narratives of the fifteenth century.

---

63   *The Book of Margery Kempe*, eds Meech *et al.*

xl) A Visionary Meditation[64]

An instance of her imaginative participation in the Biblical stories, and of her simple and familiar relationship with Christ and other Biblical figures.

Another day this creatur schul[d] yeve [give] hir to medytacyon, as sche was bodyn [commanded] befor, and sche lay stylle, nowt knowing what sche mygth best thynke. Than sche seyd to ower lord Jesu Crist, 'Jesu, what schal I thynke?' Ower lord Jesu answeryd to hir mende, 'Dowtyr, thynke on my modyr, for sche is cause of alle the grace that thu hast.' And than anoon sche saw seynt Anne gret with chylde, and than sche preyd seynt Anne to be hir mayden and hir servawnt. And anon ower Lady was born, and than sche beside [busied] hir to take the chyld to hir and kepe it tyl it wer twelve yer of age wyth good mete and drynke, wyth fayr whyte clothys and whyte kerchys [kerchiefs]. And than sche seyd to the blyssed chyld, 'Lady, ye schal be the Modyr of God.' The blyssed chyld answeryd and seyd, 'I wold I wer worthy to be the handmaiden of hir that shuld conseive the Sone of God.' The creatur seyd, 'I pray yow, Lady, yyf that grace falle yow, forsake not my servyse.' The blysful chyld passyd awey for a certeyn tyme, the creatur being stylle in contemplacyon, and sythen cam ageyn and seyd, 'Dowtyr, now am I bekome the Modyr of God.' And than the creatur fel down on hir kneys wyth gret reverens and gret wepyng and syd, 'I am not worthy, Lady, to do yow servyse.' 'Yys, dowtyr,' sche seyde, 'folwe thow me, thi servyse lykyth me wel.' Than went sche forthe wyth owyr Lady and wyth Josep, beryng wyth hyr a potel of pyment[65] and spycys therto. Than went thei forth to Elysabeth, seynt John Baptystys modir, and whan thei mettyn togyder, eythyr of hem worshepyd [honoured] other, and so thei wonyd [dwelt] togedyr wyth gret grace and gladnesse xii wokys. And than seynt John was bor [born], and owyr Lady toke hym up fro the erthe wyth al maner reverens and yaf [gave] hym to hys modyr seyng of hym that he schuld be an holy man, and blyssed hym. Sythen thei toke her leve eythyr [each] of other wyth compassyf [piteous] terys. And than the creatur fel down on kneys to seynt Elyzabeth and preyd hir sche wolde prey for hir to owyr Lady that sche mygth do

---

64   Ch. 6 (pp. 18–19). Margery refers to herself as 'the creature'.
65   'a potel of pyment': a vessel (holding two quarts) of spiced and sweetened wine.

hir servyse and plesawns. 'Dowtyr, me semyth,' seyd Elysabeth, 'thu dost right wel thi dever [duty].' And than went the creatur forth wyth owyr Lady to Bedlem and purchasyd [procured] hir herborwe [lodging] every nyght wyth gret reverens, and owyr Lady was received wyth glad cher. Also sche beggyd owyr Lady fayr whyte clothys and kerchys for to swaythyn in hir Sone whan he wer born, and, whan Jesu was born, sche ordeyned beddyng for owyr Lady to lyg in wyth hir blyssed Sone. And sythen sche beggyd mete for owyr Lady and hir blyssyd chyld. Aftyrward sche swathyd hym wyth byttyr teerys of compassion, having mend [thought] of the scharp deth that he schold suffyr for the lofe of sinful men, seyng to hym, 'Lord, I schal fare fayr wyth yow; I schal not byndyn yow soor. I pray yow beth not dysplesyd wiyth me.'

xli) She meets a Poor Pilgrim with a Crooked Back[66]

On her travels she meets a variety of interesting people, some hostile or critical, others well disposed to her. Some are sympathetic clerics, but others are simple folk and 'outsiders' like William Wever with his white beard, from Devon, or 'Rychard wyth the broke bak', whom she met on her way between Venice and Rome after her company of pilgrims had abandoned her — some saying that they would not go with her for a hundred pounds.

Than anon, as sche lokyd on the on syde, sche set [saw] a powyr man sittyng whech had a gret cowche [hump] on hys bakke. Hys clothis wer all forclowtyd [patched], and he semyd a man of fifty wyntyr age. Than sche went to hym and seyde, 'Gode man, what eyleth yowr bak?' He seyd, 'Damsel, it was brokyn in a sekenes.' Sche askyd what was his name and what cuntreman he was. He seyd hys name was Richard and he was of Erlond [Ireland]. Than thowt sche of hir confessorys wordys which was an holy ankyr [anchorite], as is wretyn befor, that seyd to hir whil sche was in Inglond in this maner, 'Dowtyr, whan yowr owyn felawshep hath forsakyn yow, God shal ordeyn a broke-bakkyd man to lede yow forth ther ye wil [wish to] be.' Than sche wyth a glad spirit seyde unto hym, 'Good Richard, ledith me to Rome, and ye shal be rewardyd for yowr labowr.' 'Nay, damsel,' he seyd, 'I wot [know]

---

66   In Ch. 30, pp. 76–7.

wel thi cuntremen han forsakyn the, and therfor it wer hard to me to ledyn the. [For t]hy cuntremen han bothyn bowys and arwys, wyth the [whec]h they myth defendyn bothyn the and hemself [themselves], and [I have] no wepyn save a cloke ful of clowtys [patches]. And yet I drede me that myn enmys shul robbyn me and peraventur taken the awey fro me and defowlyn thy body, and therfor I dar not ledyn the, for I wold not for an hundryd pownd that thu haddyst a vylany in my cumpany.' And than sche seyd ayen [replied], 'Richard, dredith yow not; God shal kepyn us bothen ryth wel, and I shal yeve yow too [two] noblys for yowr labowr.' Than he consentyd and went forth wyth hir. Sone aftyr ther cam too Grey Frerys [Franciscans] and a woman that cam wyth hem fro Jerusalem, and sche had wyth hir an asse the whech bar a chyst and an ymage therin mad aftyr our Lord. And than seyd Richard to the forseyd creatur, 'Thu shalt go forth wyth thes too men and woman, and I shal metyn wyth the at morwyn and at evyn, for I must gon on my purchase [occupation] and beggyn [beg] my levyng.' And so sche dede aftyr hys cownsel and went forth wyth the frerys and the woman. And non of hem cowde understand hir langage, and yet thei ordeyned for hir every day mete, drynke and herborwe as wel as he [they] dedyn for hemselfe and rather bettyr, that [so that] sche was evyr bownden to prey for hem. And every evyn and morwyn Richard wyth the broke bak cam and comfortyd hir as he had promysed. And the woman the which had the ymage in hir chist, whan thei comyn in good citeys, sche toke owt the ymage owt of hir chist and sett it in worshepful wyfys lappys. And thei wold puttyn schirtys thereupon and kyssyn it as thei [though] it had ben God hymselfe.

xlii) A Visiting Priest Reads to Her[67]

… ther cam a preste newly to Lynne, which had nevyr knowyn hir beforn, and, whan he sey hir gon in the stretys, he was gretly mevyd to speke wyth hir and speryd [inquired] of other folke what maner woman sche was. Thei seyden thei trustyd to God that sche was a ryth good woman. Aftyrward the preyst sent for hyr, preyng hir to come and spekyn wyth hym and wyth hys modyr, for he had hired a chawmbyr for hys modyr and for hym, and so they dwellyd togedyr. Than the sayd

---

67   In Ch. 58 (pp. 142–3).

creatur cam to wetyn [know] hys wille and speke wyth hys modyr and wyth hym and had ryth good cher of hem bothyn. Than the preyste toke a boke and red therin how owr Lord, seyng the cyte of Jerusalem, wept thereupon, rehersyng the myschevys [misfortunes] and sorwys that shulde comyn therto, for sche knew not the tyme of hyr visitacyon.[68] Whan the sayd creatur herd redyn how owr Lord wept, than wept sche sor and cryed lowde, the preyste ne hys modyr knowing no cawse of hyr wepyng. Whan hir crying and hir wepyng was cesyd, thei joyyd and wer ryth mery in owr Lord. Sithyn sche toke hir leve and partyd fro hem at that tyme. Whan sche was gon, the preste seyd to hys modyr, 'Me merveyleth mech of this woman why sche wepith and cryith so. Nevyrtheles me thynkyth sche is a good woman, and I desire gretly to spekyn mor wyth hir.' Hys modyr was wel plesyd and cownselyd that he shulde don so. And aftyrwardys the same preste lovyd hir and trustyd hir ful meche and blissed the tyme that evyr he knew hir, for he fond gret gostly comfort in hir and cawsyd hym to lokyn meche good scriptur and many a good doctor which he wolde not a [have] lokyd at that tyme had sche ne be. He red to hir many a good boke of hy contemplacyon and othyr bokys, as the Bibel wyth doctowrys thereupon, seynt Brydys boke, Hyltons boke, Boneventur, Stimulus Amoris, Incendium Amoris,[69] and swech other …

xliii) A Fire at Lynn [1420–21][70]

On a tyme ther happyd to be a gret fyer in Lynne Bischop, which fyer brent up the Gyldehalle of the Trinite and in the same town an hydows fyer and grevows [destructive] ful likely to a [have] brent the parysch church dedicate in the honowr of seynt Margarete, a solempne place and rychely honowryd, and also al the town, ne had grace ne miracle ne ben. The seyd creatur being ther present and seyng the perel and myschef [plight] of al the towne, cryed ful lowde many tymes that day and wept ful habundawntly, preyng for grace and mercy to alle the pepil. And, notwythstondyng in other tymes thei myth not enduren hir to cryen and wepyn for the plentyvows grace that owr Lord wrowt in hir, as this

---

68   See Luke 19:41-4.
69   Notes in the edition give further details of these; a translation of Margery's *Book* (for example by Windeatt, 1985) may also be consulted.
70   Ch. 67, pp. 162–3.

day for enchewyng [eschewing] of her [their] bodily perel thei myth suffyr hir to cryen and wepyn as mech as evyr sche wolde, and no man wolde byddyn hir cesyn [cease] but rather preyn hir of contynuacyon, ful trustyng and belevyng that thorw hir crying and wepyng owr Lord wolde takyn hem to mercy. Than cam hir confessor to hir and askyd yyf it wer best to beryn [carry] the Sacrament to the fyer er not. Sche seyd, 'Yys, ser, yys, for owr Lord Jesu Crist telde me it shal be ryth wel.' So hir confessor, parisch preste of seynt Margaretys cherche, toke the precyows Sacrament and went beforn the fyer as devowtly as he cowde and sithyn browt it in ageyn to the cherche, and the sparkys of the fyer fleyn abowte the church. The seyd creatur, desiring to folwyn the precyows Sacrament to the fyre, went owt at the church-dor, and, as sone as sche beheld the hedows flawme of the fyr, anon sche cryed wyth lowed voys and gret wepyng, 'Good Lorde, make it wel.' Thes wordys wrowt in hir mende inasmeche as owr Lord had seyd to hir beforn that he shulde makyn it wel, and therfor sche cryed, 'Good Lord, make it wel and sende down sum reyn er sum wedyr [storm] that may thorw thi mercy qwenchyn this fyer and esen myn hert.' Sithyn sche went ageyne into the church, and than sche beheld how the sparkys comyn into the qwer [choir] thorw the lantern of the cherch. Than had sche a newe sorwe and cryed ful lowde ageyn for grace and mercy wyth gret plente of terys. Sone aftyr, comyn in to hir thre worschepful men wyth whyte snow on her clothys, seying unto hir, 'Lo, Margery, God hath wrowt gret grace for us and sent us a feyr snowe to qwenchyn wyth the fyr. Beth now of good cher and thankyth God therfor.'

xliv) A Woman who was Out of her Mind[71]

As the seyd creatur was in a chirch of seynt Margaret to sey hur devocyons, ther cam a man knelyng at hir bak, wryngyng hys handys and schewyng tokenys of gret hevynes. Sche, parceyvyng hys hevynes, askyd what hym eylyd. He seyd it stod ryth hard wyth hym, for hys wyfe was newly delyveryd of a childe and sche was owt hir mende. 'And, dame,' he seyth, 'sche knowyth not me ne non of hir neyborys. Sche roryth and cryith so that sche makith folk evyl afeerd [terribly

---

71   Ch. 75, pp. 177–8. The woman recovers and is purified in church; it is regarded as a 'right great miracle'.

afraid]. Sche wyl bothe smytyn and bityn, and therfor is sche manykyld [manacled] on hir wristys.' Than askyd sche the man yyf he wolde that sche went wyth hym and sawe hir, and he seyd, 'Ya, dame, for Goddys lofe.' So sche went forth wyth hym to se the woman. And, whan sche cam into the hows, as sone as the seke woman that was alienyd of hir witte saw hir, sche spak to hir sadly [soberly] and goodly and seyd sche was ryth welcome to hir. And sche was ryth glad of hir comyng and gretly comfortyd be hir presens, 'For ye arn', sche seyd, 'a ryth good woman, and I beheld many fayr awngelys abowte yow, and therfor, I pray yow, goth not fro me, for I am gretly comfortyd be yow.' And, whan other folke cam to hir, sche cryid and gapyd as sche wolde an [have] etyn hem and seyd that sche saw many develys abowtyn hem. Sche wolde not suffyrn hem to towchyn hir be hyr good wyl. Sche roryd and cryid so bothe nyth and day for the most part that men wolde not suffyr hir to dwellyn amongys hem, sche was so tediows to hem. Than was sche had to the forthest ende of the town into a chambyr that the pepil shulde not heryn hir cryin. And ther was sche bowndyn handys and feet with chenys of iron that sche shulde smytyn nobody. And the seyd creatur went to hir iche day onys er twyis at the lest wey [at least], and, whyl sche was wyth hir, sche was meke anow [enough] and herd hir spekyn and dalyin [converse] wyth good wil wythowtyn any roryng er crying. And the syd creatur preyid for this woman every day that God shulde, yyf it were hys wille, restoryn hir to hir wittys ageyn. And owr Lord answeryd in hir sowle and seyd, 'Sche shulde faryn ryth wel.' Than was sche mor bolde to preyin for hir recuryng [recovery] than sche was beforn, and iche day, wepyng and sorwyng, preyid for hir recur tyl God yaf hir hir witte and hir mende ayen [again] ...

xlv) A Conversation with Christ[72]

... Than answeryd owr Lord to hir and seyd, 'I prey the, dowtyr, yeve me not ellys but lofe. Thou maist nevyr plesyn me bettyr than havyn me evyr in thi lofe, ne tho shalt nevyr in no penawns that thu mayst do in erth plesyn me so meche as for to lovyn me. And, dowtyr, yyf thu wilt ben hey in hevyn wyth me, kepe me alwey in thi mende as meche as thu mayst and foryete me not at thi mete [mealtimes], but think alwey

---

72   In ch. 77, p. 184; both participants speak in a straightforward idiomatic style.

that I sitte in thin hert and knowe every thowt that is therin, bothe good
and ylle, and that I parceyve the lest thynkyng and twynkelyng of thyn
eye.' Sche seyd ayen [in reply] to owr Lord, 'Now trewly, Lord, I wolde
I cowed lovyn the as mych as thu mythist [might] makyn me to lovyn
the. Yyf it wer possible, I wolde lovyn the as wel as alle the seyntus in
hevyn lovyn the and as wel as alle the creaturys in erth myth lovyn the.
And I wolde, Lord, for thi lofe be leyd nakyd on an hyrdil,[73] alle men
to wondryn on me for thi love, so it wer no perel to her [their] sowlys,
and thei to castyn slory and slugge on me, and be drawyn fro town to
town every day my lyfetyme, yyf thu wer plesyd therby and no mannys
sowle hyndryd, thi wil mote be fulfillyd and not myn.'

xlvi) Margery's Own Tale[74]

Accused before the Archbishop of York of preaching, she defiantly
announces 'I preche not, ser, I come in no pulpytt. I use but
comownycacion and good wordys …'. But a 'doctor' present says she
told him 'the werst talys of prestys that evyr I herde'; the Archbishop
commands her to tell the tale.

Sir, with yowr reverens, I spake but of o [one] preste be the maner of
exampyl, the which as I have lernyd went wil [wandering] in a wode
thorw the sufferawns of God for the profite of his sowle tyl the nygth
cam upon hym. He, destitute of hys herborwe [lodging], fond a fayr erber
[arbor] in the which he restyd that nyght, having a fayr pertre [pear-tree]
in the myddys al floreschyd wyth flowerys and belschyd [embellished],
and blomys ful delectabil to hys sight, wher cam a bere, gret and boistows
[rough], hogely to beheldyn, schakyng the pertre and fellyng down the
flowerys. Gredily this grevows best ete and devowryd tho fayr flowerys,
and, whan he had etyn hem, turning hys tayl-ende in the prestys presens,
voydyd hem owt ageyn at the hy[nd]yr party. The preste, having gret
abhominacyon of that lothly sight, conceyvyng gret hevynes [sorrow] for
dowte what it myth mene, on the next day he wandrid forth in his wey al
hevy and pensife, whom [and to him] it fortunyd to metyn wyth a semly
agydd man lych to a palmyr or a pilgrim, the whiche enqwiryd of the

---

73 A hurdle was used to carry prisoners to execution; the public might throw 'slurry
    and sludge' over the unfortunates.
74 In Ch. 52, pp. 126–7.

preste the cawse of hys hevynes. The preste, rehersyng the mater beforn-wretyn, seyd he conceyvyd gret drede and hevynes whan he beheld that lothly best defowlyn and devowryn so fayr flowerys and blomys and afterward so horrybely to devoydyn hem befor hym at hys tayl-ende, and he not undirstondyng what this myth mene. Than the palmyr, schewyng hymselfe the massanger of God, thus aresond [addressed] hym, 'Preste, thu thiself art the pertre, sumdel [to some degree] florischyng and floweryng thorw thi servyse seyyng and the sacramentys ministryng, thow thu do undevowtly, for thu takyst ful lytyl heede how thu seyst thi mateynes and thi servyse, so it be blaberyd [babbled] to an ende. Than gost thu to thi Messe wythowtyn devocyon, and for thi synne hast thu ful lityl contricyon. Thu receyvyst ther the frute of evyrlestyng lyfe, the sacrament of the awter, in ful febyl disposicyon. Sithen [then], al the day aftyr thu myssespendist thi tyme: thu yevist the [give yourself] to bying and selling, chopping and chongyng, as it wer a man of the world. Thu sittyst at the ale, yevyng the to glotonye and excesse, to lust of thy body, thorw letchery and unclennesse. Thu brekyst the commawndmentys of God thorw sweryng, lying, detraccyon, and swech other synnes usyng. Thus be thy mysgovernawns, lych onto the lothly ber, thu devowryst and destroist the flowerys and blomys of vertuows levyng to thyn endles dampnacyon and many mannys hyndryng lesse than [unless] thu have grace of repentawns and amending.' Than the Erchebisshop likyd wel the tale and comendyd it, seying it was a good tale. And the clerk which had examynd hir befortyme in the absens of the Erchebischop, seyd, 'Ser, this tale smytyth me to the hert.'

Chapter 2

Ballads

The question of 'medieval ballads' has excited much heated discussion, which sadly seems to have led to a recent neglect, with the result that they are often not thought of as belonging to medieval literature. The discussion has been blighted by the presence lurking in its background of two opposed and extreme views: 1) an ahistorical sense that ballads are somehow 'timeless' and 2) its opposite, a fiercely historicist view that since they are the product of a particular time and place they should be 'dated' at or very close to the time at which they are recorded. Objections can be raised against both extremes: some ballads recorded in relatively modern times seem certainly to be ancient, but questions of time and place are always there. The ballad of 'Johnnie Armstrong' (Child 169, recorded in the seventeenth century) presumably dates from soon after the death by summary execution of that Border reiver in c. 1530, although ballads with a similar type of story could well have existed. On the other hand, there is evidence that some ballads were in existence before they were 'recorded'. And the stories of some ballads seem to be very ancient, existing sometimes in differing literary forms. Child, discussing 'Tam Lin' (no. 39, recorded in a volume printed 1792) mentions a Cretan fairy tale (recorded even later), with a very similar plot, and points out a similarity with the pre-Homeric story of the forced marriage of Thetis with Peleus in Apollodorus,[1] remarking that

---

1   Probably in the *Bibliotheke*, Pseudo-Apollodorus (1st or 2nd century AD); see *OCCL* (and for the story).

   https://doi.org/10.11647/OBP.0170.02

such a long period of (possible) transmission will not seem unlikely 'to those who bear in mind the tenacity of tradition among people who have never known books'.

At this point some rough definition or description of the term 'ballad' will be useful: as, perhaps, a poem which tells a story, designed for singing or reciting (characteristically in stanzaic form), often short or shortish. The story, usually of a single action, is exciting or unusual and the teller normally concentrates on the crucial or dramatic situations or events. The method of narrative is 'impersonal'. It is simple, direct, and straightforward, making much use of direct speech and of emphatic narrative techniques (repetitions and recapitulations, and the technique of 'leaping and lingering').[2] The narrator does not psychologise, or analyse the events in depth; the story exists for its own sake. This rough definition echoes those offered by experts in ballad studies, but is deliberately wider — to escape the problem raised by some definitions, of depending exclusively on the excellent Scottish 'border ballads' in Child's collection.

Two points require a little further annotation:

1) The question of length. The majority of the examples used here are short, but *Adam Bell* (no. iv) with its 70 quatrains can hardly be called short, nor can the *Gest of Robyn Hode* (no. v), which is even longer. In fact a number of Child's ballads have 70 or more stanzas (some, but not all, recorded in *PFMS*, and 'long ballads' are also found in European balladry (for example, the long ballad of 'Marsk Stig', 101 stanzas, apparently compiled from three shorter ballads).[3] A reasonable guess might be that the length of the longer examples depends on the subject matter (a battle ballad like *Otterburn*, 70 stanzas, or the *Hunting of the Cheviot*, 64–8 stanzas,[4] might seem to require a fuller treatment), and also on the amount of material a performer had to hand, and on the nature of the audience and of the performance he was required to give: that both the *Gest* and *Adam Bell* are divided into 'fyttes' suggests at

---

2   For this phrase, in a similar context, see *Rymes*, p. 113.
3   'Marsk Stig Made An Outlaw' is in *Rymes*.
4   Both *Otterburn* and *Cheviot* are in Child; only *Otterburn* appears in this book.

least the possibility of performance in a series of stages or sittings. It is arguable that even these passages of longer narrative still maintain a sense of an essential brevity. But it is possible that *Adam Bell*, like the *Gest*, was made from pre-existing stories of adventures, and its style is similar to that of some popular romances. 'Ballads' and 'romances' are not always clearly distinguished in early accounts: see, for example, the hostile remark in Puttenham's *Arte of English Poesie* (from the later sixteenth century) on the 'small and popular musickes' sung by the 'cantabanqui ... or else by blind harpers or suchlike tavern minstrels that give a fit of mirth for a groat, and their matters being for the most part stories of old time, as the tale of Sir Topas, the reports of Bevis of Southampton, Guy of Warwicke, Adam Bell and Clymme of the Clough and such other old romances or historicall Rimes ...'.

2) The word 'impersonal' may also mislead. A reader or hearer may well feel that they have no difficulty in identifying good characters and evil ones, and, moreover, can point to explicit statements of approval or disapproval — as in the exclamation directed against the treacherous 'old wyfe' in *Adam Bell*: 'Evel mote she spede therefore!' However, such moments seem to arise from the story itself and the way it is told — the reactions of a narrator in performance rather than from the conscious artifice of the original 'author' who first put the story together. He and his 'personality' or 'individuality' remain hidden from sight. We are aware of the presence of the narrator, but not usually of the person who first put the story together, and certainly not of his personality or individuality. Hence Kittredge's words seem quite sensible: 'a ballad has no author. At all events it appears to have none.'[5] We must not underestimate the importance of performance: these poems were meant to be heard rather than read. And, to judge from the famous remark of Sidney, 'I never heard the old song of Percy and Douglas that I found not my heart moved more than with a trumpet; and yet it is sung by some blind crowder [fiddler] with no rougher vice than rude style',[6] they could move their audience.

---

5   George Lyman Kittredge, English professor and folklorist, collaborated with Child on his edition of Ballads.

6   Cited in (for example) Stewart, *Philip Sidney*, p. 114; Puttenham's comment (in the paragraph above) follows on p. 115.

To the question 'were there any medieval English ballads, or ballad-like poems?' the answer is a fairly firm yes. That the evidence of our written records is fragmentary and apparently erratic does not necessarily indicate that the material was not there. The age of enthusiastic antiquarian collectors of traditional ballads was still to come. To be 'collected' in the Middle Ages a ballad might be seen as useful for religious instruction or sermon (as is possible with *Judas*, or *Saint Stephen*), or perhaps for personal use, sometimes because of personal taste or simple chance. Sixteenth-century printers seem to have identified a popular taste for 'outlaw ballads'. Above all, we must not underestimate the power of popular memory, 'the tenacity of tradition among people who have never known books.'[7]

Our selection here tries to illustrate this in its arrangement: A) 'early texts', from the thirteenth to the sixteenth century; B) from the seventeenth-century *PFMS* — a collection whose narrow escape from destruction illustrates the fragility of our surviving corpus.[8] And C) a few 'modern' examples, which may have connections with medieval poems (chosen from a potentially long list, although in many cases the 'transmission' remains obscure).[9] This problem occurs also in the case of apparent allusions to particular ballads. For example, in the mid-sixteenth century *Complaynt of Scotland* 'the tayl of the yong Tamlene' is mentioned, as is 'Thom of Lyn', a dance.[10] These references, together with a couple in the sixteenth and seventeenth centuries, suggest very strongly that the story of the ballad of Tam Lin was known well before the text of 1792, but do not tell us about its forms or style. The remains of the early ballads and ballad-like poems, although of great interest, may now seem fragmentary or scanty, but this can be misleading. The total corpus could well have been much more extensive: we may suspect that there were more 'religious ballads', and probably more 'battle ballads' (on battles such as Harlaw, Agincourt, and Flodden,[11] or less well-known encounters); we know that there were many Robin Hood ballads beside those which appeared in manuscript or print.

---

7   See the reference to Child, above.
8   It narrowly escaped being used for lighting the fire.
9   A few later ballads, of probable medieval origin, appear in the Appendix (below); their transmission is more obscure than those in this chapter.
10   *The Complaynt of Scotland*, ed. Wedderburn, pp. 50 & 52.
11   These three are printed in Child, but were not selected for this book.

It seems very probable that the oral tradition continued alongside the 'popular' tradition, presumably with overlaps, borrowings and 'donations' between them. And it would be deeply misleading to think of all this as something totally fixed and static. The scene was probably one of constant movement, with ballads moving between the traditions, ballads constantly developing, being retold and revised, and new ones created.[12]

A. Medieval and Early Modern Ballads

i) *Judas*[13]

This poem, found in a thirteenth-century manuscript (a preacher's book), is often called the first recorded English ballad, although there have been dissenting voices, expressing doubts about its earliness and its apparent isolation. In fact it may not be totally isolated: the manuscript contains some (possibly) comparable narrative poems, called by the manuscript's editor Karl Reichl 'geistliche Spielmannsdichtung'.[14] These, the legend of Saint Margaret and a poem on the Three Kings, have something of the rapidity of narrative found in *Judas*. The matter of the poem comes from the extensive legendary material which surrounded the figure of Judas — attempts, perhaps, to explain if not exonerate his horrendous act of treachery. Child mentions a Wendish ballad in which he lost thirty pieces of silver gambling with the Jews, and then follows their suggestion that he sell his master for them. *Judas* seems to have so many of the characteristics of later ballads — rapid, abrupt transitions, repetitions, the action carried by dialogue, impersonality — that it is almost impossible not to call it a ballad.

Hit wes upon a Scere Thorsday°	*Maundy Thursday*
That ure Loverd aros,	
Ful milde were the wordes	
He spec to Judas,	

---

12   Some of the ballads in this chapter are discussed in Gray's *Later Medieval English Literature*, the section entitled Romances and Tales.

13   In *Fourteenth Century Verse and Prose* (pp. 168–9; notes pp. 256–7).

14   Clerical minstrel poems.

'Judas, thou most to Jurselem
    Oure mete° for to bugge,°   *food*   *buy*
Thritti platen° of selver   *thirty pieces*
    Thou bere° up o thi rugge.°   *must carry*   *back*

Thou comest fer i the brode stret,°   *highway*
    Fer i the brode street,
Summe of thine cunesmen°   *kinsmen*
    Ther thou meist imete.'

Imette° wid is soster   *he met*
    The swikele wimon,°   *deceitful woman*
'Judas, thou were wrthe°   *you deserve*
    Me° stende° the wid ston.   *people*   *stoned*

Judas, thou were wrthe
    Me stende the wid ston.
For the false prophete
    That tou bilevest upon.'

'Be stille,° leve° soster,   *silent*   *dear*
    Thin herte the tobreke!°   *may your heart break*
Wiste min Loverd Crist,
    Ful wel he wolde be wreke.'

'Judas, go thou on the roc,
    Heie upon the ston,
Lei thin heved° i my barm,°   *head*   *bosom*
    Slep thou the anon.'°   *quickly*

Sone so° Judas   *as soon as*
    Of slepe was awake,
Thritti platen of selver
    From hym weren itake.°   *taken*

He drou hymselve bi the top°	*tore his hair*
That al it lavede ablode;°	*streamed with blood*
The Jewes out of Jurselem	
Awenden° he were wode.°	*imagined* *mad*

Foret° hym com the riche Jeu	*towards*
That heiste° Pilatus,	*was called*
'Wolte sulle° thi Loverd	*sell*
That hette Jesus?'	

'I nul° sulle my Loverd	*will not*
For nones cunnes eiste,°	*any kind of treasure*
Nay, bote° hit be for the thritti platen	*unless*
That he me bitaiste.'°	*entrusted to*

'Wolte sulle thi Lord Crist
    For enes cunnes golde?'
'Nay, bote hit be for the platen
    That he habben wolde.'

In him com ur Lord gon,°	*came in*
As is postles° seten at mete,	*disciples*
'Wou° sitte ye, postles,	*why*
And wi nule ye° ete?	*why will you not*

'Wou sitte ye, postles,	
And wi nule ye ete?	
Ic am iboust ant isold°	*bought and sold*
Today for oure mete.'	

Up stod him Judas,	
'Lord, am I that [frec]?°	*man*
I was never o the stude°	*in the place*
Ther me the evel spec.'°	*where people spoke evil of you*

Up him stod Peter
    And spec wid al is miste,º   *might*
'Thauº Pilatus him come   *though*
    Wid ten hundred cnist[e],º   *knights*

Thau Pilatus him come
    Wid ten hundred cnist[e],
Yet ic wolde, loverd,
    For thi love fiste.'º   *fight*

'Still thou be, Peter,
    Wel I the icnowe,
Thou wolt forsake me thrienº   *thrice*
    Arº the coc him crowe.'   *before*

ii) *Saint Stephen and Herod*

This poem is found in an early fifteenth-century manuscript, a collection
of songs and carols.[15] It is a pious legend; the same miracle as in the
'Carnal [crow] and the Crane' (Child 55, recorded in Sandys *Christmas
Carols*, 1833) but probably more ancient: there it is associated with the
Three Kings and the adoration of a lion. This poem also has significant
features: a dramatic style, an impersonal question and answer pattern,
and perhaps a hint of incremental repetition ('in kyng Herowdes halle').
Although religious ballads are not frequent in Child's collection, it
seems likely that in the Middle Ages they were more numerous. For
another ballad recorded in the fifteenth century, see the riddle ballad
The Devil and the Maid; and the *PFMS King John and the Bishop* (both in
our Chapter 7, xv and xvi).

Seynt Stevene was a clerkº   *attendant*
    In kyng Herowdes halle,
And servyd him of bred and cloth
    As every kyng befalle.º   *befits*

---

15   In *The Oxford Book of Medieval English Verse*, no. 31 (also in Child, no. 22).

Stevyn out of kechon° cam   *kitchen*
  Wyth boris° hed on honde,   *boar's*
He saw a sterre° was fayr and bright   *star*
  Over Bedlem° stonde.   *Bethlehem*

He kyst° adoun the boris hed   *cast*
  And went in to the halle,
'I forsak the, kyng Herowdes,
  And thi werkes allle.

I forsak the, kyng Herowdes,
  And thi werkes alle,
Ther is a chyld in Bedlem born
  Is beter than we alle.'

'Quat eylyt° the, Stevene?   *what ails*
  Quat is the befalle?°   *has happened to you*
Lakkyt the° eyther mete or drynk   *do you lack*
  In kyng Herowdes halle?'

'Lakit me neyther mete ne drynk
  In kyng Herowdes halle;
Ther is a chyld in Bedlem born
  Is beter than we alle.'

'Quat eylyt the, Stevyn? Art thu wod,°   *mad*
  Or thu gynnyst to brede?°   *beginnest to rave*
Lakkyt the eyther gold or fe°   *reward*
  Or ony riche wede?'°   *garment*

'Lakyt me neyther gold ne fe,
  Ne non ryche wede,
Ther is a chyld in Bedlem born
  Shal helpyn us at our nede.'

'That is al so soth,° Stevyn,   *as true*
        Al so soth, iwys,°   *indeed*
As this capoun° crowe shal   *capon*
        That lyth° here in myn dysh.'   *lies*

That word was not so sone° seyd,   *no sooner*
        That word in that halle,
The capoun crew *Cristus natus est!*°   *Christ is born*
        Among the lordes alle.

'Rysyt° up, myn turmentowres,°   *rise*   *torturers*
        Be to° and al be on,°   *two*   *one (= one and all)*
And ledyt Stevyn out of this town,
        And stonyt hym wyth ston!'

Tokyn he° Stevene   *took they*
        And stonyd hym in the way,
And therefore is his evyn°   *eve*
        On Crystes owyn day.

iii) *The Battle of Otterburn*[16]

Recorded in a mid-sixteenth century manuscript; the battle took place in 1388. It is an example of a 'battle ballad'. The reference in the *Complaynt of Scotland* (also mid-sixteenth) to 'The Perssee and the Mongumrye met' may be from this version, or from the *Hunting of the Cheviot* or from an independent Scottish poem, now lost. This version seems to be firmly English. It has the characteristics of what seems to have been a well-liked type of ballad: an exciting narrative with much dialogue. It has some moments of genuine excitement, such as the cry of the Scottish knight, 'Awaken Dowglas!', culminating in a personalised battle between two chivalric heroes. According to Froissart, Otterburn was 'the hardest and most obstinate battle that was ever fought.'[17]

---

16   Child, no. 161.
17   Froissart, *Chronicles*, trans. Brereton, pp. 335–48.

The ballad is long (280 lines, 70 stanzas). Our extract (stanzas 9–25, vv. 33–100; most of the first fytte) gives the run-up to the battle and its beginning. The Scots had assembled a large army, divided into two parts: the main force towards west Carlisle; the other, under the command of James Douglas and other Scottish nobles, to Newcastle, which they attacked. Douglas marched to Otterburn. The English gathered a great army and marched there. Although superior in numbers, the English were defeated. Sir Henry Percy was captured, and Douglas killed.

… To the Newe Castell when they cam
    The Skottes they cryde on hyght,°   *on high*
'Syr Harry Perssy, and thou byste° within,   *if thou be*
    Com to the fylde and fight.

For we have brent° Northomberlonde,   *burnt*
    Thy erytage° good and right,   *heritage*
And syne° my logeyng° I have take,   *then*   *encampment*
    Wyth my brande° dubbyt many a knight.'   *sword*

Syr Harry Perssy cam to the walles,
    The Skottyssch oste for to se,
And sayd, 'And° thou hast brente Northomberlond,   *if*
    Ful sore it rewyth° me.   *grieves*

Yf thou hast haryed all Bamborowe schyre,°   *pillaged the region of Bamburgh*
    Thow hast done me grete envye:°   *harm*
For the trespasse° thow hast me done,   *offence*
    The tone° of us schall dye!'   *one*

'Where schall I byde the?'° sayd the Dowglas,   *await you*
    'Or where wylte thow com to me?'
'At Otterborne, in the high way,
    Ther mast thow well logeed be.

The roo° full rekeles° ther sche rinnes,'°   *deer*   *without fear*   *runs*
     To make the game and glee,°   *pleasure and sport*
The fawken° and the fesaunt both,   *falcon*
     Among the holtes° on hye.   *woods*

Ther mast° thow have thy welth° at wyll   *may*   *booty*
     Well looged ther mast be —
Yt schall not be long or° I com the tyll,'°   *before*   *to you*
     Sayd Syr Harry Perssye.

'Ther schall I byde the,' sayd the Dowglas,
     'By the fayth of my bodye.'
'Thether schall I com,' sayd Syr Harry Perssy,
     'My trowth I plight to the.'

A pype° of wyne he gave them over the walles,   *cask*
     For soth as I yow saye;
Ther he made the Dowglasse drynke,
     And all hys ost that daye.

The Dowglas turnyd hym homewarde agayne,
     For soth withowghten naye,°   *denial*
He toke hys logeyng at Oterborne,
     Upon a Wedynsday.

And ther he pyght° hys standard dowyn,   *fixed*
     Hys gettyng° more and lesse,   *booty*
And syne he warned hys men to goo
     To chose° ther geldynges gresse.°   *find*   *horses grass*

A Skottysshe knygh hoved° upon the bent° —   *waited*   *field*
     A wache° I dare well saye —   *sentinel*
So was he ware on° the noble Perssy   *caught sight of*
     In the dawnyng of the daye.

He pricked^o to hys pavyleon dore   *rode*
    As faste as he might ronne,
'Awaken, Dowglas!' cryed the knight,
    'For Hys love that syttes in trone.

Awaken, Dowglas!' cryed the knyght,
    'For thow maste waken wyth wynne,^o   *joy*
Yender^o have I spyed the prowde Perssye,   *yonder*
    And seven stondardes wyth hym.'

'Nay, by my trowth,' the Dowglas sayed,
    'It ys but a fayned^o taylle,   *false*
He durste not loke on my brede^o banner   *broad*
    For all Ynglonde so haylle.^o   *for the whole of England*

Was I not yesterday at the Newe Castell,
    That stondes so fayre on Tyne?
For all the men the Perssy had,
    He coude not garre^o me ones to dyne.'   *make*

He stepped owt at his pavelyon dore,
    To loke and^o it were le[s]e,^o   *if*   *false*
'Araye yow, lordynges, one and all!
    For here bygynnes no peysse!'^o   *peace*

The battle continues: 'The Perssy and the Douglas mette … They swapped together whyll that the swette … Tyll the bloode fro ther bassonnettes ranne.' Finally the Douglas is killed: 'Ther the Dowglas lost hys lyffe, And the Perssy was lede away.' He was, says the poem, exchanged for a Scottish prisoner, Sir Hugh Montgomery.

B. Poems from *PFMS*

iv) *Adam Bell, Clim of the Clough, and William of Cloudesly*[18]

This fine outlaw ballad survives in a print by William Copland (c.1560). There are fragments of an earlier printing by John Byddell (1536), a later edition (1605) by James Roberts, and a copy in *PFMS*. These, with other references in the sixteenth century, suggest that it circulated widely in the sixteenth and seventeenth centuries. Other references indicate its popularity well before the Copland print: the names of the three outlaws appear (satirically) along with those of Robin Hood and others in a Parliament Roll for Wiltshire,[19] far to the south of Cumbria, where the story is set and may have originated. An even earlier reference is probably that to 'Allan Bell', an archer in Dunbar's poem on Sir Thomas Norny.[20] The ballad seems designed to be read aloud. It has the traditional characteristics: sudden use of direct speech ('Thys nyght is come unto thys town Wyllyam of Cloudesle'), moments of dramatic intensity, and a certain impersonality — Cloudesly besieged in his house is like a scene from an Icelandic saga. But its narrative style is more relaxed than that of the shorter ballads, and it sometimes reads like a popular romance — and that makes it easier for a modern reader to read it 'on the page'. Women have a more significant role than in the Robin Hood ballads.[21] It is tempting to speculate that it may have something of the encyclopedic tendency seen in the *Gest of Robyn Hode* to incorporate everything known to the maker about the outlaws' life, even to the inclusion of Cloudesly's display of his already proven skill in archery in the 'Wilhelm Tell feat' (which is made into a little 'pitous' scene). But as it stands the poem reads well, and it must have been exciting to listen to.

These three yeomen of the north country are sworn brethren, who hunt the deer in 'Englysshe-wood' [Inglewood], and are outlawed

---

18   This, numbered Child 116, is printed with notes in *Rymes*.
19   Nigel Cawthorne, *A Brief History of Robin Hood*, mentions this document in Chapter 3 (The Hero of the Ballads). See also *Robin Hood and Other Outlaw Tales*, Knight and Ohlgren, Introduction to Adam Bell.
20   In *Selected Poems of Henryson & Dunbar*: Now Lythis of ane Gentill Knycht (and 'wyld Robein' probably refers to Robin Hood; see notes on pp. 232–3).
21   Gray marked a note here, without indicating anything further. The poem does indeed treat William's wife, and the queen, sympathetically; but this book is not about the way women are portrayed in his chosen texts so I have not followed up the idea.

'for venison'. William is a wedded man, and wishes to go to Carlisle to speak with Alice his wife and his three children. Adam Bell warns him of the danger, but he goes: 'If that I come not tomorowe, brother, By pryme to you agayne, Truste not els but that I am take Or else that I am slayne.' He is warmly received by Alice, who 'feched him meat and drynke plenty, Lyke a true wedded wyfe ...' [vv. 57–379, stanzas 15–94]

... There lay an old wyfe in that place,
　　A lytle beside the fyre,
Whych Wyllyam had found,° of cherytye　　　　*provided for*
　　More than seven yere.

Up she rose and walked full styll;°　　　　*silently*
　　Evel mote she spede° therefoore!　　　　*fare*
For she had not set no fote on ground
　　In seven yere before.

She went unto the justice hall
　　As fast as she could hye,°　　　　*hurry*
'Thys nyght is come unto thys town
　　Wyllyam of Cloudesle.'

Thereof the justice was full fayne°　　　　*glad*
　　And so was the shirife also,
'Thou shalt not travaile hether,° dame, for nought;　*struggle here*
　　Thy meed° thou shalt have or° thou go.'　　*reward* 　*before*

They gave to her a right good goune,°　　　　*gown*
　　Of scarlet it was as I heard sayne;
She toke the gyft and home she wente
　　And couched° her doune agayne.　　　　*lay*

They rysed° the towne of mery Carlel°　　*roused* 　*Carlisle*
　　In all the hast that they can.
And came thronging to Wyllyames house
　　As fast [as] they might gone.

Theyr they besette° that good yeman   *surrounded*
    Round about on every syde;
Wyllyam hearde great noyse of folks
    That heytherward they hyed.

Alyce opened a shot-wyndow,°   *hinged window*
    And loked all about;
She was ware of the justice and the shrife bothe,
    Wyth a full great route.°   *crowd*

'Alas! treason,' cryed Alyce,
    'Ever wo may thou be!
Go into my chamber, my husband,' she sayd,
    'Swete Wyllyam of Cloudesle.'

He toke hys sweard and hys bucler,
    Hys bow and hys children thre,
And wente into hys strongest chamber,
    Where he thought surest° to be.   *most secure*

Fayre Alice folowed him as a lover true,
    With a pollaxe° in her hande,   *long-handled axe*
'He shalbe deade that here cometh in
    Thys dore, whyle I may stand.'

Cloudesle bent a wel good bowe
    That was of trusty tre,°   *wood*
He smot the justice on the brest
    That hys arrowe brest° in thre.   *broke*

'Gods curse on his hart,' saide William,
    'Thys day thy cote° dyd° on —   *coat of mail*   *put*
If it had ben no better than myne,
    It had gone nere thy bone.'

'Yelde the, Cloudesle,' sayd the justice,
    'And thy bowe and thy arrows the fro!'º   *[yield] from you*
'Gods curse on hys hart,' sayde fair Alice,
    'That my husband councelleth so.'

'Set fyre on the house,' saide the sherife,
    'Syth it wyll no better be!
And brenneº we therin William,' he saide,   *burn*
    'Hys wyfe and children thre.'

They fyred the house in many a place.
    The fyre flew up on hye,
'Alas!' then cryed fayr Alice,
    'I se we shall here dy!'

William openyd hys backe window,
    That was in hys chamber on hye,
And wyth shetes let hys wyfe downe
    And hys children thre.

'Have here my treasure!' sayde William,
    'My wyfe and my children thre;
For Christes love do them no harme,
    But wrekeº you all on me!'   *avenge*

Wyllyam shot so wonderous well
    Tyll hys arrows were all go,º   *gone*
And the fyre so fast upon hym fell,
    That hys bowstryng brentº in two.   *burnt*

The sperclesº brent and fell hym on,   *embers*
    Good Wyllyam of Cloudesle.
But then was he a wofull man, and sayde,
    'Thys is a cowards death to me.

Lever° I had,' sayde Wyllyam,   *rather*
　　'With my sworde in the route to renne°   *run*
Thenne here among myne ennemyes wode°   *furious*
　　Thus cruelly to bren.'

He toke hys sweard and hys buckler,
　　And among them all he ran;
Where the people were most in prece,°   *crowd*
　　He smot downe many a man.

There might no man stand° hys stroke,   *withstand*
　　So fersly on them he ran;
Then they threw wyndowes and dores on him
　　And so toke° that good yeman.   *captured*

There they hym bounde both hand and fote,
And in depe dungeon hym cast,
'Now, Cloudesle' sayde the hye justice,
'Thou shalt be hanged in hast.'

'One vow shal I make,' syde the sherife.
　　'A payre of new galowes shall I for the make,
And al the gates of Caerlel° shalbe shutte,   *Carlisle*
　　There shall no man come in therat.

Then shall not helpe Clim of the Cloughe,
　　Nor yet [shall] Adam Bell,
Though they came with a thousand mo,
　　Nor all the devels in hell.'

Early in the mornyng the justice uprose,
　　To the gates fast gan he gon,
And commaunded to be shut full cloce°   *tightly*
　　Lightile° everychone.°   *quickly*   *everyone*

Then went he to the market-place,
    As fast as he coulde hye;
A payre of new gallous there dyd he up set,
    Besyde the pyllory.

A lytle boy stod them amonge,
    And asked what meaned that gallow-tre;
They sayde, 'To hange a good yeaman,
    Called Wyllyam of Cloudeslie.'

That lytle boye was the towne swine-heard,
    And kept fayre Alyse swine;
Full oft he had sene Cloudesle in the wodde,
    And geven hym there to dyne.

He went out of a creves° in the wall,   *gap*
    And lightly to the woode dyd gone;
There met he with the wyght° yonge men,   *sturdy*
    Shortly and anone.°   *speedily*

'Alas!' then sayde that lytle boye,
    'Ye tary here all to longe;
Cloudesle is taken and dampned to death,
    All readye for to honge.'

'Alas!' then sayde good Adam Bell,
    'That ever we see this daye!
He might her with us have dwelled,
    So ofte as we dyd hyim praye.

He might have taryed in grene foreste,
    Under the shadowes sheene,°   *beautiful*
And have kepte both hym and us in reaste,°   *peace*
    Out of trouble and teene.'°   *harm*

Adam bent a ryght good bow,
    A great hart sone° had he slayne;   *at once*
'Take that, chylde', he sayde, 'to thy dynner,
    And bryng me myne arrowe agayne.'

'Now go we hence,' sayed these wight yong men,
    'Tary we no lenger here;
We shall hym borowe,° by Gods grace,   *ransom*
    Though we bye it full dere.'°   *pay for it dearly*

To Caerlel went these good yemen,
    In a mery mornyng of Maye;
Her is a fyt of Cloudesli,
    And another is for to saye.[22]

And when they came to mery Caerlell,
    In a fayre mornyngtyde,
They founde the gates shut them untyll°   *against them*
    Round about on every syde.

'Alas!' than sayd good Adam Bell,
    'That ever we were made men!
These gates be shyt so wonderly well,
    That we may not come herein.'

Than spake Clymme of the Cloughe,
    'With a wyle° we wyll us in brynge;°   *trick*   *get*
Let us say we be messengers,
    Streyght comen from oure kynge.'

Adam sayd, 'I have a letter wryten wele,
    Now let us wisely werke;
We wyll say we have the kynges seale —
    I holde the porter no clerke.'

---

22   This is the end of the first 'fytte' and the beginning of Part II.

Than Adam Bell bete on the gate,
    With strokis greate and stronge;
The porter herde suche a noyse therate,
    And to the gate he thronge.º   *hurried*

'Who is there nowe,' sayd the porter.
    'That maketh all this knockynge?'
'We be two messengers,' seyd Clymme of the Cloughe,
    'Becomen streyght frome oure kynge.'

'We have a letter,' sayd Adam Bell,
    'To the justice we must it brynge;
Let us in, oure message to do,
    That we were agayne to oure kynge.'

'Here cometh no man in,' sayd the porter,
    'By hym that dyed on a tre,
Tyll a false thefe be hanged,
    Called Wyllyam of Cloudysle.'

Than spake that good yeman Clym of the Cloughe,
    And swore by Mary fre,º   *gracious*
'If that we stande long without
    Lyke a thefe hanged shalt thou be.

Lo, here we have the kynges seale;
    What, lordane,º arte thou wode?'º   *fool*   *mad*
The porter had wendeº it had been so,   *thought*
    And lightly dyd of his hode.º   *took off his hood*

'Welcome be my lordes seale,' sayd he,
    'For that ye shall come in,'
He opened the gate right shortly —
    An evyll openynge for hym!

'Nowe we are in,' sayd Adam Bell,
    'Therof we are full fayne;
But Cryst knoweth that herowed° hell,   *harrowed*
    How we shall come oute agayne.'

'Had we the keys,' sayd Clym of the Clowgh,
    'Ryght well than sholde we spede;
Than might we come out well ynough,
    Whan we se tyme and nede.'

They called the porter to a councell,
    And wronge hys necke in two.
And kest hym in a depe dungeon,
    And toke the keys hym fro.

'Now am I porter,' sayd Adam Bell;
    'Se, broder, the keys have we here;
The worste porter to mery Carlyl,
    That ye had this hondreth yere.

Now wyll we oure bowes bende,
    Into the towne wyll we go,
For to delyver our dere broder,
    Where he lyeth in care and wo.'

Then they bent theyr good yew bowes,
    And loked theyr stringes were round;°   *in proper shape*
The market-place of mery Carlyll
    They beset in that stounde,°   *time*

And as they loked them beside,
    A payre of newe galowes there they se,
And the justyce with a quest of swearers,°   *inquest of jurors*
    That had juged Clowdysle there hanged to be.

And Clowdysle hymselfe lay redy in a carte,
    Fast bounde bothe fote and hande,
And a strong rope aboute his necke,
    All redy for to be hanged.

The justyce called to hym a ladde;
    Clowdysles clothes sholde he have,
To take the mesure of that good yoman,
    And therafter to make his grave.

'I have sene as greate a merveyll,' sayd Clowdesle,
    'As bytwene this and pryme,°   *Prime*[23]
He that maketh thys grave for me,
    Hymselfe may lye therin.'

'Thou spekest proudely,' sayd the justyce;
    'I shall hange the with my hande.'
Full well that herde his bretheren two,
    There styll as they dyd stande.

Than Clowdysle cast hys eyen aside,
    And sawe his bretheren stande,
At a corner of the market-place,
    With theyr good bowes bent in theyr hand,
Redy the justyce for to chase.

'I se good comforte,' sayd Clowdysle,
    'Yet hope I well to fare;
If I might have my hands at wyll,
    Ryght lyttell wolde I care.'

Than bespoke° good Adam Bell,   *spoke*
    To Clymme of the Clowgh so fre;°   *bold*
'Broder, se ye marke the justice well;
    Lo, yonder ye may him se.

---

23   The first hour of daytime, about 6 am (the second canonical hour, see *OED*).

And at the sheryf shote° I wyll,   *shoot*
    Strongly with an arowe kene' —
A better shotte in mery Carlyll,
    Thys seven yere was not sene.

They loused° theyr arowes bothe at ones,   *released*
    Of no man had they drede;
The one hyt the justice, the other the sheryf,
    That bothe theyr sydes gan blede.

All men voided,° that them stode nye,   *moved away*
    Whan the justice fell to the grounde,
And the sheryf fell nyghe hym by;
    Eyther° had his dethes wounde.   *each*

All the citezeyns fast can° fle,   *did*
    They durste no kenger abyde;
There lightly they loused Clowdysle,
    Where he with ropes lay tyde.

Wyllyam sterte° to an officer of the towne,   *rushed*
    Hys axe out his hande he wronge;°   *wrenched*
On eche syde he smote them downe,
    Hym thought° he had taryed to longe.   *it seemed to him*

Wyllyam sayd to his bretheren two,
    'Thys daye let us togyder lyve and deye;
If ever you have nede as I have nowe,
    The same shall ye fynde by me.'

They shyt° so well in that tyde,°   *shot*   *time*
    For theyr strynges were of sylke full sure,
That they kepte° the stretes on every syde;   *held*
    That batayll dyd longe endure.

They fought togyder as bretheren true,
    Lyke hardy men and bolde;
Many a man to the grounde they threwe,
    And made many an herte colde.

But whan theyr arowes were all gone.
    Men presyd on them full fast;
They drewe theyr swerdes than anone,º   *at once*
    And theyr bowes from them caste.

They wente lightlyº on theyr waye,   *quickly*
    With swerdes and buckelers rounde;
By that it was the myddes of the daye,
    They had made many a wounde.

There was many an oute-horn in Carlyll blowne[24]
    And the belles backwarde dyd they rynge;
Many a woman sayd alas,
    And many theyr hands dyd wrynge.

The mayreº of Carlyll forth come was,   *mayor*
    And with hym a full grete route,º   *company*
These thre yomen dreddeº hym full sore,   *feared*
    For theyr lyves stode in doubte.

The mayre came armed, a full greate pace,º   *hastily*
    With a pollaxe in his hande;
Many a stronge man with hym was,
    There in that stoureº to stande.   *conflict*

The mayre smote at Cloudysle with his byll,º   *axe, halberd*
    His buckeler he brastº in two;   *broke*
Full many a yoman with grete yll,
    'Alas, treson!' they cryed for wo.

---

24   See *A Dictionary of the Older Scottish Tongue*: a horn would be blown to bring people
    out. Bells (next line) were rung backwards to sound the alarm.

'Kepe we the gates fast!' they bad,°   *bade*
   'That these traytours theroute not go.'

But all for nought was that they wrought,
   For so fast they downe were layde
Tyll they all thre, that so manfully fought,
   Were gotten without at a brayde.°   *outside in a moment*

'Have here your keys!' sayd Adam Bell.
   'Myne office I here forsake;
Yf ye do by my councell,
   A newe porter ye make.'

He threwe the keys there at theyr hedes,
   And bad them evyll to thryve,
And all that letteth any good yoman
   To come and comforte his wive.°   *wife*

Thus be these good yomen gone to the wode,
   As light as lefe on lynde;°   *tree*
They laughe and be mery in theyr mode,°   *mind*
   Theyr enemyes were farre behynde ...

In Inglewood, Cloudesly is reunited with Alice and his children.
The outlaws decide to go to the king to obtain a charter of peace. The
queen pleads for mercy to be shown to them, and the king somewhat
reluctantly agrees. Messengers arrive with news of the carnage they have
caused in the north, but the king has now given his word ('I wyll se these
felowes shote, That in the north have wrought this wo'), and they give a
demonstration, with Cloudesly performing the feat of shooting an apple
on the head of his seven-year-old son. The king and the queen give them
offices at court; the three go to Rome to be absolved of their sins, they
return to stay with the king, and die good men all three: 'Thus endeth the
lyves of these good yemen, God sende them eternall blysse, And all that
with hand-bowe shoteth, That of heven they may never mysse!'

v) *A Gest of Robyn Hode*[25]

Of all the outlaw ballads and stories, the tales of Robin Hood and his companions and enemies seem to have been the most popular. Robin Hood remains an elusive figure. The careful and informative work of medieval historians has not so far produced a historical prototype satisfactory to everyone.[26] The earliest reference seems to be the 'Robehod fugitivus' (possibly a nickname) in a Berkshire document of 1262.[27] The surviving medieval stories do not help us with information about his origins: he is a 'yeoman', but we are not told the reasons for his outlawry; he seems to exist, fully formed, as the outlaw hero. 'Rhymes of Robin Hood' are alluded to by Langland in the later fourteenth century. The stories sometimes furnished the plots for folk plays.[28] They clearly existed in large numbers; in spite of great losses we have a small but varied group of surviving texts.[29] Of these the longest and most ambitious work is the *Gest of Robyn Hode*, which survives only in printed versions and some fragments.[30] Modern editions are usually based on the Antwerp edition, supplemented by Wynkyn de Worde's. It is a long poem (456 stanzas) almost certainly based on earlier Robin Hood ballads, probably put together in the mid-fifteenth century as a 'ballad-romance', a popular epic, or a 'long ballad' as found in some European examples, or in *Adam Bell*. Three stories are woven together: the adventures of Robin Hood with a knight, with the sheriff of Nottingham, and with the king. Our extract, the third 'fytte', tells how Robin's follower Little John tricked the sheriff and delivered him to Robin.

Fytte 1 briefly introduces Robin Hood and some of his men in Barnsdale (Yorks). Little John, remarking 'It is fer dayes, God sende us a gest, That we were at oure dynere!', is sent with two companions to Watling Street, to find some unknown guest who can be invited to dinner (for which he will pay). They meet a sorrowful knight: 'All dreri was his semblaunce, He rode in simple aray; A soriar man than he was one Rode never in somer day.' He is brought to Robin in the wood, and

---

25   In *Rymes*.
26   See Introduction to this text, in *Rymes*.
27   See Norman Davies, *The Isles: A History*, p. 333.
28   See chapter 10, below.
29   *Rymes* contains a goodly collection, as does *Robin Hood* eds Knight and Ohlgren.
30   The Introduction to this text, in *Rymes*, lists printed versions and fragments.

given dinner: 'Brede and wyne they had right ynoughe, And umbles of the dere, Swannes and fessauntes they had full gode, And foules of the ryvere.' But when the question of payment is raised, the knight says he has only ten shillings. This is checked by Little John, and the knight's story emerges: to save his son, who slew a knight, his goods have all been sold, and his lands are pledged to the abbot of St Mary's Abbey for four hundred pounds; the only security he has is Our Lady, and payment is due. Robin produces the four hundred pounds, and the knight is given clothes and a horse; Little John is to be his 'knave' [servant]. In Fytte 2 the grateful knight comes to St Mary's to pay the abbot. The abbot and most of the monks are thinking only of the money. The knight arrives, in simple garments, and tests the abbot by sayng that that he has not brought a penny. A furious scene follows, and the knight departs, leaving the four hundred pounds: 'Have here thi golde, sir abbot … Had thou ben curtes at my comynge, Rewarded shuldest thou have be.' After a year has passed, and the knight has four hundred pounds, he sets off to pay Robin Hood. On the way he sees a great wrestling contest, and helps a yeoman who is a stranger. And here Fytte 3 begins …

The Third Fytte, An Adventure of Little John (alias Grenelef)

Lyth° and lystyn, gentilmen,	*attend*
All that nowe be here,	
Of Litell Johnn, that was the knightes man,	
Goode myrth[es] ye shall here.	

It was upon a mery day		
That yonge men wolde go shete,°	*to shoot*	
Lytell John fet° his bowe anone,°	*fetched*	*quickly*
And sayde he wolde them mete.		

Thre tymes Litell John shet aboute,	
And alwey he slet the wande;°	*split the stick*[31]

---

31   As everybody knows, Robin and his fellows could shoot at a peeled wand set in the ground at long range, splitting it every time.

The proude sherif of Notingham
    By the markes° can stande.°   *targets*   *stood*

The sherif swore a full greate othe,
    'By hym that dyede on a tre,°   *died on a cross*
This man is the best arschere°   *archer*
    That evere yet sawe I [me].

Sey me nowe, wight° yonge man,   *brave*
    What is nowe thy name?
In what countre were thou borne,
    And where is thy wonynge wane?'°   *dwelling place*

'In Holdernes,° sir, I was borne,   *Holderness*[32]
    Iwys al of my dame,
Men cal me Reyno[l]de Grenelefe.
    Whan I am at home.'

'Sey me, Reyno[l]de Grenelefe,
    Wolde thou dwell with me?
And every yere I woll the gyve
    Twenty marke to thy fee.'°   *wages*

'I have a maister,' sayde Litell John,
    'A curteys knight is he —
May ye leve° gete of hym,   *permission*
    The better may it be.'

The sherif gate° Litell John   *got*
    Twelve monethes of° the knight;   *from*
Therfore he gave him right anone°   *immediately*
    A gode hors and a wight.°   *strong*

---

32   East Yorkshire; a flat marshy area, east of Hull.

Nowe is Litell John the sherifes man,
    God lende° us well to spede!°   *grant*   *prosper*
But alwey thought Lytell John
    To quyte hym wele his mede.°   *pay his deserts*

'Nowe so God me helpe,' sayde Litell John,
    'And by my true leutye,°   *loyalty*
I shall be the worst servaunt to hym
    That ever yet had he.'

It fell upon a Wednesday
    The sheriff on huntynge was gone,
And Litel John lay in his bed,
    And was foriete° at home.   *forgotten*

Therfore he was fasting°   *without food*
    Til it was past the none,
'Gode sir stuarde,° I pray to the,   *steward*
    Gyve me my dynere,' saide Litell John.

'It is longe for Grenelefe
    Fastinge thus for to be,
Therfore I pray the, sir stuarde,
    Mi dyner gif [thou] me.'

'Shalt thou never ete ne drynke,' sayde the stuarde,
    'Tyll my lorde be come to towne!'
'I make myn avowe to God,' sayde Litell John,
    'I had lever° to crake thy crowne!'   *would rather*

The boteler° was full uncurteys,   *butler*
    There he stode on flore.
He start to the botery
    And shet fast the dore.

Lytell John gave the boteler suche a tap°   *blow*
    His backe went nere in two —
Though he lived an hundred ier°   *years*
    The wors[e] shuld he go.

He sporned° the dore with his fote,   *kicked*
    It went open wel and fine,
And there he made a large lyveray°   *took a good allowance*
    Bothe of ale and of wyne.

'Sith ye wol nat dyne,' sayde Litell John,
    'I shall gyve you to drynke —
And though ye lyve an hundred winter,
    On Lytell John ye shall thinke.'

Litell John ete, and Litel John drank,
    The while that he wolde.
The sherife had in his kechyn a coke,°   *cook*
    A stoute° man and a bolde,   *strong*

'I make myn avowe to God,' sayde the coke,
    'Thou arte a shrewde hynde°   *wicked servant*
In ani hous for to dwel,
    For to aske thus to dyne.'

And there he lent° Litell John   *gave*
    God° strokis thre,   *good*
'I make myn avowe to God' sayde Lytell John,
    'These strokis liked° well me.   *pleased*

Thou arte a bolde man and hardy,
    And so thinketh me;°   *seems*
And or° I pas fro this place   *before*
    Assayed° better shalt thou be.'   *tested*

Lytell John drew a ful gode sworde,
    The coke toke another in hande —
They thought no thynge° for to fle,   *not at all*
    But stiffly° for to stande.   *resolutely*

There they faught sore° togedere   *fought bitterly*
    Two myle way° and well more,   *the time taken to go two miles*
Myght neyther other harme done°   *do harm*
    The mountnaunce° of an owre.°   *length*   *hour*

'I make myn avowe to God,' sayde Litell Johnn,
    'And by my true lewte,
Thou art one of the best swordemen
    That ever yit sawe I [me].

Cowdest thou° shote as well in a bowe,   *if you could*
    To grene wode thou shuldest with me,
And two times in the yere thy clothinge
    Chaunged shulde be,

And every yere of° Robyn Hode   *from*
    Twenty merke to thy fe.'°   *reward*
'Put up thy swerde,' saide the coke,
    'And felowes woll we be.'

Thenne he fet° to Lytell Johnn   *fetched*
    The nowmbles of a do,°   *entrails of a doe*
Gode brede and full gode wyne —
    They ete and drank theretoo.

And when they had dronkyn well
    Theyre trouthes togeder they plight
That they wo[l]de be with Robyn
    That ilke° same nyght.   *very*

They dyd them° to the tresourehows°   *went   treasure-house*
    As fast as they myght gone,
The lokkes that were of full gode stele°   *steel*
    They brake them everichone.

They toke away the silver vessell,
    And all that they might get —
Pecis,° masars° ne sponis   *vessels   cups*
    Wolde they not forget.

Also [they] toke the gode pens,
    Thre hunred pounde and more,
And did them st[r]eyte° to Robyn Hode,   *went straight*
    Under the grene wode hore.°   *grey*

'God the save, my dere mayster,
    And Criste the save and se!'°   *watch over*
And thanne sayde Robyn to Litell John,
    'Welcome myght thou be!

Also be that fayre yeman
    Thou bryngest there with the;
What tydynges fro Noty[n]gham?
    Lytill Johnn, tell thou me.'

'Well the gretith the proude sheryf,
    And sende[th] the here by me
His coke° and his silver vessel   *cook*
    And thre hundred pounde and thre.'

'I make myne avowe to God,' sayde Robyn,
    'And to the Trenyte,
It was never by his gode wyll
This gode° is come to me.'   *goods*

Lytyll John there hym bethought
    On a shrewde wyle.°   *cunning trick*
Fyve myle in the forest he ran,
    Hym happed° all his wyll.   *came to pass*

Than he met the proude sheryf
    Huntynge with howndes and horne —
Lytell John coude° of curtesye,   *knew*
    And knelyd hym beforne,

'God the save, my dere mayster,
    And Criste the save and se!'
'Reynolde Grenelefe,' sayde the sheryf,
    'Where hast thou nowe be?'

'I have be in this forest,
    A fayre syght can° I se,   *did*
It was one of the fairest syghtes
    That ever yet sawe I me.

Yonder I sawe a right fayre harte°   *hart*
    His coloure is of grene,
Seven score of dere upon a herde°   *in a herd*
    Be with hym all bydene.°   *together*

Their tyndes° are so sharpe, maister,   *antlers*
    Of sexty and well mo,
That I durst not shote for drede,
    Lest they wolde me slo.'°   *slay*

'I make myn avowe to God,' sayde the sheryf,
    'That syght wolde I fayne° se.'   *gladly*
'Buske you thederwarde,° mi dere mayster,   *hasten thither*
    Anone,° and wende with me.'   *quickly*

The sheriff rode, and Litell Johnn
    Of fote he was full smerte,º   *nimble*
And whane they came before Robyn,
    'Lo, sir, here is the mayster-herte.'

Still stode the proude sheryf.
    A sory man was he,
'Wo the worthe,º Raynolde Grenelefe!   *a curse on you*
    Thou hast betrayed nowe me.'

'I make myn avowe to God,' sayde Litell John,
    'Mayster, ye be to blame,
I was mysservedº of my dynere   *badly served*
    Whan I was with you at home.'

Sone he was to souper sette,
    And served well with silver white,
And whan the sheryf sawe his vessel,
    For sorowe he might not ete.

'Make glad chere,' sayde Robyn Hode,
    'Sheryf, for charite,
And for the love of Litill John
    Thy lyfe I graunt to the.'

Whan they had souped well,
    The day was al gone;
Robyn commaude[d] Litell John
    To drawe of his hosen and his shone,º   *stockings and shoes*

His kirtell,º and his cote of pie,º   *tunic*   *short jacket*
That was fured well and fine,
And to[ke] hym a grene mantel
    To lapº his body therin.   *wrap*

Robyn commaundyd his wight yonge men,
 Under the grene wode tree,
They shulde lye in that same sute,º   *manner*
 That the sherif myght them see.

All nyght lay the proude sherif
 In his brecheº and in his [s]chert,º   *breeches* *shirt*
No wonder it was, in grene wode
 Though his sydes gan to smerte.º   *ache*

'Make glade chere,' sayde Robyn Hode,
 'Sheryf, for charite,
For this is our ordre iwys,º   *indeed*
 Under the grene wode tree.'

'This is harder order,' sayde the sheryef,
 'Than any ankir or frereº —   *anchorite or friar*
For all the golde in mery Englonde
 I wolde nat longe dwell her.'º   *here*

'All this twelve monthes,' sayde Robin,
 'Thou shalt dwell with me —
I shall the teche, proude sherif,
 An outlawe for to be.'

'Orº I be here another nyght,' sayde the sheyif, *before*
 'Robyn, nowe pray I the,
Smyte ofº mijn hede rather tomorowe, *smite off*
 And I forgyve it the.

'Lat me go,' than sayde the sheryf,
 'For saynte charite,
And I woll be the best[e] frende
 That ever yet had ye.'

'Thou shalt swere me an othe', sayde Robyn,
   'On my bright bronde,°   *sword*
Shalt thou never awayte me scathe°   *lie in wait to do me harm*
   By water ne by lande,

And if thou fynde any of my men,
   By nyght or [by] day,
Upon thyn othe thou shalt swere
   To helpe them tha[t]° thou may.'   *as far as*

Nowe hathe the sherif sworne his othe,
   And home he began to gone —
He was as full of grene wode
   As ever was hepe° of stone.   *hip*[33]

In fytte 4 Robin is still waiting for his money: 'I drede Our Lady be wroth with me, For she sent me nat my pay'. Little John is sent up to Watling Street to find 'some unknown guest'. He finds two black monks from the abbey and their retinue. One is taken to Robin. He has never heard of Mary as a 'borowe', but Robin tells him that he is her messenger. He says that he has only twenty marks, but Little John's checking reveals eight hundred pounds and more: 'Our Lady hath doubled your cast [throw, outlay]', he remarks to Robin. Now the knight arrives with his four hundred pounds. Robin tells him to keep it and use it well: 'Our Lady by her selerer Hath sent to me my pay.' The following Fyttes relate the other stories of Robin's adventures, ending with his brief stay in the king's court, his return to the greenwood, and his death.

vi) *Sir Aldingar*[34]

Percy used this in his *Reliques* (1765);[35] Scott used another version in the 'Minstrelsy of the Scottish Border' (1803). The ballad has parallels

---

33   Rose-hips, or haws (of thorn) are more 'stone' than fruit.
34   *PFMS*, vol i, p. 165 ff.
35   For the *Reliques*, see Hales and Furnivall Forewords (to *PFMS*), pp. xxii–iii & xxxvii ff: a discussion of the contents and their importance.

in Scandinavian ballads. A very similar story is told by William of Malmesbury (see Chapter 4 (ii), below).

Sir Aldingar is the treacherous steward of the king. He desires to sleep with the queen, but she rejects him. In anger 'he sought what meanes he cold find out, In a fyer to have her brent.' A blind and lame leper is placed on the queen's bed, and Aldingar tells the king that it is the queen's new love. The queen laments and describes a dream she has had: a griffin carried her crown away and would have forced her into his nest, but a merlin came flying from the east and killed it. She asks for a champion to fight for her: one must be found within forty days or else she will be burnt. One messenger can find no-one, and the other only a little child, who 'seemed noe more in a mans likenesse Then a child of four yeeres old.' He sends the messenger back with a greeting for the queen, and a message to remember her dream: 'When bale is att hyest, boote is att next.'[36] The queen is gladdened, but is put into a tun ready to be burnt. The little child comes riding out of the east, and demands that Aldingar be brought. The steward thinks little of him, but … [vv. 167–202]

… The little one pulld forth a well good sword,
    Iwiis, itt was all of guilt,°   *gilded metal*
It cast light there over that field,
    It shone all of guilt.

He stroke the first stroke att Aldingar,
    He stroke away his legs by his knee,

Sayes, 'Stand up, stand up, thou false traitor,
    And fight upon thy feete,
For and thou thrive as thou begins,
    Of a height wee shalbe meete.'

---

36 'When things are at their worst, hope is at hand'. A common proverb; see Whiting
    B 18 & 22.

'A preist! A preist!' says Aldingar,
    'Me for to houzle and shrive!º   *give the sacrament and absolution*
A preist! A preist!' says Aldingar,
    'While I am a man living alive!

I wold have laine by our comlie queene,
    To it shee wold never consent;
I thought to have betrayd her to our king,
    In a fyer to have had her brent.

There came a lame lazarº to the kings gates,   *leper*
    A lazar both blind and lame;

I tooke the lazar upon my backe,
    In the queenes bed I did him lay.
I bad him "lie still, lazar", where he lay,
    Looke he went not away,
I wold make him a whole man and a sound
    In two houres of a day.

Ever alacke!' says Sir Aldingar,
    'Falsing never doth well.

Forgive, forgive me, queene, madam[e]
    For Christs love forgive me!'
'God forgave his death, Aldingar,
    And freely I forgive thee.'

'Now take thy wife, thou king Harry,[37]
    And love her as thou shold,
Thy wiffe shee is as true to thee
    As stone that lies on the castle wall.'

---

37   This king may be the same as King Henry, in Gunnhild (chapter 4, below).

vii) *Glasgerion*[38]

Used by Percy in the *Reliques*;[39] Chaucer mentions 'the Bret Glascurion' among the harpers in his *House of Fame* (v. 1208). He seems to be the Welsh tenth-century Y Bardd Glas Keraint, the Blue [i.e. chief] Bard Geraint, of whom little is known. He may well be the Glasgerion of the ballad. His harping skill is described at the beginning of the ballad; in a later Scottish ballad collected from the recitation of an old woman (Robert Jamieson's Popular Ballads and Songs from Tradition, 1806, Child's version B) the harper, there called Glenkindie, was the 'best harper That ever harpd on a string ... He'd harpit a fish out o saut water, Or water out o a stane, Or milk out o a maiden's breast, That bairn had never nane'.

Glasgerion is a king's son and an excellent harper. The king's daughter of Normandy is so moved by his playing that she invites him to her bower when men are at rest. He tells his boy, Jack, of this, and Jack tells him to sleep and he will awaken him before cockcrow ... [vv. 33–96]

... But upp then rose that lither⁰ ladd,	*wicked*
And did on hose and shoone,	
A coller he cast upon his necke,	
Hee seemed a gentleman,	
And when he came to that ladies chamber,	
He thrild upon a pinn,⁰	*rattled the door-pin*
The lady was true of her promise,	
Rose up and let him in.	
He did not take the lady gay	
To boulster nor to bed,	
But downe upon her chamber flore	
Ful soone he hath her layd.	

---

38 *PFMS* vol. i, p. 246 ff.

39 For the *Reliques*, see Hales and Furnivall Forewords (to *PFMS*), pp. xxii–iii & xxxvii ff.

He did not kisse that lady gay
    When he came nor when he youd,º   *went*
And sore mistrusted that lady gay
    He was of some churles blood.

But home then came that lither ladd,
    And did of his hose and shoone,
And cast that coller from about his necke —
    He was but a churles sonne,
'Awaken,' quoth hee, 'my master deere,
    I holde it time to be gone,

For I have sadled your horsse, master,
    Well bridled I have your steed —
Have I not served a good breakfast,
    When time comes I have need?'

But up then rose good Glasgerryon,
    And did on both hose and shoone,
And cast a coller about his necke,
    He was a kings sonne.

And when he came to that ladies chamber
    He thrild upon a pinn —
The lady was more then true of promise,
    Rose up and let him in.

Saies, 'Whether have you left with me
    Your braclett or your glove?
Or are you returned backe againe
    To know more of my love?'

Glasgerryon swore a full great othe,
    By oake and ashe and thorne,
'Lady, I was never in your chamber
    Sith the time that I was borne.'

'O! then it was your little foote page
    Falsly hath beguiled me!'
And then shee pulld forth a little penknife,
    That hanged by her knee,
Says, 'There shall never noe churles blood
    Spring within my body!'

But home then went Glassgerryon,
    A woe° man, good [Lord] was hee,   *sorrowful*
Sayes, 'Come hither, thou Jacke my boy,
    Come thou hither to me.

For if I had killed a man tonight,
    Jacke, I wold tell it thee,
But if I have not killed a man tonight,
    Jacke, thou hast killed three!'

And he puld out his bright browne° sword,   *gleaming*
    And dryed it on his sleeve,
And he smote off that lither ladds head,
    And asked noe man noe leave.

He sett the sworde point till his brest,
    The pumill° till a stone —   *pommel*
Thorrow that falsnese of that lither ladd
    These three lives werne all gone.

C. Some Later Ballads

Some ballads recorded in later times which possibly have some link with medieval tales or ballads. The list is a long one, and the connections are often uncertain.

viii) *Fair Annie*[40]

The story behind this Scottish ballad, recorded in Scott's 'Minstrelsy of the Scottish Border' (1802) and Robert Jamieson's 'Popular Ballads and Songs from Tradition' (1806), seems to be somehow related to that of Marie de France's *Lai le Freine*, in which twins are separated soon after birth. One is a foundling, left with only a rich robe (compare *Emaré* in our chapter Romances, iii) and a ring. She grows up to be a gentle and patient woman. She is loved by a knight, but when he is persuaded to marry he chooses a nobly born lady, who is in fact Freine's twin. Freine is in the hall when the bride arrives, but thanks to the robe and the ring is 'recognised', and marries the knight herself. This lai was translated into Middle English in the fourteenth century, but survives only in an incomplete form: the recognition scene and the denouement are lost. A Scandinavian ballad exists in Danish and Swedish, and there are versions in Dutch and German. The Scottish ballad begins with Annie's lord informing her that he is going across the sea to bring home 'a braw bride'; Annie, who has borne him seven sons, welcomes the new bride, but laments bitterly …

… When bells were rung, and mass was sung,
   And a' men bound to bed,
Lord Thomas and his new come bride
   To their chamber they ere gaed.º   *gone*

Annie made her bed a little forbyeº   *nearby*
   To hear what they might say,
'And ever alas!' fair Annie cried,
   'That I should see this day!

---

40   Child, no. 62 (in vol. ii), stanzas 21 to end.

Gin° my seven sons were seven young rats,   *if*
    Running on the castle wa',°   *wall*
And I were a grey cat mysell,
    I soon would worry them a',

Gin my seven sons were seven young hares,
    Running oer yon lilly lee,°   *beautiful field*
And I were a grey hound mysell,
    Soon worried they a' should be.'

And wae and sad fair Annie sat,
    And drearie was her sang,
And ever as she sobbd and grat,°   *wept*
    'Wae to the man that did the wrang!'

'My gown is on,' said the new come bride,
    'My shoes are on my feet,
And I will to fair Annie's chamber,
    To see what gars her greet.°   *makes her weep*

What ails ye, what ails ye, fair Annie,
    That ye make sic a moan:
Has your wine barrels cast the girds°   *hoops*
    Or is your white bread gone?

O wha° was't your father, Annie,   *who*
    Or wha was't your mother?
And had ye ony sister, Annie,
    Or had ye ony brother?'

'The earl of Wemyss was my father,
    The countess of Wemyss my mother,
And a' the folk about the house
    To me were sister and brother.'

'If the earl of Wemyss was your father
    I wot sae° was he mine —   *so*
And it shall not be for lack o' gowd°   *gold*
    That ye your love shall tine,°   *lose*

For I have seven ships o' mine ain,°   *own*
    A' loaded to the brim,
And I will gie them a' to thee,
    Wi four to thine eldest son.
But thanks to a' the powers in heaven
    That I gae maiden hame!'

ix) *The Three Ravens*

Child no. 26. Recorded in 1611, it was apparently very popular, but is now less well known than the generally similar 'Twa Corbies' (in Scott's 'Minstrelsy'). See also 'The New-Slain Knight' (Child no. 263). A perhaps remote resemblance to the image of the wounded knight, in the enigmatic Corpus Christi Carol, has been suggested;[41] and it is possible that famous poem is a 'religious' version derived from a ballad of a slain knight such as this.

There were three ravens sat on a tree.
    Downe a downe, hay down, hay downe
There were three ravens sat on a tree,
    With a downe
There were three ravens sat on a tree,
They were as blacke as they might be,
With a downe derrie, derrie, derrie, downe, downe.

The one of them said to his mate,
'Where shall we our breakefast take?'

---

41   The Corpus Christi Carol (see below, in ch. 7) is number 247 in *The Oxford Book of Medieval Verse*.

'Downe in yonder green field,
There lies a knight slain under his shield,

His hounds they lie downe at his feete,
So well they can their master keepe.

His haukes they flie so eagerly
There's no fowle dare him come nie.'

Downe there comes a fallow doe,
As great with yong as she might goe.

She lift up his bloudy hed,
And kist his wounds that were so red.

She got him up upon her backe,
And carried him to earthen lake.º   *pit*

She buried him before the prime,
She was dead herselfe ere evensong time.

God send every gentleman,
Such haukes, such hounds, and such a leman.

x) *Thomas the Rhymer*[42]

Child no. 37; the best known version is that of Mrs Brown in the early nineteenth century. The ballad has some intriguingly close parallels with the late medieval English romance *Thomas of Erceldoune*: see our chapter Romances (ix). Even older than Mrs Brown's, and even closer to

---

42   See [Thomas] *The Romance and Prophecies of Thomas of Erceldoune*, ed. Murray, where two other versions of *Thomas the Rhymer* are printed at pp. liii–v; but Gray probably used Child 37 C*, which is different again (in the 5-volume Child, see vol. 4 pp. 454–5, *sub* 37). The Ballads are also available in a 1904 one-volume Student's Cambridge edition, where versions A and C* are on pp. 63–6.

the romance is Child's version C from Scott's 'Materials for the Border Minstrelsy': Mrs Greenwood (1806) 'from the recitation of her mother and aunt, both of them then over 60, who learnt it in childhood from a very old woman, at Longnewton, near Jedburgh.'

Thomas lay on the Huntlie bank,
    A spying ferlies° wi his eee,°   *wonders*   *eye*
And he did spy a lady gay,
    Come riding down by the lang lee.

Her steed was o the dapple grey,
    And at its mane there hung bells nine;
He thought he heard that lady say,
    'They gowden bells sall a' be thine.'

Her mantle was o velvet green,
    And a' set round wi jewels fine;
Her hawk and hounds were at her side,
    And her bugle-horn wi gowd did shine.

Thomas took aff baith cloak and cap,
    For to salute this gay lady:
'O save ye, save ye, fair Queen o Heavn,
    And ay weel° met ye save and see!'°   *ever well*   *protect*

'I'm no the Queen o Heavn, Thomas;
    I never carried my head sae hee;
For I am but a lady gay,
    Come out to hunt in my follee.°   *park*[43]

Now gin° ye kiss my mouth, Thomas,   *if*
    Ye manna miss my fair bode;°   *offer*

---

43   Pleasure-park. Here, and for a matching verse in *Thomas of Erceldoune* (*pace* Child's glossary for the ballad; there is no glossary in the edition of *Erceldoune*), see Mawer, '*La Folie* in Place-names'.

Then ye may een° gang hame and tell   *even*
    That ye've lain wi a gay ladee.'

'O gin I loe° a lady fair,   *love*
    Nae ill tales o her wad I tell,
And it's wi thee I fain wad gae,°   *would go*
    Tho it were een to heavn or hell.'

'Then harp and carp,° Thomas,' she said,   *speak, tell tales*
    'Then harp and carp alang wi me;
But it will be seven years and a day
    Till ye win back to yere ain° countrie.'   *your own*

The lady rade, True Thomas ran,
    Untill they cam to a water wan;°   *dark*
O it was night and nae delight.
    And Thomas wade aboon° the knee.   *above*

It was dark night, and nae starn-light.°   *star-light*
    And on they waded lang days three,
And they heard the roring o a flood,
    And Thomas a waefou° man was he.   *woeful*

Then they rade on, and farther on,
    Untill they came to a garden green;
To pu° an apple he put up his hand,   *pull*
    For the lack o food he was like to tyne.°   *perish*

'O haud° yere hand, Thomas,' she cried,   *hold*
    'And let that green flourishing be;
For it's the very fruit o hell.
    Beguiles baith man and woman o yere countrie.

But look afore ye, True Thomas,
    And I shall show ye ferlies three;

Yon is the gate° leads to our land,   *road*
    Where thou and I sae° soon shall be.   *so*

And dinna ye see yon road, Thomas,
    That lies out-owr° yon lilly lee?°   *beyond*   *lovely lea*
Weel° is the man yon gate may gang,°   *well*   *go*
    For it leads him straight to the heavens hie.

But do you see yon road, Thomas,
    That lies out-owr yon frosty fell?
Ill is the man yon gate may gang,
    For it leads him straight to the pit o hell.

Now when ye come to our court, Thomas,
    See that a weel-learned man ye be;
For they will ask ye one and all,
    But ye maun° answer nane but me.   *must*

And when nae answer they obtain,
    Then will they come and question me,
And I will answer them again°   *in reply*
    That I gat yere aith° at the Eildon tree.   *oath*

Ilka° seven years, Thomas,   *every*
    We pay our teindings° unto hell,   *tithings*
And ye're sae leesome° and sae strang   *pleasing*
    That I fear, Thomas, it will be yeresell.'°   *yourself*

Chapter 3

Romances

The romance is one of the most important and distinctive literary forms in the Middle Ages. 'Romance' is a French word, and as a literary form it developed in French courts and literary circles; although the antecedents of medieval romance go back to the Greek romance.[1] French romances could certainly be genuinely 'courtly', as in the twelfth-century poems of Chrétien de Troyes, but they were not all an exclusively élite form of literature: underneath the elegant narratives we can sometimes discern folktale patterns and motifs. Marie de France says that some of her sophisticated lais are related to ancient Breton stories. Even in medieval France we begin to feel that 'courtly' and 'popular' are terms which do not denote totally self-contained and mutually exclusive categories but, rather more vaguely, points on a continuous spectrum. This seems even more likely when we turn to Middle English romance, where many examples have survived, quite a few of them from French originals.

There is here a substantial body of what is commonly called 'popular' romance, probably one step away from the lost orally transmitted (sometimes orally created) romances of the minstrels, sometimes inheriting or imitating their stylistic patterns like a formulaic but expressive diction. Chaucer's own tale of *Sir Thopas* is a brilliant burlesque of popular romances. It has a number of their common characteristics: division into 'fits' or sections each beginning with a call

---

1   For example, the story of Apollonius of Tyre. Similar 'romance-type' tales are found around the world.

   https://doi.org/10.11647/OBP.0170.03

to attention; sudden, sometimes melodramatic, events and adventures (here involving an 'elfqueene' and a giant, Sir Olifaunt); very simple formulaic diction. Chaucer's burlesque produces a narrative which is exquisitely awful, and is broken off by the Host with a remark about doggerel. However, the burlesque is not completely destructive. The popular romances and their shortcomings are lost to sight in a cloud of joyously impossible comedy. We are left with the strong feeling that Chaucer secretly loved these romances: he certainly has a detailed knowledge of them, and alludes to several (for example, *Guy of Warwick*). And in fact, most of the surviving popular romances are not as awful as *Sir Thopas*. They show distinct signs of literary quality, and the whole corpus reveals a remarkable variety. Some would find a place at one end or other of our spectrum. *Emaré*, with its repetitions and formulae, seems close to the 'oral' pole, whereas one has to look very closely at the Auchinleck copy of *Sir Orfeo* in order to see the formulae, which have been skilfully worked into a polished narrative style. Again in popular romances we find echoes of folktale motifs and patterns: Cinderella-type stories, for instance. Some have connections with later ballads (though the details of any connection often remain mysterious); and the occasional romance in quatrains, like *The Knight of Curtesy* (which uses the legend of the 'eaten heart')[2] or *Thomas of Erceldoune* (clearly related to *Thomas the Rhymer*), sometimes sound like long ballads. Like the early outlaw ballads (see Chapter 2), most of these romances have a direct, formulaic and expressive style, often more impressive in the hearing, rather than in reading on the page. Typically, too, most share a liking for simple stanza forms, like couplets or the common twelve-line tail-rhyme stanza.

In order to illustrate briefly the variety of this extensive body of literature, I have decided to opt for extracts — two longer ones from *Havelok* and *Sir Orfeo*, romances admired by critics — and a series of shorter examples from less well-known works, which illustrate their treatment of individual scenes or dramatic moments in the narrative (many of them showing mortals in eerie and perilous situations). Adventures are an important and central feature of the romance, whether sophisticated and 'literary' or 'popular'.

---

2   See '*The Knight of Curtesy and the Fair Lady of Faguell*', ed. McCausland; and *Simple Forms* pp. 96–7.

i) *Havelok*

A romance of just over three thousand lines, written probably in the late thirteenth century, or possibly at the beginning of the fourteenth. Havelock story material was in circulation earlier: in the Anglo-Norman chronicler Gaimar's *Estoire* (c. 1135–40) and in the French *Lai d'Havelok* (c. 1190–c. 1220) which is based on Gaimar. The Middle English romance is remarkable for its realism and for its interest in the lives of humbler folk. The parallel stories of Havelock and Goldeboru are well told. The author has been called 'an unobtrusively sophisticated writer'.[3]

(a) King Ethelwold of England dies, leaving his daughter Goldeboru in the protection of Godrich, the Earl of Cornwall. The Danish king Birkabeyn also dies, and leaves his son Havelock in the protection of Earl Godard. Both protectors are treacherous. Godard seizes the throne of Denmark and imprisons Havelock and his sisters … [vv. 447–80]

… onon he ferde°	*went*	
To the tour ther he° woren sperde,°	*they*	*shut up*
Ther he greten° for hunger and cold.	*wept*	
The knave,° that was somdel° bold,	*boy*	*quite*
Kam him ageyn,° on knes him sette,	*to meet him*	
And Godard ful feyre° he ther grette.°	*courteously*	*greeted*
And Godard seyde, 'Wat is yw?°	*what is the matter with you?*	
Hwi grete ye and goulen° nou?'	*howl*	
'For us hungreth swithe sore,'°	*because we are very hungry*	
Seyden he, 'we wolden more,		
We ne have to hete, ne we ne have		
Herinne neyther knith ne knave°	*knight nor servant*	
That yeveth us drinken, ne no mete,		
Halvendel° that we moun° ete.	*half*	*can*
Wo is us that we weren born!		
Weilawei,° nis it no korn°	*alas!*	*is there no corn*
That men micte° maken of bred?	*could*	

---

3 In *Middle English Verse Romances* (ed. Sands). Extracts and commentary (including other Havelock references) are in *Early Middle English Verse and Prose*, eds Bennett and Smithers (revised edn. 1985): pp. 52–64 & 288–97. The spelling 'Havelock' denotes a range of romances and tales about this character.

Us hungreth, we aren ney° ded.'	*almost*
Goderd herde here wa;°	*misery*
Therof yaf he nouth a stra.°	*not a straw*
But tok the maydnes bothe samen,°	*together*
Also it were upon his gamen,°	*sport*
Also he wolde° with hem leyke,°	*as if he wished* *play*
That weren for hunger grene and bleike;°	*pale and sickly*
Of bothen he karf° on two here throtes,	*cut*
And sithen° hem al to grotes.°	*then* *small pieces*
Ther was sorwe, woso° it sawe,	*whoever*
Hwan the children bi the wawe°	*wall*
Leyen and sprauleden° in the blod;	*lay and sprawled*
Havelok it saw, and therbi stod.	
Ful sori was that seli knave.°	*innocent boy*
Mikel dred° he mouthe° have,	*great fear* *might well*
For at hise herte he saw a knif	
Forto reven° him hise lyf.	*deprive*

(b) Godard hands over Havelock to Grim, a fisherman, and orders him to be killed. However, Grim sees a wonderful light shining from the boy's mouth, and a royal birthmark, and realises he is the destined king; he flees with him and his own family to England, settling at the mouth of the Humber, where Grimsby now stands. As Havelock grows up, he realizes how difficult life is for Grim. [vv. 785–862]

Thusgate° Grim him fayre ledde;	*in this way*
Him and his genge° wel he fedde	*household*
Wel tweif winter other° more.	*or*
Havelok was war that Grim swank° sore	*toiled*
For his mete, and he lay at hom;	
Thouthe: 'Ich am nou no grom°	*child*
Ich am wel waxen° and wel may eten	*grown*
More than evere Grim may geten.	
Ich ete more, bi God on live,	
Than Grim an his children five!	
It may nouth ben thus longe.	

Goddot,° y wile with the gange,°   *God knows* *go*

Forto leren° sum gode to gete;°   *learn* *win*

Swinken ich wolde for mi mete.

It is no shame forto swinken;

The man may wel eten and drinken

That nouth ne have but on swink long.° *in proportion to his work*

To liggen° at hom it is ful strong.°   *lie* *disgraceful*

God yelde° him, ther I ne may,   *reward*

That haveth me fed to this day.

Gladlike I wile the panieres bere;

Ich woth ne shal it me nouth dere,°   *harm*

They° ther be inne a birthene gret,°   *although* *great burden*

Also° hevi as a neth.°   *as* *ox*

Shal ich nevere lengere dwelle;°   *delay*

Tomorwen shal Ich forth pelle.'°   *hasten*

On the morwen, hwan it was day,

He stirt up° sone and nouth° ne lay,   *leapt up* *did not*

And cast a panier on his bac,

With fish giveled° als a stac,°   *heaped up* *haystack*

Also michel° he bar him one°   *much* *by himself*

So he° foure, bi mine mone.°   *as if he were* *opinion*

Wel he it bar, and solde it wel.

The silver he brouthe hom il del.°   *in full*

Al that he therefore tok;

Withheld he nouth a ferthinges nok.° *a fraction of a farthing*

So yede he forth ilke day,

That he nevere at home lay,

So wolde he his mester° lere.°   *trade* *learn*

Bifel° it so, a strong dere°   *happened* *severe shortage*

Bigan to rise of korn of° bred,   *for*

That Grim ne couthe no god red°   *way*

Hw° he sholde his meine° fede.   *how* *household*

Of° Havelok havede he michel drede,° *for* *fear*

For he was strong, and wel mouthe ete

More thanne hevere° mouthe be gete,° *ever* *obtained*

Ne he ne mouthe on the se take
Neyther lenge° ne thornbake,°   *ling*   *skate*
Ne non other fish that douthe,°   *was of value*
His meyne feden with he mouthe.°   *with which he could feed*
Of Havelok he havede kare,°   *anxiety*
Hwilgat° that he micthe fare;   *how*
Of his children was him nouth,°   *not at all*
On Havelok was al his thouth,
And seyde, 'Havelok, dere sone,
I wene that we deye mone°   *must die*
For hunger, this dere° is so strong,   *famine*
And hure mete is ute° long.   *exhausted*
Betere is that thu henne gonge°   *go hence*
Than thu here dwelle longe;
Hethen° thou mayt gangen to late.°   *from here*   *too late*
Thou canst ful wel the ricthe gate°   *direct road*
To Lincolne, the gode borw;°   *town*
Thou havest it gon ful ofte thoru.
Of me ne is me nouth a slo.⁴
Betere is that thu thider go,
For ther is mani god man inne;
Ther thou mayt thi mete winne.
But wo is me thou art so naked!
Of mi seyl y wolde the were maked
A cloth thou mithest inne gongen,°   *travel*
Sone, no cold that thu ne fonge,'°   *catch*
He toke the sheres of° the nayl.   *from*
And made him a couel of the sayl,   *cloak*
And Havelok dide it sone° on;   *at once*
Havede neyther hosen ne shon,°   *stockings nor shoes*
Ne none kines other wede;°   *any other sort of garment*
To Lincolne barfot he yede.°   *went*

---

4   For me, it is not worth a sloe (= I can't do anything).

(c) In England the traitor Godrich, who has promised a fine marriage for Goldeboru, is determined to end her claim to the English throne. Havelock, now a strong young man, has found work in Lincoln, and becomes a scullion in Godrich's household. Godrich marries Goldeboru to the supposed scullion. Her sorrow is ended by a supernatural sight. [vv. 1247–74]

On the nith,° als Goldeborw lay,	*in the night*	
Sory and sorwful was she ay,°	*ever*	
For she wende° she were biswike,°	*thought*	*tricked*
That she [we]re yeven° unkyndelike.°	*given*	*beneath her station*
O nith saw she therinne a lith°	*light*	
A swithe fayr, a swathe bryth,°	*very bright*	
Also brith, also shir,°	*radiant*	
So it were a blase° of fir.	*flame*	
She lokede north and ek south,		
And saw it comen out of his mouth		
That lay bi hire in the bed;		
No ferlike° thou she were adred!°	*wonder*	*afraid*
Thouthe she, 'Wat may this bimene?°	*signify*	
He beth heyman° yet, als y wene;	*will be a lord*	
He beth heyman er° he be ded.'	*before*	
On hise shuldre of gold red		
She saw a swithe noble croiz.°	*cross*	
Of an angel she herd a voyz,		
'Goldeborw, lat thi sorwe be,		
For Havelok, that haveth spuset the,°	*married thee*	
Is kings sone and kings eyr;°	*heir*	
That bikenneth° that croyz so fayr.	*demonstrates*	
It bikenneth more, that he shal		
Denemark haven° and Englond al;	*possess*	
He shal ben king strong and stark°	*mighty*	
Of Engelond an Denemark:		
That shalt thu wit thin eyne sen,		
And thou shalt quen and levedi ben.'		

Eventually, Grim takes Havelock and Goldborough to Denmark, where Havelock is recognised as the destined king by Earl Ubbe. He defeats Godard, becomes king of Denmark, then goes back to England where he defeats Godrich and becomes king of England.

ii) *Sir Orfeo*[5]

The story of Orpheus and Eurydice was a favourite in the Middle Ages. The happy ending given to it here is not unique. Possibly Celtic stories also lie in the background (cf. the Irish tale of the *Wooing of Etainn*),[6] and stories of the recovery of mortals from the otherworld or of those taken by the fairies.[7] The Middle English romance was probably written in the later thirteenth century or the early fourteenth. This story, and other popular Orpheus stories, lived on — into a Scottish romance and a Shetland ballad recorded in the nineteenth century (Child No. 19). There is a reference to a French 'lai d'Orphey', but this has not survived. This romance is remarkable for its sensitivity to human emotion, its insistence on the virtues of faithfulness and courage, and its narrative skill. For all its literary art, it has many of the characteristics of popular romance. Interestingly, though Orfeo is a 'heigh lording', he is also a minstrel (we are given some details of performance in vv. 25 ff, 267 ff, 361 ff).

(a) Orfeo, a king and a great harper, is married to the beautiful Heurodis. One day at the beginning of May she goes out with her maidens, and falls asleep under a tree. When she awakes she shows signs of a terrible distress. Taken back to her chamber, she describes how in her sleep she was visited by a large company of mysterious knights and ladies, and was commanded by their king to return to the tree on the following day; if she offers any resistance she will be torn apart, and still carried off. The next day Orfeo with a body of men escorts her to the tree. But she is snatched away 'with fairy forth ynume'. Orfeo is distraught, and decides to go alone into the wilderness, leaving his kingdom in the care of his steward … [vv. 219–330][8]

---

5   In *Middle English Verse Romances* (Sands; other editions are listed).
6   See Kittredge, 'Sir Orfeo'.
7   For example, the first story from Walter Map, above.
8   In Sands, the passage is vv. 195–306; there is a 'prologue' printed in some editions, which explains the differing line-numbers. But the passages are easy to identify, whichever edition the reader consults.

Tho was ther wepeing in the halle,

And grete cri among hem alle;

Unnethe° might old or yong   *scarcely*

For wepeing speke a word with tong.

Thai kneled adoun al yfere,°   *together*

And praid him, yif his wille were,

That he no schuld nought fram hem go.

'Do way,'° quath he, 'it schal be so.'   *Enough!*

Al his kingdome he forsoke;

Bot a sclavin° on him he toke.   *pilgrim's cloak*

He no hadde kirtel no hode,°   *kirtle nor hood*

Schert [no] non other gode,°   *belongings*

But his harp he toke algate°   *at any rate*

And dede him° barfot out atte yate;°   *went*   *at the gate*

No man most with him go.

O way!° What ther was wepe and wo,   *Alas!*

Whan he that hadde ben king with croun

Went so poverlich° out of toun.   *in such poor array*

Thurth wode and over heth°   *heath*

Into the wildernes he geth.

Nothing he fint° that him is ays,°   *finds*   *comfort*

Bot ever he liveth in gret malaise.

He that hadde ywerd° the fowe and griis⁹   *worn*

And on bed the purpur biis;°   *fine linen*

Now on hard hethe he lith;

With leves and gresse he him writh.°   *covers*

He that hadde had castels and tours,

River, forest, frith with flours,°   *woodland with flowers*

Now, thei° it comenci to snewe and frees,°   *though*   *freeze*

This king mot make his bed in mese.°   *moss*

He that had yhad knightes of priis°   *of value*

Bifor him kneland, and levedis,°   *ladies*

Now seth° he nothing that he liketh,   *sees*

---

9   'variegated fur and grey fur': this phrase indicates opulence (the striped fur may have been squirrel specially imported from Russia).

But wilde wormes° bi him striketh.°	*serpents*	*glide*
He that had yhad plente		
Of mete and drink, of ich deynte,°	*every delicacy*	
Now may he alday° digge and wrote°	*all day long*	*grub*
Er he finde his fille of rote.°	*roots*	
In somer he liveth bi wild frut		
And berien bot gode lite;°	*very little*	
In winter may he nothing finde		
Bot rote, grases and the rinde.°	*bark*	
Al his bodi was oway duine°	*wasted away*	
For missays,° and al tochine;°	*discomfort*	*scarred*
His here of his berd, blac and rowe,°	*rough*	
To his girdelstede° was growe.	*waist*	
Lord! who may telle the sore°	*distress*	
This king sufferd ten yere and more?		
His harp, whereon was al his gle,°	*minstrelsy*	
He hidde in an holwe tre,		
And when the weder was clere and bright,		
He toke his harp to him wel right,		
And harped at his owhen° wille,	*own*	
In alle the wode the soun gan schille,°	*resound*	
That alle the wilde bestes that ther beth°	*are*	
For joie abouten him thai teth,°	*come*	
And alle the foules that ther were		
Come and sete on ich a brere°	*twig*	
To here his harping affine,°	*to the end*	
So miche melody was therin.		
And when he his harping lete° wold,	*leave*	
No best bi him abide nold.°	*would not*	
He might se him besides		
Oft in hot undertides°	*noon times*	
The king o fairy with his rout°	*company*	
Com to hunt him al about		
With dim cri and bloweing,		
And houndes also with him berking;		

Ac no best thai no nome,° — *caught*

No never he nist° whider thai bicome.° — *knew not* — *went*

And other while he might him se

As a gret ost bi him te,° — *come*

Wele atourned,° ten hundred knightes, — *equipped*

Ich yarmed to his rightes,° — *properly*

Of cuntenaunce° stout° and fers, — *appearance* — *strong*

With mani desplaid baners,

And ich his swerd ydrawe° hold; — *drawn*

Ac never he nist whider thai wold.° — *would go*

And other while he seiye other thing:

Knightes and levedis com daunceing

In queynt° attire, gisely,° — *elegant* — *skilfully*

Queynt pas and softly;

Tabours and trunpes° yede hem bi,° — *drums and trumpets* — *beside*

And al maner menstraci.° — *minstrelsy*

And on a day he seiye him biside

Sexti levedis on hors ride,

Gentil and jolif° as brid on ris;° — *merry* — *spray*

Nought o man amonges hem ther nis.° — *is not*

And ich a faucon on hond bere,

And riden on haukin bi o rivere.

Of game thai founde wel gode haunt,° — *plenty*

Maulardes,° hayroun° and cormeraunt. — *mallards* — *heron*

The foules of the water ariseth;

The faucons hem wele deviseth;° — *aim at*

Ich faucon his pray slough.° — *slew*

That seiye Orfeo, and lough:° — *laughed*

'Parfay,'° quath he, 'ther is fair game. — *Indeed*

Thider ichil,° bi Godes name; — *I will go*

Ich was ywon° swiche werk to se.' — *accustomed*

He aros and thider gan te.° — *went*

To a levedi he was ycome,

Biheld, and hath wel undernome° — *realised*

And seth bi al thing that it is

His owhen quen, dam Heurodis.

Yern° he beheld hir and sche him eke,°   *eagerly*   *also*

Ac° neither to other a word no speke.   *but*

For messais that sche on him seiye

That had ben so riche and so heiye,

The teres fel out of her eiye.

The other levedis this yseiye.

And maked hir oway to ride;

Sche most with him no lenger abide.

(b) But the determined Orfeo takes up his harp and rides after the ladies, into a rock. He finds himself in a beautiful land with a fine castle. Introducing himself as a minstrel he enters, and plays for the king, who is entranced by his music. [vv. 435–74][10]

Bifor the king he sat adoun,

And tok his harp so miri of soun,

And tempreth° it as he wele can,   *tunes*

And blisseful notes he ther gan.°   *began*

That al that in the palays were

Com to him forto here,

And liggeth° adoun to his fete,   *lie*

Hem thenketh his melody so swete.

The king herkneth and sitt ful stille

To here his gle° he hath gode wille.   *music*

Gode bourde° he hadde of his gle;   *enjoyment*

The riche quen also hadde he.°   *she*

When he hadde stint° his harping,   *ceased*

Than seyd to him the king,

'Menstrel, me liketh wele thi gle.

Now aske of me what° it be;   *whatever*

Largelich ichil° the pay.   *generously I will*

Now speke, and tow might assay.'°   *put it to the test*

'Sir,' he seyd, 'ich biseche the

_____

10   In Sands, these are vv. 411–50.

Thatow woldest yive me		
That ich° levedi bright on ble°	*same*	*complexion*
That slepeth under the ympetre.'°	*orchard tree*	
'Nay,' quath the king, 'that nought nere.°	*could not be*	
A sori couple of you it were,		
For thou art lene, rowe° and blac,	*rough*	
And sche is lovesum,° withouten lac;°	*beautiful*	*blemish*
A lothlich° thing it were forthi°	*hateful*	*therefore*
To sen hir in thi compayni.'		
'O sir,' he seyd, 'gentil king,		
Yete it were a wele fouler thing		
To here a lesing° of thi mouthe.	*falsehood*	
So, sir, as ye seyd nouthe,°	*just now*	
What ich wold aski have y schold,		
And nedes thou most thi word hold.'		
The king seyd, 'Sethen it is so,		
Take hir bi the hond and go,		
Of hir ichil thatow be blithe.'°	*happy*	
He kneled adoun and thonked him swathe.°	*greatly*	
His wiif he tok bi the hond,		
And dede him swathe out° of that lond.	*went quickly*	

Disguised as a minstrel 'of poor life' he takes Heurodis with him back to his own city. He plays before the steward, who recognises his harp. He reveals his identity, is restored to his kingdom, and after his death the faithful steward becomes king.

iii) *Emaré*

A simple romance, with direct style, repetitions, and formulae, perhaps suggesting it is not too far removed from oral storytelling; but one which it is easy to underestimate. With its symmetrical plot it tells a 'pitous' story of a suffering woman, a calumniated queen. It is a 'test' story; it has similarities with the Constance story (Chaucer's Man of Law's Tale, Gower's tale of Constance) or Chaucer's story of Griselda. Behind it lies the folk tale of the 'Maiden without Hands'.[11] Emaré's wonderful garment, a present from the 'riche kynge of Cesile' may have originally been a fairy present.

(a) Emaré, the beautiful daughter of the emperor Artyrus, excites the passion of her father. When she refuses his incestuous desire, he has her cast out in a rudderless boat, clad in a robe of rich, gold, ornamented cloth. Her boat is blown far away by the wind; the emperor repents, but it is too late ... [vv. 313–60]

The lady fleted° forth alone.	*floated*	
To God of heven she made her mone°	*lament*	
And to hys modyr also,		
She was driven wyth wynde and rayn		
Wyth stronge stormes her agayn,°	*against*	
Of the watur so blo.°	*dark*	
As y have herd menstrelles syng yn sawe,°	*tales*	
Hows ny° lond myghth she non knowe,°	*nor*	*make out*
Aferd° she was to go.	*afraid*	
She was so driven fro wawe to wawe		
She hyd her hede and lay full lowe,		
For° watyr she was full woo.°	*because of*	*in great misery*
Now this lady dwelled thore		
A good sevennyghth and more,		
As hyt was Goddys wylle.		
Wyth carefull° herte and sykyng° sore,	*sorrowful*	*sighing*
Such sorrow was here yarked° yore,°	*destined for*	*long ago*
And ever lay she styll.		
She was driven ynto a lond,		
Thorow the grace of Goddes sond,°	*dispensation*	
That all thing may fulfylle.		
She was on the see so harde bestadde,°	*beset*	

---

11   *Emaré* is in *Six Middle English Romances*, ed. Mills. For the Handless Maiden, see Bliss *Naming and Namelessness*, the section entitled Unknown Women esp. *La Manekine* (and index).

For hungur and thurste almost madde:

  Woo worth wederus yll!º   *a curse on bad storms*

She was dryven into a lond

That hyghthº Galys, y unthurstond: *was called*

  That was a fayr countre.

The kyngus steward dwelled ther bysyde,º   *nearby*

In a kastell of mykyll pryde:º   *much splendour*

  Syr Kadore hyght he.

Every day he wolde go,

And take wth hym a sqwyer or two,

  And play hym by the see.

On a tyme he toke the eyr

Wyth two knyghtus gode and fayr;

  The wedur was lythe of le.º   *calm and peaceful*

A bootº he fond by the brymº   *boat*   *edge*

And a glysteryng thing theryn:

  Therof they hadde ferly.º   *wonder*

They went forth on the sond   *sand*

To the boot, y unthurstond,

  And fond theryn that lady.

She hadde so longe metelesº be   *without food*

That hym thowht gret deleº to se;   *distress*

  She was yn poyn[t] to dye.º   *at the point of death*

They askede her what was her name;

She changed hyt ther anone,º   *at once*

  And seyde she hetteº Egaré.[12]   *was called*

(b) Sir Kadore cares for her, and his king falls in love with her and marries her. They live happily for a time, and while the king is away fighting she bears a son, Segramour. A letter to him from Sir Kadore, telling him of this, is intercepted by the king's wicked mother who hates

---

12 Egaré means lost or strayed.

Egaré/Emaré. Another letter is substituted, saying that her offspring
was a devil. The king laments, but sends a letter saying that she should
be well cared for. This too is intercepted by his mother and replaced
with another saying that she should be cast out on the sea with her child
and her splendid robe. The steward is unable to prevent this, and the
two are cast adrift. [vv. 637–708]

Then was ther sorrow and myche woo,	
When the lady to shype shulde° go;	*had to*
They wepte and wronge her hondus.	
The lady that was meke and mylde	
In her arme she bar her chylde,	
And toke leve of the londe.	
When she wente ynto the see	
In that robe of riche ble,	
Men sowened° on the sonde.°	*swooned* *sand*
Sore they wepte and sayde, 'Alas,	
Certys thys ys a wykked kase.°	*event*
Wo worth dedes wronge!'°	*evil deeds*

The lady and the lytyll chylde	
Fleted forth on the watur wylde,	
Wyth full harde happes.°	*misfortunes*
Her surkote° that was large and wyde,	*robe*
Therwith her visage she gan hyde,	
Wyth the hynthur lappes;°	*back folds*
She was aferde of the see	
And layde her gruf° uponn a tre,°	*face down* *beam*
The chylde to her pappes.°	*breasts*
The wawes that were grete and strong	
On the bote faste they thronge,	
Wyth mony unseemly rappes.°	*blows*

And when the chyld gan to wepe
Wyth sory herte she songe hyt aslepe
    And putte the pappe yn hys mowth.

And syde, 'Myghth y onus gete̥ lond,   *get to*
Of the watur that ys so stronge.̥   *severe*
    By northe or by sowthe,
Wele owth y to warye̥ the, see,   *ought I to curse*
I have myche shame yn the!'
    And evur she lay and growth.̥   *lamented*
Then she made her prayer
To Jesu and hys modur dere,
    In all that she kowthe.

Now thys lady dwelled thore
A full sevenenyght and more,
    As hyt was Goddys wylle;
Wyth karefull herte and sykyng sore,
Such sorrow was her yarked yore,
    And she lay full stylle.
She was driven toward Rome,
Thorow the grace of God yn trone,̥   *throne*
    That all thing may fulfylle.
On the see she was so harde bestadde,
For hungur and thurste allmost madde,
    Wo worth chawnses ylle!̥   *evil events*

A marchaunte dw[el]led yn that cyte.
A ryche mon of gold and fee.̥   *property*
    Jurdan was hys name.
Every day wolde he
Go to playe hym by the see,
    The eyer forto tane,̥   *air to take*
He wente forth yn that tyde,̥   *time*
Walkynge by the see sy[d]e,
    All hymselfe alone.
A bote he fonde by the brymme
And a fayr lady therynne,
    That was right wobygone.

The cloth on her shon so bryth
He was aferde of that sight,
    For glysteryng of that wede;º   *garment*
And yn hys herte he thowghth rightº   *thought indeed*
That she was non erdyly wyght;
    He sawe nevur non such yn leede.º   *the world*
He sayde, 'What hette ye,º fayr ladye?'   *is your name*
'Lord,' she sayde, 'y hette Egarye,
    That lye her yn drede.'º   *fear*
Up he toke that fayre ladye
And the yonge chylde her by,
    And hom he gan hem lede.

[Jurdan and his wife care for her, and Segramour grows up. In a final scene, Emaré is at last reunited with her husband and her father, who have come to Rome to do penance.]

iv) *Octavian*[13]

Written perhaps in the first half of the fourteenth century, *Octavian* tells the story (widespread in Europe) of another calumniated woman and her sons, stolen by wild creatures.

Florence, wife of the emperor Octavian, bears twin sons (Florentyn and Octavian). Thanks to the hostility of a cruel mother-in-law she and her babies are driven out into the forest, and both children are carried off by animals. [vv. 325–84]

Be that sche had hur children dyght,º   *made ready*
Hyt was woxeº derke nyght,   *become*
    As sche sate be the welle;
In the erberº downe sche lay   *grassy spot among trees*
Tyll hyt was dawning of the day
    That fowlysº herde sche yelle.º   *birds*   *cry*
There came an ape to seke hur pray;

---

13   In *Six Middle English Romances* (ed. Mills).

Hur oon chylde sche bare away
    On an hye hylle.
What wondur was, thogh sche were woo?
The ape bar the chylde hur fro!
    In swownyng downe sche felle.

In all the sorowe that sche in was,
There come rennyng a lyenas,°   *lioness*
    Os wode as sche wolde wede;°   *as frenzied as if she would go mad*
In swownyng as the lady lay,
Hur wodur° chylde sche bare away,   *other*
    Hur whelpys° wyth to fede.   *cubs*
What wondur was thogh sche woo° ware?   *in misery*
The wylde beestys hur chyldyr away bare;
    For sorowe hur herte can blede,
The lady sett hur on a stone
Besyde the welle and made hur mone,
    And syghyng forthe sche yede.

There came a fowle that was feyre of flight°   *beautiful in flight*
(A gryffyn he was callyd be right)
    Ovyr the holtys hore;°   *grey woods*
The fowle was so moche of might°   *great in strength*
That he wolde bare a knight
    Well armyd thogh he ware.°   *even though he were*
The lyenas wyth the chylde up toke he
And into an yle of the see
    Bothe he tham bare.
The chylde slept in the lyenas mowthe;
Of wele nor wo° nothing hyt knowyth,   *good fortune or misery*
    But God kepe hyt from care!

Whan the lyenas had a fote on londe,°   *the ground*
Hastyly sche can upstonde,°   *reared up*
    As a beste that was stronge and wylde.

Thorow Goddys grace the gryffyn she slowe
And sythen ete of the flesche ynowe⁰   *plenty*
   And leyde hur downe be⁰ the chylde.   *by*
The chylde soke⁰ the lyenas,   *suckled from*
As hyt Goddys wylle was,
   Whan hyt the pappys⁰ feled;⁰   *teats*   *felt*
And when the lyenas began to wake,
Sche lovyd the chylde for hur whelpys sake
   And therwyth sche was full mylde.⁰   *peaceful*

Wyth hur fete sche made a denne
And leyde the lytull chylde theryn
   And kepte⁰ hyt day and nyght;   *guarded*
And when the lyenas hungurd sore,
Sche ete of the gryffyn more,
   That afore was stronge and wyght.
As hyt was Goddes owne wylle,
The lyenas belafte⁰ the chylde style:⁰   *left*   *at peace*
   The chylde was feyre and bright.
The lady sett hur on a stone,
Besyde the welle and made hur mone
   As a wofull wyght.⁰   *creature*

[After many adventures, the brothers, now proven warriors, are reunited and the mother-in-law is burnt.]

v) *Sir Gowther*

This romance, dated around 1375 in Mills,[14] is a version of the widespread legend of Robert the Devil, in which a young child, begotten by a devil, finds salvation after a disorderly and sinful youth.

A duke and his wife have been married for ten years, but have no child. In desperation the wife prays for a child by any means ... [vv. 58–81]

---

14   *Six Middle English Romances.*

Tho lade sykud° and made yll chere,°	*sighed*	*was unhappy*
That all feyled° hur whyte lere,°	*grew dull*	*white face*
For shu conseyvyd noght,°	*had not conceived*	
Scho preyd to God and Mare mylde		
Schuld gyffe hur grace to have a chyld,		
On what maner scho ne roghth.°	*did not care*	
In hur orchard, apon a day,		
Ho meyt° a man, tho sothe to say,	*she met*	
That hur of luffe besoghth;°	*besought*	
As lyke° hur lorde as he might be —	*similar*	
He leyd hur down under a tre,		
With hur is° wyll he wroghtth.°	*his*	*took*

When he had is wylle all don,		
A felturd fende° he start up son,	*shaggy fiend*	
And stode and hur beheld.		
He seyd, 'Y have geyton° a chylde on the	*begotten*	
That in is yothe full wylde schall bee		
And weppons wyghtly weld.'°	*powerfully wield*	
Scho blessyd hur° and fro hym ran;	*crossed herself*	
Into hur chambur fast ho wan,°	*came*	
That was so bygly byld;°	*strongly made*	
Scho seyd to hur lord, that lade myld,		
'Tonyght we mon° geyt chyld,	*must*	
That schall owre londus weld.'°	*rule*	

The boy, Gowther, grows up to be a very strong and very 'wild' young man who terrorises everyone in the neighbourhood. His supposed father dies of sorrow. When he is called 'a devil's son' by an earl, Gowther forces his mother to tell the story of his conception. He goes to Rome, and begins a life of penitence as 'Hob the Fool'. He rescues the emperor's daughter from the Saracens, is recognised by her, and marries her. He is absolved by the Pope, becomes the ruler of Almayne, and is venerated as a saint.

vi) *Chevelere Assigne*[15]

A fourteenth-century century romance in alliterative long lines. It is a version of the Swan-Knight legend (cf. Lohengrin, the son of Parzival in German romance); though it is not here associated, as it often was from the late twelfth century, with the name of Godfrey of Bouillon, one of the leaders of the First Crusade.

An episode in which the innocent young knight Enyas (Helyas, in other Middle English stories) is instructed in the art and method of single combat. The scene is treated with a touching and attractive comedy (as in some scenes in the English *William of Palerne*).[16] Bewtrys (Beatrice), wife of king Oriens of Lyon, is delivered of six sons and a daughter, born simultaneously, each with a silver chain around the neck. Her wicked mother-in-law, Matabryne, orders her man Markus to drown the children, but out of pity he spares them and leaves them in the forest, where they are reared by a hermit. But Malkedras, a wicked forester, sees them, and tells Matabryne who sends him to kill them and bring her the silver rings from their necks. He finds six children; the seventh, Enyas, has gone into the forest with the hermit in search of food. When the chains are cut, the six children become swans, and fly to a nearby river. Matabryne wishes that Beatrice should be burnt, but the young Enyas offers to fight on her behalf: he must do battle with Malkedras. [vv. 287–313]

A knyghte kawghte hym by the honde, and ladde hym of the rowte.
'What beeste is this,' quod the child, 'that I shall on hove?'[o]   *ride*
'Hit is called an hors,' quod the knyghte, 'a good and an abull.'[o]   *useful*
'Why eteth he yren?'[o] quod the chylde, 'Wyll he ete noghth elles?   *iron*
And what is that on his bakke, of byrthe or on
        bounden?'[o]   *from birth, or fastened*
'Nay, that in his mowth men callen a brydell,
And that a sadell on his bakke, that thou shalt in sytte.'

---

15   *The Romance of the Chevelere Assigne*, ed. Gibbs. If Gray used this edition, he silently
     deleted letters added by the editor (such as 'e' at the ends of words marked in italic
     type).
16   *William of Palerne*, ed. Skeat.

'And what hevy kyrtell° is this with holes so thykke,   *coat*

And this holowe on° on my hede? I may not here.'°   *hollow one*   *hear*

'An helme men kallen that on and an hawberke° that other.'   *coat of mail*

'But what broode on is this on my breste? Hit bereth° adown my   *weighs*
     nekke.'

'A bryghte shelde and a sheene,° to shelde the fro strokes,'   *shining*

'And what longe on is this that I shall up lyfte?'

'Take that launce up in thyn honde, and loke° thou hym hytte;   *see that*

And whenne that shafte is schyvered,° take   *shattered*
     scharpelye° another.'   *quickly*

'Ye, what yf grace be we to grownde wenden?'°   *go*

'Aryse up lightly on the fete, and reste the no lengur.°   *longer*

And thenne plukke out thy swerde, and pele° on hym faste,   *strike*

Allwey eggelynges down° on all that thou fyndes.   *edge downwards*

His ryche helm nor his swerde rekke° thou of   *care*
     neythur;°   *neither*

Lete the sharpe of thy swerde schreden hym small.'

'But woll not he smyte ayeyne, whenne he feleth smerte?'

'Yys, I knowe hym full wele, both keenly and faste.

Evur folowe thou on the flesh tyll thou haste hym falleth,°   *felled him*

And sythen smyte of his heede; I kan sey the no furre.'°   *further*

'Now thou haste tawghte me,' quod the childe, 'God I the
     beteche;°   *commend*

For now I kan of the crafte more thenne I kowthe.'

Enyas overcomes Malkedras; Matabryne herself is burnt; Beatrice is released. Five chains are returned to the swans, who become human once more; the sixth child, who must remain a swan, laments bitterly. The others are baptised: 'thus the botenynge of God browghte hem to honde.'[17]

---

17   Thus the help of God brought them to a happy end.

vii) *The Turke and Gowin*[18]

A romance (probably written around 1500) which survives, in an incomplete form, in the mid-seventeenth century *PFMS*. Arthurian tales, and especially stories about Sir Gawain, often find their way into popular romance. The Percy Folio Grene Knight tells the story of Sir Gawain and the Green Knight; and others, like this, have similarities with that story.

A strange man — broad and shaped like a Turk — enters when Arthur is sitting at table, and asks for an exchange of buffets (compare *Sir Gawain and the Green Knight*). Gawain accepts the challenge. He accompanies the Turk, into a hill and to the castle of the king of Man, through a series of often fantastic adventures and tests of strength. At the end, the Turk, bearing a basin of gold, asks Gawain to cut his head off … [vv. 268–94]

… He tooke forth a bason of gold
As an emperour washe shold,
    As fell for his degree.

He tooke a sword of mettle free,°	*noble metal*
Saies, 'If ever I did any thing for thee,	
Doe for me in this stead;°	*place*
Take here this sword of steele	
That in batell will bite weele,°	*well*
Therwith strike of my head.'	

'That I forefend!'° said Sir Gawaine,	*forbid*
'For I wold not have thee slaine	
For all the gold soe red.'	
'Have done, Sir Gawaine, I have no dread,	
But in this bason let me bleed	
That standeth here in this steed,	

---

18   In *Sir Gawain: Eleven Romances and Tales* (Hahn's edition differs slightly from Gray's here).

And thou shalt see a new play,
With helpe of Mary that mild ma[y]
    That saved us from all dread.'
He drew forth the brand° of steele,   *sword*
That in battell bite wold weele,
    And there stroke of his head.

And when the blood in the bason light,°   *fell*
He stood up a stalwortht knight
    That day, I undertake,°   *guarantee*
And song, *Te deum laudam*[*u*]*s*.[19]
Worshipp be to our lord Jesus
    That saved us from all wracke!'°   *disaster*

They return to Arthur's court, and the Turk, now Sir Gromer, a stalwart knight, is made king of Man.

viii) *Sir Lambewell*[20]

Marie de France's lai of *Lanval* survives in two Middle English versions: *Sir Landevale* (early fourteenth century) and Thomas Chestre's *Sir Launfal* (later fourteenth). The former lives on in two popular versions. *Sir Lambewell* (632 lines, in *PFMS*) ia a good example of popular romance, which has probably passed through a series of copyists and retellers.

Lambewell is a young knight at Arthur's court who is far from home and who has spent much of his wealth. In his distress he is helped by a fairy mistress, who in typical fashion imposes a taboo: he must not reveal her to anyone. But, taunted by Guinevere, he does. He is no longer visited by his mistress, and he is accused of slandering the queen. But just before the judges speak, his beautiful mistress rides into the town, with a sparrowhawk on her hand, and three white greyhounds running beside her ... [vv. 523–38 & 600–30]

---

19   *Te Deum Laudamus* (We praise thee, O God) is not a psalm, but has been a song of praise in the Church since early Christian times.
20   In *PFMS* (vol i), p. 142 ff.

… Wife and child, yonge and old,
All came this lady to beholde,
And all still upon her gazing
As people that beheld the sacring;º   *consecration of the Host*
And all they stood still in their study,º   *amazement*
And yet they thought them never weary,
For there was never man nor woman that might
Be weary of this ladies sight.
As soone as Sir Lambwell did her see,
On all the people cryed hee
'Yond comes my life and my liking!º   *delight*
Shee comes that me out of baileº shall bring!   *torment*
Yond comes my lemman,º I make you sure;   *beloved*
Treulie shee is the fairest creature
That ever man see before indeed,
Looke where shee rydes upon her steed!' …

… Th[e] king and theº prayd, everyone;   *they*
But for all that ever he cold doe,
Not a word shee wold speake him too,
But obayd her to the king soe h[e]nd,º   *courteous*
And tooke her leave away to wend.
Then Lambewell saw that shee wold fare,º   *go*
His owne hart he tookeº to him there;   *took courage*
When shee turned her horse to have gone,
He leaped upon, sooneº anon,   *immediately*
Upon her palfray; whatsoever betide,
Behind her he wold not abide;
And he said, 'Madam, with reason and skill
Now goe which way so ere you will,
For when you light downe, I shall stand.
And when you ryd, all at your hande,
And whether it be for waile or woeº   *good or ill*
I will never depart you froe.'
This lady now the right way nummº   *took*

With her maids all and some,
And shee brought Sir Lambwell from Carlile
Farr into a jolly° il[e]   *pleasant*
That clipped was A[v]ilion,
Which knoweth well every Briton;
And shee came there, that lady faire,
Shee gave him all that he found there,
That was to say, all manner of thing
That ever might be to his likinge;
And further of him hard° no man,   *heard*
Nor more of him tell can,
But in that iland his life he spend,
Soe did shee alsoe tooke her end.°   *ended her life*

ix) *Thomas of Erceldoune*[21]

This fifteenth-century romance has very clear similarities with the ballad of *Thomas the Rhymer* (see our chapter Ballads, no. x), but the nature of the relationship is not certain. Many scholars have thought that the ballad is derived from the romance, but recently it has been argued that the romance has itself been formed from earlier tales or possibly ballads (which may have lived on separately). Certainly, the romance has some unusual features: the first-person narrative at the beginning, the unusual quatrain form and the relative lack of 'story'. It ends with a long series of prophecies, but these may well have been added later.

a) vv. 25–36 & 69–108[22]

Als I me wente this endres daye,
Full faste in mynd makand my mone,°   *lament*
In a mery mornynge of Maye,
In Huntle bankkes myselfe allone.

---

21 [Thomas] *The Romance and Prophecies of Thomas of Erceldoune*, ed. Murray.
22 This first part is on p. 2 of the edition (the Thornton text); the next begins on p. 5; the edited text is not set out in quatrains.

I herde the jaye, and the throstyll coke,°   *male thrush*
The mawys° menyde° hir of hir songe,   *song-thrush*   *sang plaintively*
The wodewale° beryde° als a belle,   *oriole woodpecker*   *cried*
That alle the wode abowte me ronge.

Allone in longynge thus als I laye,
Undyrenethe a seemly tree,
[Saw] I whare a lady gaye
[Come rydyng] over a longe lee° …   *meadow*[23]
… [She led three grehoundes in a leshe],
And sevene raches° by hir thay rone,°   *hounds*   *ran*
Scho bare an horne abowte hir hales,°   *neck*
And undir hir belte full many a flone.°   *arrow*

Thomas laye and sawe that syghte,
Undirnethe ane semly tree;
He sayd, 'Yone es Marye moste of myghte,
That bare that childe that dyede for mee.

Bot if° I speke with yone lady bryghte,   *unless*
I hope° myne herte will bryste° in three!   *think*   *break*
Now sall I go with all my myghte,
Hir for to mete at Eldoune tree.'

Thomas rathely° upe he rase,   *quickly*
And he rane over that mountayne hye;
Gyff° it be als the storye sayes,   *if*
He hir met at Eldone tree.

He knelyde downe upon his knee,
Undirnethe that grenwode spray;°   *branch*
And sayd, 'Lufly ladye! Rewe° one mee,   *have mercy*
Qwene of hevene, als thou wele maye!'

---

23   An extensive meadow, or this may be a place-name (the edition has no explanatory
     notes; cf. the 'lilly lee' in *Thomas the Rhymer*.

Then spake that lady milde of thoghte,
'Thomas, late swylke° words bee;   *such*
Qwene of hevene ne am I noghte,
For I tuke° never so heghe degree.°   *assumed*   *degree*

Bote I ame of ane other countree,
If I be payrelde° moste of prysse;°   *clothed*   *excellence*
I ryde aftyre this wylde fee,°   *animals*
My raches rynnys at my devyse.'°   *command*

'If thou be parelde moste of prys[e],
And here rydis thus in thy folye²⁴
Of lufe, lady, als thou erte wysse,
Thou gyffe me leve to lye the bye.'

Scho sayde, 'Thou mane, that ware folye,
I praye the, Thomas, thou late me bee;
For I saye the full sekirlye,°   *certainly*
That synne will fordoo° all my beaute.'   *destroy*

'Now, lufly ladye, rewe one mee,
And I will evermore with the duelle;
Here my trouthe I will the plyghte,
Whethir thou will in hevene or helle' …

[Thomas makes love to her and she is transfomed into an ugly and fearsome sight. Then she leads him into Eildon Hill … b): vv. 157–222]²⁵

… 'Thomas, take leve at sonne and mone,
And als at lefe that grewes° on tree;   *grows*
This twelmoneth sall thou with me gone,
And medillerthe° sall thou none° see.'   *earth*   *not at all*

---

24 cf. 'follee' in *Thomas the Rhymer*. The word usually means 'folly', but other meanings
    include 'park', a place for hunting and other activities.
25 This section begins on p. 9 of the edition.

He knelyd downe appone his knee,
Undirnethe that grenewod spraye,
And sayd, 'Lufly lady, rewe on mee,
Mylde qwene of hevene, als thou beste maye,

Allas!' he sayd, 'and wa es mee,
I trowe my dedis wyll wirke me care.
My saulle, Jesu, byteche I the,
Whedir some° that ever my banes° sall fare.'   *wherever*   *bones*

Scho ledde hym in at Eldone hill,
Undirnethe a derne° lee,   *secret*
[Whare it was] dirke° als mydnyght myrke,   *dark*
And ever the water till° his knee.   *to*

The montenans° of dayes three,   *space*
He herde bot swoghynge° of the flode;   *rumbling*
At the laste, he sayde, 'full wa is mee!
Almaste I dye for fawte of f[ode].'

Scho lede hym intill a faire herbere,°   *arbour*
Whare frwte was g[ro]wan[d gret plentee],
Pere and appill, bothe ryppe thay were,
The date and als the damasee,°   *damson*

The fygge and als so the wyneberye.°   *bilberry or grape*
The nyghtgales byggande° on their neste,   *dwelling*
The papejoyes° faste abowte gan flye,   *parrots*
And throstylls sange wolde hafe no reste.

He pressede° to pulle frowyte with his hande,   *pressed forward*
Als mane° for fude that was nere faynt,   *like a man*
Scho sayd, 'Thomas, thou late thame stande,
Or ells the fende the will atteynt;°   *seize*

If thou it plokk,° sothely to saye,   *pluck*
Thi saule gose to the fyre of helle;
It comes never owte or° domesdaye,   *before*
Bot ther in payne ay for to duelle.

Thomas, sothely I the hyghte,°   *command*
Come lygge thyne hede downe on my knee,
And [thou] sall se the fayreste syghte,
That ever sawe mane of thi contree.'

He did in hye° als scho hym bade;   *haste*
Appone hir knee his hede he layde,
For hir to paye° he was full glade,   *please*
And thane that lady to hym sayde,

'Seese thou nowe yone faire waye,
That lygges over yone heghe mountayne?
Yone es the waye to hevene for aye,
Whene synfull sawles are passed ther payne.

Seese thou nowe yone other waye,
That lygges lawe bynethe yone rysse?°   *brushwood*
Yone es the waye, the sothe to saye,
Unto the joye of paradyse.

Seese thou yitt yone thirde waye,
That ligges undir yone grene playne?
Yone es the waye, with tene and traye,
Whare synfull saulis suffiris thaire payne.

Bot seese thou nowe yone ferthe waye,
That lygges over yone depe delle?
Yone es the waye — so waylawaye! —
Unto the birnande fyre of helle.

Seese thou yitt yone faire castelle,
[That standis over] yone heghe hill?
Of towne and towre it beris the belle —
In erthe es none lyke it until.

For sothe, Thomas, yone es myne awenne,º   *own*
And the kynges of this countree ...'

He is commanded to speak only to her when he is in her lord's castle.
Thomas stands still and looks at her. She is once more 'fayre and gude',
riding on her palfrey with her hounds; she leads him to the castle, where
he sees ladies making music, knights dancing, and feasting: there was
'revelle, gamene and playe'. He stays there until (relapsing momentarily
into first-person narrative, 'till one a daye, so hafe I grace, My lufly lady
sayde to mee') he is told to make ready for the jouney back to 'Eldone
tree'. He says that he has only been in the castle for three days; she tells
him that he has been there for three years and more (seven years and
more according to the Cambridge MS).[26] She says that on the following
day the foul fiend of hell will come and 'amange this folke will feche his
fee' and 'thou arte mekill mane and hende — I trowe full wele he wolde
chese the' (v. 292), and she takes him back to 'Eldonne tree'. The first
Fytte ends here. In the following two fyttes, in response to his request
to be told of 'some ferly' she tells him a long series of prophecies, until
at last he allows her to go ... to Helsdale in the north, reputed to be the
home of fairies and witches.

---

26   In Murray's edition, p. 17 (v. 286).

Chapter 4

Tales and Legends

This section gives some popular examples of the vast number of short tales, in both prose and verse, which have survived from the Middle Ages. 'Tale' and 'legend' are terms which in medieval English can more easily overlap than in modern English: together they are the equivalent of the German Sage (story). In Middle English 'legend' is used of the story or life of a saint, and also more generally for story or 'account'. It does not seem to have had the common modern meaning of 'non-authentic' or non-historical, although there were certainly people in the Middle Ages who questioned the truth of some legends (such as that King Arthur did not die in his last battle, but lived on). The etymological background of the two English words are of interest: 'tale' is associated with 'telling' or 'speaking'; 'legend' (from Latin, meaning that which is read) with 'reading'. Both activities are significant in the performance and transmission of tales and legends. The two activities, however, were not then mutually exclusive. Tales and legends were spoken, by storytellers or preachers, or sung, by entertainers or minstrels; and also read by the newly literate. But 'reading' was sometimes reading aloud, in public streets or private rooms.[1]

However the tales and legends were experienced, it is very clear that medieval 'folk' loved them: Chaucer's Pardoner remarks 'lewed peple loven tales olde', though he also has a cynical eye on the money to be earned. However, it is difficult to overestimate the vast scope

---

1   See 1 xlii and 4 ii. 1 xlii is about the priest reading to Margery, in chapter 1 above; 4 ii is the story of Gunnhild, below: 'sung of in our time in the public streets'.

  https://doi.org/10.11647/OBP.0170.04

and variety of these 'tales olde', some of which go back to the very beginnings of recorded literature. It is as if we are confronted by a vast ocean of stories.[2] And the stories are not only of an almost infinite variety, but they seem wonderfully flexible. They are constantly changing, being retold or reshaped, being turned into various literary forms, crossing linguistic or geographical boundaries, sometimes making their way into highly sophisticated literary works like the *Decameron*[3] or the *Canterbury Tales*. Attempts at classifying them are fraught with difficulties. Here we simply offer some examples of some significant 'kinds'. The very common 'comic tales' and 'animal stories' are given their own chapters.[4] This chapter serves as an introduction, and has examples of kinds such as anecdotes, exemplary stories, local legends, religious legends and saints' lives. Some of these continued to flourish: anecdotes are still with us, still circulating by word of mouth and feeding a taste for gossip and satire. In the Middle Ages they also appear in chronicles, and sometimes, it seems, had a role in providing what became in the hands of chroniclers 'historical material' itself. Other kinds have a significance that we do not always recognise. 'Exemplary story' or 'exemplum' sounds at first to be a rather dull category. But the examples are often far from dull: they aim to entertain as well as to instruct. And they have a considerable literary influence: in general, helping to form the 'mentalites' of sophisticated authors, all of whom must have heard them. In particular: we sometimes find echoes of their simple, pungent style in literary storytelling, and even in 'mystical' works when their authors turn to stories (compare Julian of Norwich's description of Christ as a lord in his house, presiding over a stately and joyous feast, or her tale of the Lord and the Servant;[5] and Margery Kempe's own exemplum,[6] which wins the approval of the archbishop).

Many of these tales are told in a manner which seems close to the speaking voice of an oral taleteller. It is very likely that behind our

---

2   Gray's chapter on different kinds of narrative, in *Simple Forms*, is entitled The Ocean of Story.

3   The *Decameron* is a collection of stories or *novellas* written in Italian, in the fourteenth century, by Giovanni Boccaccio.

4   Chapter 5, Merry (Comic) Tales; and chapter 6, Animal Tales.

5   Julian of Norwich, *Revelations of Divine Love*, trans. Wolters, chapters 14 & 51.

6   Extract xlvi, Margery's Own Tale, in chapter 1 (Voices from the Past) above.

examples recorded in manuscript or print there lies a mass of oral stories, now lost forever. This lost corpus would have contained examples of what the Swiss folklorist Max Lüthi thought of as two basic forms in the prehistory of narrative: the Volksmärchen or folktale (with its strange magical clarity, its absolute demands, its simple 'one-dimensionality'), and Volkssage or traditional story (with a more 'historic' setting in a more familiar world, and some concern with human emotions and relationships). These basic forms also lie behind our recorded copies of narrative ballads and popular romances. Many of our recorded examples of tales and legends seem close to the Volkssage, but we sometimes catch glimpses of the simpler Volksmärchen and its motifs.[7]

A. Anecdotes and Tales in Chronicles

As well as the 'lewed peple', chroniclers loved tales and anecdotes. Some of the stories they used are still remembered: Cnut and the sea, Alfred and the cakes; or Lady Godiva of Coventry, who rescued the town from the servitude of an oppressive tax by riding naked (veiled by her long hair) through the streets. And there are very many others, on a variety of topics. William of Newburgh records the finding of fairy children, the Lanercost chronicle records a story of King Arthur living on after his last battle, and there are gossipy stories about Fair Rosamund, the mistress of Henry II.[8] Here we have two anecdotes from early medieval chroniclers, concerning the warrior Siward, whose fame lived on in later lore, and of Gunnhild, whose trials seem to have later become the ballad of *Sir Aldingar*.

i) Siward[9]

About this time [1054] Siward the brave earl of Northumbria, almost a giant in size and very tough in both hand and mind, sent his son to subjugate Scotland. When messengers reported his death in battle to

---

7   See *Simple Forms*, Chapter 7, for a fuller discussion of points raised in this introduction, including references.

8   These well-known stories can easily be found by consulting reference works, or the internet; space does not permit detailed descriptions of texts not selected for inclusion in this anthology.

9   In Henry of Huntingdon's *Chronicle*, trans. Forester, pp. 204 & 205.

his father, he said 'Did he receive the lethal wound in his front or in his back?' 'In the front', said the messengers. And he said, 'I rejoice wholeheartedly, for I would not consider any other death worthy of me or my son.' And so Siward left for Scotland and overcame its king in battle, ravaged the whole kingdom and subjected it to himself ...

... In the next year [1055] the stern earl Siward was smitten by a 'flux', a discharge from or in the stomach, and, sensing that death was imminent, said 'How deeply shameful it is to me not to have been able to die in the many battles I have fought but am left to die with dishonour in the manner of cows. Put on my invincible breastplate, gird my sword about me, place my shield in my left hand, and my axe adorned with gold in my right, so that the most courageous of warriors may die dressed like a warrior.' He spoke thus and, fully armed, as he had said, breathed out his spirit.

ii) Gunnhild[10]

Harthcnut ... sent his sister Gunnhild, the daughter of Cnut by Emma, a maiden of outstanding beauty, who in the time of her father was sighed for by many wooers, but not won, in marriage to Henry the emperor of the Germans. Thronged and distinguished was that wedding festivity, and it is still sung of in our time in the public streets. The maiden of so great a name was led to the ship surrounded by all the princes of England ... She came thus to her husband, and for a long time she cherished her matrimonial vows. However, finally she was accused of adultery, and she put forward a little boy, a nursling who kept her pet starling, to battle in a duel with her denouncer, who was a man of gigantic build, since her other servants avoided it out of laziness and fear. And so, when combat was joined, through a miracle from God, the accuser was cut down in the hollow of the knee, and fell. Gunnhild, rejoicing in their unhoped for triumph, gave her husband notice of separation; nor could she be prevailed upon any longer by threats or enticements to come to his bedchamber again, but taking the religious veil, in the service of God, she grew old gently and peacefully.

---

10 The source is William of Malmesbury's *Kings Before the Norman Conquest* (trans. Stephenson), p. 179; it is also in Gray's *From the Norman Conquest*, pp. 66–7.

B. Moral Tales, Exempla

These are very common, and were often used in sermons: the brief stories could be elaborated or adapted in various ways by preachers. Probably oral 'performance' would make them more emphatic and memorable than when read on the page. Sometimes they could form the basis for more 'literary' versions, sometimes they themselves are abbreviated 'epitomes' of longer versions. They are to be found in various story-collections: Dives and Pauper, Jacob's Well, the Book of the Knight of Latour Landry.[11] This selection is from *The Alphabet of Tales*.[12]

iii) The Cursed Dancers[13]

… a preste that hight Tulius on a tyme opon the Yole-evyn said mes in a kurk of saynt Magnus. And ther was in the kurk-garthe [churchyard] a grete meneya of men and women dawnssand in a cercle and syngand carals, and lettid [hindered] dyvyne serves with ther noyse and ther cry. And this preste commaundid thaim to lefe, and thay wold not for hym. And when he saw thai wold not lefe, in his mes he prayed unto God and saynt Magnus that it mot please thaim at [that] thai suld abide so still unto the yere end; and so thai did. And all that yere nowder rayn nor snaw fell opon thaim, nor thai wer never hongrie nor thrustie … bod [but] ever thai went aboute syngand carals as thai had be mad folk. And ther was a yong man that had his sister emang thaim, and he tuke hur be the arm and wold hafe drowen hur fro thaim, and he pullid of hur arm, and ther come no blode further [forth], bod sho dawnsid on still, and thus thai did all the yere to [until] it was passed. And than Hubertus at was bysshopp of Colayn [Cologne] [com] and assoylid thaim and lowsid thaim oute of this band, and recownceld ther befor the altar. And ther dyed of thaim ther a man and ii women, and all the toder [others] slepid .iii. dayes and .iii. nyghtes togeder, and som of thaim had a trembling of all ther bodie evur after ewhils [whilst] thai liffid. And this happened in a town of Ducheland [Germany] in the yere of owr Lord m.l.x.

---

11 As explained above, space does not permit detailed reference to works not excerpted for this anthology (*Jacob's Well* is mentioned again below, among Animal Proverbs).

12 *An Alphabet of Tales*, ed. Banks, in EETS.

13 Tale CCXV, *Chorizare*. A version of this story, The Dancers of Colbek, is printed in *Fourteenth Century Verse and Prose*. Another is in William of Malmesbury (*Kings*, p. 158).

iv) A Merry Poor Man[14]

... Ther was a pure man that with the labur off his handis unnethis [scarcely] cuthe get his liflod [livelihood], for when he had suppid, ther lefte right noght over night unto in the morning; and evur he was merie, to so mekull that everilk night, when he was in his bed with his wife, he wolde, and sho [she], syng a sang merelie at [that] all ther neghburs mott here, and than thai wold fall on slepe. So ther neghburs had grete mervall theroff, and one of thaim said, 'I sall make swilk [such] a way at I sall gar [cause] hym lefe hys syngyng'. And in presens of som of his neghburs, opon a night he tuke a sachell full of sylver, and lete fall afor [before] this pure mans dure [door]. And when at he rase and sulde go furth to seke his liflod, he fande this bagg, and he tuke it up and turnyd agayn therwith into his howse and hid it. So on the night after, als tyte [as soon] as he was in his bed, he umthoght [considered] hym in his mynde what he wolde do therwith; and he was ferd therfor that he war not culpid [found guilty] with felony therfor, and also at no thevis sulde stele it from hym, or if so be at he boght or solde therwith, or boght any lande, he mond [would] be suspecte, unto so mekull at he was so occupyed in his thoght that at that nyght he sang not, nor was not merie, bod a grete while after he was passand [very] hevie and thoghtfull. And than his neghburs askid hym whi he was so hevie, and whi he sang nott as he was wunte to do; and he wolde nott tell thaim the treuth. And than he at aght [owned] this money said unto hym, 'I knaw the treuth; for suche a day and in suche a place thou fande my money, and tuke it up at I and my neghburs saw, and had it into thi howse.' And when he hard this he wex [grew] ferd and shamefull, and sayd, 'Woo wurth [befall] that money that hase turment me thus, for sen [since] that I fand it I had never joy in my harte; and I hafe bene trubbled in my witt ever syne, mor than ever I was before when I with grete labur of my bodie and my handis gat my meat [food]. And therfor take thi money thi selfe agayn, at I may syng and be mery as I was wunte to done.' And so he did; and fro [after] it was gone, this pure man made als merie as evur did he.

---

14 Tale CCLXXVI, *Diuicijis preponende sunt condiciones bone.*

v) Alexander and the Pirate[15]

… Ther was a maister of a ship that hight [was called] Dironides, and he was a grete robber be the se; so on a tyme hym happend to be taken and broght befor kyng Alexander. And kyng Alexander askid hym whi he usid suche ribburi [robbery] with his shupp; and he answerd agayn and said, 'Whi laburs thou to hafe dominacion of all this werld, and I that usis bod [but] a little schup, I am callid a thefe, and thou that usis to rob and refe with a grete navie of schuppis erte callid ane emperour? And forsuthe, thou sall verelie know, that, and [if] rightwusnes be removid away, what er kyngisdomis? Not els bod grete thyfte; and what er little kyngdoms? Not els bod little thifte. And thus, thou erte a grete thefe, and I am bod a little thefe.'

vi) Envy is found even in Little Girls[16]

… In Freseland in a nonrie there was ii little maydens that lernyd on the buke, and ever thai strafe [strove] whethur [which] of thaim shulde lern mor than the toder. So the tane [one] of thaim happend to fall seke, and sho garte [caused] call the priores unto hur and sayd, 'Gude ladie, suffer nott my felow to lern unto [until] I cover [recover] of my sekenes. And I sall pray my moder to gif me vi d. and that I sall giff you and [if] ye do so; for I drede that whils I am seke that sho sall pas me in lernyng, and that I wolde not at sho did'; and at this wurde the priores smylid and had grete mervayle of the damysell consyte [thought].

vii) A Lecherous Woman is carried off to Hell[17]

We rede of a prestis concubyne, that when she was bown to dye sho cried opon thaim at was aboute hur with grete instans, and bad thaim gar make hur a payr of hy bottois [boots] and put thaim on hur leggis for thai war passand necessarie unto hur, and so thai did. And opon the night after, the mone shane bright, and a knight and his servand was rydand in the feldis togedur, and ther come a woman rynand fast unto thaim, cryand, and prayed thaim helpe hur. And onone this knught light

---

15 Tale CCCXXXIV, *Fures possunt dici multi principes et prelati.*
16 Tale CCCXCVI, *Inuidia aliqualis eciam in puellis paruis reperitur.*
17 Tale CCCCLVI, *Luxuriosam mulierem diabolus ad infernum portauit.*

and betaght his man his hors, and he kennyd [recognised] the womman
wele enogh, and he made a cercle abowte hym wth his swerd, and tuke
hur in unto hym; and sho had nothing on bod [but] hur sarke [shirt] and
thies buttois. And belife he harde a blaste of ane ugsom horn at [that] a
hunter blew horrible, and huge barkyng of hundis. And als sone as thai
hard, this womman was passand ferde. And this knight spirrid [asked]
hur whi sho was so ferd, and sho tellid hym all; and he light [alighted]
and tuke the tressis of hur hare and wappid it strayte abowte his arm,
and in his right arm he helde his swerd drawen. And belife [at once] this
hunter of hell come at hand, and than this womman said, 'Lat me go,
for he commys.' And this knight held hur still, and this womman pullid
faste and wolde hafe bene away. So at the laste sho pullid so faste at all
hure hare braste of hur heade, and sho ran away and this fend folowd
after and tuke hur, and keste hur overthwarte behind hym on his hors at
[so that] hur hede and hur armys hang down on the ta [one] syde, and
hur legis on the toder syde. And thus, when he had his pray, he rade
his ways, and be [by] than it was nere day. And this knight went in the
morning unto the town, and he fand this womman new dead, and he
teld all as he had sene, and shewid the hare at was wappid abowte his
arm. And thai lukyd hur head ther sho lay, and thai fande how all the
hare was plukkid of be the rutis.

viii) The Weeping Puppy[18]

A common story, told by Petrus Alfonsi and others. Sometimes the
elements of a 'merry tale' in it are developed (cf. the Early Middle
English *Dame Sirith*),[19] but here it is firmly moral with the title *Mulier
mediatrix aliam ad peccatum inducit*: a female go-between leads another
woman into sin.

Petrus Alphonsis tellis how som tyme ther was a wurshupfull man that
went on pylgramage, and he had a gude wyfe and a chaste. So ther was
a yong man that luffid hur passandly, and wolde hafe giffen hur grete
giftis to hafe had his luste on hur, and sho wolde not on no wyse. So at the
laste he fell seke for sorrow at he mot not spede [succeed], and lay in his

---

18   Tale DXXXVII (the title is as Gray gives it).
19   In *Early Middle English Verse and Prose*; it is also (moralized) in *A Hundred Merry Tales*
      (ed. Zall), pp. 33–5.

bed. So ther come in ane olde wyfe and vysitt hym and askid hym what was the cauce at he was seke for. And he oppynd his herte unto hur and tolde hur all that hym aylid. And sho said hym thurte [he needed] not be seke herfor, sho cuthe help hym well enogh. And he promysid hur a gude rewarde to helpe hym. So sho had a little bykk [bitch] whelpe; and sho held it fastand ii dayes. So on the iii day sho made a cake of mustard and mele and gaff it, and it ete it; and for bytuernes of the musterd it began hugely to grete [weep], and the een [eyes] therof to ryn. So sho went unto this gude wyfe hows, and this whelpe folowid hur. And sho, becauce sho was ane olde wyfe, welcomyd hur fayre, and gaff hur meat and drynk. So at the laste sho askid hur what this whelpe aylid to wepe thus. And sho answserd and said, 'Dere dame, it is no mervell if I make sorow and wepe, for this whelpe was my doghter, and was a full leall [loyal] maydyn, and a gude and a fayr. And becauce sho wolde not consent unto a yong man that luffid hur, to be his luff, thus sho was shapen to be a biche whelpe.' And with that sho lete as sho swownyd and wepid sore. So this gude wyfe made mekull sorow, and said, 'What mon I do? Allas! for I am in the same cace; for a yong man luffis me and I have dispysid hym, and I am aferd that I sall oght [have to] be mysshapend.' And than the olde wyfe answserd and cownceld hur to consent unto hym, and latt hym hafe his liste at [so that] sho wer not forshapyn and made a byche whelpe. And sho prayed hur to go for hym, and so sho did and fechid hym unto this womman, and ther he had his luste and his desire, and this false alde when [woman] had a gude rewarde of ather [each] partie.

ix) Pope Joan[20]

We rede in cronicles how som tyme ther was a yong damysell, and a luff [lover] of hurs went away with hur and broght hur in mans clothyng unto Rome, and ther sho went unto the scule and wex [became] so parfyte in connyng [learning] that sho had no make [equal] in all Rome. So at the laste, be ane hole consent, sho was chosyn to be pope, and was made pope. And when she was pope hur luff lay with hur and gatt hur with chylde, so he wiste not at sho was with childe to [until] sho

---

20   Tale DCI, *Papa. Papa mulier creatur*. This well-known legend has been told and retold by many, including the novelist Lawrence Durrell.

was evyn at travellyng [labour]. So hur happened on a day to com in procession fro saynt Peturs unto saynt John Latarenens [Lateran], and ther sho began to travel, and bare hur chylde betwixt Colliseum and saynt Clemett kurk; and ther sho dyed, and ther thai berid hur. And becauce of that detestable dead [deed], the pope usid never syne to com theraway with procession, and herefor hur name is nott putt emang [among] other popes namis in the Martiloge.

x) The Fate of an English Witch[21]

... som tyme ther was in Englond a womman that usid sorcerie. And on a day as sho was bown [ready] to eatt, sho hard a craw [crow] cry beside hur, and sodanlie the knyfe that was in hur hande fell. And hereby sho demyd at [that] hur dead [death] drew nere, and so sho fell seke, bown to dye. And sho sent after a monk and a non that was hur childer and chargid thaim in hur blissyng that anone [as soon] as sho war dead thai sulde sew hur in a harte-skyn, and than at thai sulde close hur in a tombe of stone, and at thai sulde feste [fasten] the coveryng theron stronglie bothe with lead and strong yrn, and at thai sulde close this stane and bynde it aboute with iii strang chynys [chains], and than at thai sulde do mes [Mass] and pray for hur aboute hur bodye. And if sho lay so sekurlie [securely] iii dayes, than sho chargid thaim to bery hur upon the iiii day in the erth. And so all this was done, and ii furste nyghtis, as clerkis was sayand ther prayers aboute hur, fendis [fiends] brak the yatis [gates] of the kurk, and come in unto hur and brak ii of the chynys that was at ather end; and the myddyll chyne abade [remained] still hale [whole]. And upon the iii nyght aboute cokkraw [cockrow], ther come in suche a throng of fendis at thai at saw it semyd at the temple turnyd upsadown. So ther come a fend at was maste ugsom [horrible] of all, and hyer than any of the toder [others] was, and he come unto this tombe and called hur be hur name and bad hur ryse. And sho answerd agayn and sayde sho mot not for the bondis at was bon [bound] aboute the tombe. And he bad lowse thaim. And onone [instantly] at his commandment the chyne braste [broke] as it had bene hardis [coarse flax], and the covering of the tombe flow [flew] off. And ther he tuke hur oppynlie befor all men and

---

21   Tale DCCXXVIII, *Sortilegi puniuntur*.

bar hut oute of the kurk. And ther befor the yatis ther was ordand a blak hors, and that ane uglie, and hereoppon was sho sett. And than onone sho and all this felowshup vanysshid away.

C. Local Legends

According to Westwood and Simpson, editors of *The Lore of the Land* (a vast and valuable collection of English examples), local legend is 'a kind of folktale which centres on some specific place, person, or object which really exists or has existed within the knowledge of those telling and hearing the story; it means a great deal to those living in a particular area, or visiting and exploring it, but in most cases has not become widely known outside its own community.'[22] It could therefore, in theory, be easily distinguishable from the more general and less geographically specific 'legend'. However, it is not always easy when dealing with possible medieval examples to isolate or distinguish them in this way, for two obvious reasons. First, because we do not have precise details of their transmission, and also because the world of medieval story is characterised by movement: stories travel about, often very widely. They are retold, adapted for various purposes, and may be attached to various places where they may find a new home. References to places may sometimes be rather arbitrary: according to the prologue to *Sir Orfeo*, Winchester used to be called Thrace. Alexander Neckham says that Cirencester (where he was abbot) received the name of *Urbs Passerum* because the Saxon invaders devised a cunning plan to overcome the British defenders by sending in sparrows with burning straws fastened to their tails to burn the roofs of houses; this story is also found in Gaimar and other writers, but apparently similar stories and stratagems are found elsewhere.[23] Geoffrey of Monmouth says that the Saxon Hengist asked Vortigern for enough land as can be encircled by a single thong.[24] By finely cutting the hide of a bull he made one long enough to mark out ground for a great fortress. The place took its name from the thong, *Castrum Corrigie*

---

22 Introduction, p. 3.
23 See Gaimar's *Estoire*, note to vv. 856–70.
24 Geoffrey, trans. Thorpe, pp. 158–9.

(modern Caistor). The story is similar to that in Virgil, of Dido and the founding of Carthage.[25] Henry of Huntingdon's brief story of the Brave Man of Balsham may well be a traditional local legend: when the Danes had ravaged East Anglia and burnt Cambridge they went through the Gog Magog hills and came to Balsham, where they killed everyone they found, throwing the children up in the air and catching them on the sharp points of their spears. But one man, 'worthy of widespread fame' went up the steps of the church tower, 'which stands there at this day',[26] and 'made secure as much by the position as by his bravery' fought the whole army.[27] However, though there are similar stories of a lone hero resisting a great force, like local legends recorded later, medieval examples are often associated with strange or eerie places. Stonehenge had aready produced one: according to Geoffrey of Monmouth the stones were transported to England by Merlin from Ireland, where they were called the Giants' Ring because giants had brought them there from Africa.[28] We give a few examples from the twelfth-century chronicler Gervase of Tilbury, who seems to have a particular interest in this type of story.

xi) Peak Cavern: a passageway to the Antipodes[29]

In greater Britain there is a castle placed among mountains, to which the people have given the name of the Peak. Its defences are almost impregnable, and in the hill is a cavernous opening which from time to time belches out, and very powerfully, a wind, like a pipe. The people marvel whence such a wind comes, and among other things which happen there causing further wonder, I have heard from a very religious man, Robert, Prior of Kenilworth, who originated from that area, that

---

25 The agreement was for an area no larger than could be covered by a single hide; cutting the hide into thin strips made a much larger area possible. See *OCCL* for Dido, whose task was to use a single hide; in Mannyng's *Chronicle* (vv. 7499–512) he asks for as much land as can be covered by a single 'boles hyd'.

26 This is an example of the 'still-there' motif, gleefully exploited by medieval authors to prove the veracity of their narrative.

27 Henry of Huntingdon's *Chronicle*, the year 1010 (pp. 188–9 in Forester's translation).

28 Geoffrey trans. Thorpe, pp. 196–7.

29 Of the four passages from Gervase in this anthology, just this one matches the passage numbered (c) in Gray's *From the Norman Conquest* (pp. 90–1). As before, he has clearly made his own translation. See Gervase, ed. and trans. Banks and Binns, pp. 642–5.

when the nobleman William Peveril owned the castle with the adjoining estate, an active and powerful man, rich in diverse livestock, one day his swineherd was dilatory in the duty entrusted to him, and lost a pregnant sow, of a very superior kind. Fearing therefore the sharp words of his lord's steward, he pondered whether by any chance the sow might have stolen into the famous, but yet uninvestigated, cave of Peak. He decided that he would explore that hidden place. He went into the cavern at a time when it was without any wind, and after travelling for a long time he completed his journey and at length came out from the darkness, free, into a bright place, a spacious level plain of fields. Going into the land, which was extensively cultivated, he found reapers gathering ripe produce, and among the hanging ears of corn he recognised the sow, which had brought forth from herself little pigs. Then the swineherd, amazed and rejoicing that his loss was repaired, related the events, just as they had happened, to the bailiff of that land; he was given back the sow, and sent off joyfully; and led forth his herd of pigs. A wonderful thing: coming back from the subterranean harvest he saw the wintry cold continuing in our hemisphere, which I have been rightly led to ascribe to the absence of the sun and its presence elsewhere.

xii) Laikibrais; Saint Simeon's Horn, and a mysterious Dog[30]

There is in greater Britain a forest,[31] filled with many kinds of game, which looks upon the town of Carlisle. Almost in the middle of this forest is a valley fenced around by hills near a public road. Every day at the first hour is heard a sweet sound of bells, and for this reason the local inhabitants have called that deserted spot Laikibrais in the Gallic (Welsh, *or* French) language.

In this same forest a more marvellous event happened. There was a town named Penrith within the borders of that forest. A knight, springing from that town, when he was hunting in the forest far removed from the noise of men, was alarmed by a sudden tempest with thunder and lightning flashes. When, here and there, flashes of lightning set the forest on fire, he glimpsed a large hound passing, becoming visible in

---

30 In Gervase, ed. and trans. Banks and Binns, pp. 690–5.
31 Inglewood Forest; the 'lake that cries' is probably the fabled Tarn Wathelyn (see note in edition).

the storm, and fire was flashing from its throat. The knight, terrified by such an amazing vision, was unexpectedly met by another knight carrying in his hand a hunting horn. Filled with fear, he approached this figure, and revealed the reason for his fear. 'Hearken,' said the sudden arrival comfortingly, 'Put aside your fear. I am Saint Simeon, whom you called on and entreated in the midst of the lightning. I give you this horn for the perpetual defence of yourself and your household, so that whenever you are afraid of lightning or thunder you can blow the horn and at once all fear of threatening danger will disappear, nor will lightning have any power within the area where the sound of the horn may be heard.' Upon this Saint Simeon inquired if our knight had seen anything which had excited any amazement or wonder in him. In reply he said that he had seen a hound with fire blazing from its open mouth. Saint Simeon vanished in search of it, leaving the horn with the knight as a remembrance of the happening and as a lasting protection for his household. It has been seen by many, and marvelled at. It is lengthy, and twisted back in the style of hunting horns, as if it were made from the horn of an ox. And furthermore the dog which we spoke of went into a priest's house on the edge of that town, making its way through the entrance apparently firmly closed against it, and set fire to his house with its unlawfully begotten family.

xiii) Wandlebury Ring[32]

In England, on the edges of the diocese of Ely, is a town, Cambridge by name; and nearby, within its area, a place which men call Wandlebury, because the Vandals camped there as they were devastating parts of Britain and destroying the Christians. There, on the peak of a small hill where they set up their tents, is a circular plain, enclosed by ramparts, with a single entrance in the manner of a gate offering access. There is a tale from ancient times supported by popular account that if a knight goes into this level area after nightfall, when the moon is shining, and cries aloud 'Let a knight come forth against a knight!' at once a knight will hasten out against him, prepared for combat, and with their horses galloping together he either unhorses his opponent or is himself thrown

---

32   *Ibid.* pp. 668–73.

down. But first, a knight must enter the circle through that entrance alone, though his companions are not prevented from seeing the conflict from outside …

To support the truth of this tale, Gervase cites the case of Osbert FitzHugh, a twelfth-century knight who put it to the test: he felled his adversary, and captured his horse, but was wounded in the thigh. The challenger disappeared. The horse was black, with grim wild eyes; at cockcrow it broke loose, galloped off, and disappeared. Every year, on the same night and at the same time, Osbert's wound would break open again.

xiv) A Mysterious Drinking Horn[33]

Another event no less marvellous, and well enough known, happened in greater Britain. There was in the county of Gloucestershire a hunting forest,[34] filled with bears, stags and all kinds of game found in England. Here in a dale filled with trees was a little knoll, its top as high as a man's stature on which knights and huntsmen are accustomed to ascend when, tired by the heat and thirst, they tried to find a remedy for their condition. Thanks to this place and its nature, if anybody leaving his companions climbed up it by himself, and then, as if he was talking to another person, were to say 'I am thirsty', immediately, and unexpectedly, a cupbearer was standing by his side, impressively attired, and with a cheerful countenance holding in his hand and offering to him a great horn, like that used by he English in olden times for a drinking goblet. A nectar of unknown but most pleasant taste was offered to him; when he drank it all the heat and tiredness of his warm body would vanish, so that anybody would imagine not that he had been toiling away, but wished to seize the opportunity to toil once again. When he had drunk the nectar the attendant offered him a towel to dry his mouth, and having done his service he vanished, nor did he look for a reward for his trouble, nor conversation and inquiry …

---

33 *Ibid*. pp. 672–5.
34 Probably the Forest of Dean.

This lasted for many years, until one day a knight out hunting did not return the horn according to the proper custom, but kept it for himself. However, the earl of Gloucester did not wish to countenance a theft and gave the horn to King Henry.

D. More 'free-standing' Literary Examples

More 'free-standing' literary examples (of which there are many), represented by a story about Hereward and a nice moral tale, *The Childe of Bristowe.*

xv) *Hereward*

The deeds of the eleventh-century English hero Hereward were celebrated by the people in songs and dances, and apparently in oral tales. Some made their way into the twelfth-century French verse chronicle of Gaimar, *L'Estoire des Engleis,* others into the Latin *Gesta Herewardi,* and *The Book of Ely.*[35]

The English rebelling against William the Conqueror around Ely and its fens were surrounded by the Conqueror's forces, and eventually begged for mercy ...

... Except Hereward, who was so noble.
With a few men he escaped, and with him
Geri, one of his relatives,
And five companions with them.
A man who brought fish to the guards
Along the marshes, acted
As a good and courteous man:
Sheltered them in a boat of reed,
Completely covered them with rushes;
And began to row towards the guards,

---

35   The following extract is from Gaimar's *Estoire,* vv. 5492–544 (ed. Bell). Gaimar's patron was a Lincolnshire noblewoman. Gray will have made his own translation (see also his *From the Norman Conquest,* pp. 154–6).

And when one evening it began to darken,
Came close to the dwellings with his boat.
The French were in a tent,
The viscount Guy was their leader;
He recognized the fisherman,
And they knew that he often came,
So none of them took note of him;
They saw the fisherman rowing.
It was night, and they sat at meat.
Out of the boat came Hereward,
He was as fierce as a leopard,
And his companions followed him.
They made for the tent under a bush,
With them went the fisherman —
Hereward was formerly his lord.
What can I say? Those knights
Were taken by surprise as they ate.
They came in with axes in their hands,
And were not unskilled in striking hard;
They killed six and twenty Normans
And twelve Englishmen were killed there.
Terror spread throughout the dwellings,
And everyone took to flight.
They abandoned horses still saddled,
Onto which the outlaws mounted
At leisure and in safety;
They had no trouble there at all,
And went away happy at their misdeeds.
Each one picked out a very good horse.
The woods were near, and they entered them,
They did not lose their way,
They knew all that country very well!
There were many of their friends there.
At a town which they came to
They found ten of their close friends

And these joined up with Hereward.

Once they were eight, now more than ten,

Ten and eight are the companions now;

Before they passed Huntingdon

They had a hundred men, well armed,

Close liegemen of Hereward ...

xvi) *The Childe of Bristowe*[36]

A man who has studied law and learnt how to beguile poor men has a son on whom he dotes. In order to make his son rich he 'rought not whom he beguiled'. The young child, set to learning, becomes 'wise and witty' and fears 'al dedis derke'. The father is keen for him to study law, so that no one will be able to beguile him, but the son has other ideas. 'The child answerd with a softe sawe: They fare ful well that lerne no lawe, And so I hope to do'; he fears to imperil his soul 'for any wynnyng of worldes welthe', and is determined to be a merchant: 'that good getyn by marchantye' is 'trouthe'. He goes to Bristol and is engaged to a merchant there, 'a just trew man', for seven years. He does well, loves God, and 'al marchauntz loved hym, yong and olde.' Meanwhile his father continues his dubious behaviour until he falls sick and draws towards his end. On his deathbed he discovers that no one in the neighbourhood is prepared to be his executor; he sends for his son and heir ('moche good have y gadred togeder With extorcion and dedis lither' — all for the son) and eventually persuades him to be his attorney. But the son binds him with another charge: that a fortnight after his death his spirit should appear and report on his fate. When the father dies, the son arranges for masses, sells his father's goods, and distributes the proceeds to the poor. But the gold is soon gone ... [stanzas 39–46]

... By than the fourtenyght was broght to ende,

The child to the chamber gan wende,

    Wher his fader dyed.

Adoun he knelid half a day;

---

36   In Camden *Miscellany*, ed. Hopper, vol. IV.

Al the good prayers that he couthe say,
    His fader for to abide.º   *wait for*

Betwene mydday and underº   *afternoon*
Ther cam a blast of lightning and dunder
    Thurgh the walles wide,
As al the place on fire had be;
The child seid '*Benedicite!*'º   *God bless!*
    And fast on God he cryde.

And as he sate on his prayere,
Sone before hym gan appere
    Foule tydynges betwene,º   *meanwhile*
His faders soule brennyngº as glede;   *burning*
The devel bi the nekke gan hym lede
    In a brennyng cheyne.

This child seid, 'I conjure the,
Whatsoever thu be, speke to me.'
    That other answerd ageyne,
'Y am thy fader that the begate;
Now thu may se of myn astate;º   *condition*
    Lo, how y dwelle in peyne.'

The child seid, 'Ful woo is me,
In this plyte that [y] yow se;
    It pershethº myn hert sore.'   *pierces*
'Sone,' he seid, 'thus am y led
For because of my falshed
    That y used ever more.

Mi good was getyn wrongfully,
Butº it myght restord be,   *unless*
    And asethº be made therefore,   *compensation*
A C yer thus shal I do;

Gef me my trouthe;° y were ago;   *pledge,*
    For til than my soule is lore.'°   *lost*

'Nay, fader, that shal not be,
In better plite y wol yow se,
    Yf God wol gef me grace;
But ye shal me your trouthe plighte,
This same day fourtenyht
    Ye shal appere in this place.

And y shal labore yf y may
To bring your soule in better way,
    Yf y have lyf and space.'
He graunted hym in gret hast;
With that ther cam a donder blast
    And both ther way gan passe.

[The son goes back to Bristol and borrows money from his master; he arranges
for those who have suffered because of his father to be recompensed. But once
again … stanzas 57–64]

By that the fourtenyht was come,
His gold was gone, al and some;
    Then had he no more.
Into the chamber he went that tide,
The same that his fader in dyde,°   *died*
    And knelid, as he dud ore.°   *did previously*

And as he sate in his prayere,
The spiret before hym gan appere
    Right as he dud before,
Save the cheyn away was caught;
Blak he was, but he brent noght,
    But yet he was in care.°   *sorrow*

'Welome, fader,' seid the childe,
'I pray yow with wordes mylde,
    Tel me of your astate.'

'Sone,' he seid, 'the better for the,
Yblessid mote° the tyme be   *may*
   That ever I the begate!

Thou hast relevyd me of moche wo —
My bitter chayne is fal me fro
   And the fire so hote —
But yet dwel y stille in peyn,
And ever must, in certayn,
   Tyl y have fulfilled my day.'

'Fader,' he seid, 'y charge yow tel me
What is moste ayens° the.   *against*
   And doth yow most disese.'
'Tethynges° and offrynges, sone,' he sayd,   *tithes*
'For y them never truly payd,
   Wherfor my peynes may not cesse,

But it be restored agayn
To as many churches, in certayne,
   And also mykel encresse.
Alle that for me thu dos pray
Helpeth me not to the uttermost day
   The valure of a pese.°   *value of a pea*

Therfor, sone, I pray the
Gef me my trouthe° y left with the,   *pledge*
   And let me wynde° my way,'   *wend*
'Nay, fader,' he seid, 'ye gete it noght,
Another craft° ther shal be soght,   *device*
   Yet efte y wille assay.°   *try*

But your trouthe ye shal me plight.
This same day a fourtenyht
   Ye shal come ageyn to your day;
Ye shal appere here in this place,

And I shal loke, with Goddes grace,
>   To amend yow yf y may.'

[The spirit leaves, and the son returns to Bristol to ask his master yet again for 'a litel summe of gold' … stanza 67]

His maister seid, 'Thu art a fole —
Thu hast bene at som bad scole;
>   By my feith, y holde the mad,
For thu hast played atte dice,
Or at som other games nyce'º …   *foolish*

[But the son says that he will sell him his own body 'for ever to be thy lad', and the master, who loves him, gives him more than he has asked for. He is allowed a further fortnight's leave … stanzas 72–83]

He sought alle the churches in that contreº   *region*
Where his fader had dwelled by,
>   He left not one behynde.

He made asethº with hem echon.   *compensation*
By that tyme his gold was gone,
>   They couthe aske hym no mare;
Save as he went by the street,
With a pore man gan he mete,
>   Almost naked and bare.

'Your fader oweth me for a semeº of corn.'   *load*
Down he knelid hym beforn;
>   'And y hym drad full sare.
For your fader soules sake,
Som amendes to me ye make,
>   For Hym that Marie bare.'

'Welawey!' seid the yong man,
'For my gold and silver is gan;
>   I have not for to pay.'
Off his clothes he gan take,
And putt hem on the pore manis bake,
>   Chargyng for hys fader to pray.

Hosen and shon he gave hym tho,
In sherte and breche he gan go;
    He had no clothes gay.
Into the chamber he wente that tide°   *time*
The same that his fader on dyde,°   *died in*
    And knelid half a day.

When he had knelid and prayed long,
Hym thought he herd the myriest song,
    That any erthely man might here;
After the song he sawe a light,
As thow° a thousand torches bright,   *though*
    It shone so faire and clere.

In that light, so faire lemand°   *shining*
A naked child in angel hand
    Before hym did appere,
And seid, 'Sone, blessed thu be,
And al that ever shale come of the,
    That ever thu goten were.'

'Fader,' he seid, 'ful wel is me.
In that plite that y now se,
    Y hope, that ye be save,'
'Sone,' he seid, 'y go to blisse,
God almyghti quyte the this,
    Thi good ageyn to have.

Thu hast made the ful bare
To aqueynche me of mykel care;
    My trouthe, good sone, y crave.'
'Have your trouthe,' he seid, 'fre,
And of thi blessing y pray the,
    Yf that ye wold fochesave°   *grant*

In that blessyng mote thu wone°   *dwell*
That Oure Lady gaf here sone,
    And myn on the y lay.'[37]
Now that soule is gone to blisse
With moche joye and angelis,
    More than y can say.

This child thanked God almyght
And his moder Marye bryght,
    Whan he sey° that aray.   *saw*
Even to Bristow gan he gon
In his sherte and breche alon;
    Had he no clothes gay.

When the burges the child gan se,
He seid then, '*Benedicite*!
    Sone, what araye is this?'
'Truly, maister,' seid the childe,
'Y am come me to yelde°   *surrender myself*
    As your bonde man.'

[His master hears the full story, and is impressed: 'but fewe sones bene of tho
That wole serve here [their] fader so.' He makes the son his 'felow' and heir,
and has him married to a worthy man's daughter. When his master dies, he
inherits all his goods ... stanza 93]

Thus hath this yong man kevered°   *recovered*
First was riche and sitthen° bare,   *then*
And sitthen richer then ever he was ....

---

37   It is thought that 'with God's blessing and mine' is a typical formula used for, or
    with refererence to, a child. Agnes Paston uses it in a letter to her son.

E. Religious Tales and Saints' Legends[38]

xvii) *Mary of Nemmegen*[39]

Mary meets the Devil: Mary has been angrily refused lodging for the night by her aunt, and is in despair …

… She departed fro hyr with a hevy harte out of the towne of Nemmegen in the evening, and at the laste she went so longe tyll she cam to a thycke hegge, where that she satt hyr downe, wepynge and gyvynge hyrselfe unto the dyvell, and sayd, 'Woo be to the, my aunte! This may I thanke the, for nowe care I nat whether that I kyll myself, or whether that I goo to drowne me, and I care nat whether the dyvell or God come to me and helpe me — I care nat whether of them two it be!'

The dyvell, that is at all tymes reddy for to hauke after dampned sowles, heryng these words of Marye, turned hym into the lekenes of a man, but he had but one yee [eye], for the dyvell can never turne hym in the lykenes of a man, but [unless] he hathe some faute. And than sayd he to his selfe, 'Nowe wyll I goo suger my words for to speke unto this mayde that I desplease hyr nat, for men must speke sweetly to women.' And with these words sayde he to Mary, 'O fayer mayde, why syt you here thus wepyng? Hathe there any man that hathe dyspleased you or done you wronge? If that I knewe hym, I shulde be awrokyn [avenged] on hym!' Than Mary, herynge his voyce, loked besyde hyr and sawe a man stande by hyr, wherof she was afrayde, and sayde, 'Helpe, God, I am wayted [spied upon]!' The devell sayd unto Mary, 'Fayer mayde, be nat afrayde, for I wyll nat do unto you no maner of harme, but doo you good. For your fayernes men muste love you, and if that ye wyll consent unto me, I shall make you a woman above all other women, for I have more love unto you than I have to any other woman nowe lyvyng.' Than sayde Mary, 'I syt here halfe mad and in dyspayer. I care nat whether that I gyve myself to God or to the dyvyll so that I were out of this thraldome and mysarye, but I pray you showe unto me who that ye be.' The dyvyll answered to hyr, 'I am a master of many scyances, for that [whatever] I take on me to

---

38   The latter are often found in abbreviated form in sermons or adapted as exempla. Gray left an extra sub-heading here, for more Saints' Lives which he never inserted; it has been necessary to collapse the sections.

39   *Mary of Nemmegen*, ed. Raftery, pp. 26–8.

do I brynge it unto a ende, and if that ye wyll be my paramoure, I shall tech to you all the forsayde scyances, so that there is the worlde shall passe you.' Than sayd Mary to the dyvyll, 'I praye you, showe unto me what ye be, and what your name is.' Than sayd the dyvell, 'What recketh [care] you what I be? I am nat the beste of my kynne. And [if] ye wyll nat be displeased, my name is Satan with the one yee, that is well knowen amonges good fellowes.' Than sayd Mary, 'Nowe perseyve I well that ye be the dyvell.' 'That is al one [all the same] who I be, for I bere unto you good love.' Than sayd Mary, 'I wold nat be afrayd of hym if that it were Lusyfer hymselfe!' Than sayde the dyvell to Marye, 'Fare mayde, wyll ye be my love? I shall teche unto you al the scyances aforesayde, and I shall gyve unto you manye other costely jewelles and also money at youre pleasure, so that ye shall lacke nothynge at all and you shall have all your owne pleasure to do that thynge that ye wyll desire, so that there is noo woman shall have the pleasure that ye shall have.' Than sayde Marye to the dyvyll, 'Or that [before] ye lye with me, ye shall teche to me the forsayde scyances.' Than sayde the dyvyll, 'I am contente — aske what that ye wyll, and ye shall have it.' Than sayde Mary, 'I wyll have nygromancy [necromancy] for one, for I have a unkyll that hathe a boke therof, and when that he lyste, he wyll bynde the fynde [fiend] therwith.' Than sayd the dyvell, 'O fayer mayde, what ye desire ye shal have, but I occupy [employ] nat that science myself, for it is so daungerouse, for when that ye begyn for to counger [conjure] and if ye mysse one letter in redynge, the geste [spirit] that ye call for wyll breke your necke, and therefore I counsayll you nat to lerne that science.' Than sayd Mary, 'If that it be so, that science wyll I nat lerne.' Than was the dyvyll glad, and sayde to his selfe, 'Now have I turned hyr mynde fro that science, for if that she culde nygromancy, then when she were angery with me, then wolde she bynde me therwith ...'.

He also dislikes her name, because he and his fellows have suffered from a Mary in the past. He persuades her to be called Emmekyn. She becomes his paramour. They travel around together, and eventually return to Nemmegen. There Mary is converted by a play about sinful living. The devil tries to kill her, but she survives. The pope imposes on her the penance of wearing three iron rings. She enters a nunnery, and when she dies an angel frees her from the rings as a sign of God's forgiveness.

xviii) Saint George and the Dragon[40]

As the saint rides by, he sees a damsel standing and mourning …

… And when he saw the aray of thys damesell, hym thought well that hyt schuld be a woman of gret renon, and askyd hur why scho stode ther with soo mornyng a chere. Than answered scho and sayde, 'Gentyll knyght, well may I be of hevy chere, that am a kyngys doghtyr of thys cyte, and am sette here for to be devoured anon of a horrybull dragon that hath eton all the chyldyr of thys cyte. And for all ben eton, now most I be eten; for my fader yaf the cyte that consell. Wherfor, gentyll knyght, gos [go] hens fast and save thyselfe, lest he les [destroy] the as he wol me!' 'Damesell,' quod George, 'that wer a gret vyleny to me, that am a knyght well i-armed, yf I schuld fle, and thou that art a woman schuld abyde.' Than wyth thys worde, the horrybull best put up his hed, spyttyng out fure, and proferet batayll to George. Then made George a cros befor hym, and set hys spere in the grate [rest], and wyth such might bare down the dragon into the erth, that he bade this damysell bynd hur gurdull aboute his necke and led hym aftyr hur into the cyte. Then this dragon sewet [followed] her forth, as hyt had ben a gentyll hownde, mekly without any mysdoyng.

xix) Saint Julian[41]

We rede how that when saynt Julyan was a yong man and went on huntyng, he pursewid on a tyme after a harte. And this harte turnyd agayn and spak unto hym and sayd, 'Thow that mon [is destined to] sla bothe thi fadir and thi moder, wharto pursewis thou me?' And he had grete wonder herof, and becauce [so that] this sulde not happyn hym, he went away oute of a fer contreth and servid a wurthi prince; and he made hym a knyght and gaff hym a warde, a grete gentylwomman, unto his wife. And his fadur and his moder at home, hafyng grete sorrow that he was gone oute of the contrey fro thaim, went and soght hym many mylis. So on a tyme when he was furthe [away], be a sodan cace [sudden chance] thaim happynd to com unto his castell. And be wurdis at [that]

---

40   *John Mirk's Festial*, vol. 1 item 30 in the EETS edition (the episode appears on p. 118); Gray also included it in *Simple Forms* p. 142 (within Saints' Legends, pp. 139–43).

41   See *Gilte Legende*, EETS OS 327 (vol. 1, pp. 143–4), in which this Julian is one of several Julians. Gray's version is close, but not exactly as printed in the EETS edition.

thai said ther his wyfe understude at thai was fadir and moder unto hur
husband, be all the proces at sho had hard [heard] hur husband say. And
when sho had made thaim wele to fare, sho laid thaim samen [together]
in hur awn bedd. And this Julian come home sodanlie in the mornyng
and wente unto his chamber, and fand thaim ii samen in the bed. And
he, trowyng that it had bene one that had done avowtry [adultery] with
his wyfe, he slew thaim bothe and went his ways. And he mett his wife
fro the kurkward [coming from the church], and sho tolde hym how his
fadir and his moder was commen, and how sho had layd thaim in hur
awn bedd. And than he began to wepe and make sorow, and said, 'Lo!
that at the harte said unto me, now I, a sory wriche, hafe fulfillid itt.'
And than he went oute of contre and did penans, and his wyfe wolde
never forsake hym. And ther thai come unto a grete water, ther many
war perisschid, and ther he byggid a grete hostre, and all that ever come
he herbard [lodged] thaim, and had thaim over this watyr. And this
he usyd a lang tyme. So on a nyght aboute mydnyght, as he layin his
bed and it was a grete froste, he hard a voyce cry petifullie, and sayd,
'Julian! Com and feche me owr, I pray the!' And he rase onone [at once]
and went our the water, and ther he fand a man that was nerehand
frosyn to dead, and he had hym our, and broght hym into his howse
and refresshid hym, and laid hym in his awn bed and happid [covered]
hym. And within a little while he that was in the bed, that semyd seke
and like a leppre, ascendid unto hevyn and sayd on this maner of wyse,
'Julyan! Almighti God hase reseyvid thi penans. And within a little
while ye bothe shall com unto Hym.' And with that he vanysshid away.

xx) A Saintly Fool[42]

… Som tyme ther was in a monasterie of nonnys a maydyn, and for
Goddis luff sho made hur selfe evyn as a fule, and meke and buxhom
[obedient] to everilk bodis commandment; and sho made hur selfe
so vile, and so grete ane underlowte [underling], that ilkone uggid
[everyone felt apprehensive] with hur, bod [but] ilkone strak hur and
skornyd hur, and evur sho tuke it in plesans. So sho passed never the
kichyn, bod bade ther, and wasshid dysshis and skowrid pottys, and
did all maner of fowle labur. And sho satt never at meat, bod held hur

---

42   In the *Alphabet of Tales*, number CCCXXII, *Fatuitas*.

selfe content with crombys and crustis that war lefte at the burd [table]; and therwith sho liffid, and sho war [wore] nevur shone nor hose, and sho had nothing on hur head bod revyn [torn] clothis, and raggid. And sho was servyciable to everilk creatur, and wold do no bodye wrong, and what at evur was done unto hur, ther was none at hard hur gruche therwith. So emang all thies, be the commawndement of ane aungell, saynt Patryk, at was a holie man and liffid in wildrenes, come unto this same monasterie, and callid befor hym all the nonnys and all the susters of the place, at he might se thaim, and sho come not. And than he said, 'Ye er not all here.' And thai said, 'Yis, fadur, we er all here, outtakyn one that is bod a fule.' And he bad thaim call hur; and als sone as he saw hur he knew in his spiritt that sho was mor halie than he. And he fell down on his kneis befor hur an said, 'Spirituall moder, giff me thi blissyng!' And sho fell down on kneis before hym and said, 'Nay, fathur, rather thou sulde blis me.' And with that the susters of the howse had grete wonder, and said unto hym, 'Fathir, suffer not this enjorie, for sho is bod a fulle.' And he said, 'Nay, sho is wise, and ye er bod fules, for sho is bettyr than owder ye or I.' And than all the susters fell on ther kneis befor hur, and askyd hur forgifnes of wrangis and injuries that thai had done unto hur [and] scho forgiffes thaim ilkone with all hur harte.

xxi) The Virgin Mary saves a Thief on the Gallows[43]

We rede in hur 'Meracles' how som tyme ther was a thefe, and he had a grete devocion unto our Ladie, and said hur salutacion oft unto hur. So at the laste he was takyn with thift and hanged, and our Ladie come and held hym up iii dayes, hur awn handis, so that he felid no sare. So thai that hanged hym happened be cace [chance] to com by hym away, and fand hym mery and liffand [living]. And thai trowed he had not bene wele hanged. And thai wer avysid [thought] to have stykkid hym with a swerd as he hang. And as thai wold hafe stryken hym, our Lady putt it away with hur hand, so at thai noyed [harmed] hym noght. And he told thaim how our Ladie helpid hym, and thai tuke hym down and lete [released] him. And he went unto ane abbay, and ther servid our Ladie ewhils [whilst] he liffid.

---

43   In *Alphabet of Tales*, number CCCCLXIV, *Maria deuotos sibi a morte liberat*. In *From the Norman Conquest* (pp. 229–31) Gray gives Adgar's version of the tale, in which the thief's name is Ebbo.

Chapter 5

Merry Tales

The short comic tale seems to have been a favourite form in medieval popular literature.[1] Large numbers survive, and they show considerable variety, reflecting the variety of the wider medieval comic tradition. I will try to give some idea of this variety, in topic, form, and treatment. Medieval comedy is sometimes crude and vulgar, sometimes more detached and witty, offering some kind of entertainment or 'game'. It may be genial, but sometimes seems darker and more cruel, finding entertainment in physical as well as in moral deformity. It makes enthusiastic use of cunning tricks and tricksters, adroit answers, ingenuity and intelligence. Some tales seem totally amoral, and would no doubt have needed the defence offered in Chaucer's dictum, 'men shal nat maken ernest of game'. And yet some are curiously similar to moral, exemplary tales (as in *The Wright's Chaste Wife*).

Tales appear in both verse and prose and take many forms — too many for them all to be represented here. We have only one example of the fabliau (a word used of verse tales which flourished in France from the twelfth century, but part of a wider and much earlier tradition, and which were given highly sophisticated treatment by Chaucer). Fabliaux and fabliau-like tales characteristically give vigorous expression in terse and simple style to a decidedly non-idealistic view of life. The setting is non-courtly, the characters are often tradesmen, merchants,

---

1   Gray called this chapter 'Comic Tales', but 'Merry' in the table of contents. I retain 'Merry' so as to match his chapter-title in *Simple Forms*.

 https://doi.org/10.11647/OBP.0170.05

and their womenfolk, clerics and students. Plot and action are very important, as is direct speech and conversation. There is a combination of realism (especially in 'local' details) with a plot that is decidedly non-realistic — much more so than that of a romance, though not usually as extreme as the wild 'eldritch' fantasy of some Scottish comic tales. Much fun is had with stereotype: old men with young wives, lecherous clerics and monks, women as objects of desire and adept at fulfilling their own desires. Fabliaux in the narrow sense, like those in French verse, are rare in English before Chaucer; the Early Middle English *Dame Sirith*, a version of the story of the 'weeping puppy', is an early example.[2] But many of the comic tales printed here have distinctly fabliau-like elements, such as the magically adhesive Basin in number i. To encourage a comparison in literary treatment I have included extracts from two examples of a popular comic tale, in which a ruler meets one of his subjects and is entertained by him, but not recognised. And to remind us of the long continuity of the merry tale I have included examples from a late flowering from the age of printing, examples of the jestbooks of the sixteenth and later centuries.

i) The Tale of the Basyn[3]

An example of a simple comic story with a happy ending, based on a folktale motif: 'all stuck together'; a well-known example is Grimms' 'The Golden Goose'.[4]

'Off talys and trifulles many man tellys; Summe byn trew and sum byn ellis [otherwise].' There were two brothers: a parson, sensible, 'a good clerke' and rich; the other, his father's heir, feckless and 'a febull husbande' ruled by his wife: 'He durst not onys speke a worde When she bade be stille'. He and his wife spend all their money and he has to ask for money from his brother. That is soon gone, and he has to ask

---

2   The Weeping Puppy, see chapter 4 number viii above.
3   The Tale of the Basin is in *Ten Fifteenth-century Comic Poems*, ed. Furrow, although it is unlikely Gray used this edition; see also *Medieval Comic Tales*, where it is called The Tale of the Pot (sc. chamber-pot).
4   *Grimms' Fairy Tales* (London, n.d; a previous owner has dated his copy 1896). This well-known and finely-illustrated edition does not give story-numbers; The Golden Goose (Grimms' number 64) is pp. 197–200. The story is found in Andrew Lang's *Red Fairy Book* (and elsewhere).

again. The parson agrees, but warns him and discovers why he 'lyves
in dispayre': there is a merry priest, Sir John, who 'harpys and gytryns
[plays the gittern] and syngs … wresttels and lepis and casts the ston
alsso.' The parson instructs his brother to obtain 'the vessell owt of the
chambur — the same that thei make water in', and bring it to him. This
done, the parson performs a 'prive experiment' on it, and the brother
takes it back home and places it beside the bed in the chamber. He
rides away, to the delight of his wife, who prepares a feast for Sir John.
[vv. 125–223]

… She sent after sir John
Prively at a posturne yate, as still as any ston.
They eton and dronken, as thei were wonte to done
Till that thaym list to bedde for to gon,
    Softly and stille.
Within a litull while sir John con wake,
And nedis° water he most make;   *of necessity*
He wist° wher he shulde the basyn take,   *knew*
    Right at his owne wille.

He toke the basyn to make watur in
He mught not get his hondis awey, all this worde° to wyn;   *world*
His handis fro the basyn myght he not twyn.°   *separate*
'Alas!' seid sir John, 'how shall I now begynne,
    Here is sum wychcrafte!'
Faste the basyn con he holde,
And alle his body tremeld° for colde —   *shook*
Lever° than a .c. pounde he wolde,   *rather*
    That hit were him rafte.°   *pulled*

Ryght as a chapmon shulde sell his ware,
The basyn in the chaumbeur betwix his hondis he bare.
The wyfe was agrevyd he stode so long thare
And askid why so, hit was a nyce fare,°   *foolish behaviour*
    So stille ther to stonde.
'What, woman,' he seid, 'in gode fay,°   *faith*

Thu must helpe, gif thou may,
That this basyn were away,
    Hit will not fro my honde.'

Upstert the godewyfe, for nothyng wolde she lette,°   *refrain*
And bothe hir hondis on the basyn she sette.
Thus sone wer thai bothe fast, and he never the bette;°   *better*
Hit was a myssefelisshippe a man to have imette,
    Be day or be nyght.
They began clepe° and crye   *call out*
To a wenche that lay thaim bye,
That she shulde come on hye°   *quickly*
    To helpe yif she myght.

Upstert the wench, er she was halfe waked,
And ran to hir maistrys all baly° naked.   *belly (= completely)*
'Alas,' seid her maistrys, 'who hase this sorow maked?
Helpe this basyn wer awey, that oure sorow were slakyd.°   *relieved*
    Here is a sory chaunce!'°   *happening*
To the basyn the wenche she raste,
For to helpe had she caste —
Thus were they sone alle thre fast,
    Hit was a nyce daunce …
[They dance all night until sunrise. The priest's clerk rings the 'day-bell' for his master to say Matins, and he comes and sees the priest's plight]
… Anon as sir John can se, he began to call;
Be that worde thei come down into the hall.
'Why goo ye soo?' quod the clerke, 'hit is shame for you alle.
Why goo ye so nakyd? Foule mot yow falle.
    The basyn shalle yow froo.'
To the basyn he made a brayde,°   *tried to grab*
And bothe his hondis theron he leyde —
The furst worde that the clerke seyde,
    'Alas! what shall I doo?'

The carter fro the halle-dure° erth can he throw,   *door of the hall*

With a shevell° in his hande, to make it clene, I trowe   *shovel*

When he saw thaym go rounde upon a row.

He wende hit hade bene folys° of the fayre he tolde it in his   *fools*

    saw°   *speech*

    He seide he wolde assay iwysse;

Unneth he durst go in for fere,

Alle save the clerke nakyd were —

When he saw the wench go there,

    Hym thoght hit went amysse.

The wench was his special,° that hoppid on the rowte —   *sweetheart*

'Lette go the basyn, er thu shalle have a clowte!'°   *blow*

He hit the wenche with a shevell above on the [t]owte;°   *bottom*

The shevyll sticked then fast, withowte any dowte,

    And he hengett° on the ende.   *hung*

The carter with a sory chaunce

Among thaim all he led the daunce;

In Englonde, Scotllond, ne in Fraunce

    A man shulde non sich fynde.

The godeman and the parson came in that stounde,

Alle that fayre feliship dawnsyng thei founde,

The godeman seid to sir John, 'be cockis° swete wounde,   *God's*

Thu shalle lese° thine harnesse° or a .c. pounde —   *lose*   *privy*
    member

    Truly thu shalle not chese.'°   *choose*

Sir John seid, 'in good fay,°   *faith*

Helpe this basyn were awey,

And that mone° will I pay,   *money*

    Er I this harnes lese.'

The parson charmyd the basyn that it fell thaim fro,

Every man then hastely on thaire wey can goo:

The preest went out of contre for shame he hade thoo,

And then thai levyd° their lewtnesse,° and did no more soo,   *gave up* *folly*

But wex° wyse and ware.   *became*
Thus the godeman and his wyfe
Levyd togeder withowt stryfe.
Mary, for her joyes fyfe,[5]
    Shelde us alle fro care.

ii) The King and the Hermit

The possibilities, usually comic or satirical, of the 'unrecognised' or disguised ruler forced to meet one of his subjects seems to have fascinated popular storytellers. Of the various examples, two are relatively well-known: 'John the Reeve' (in *PFMS*, vol ii, 550), and the Scottish *Rauf Coilyear*. We include extracts from the second (iii below); and from *The Kynge and the Hermyt*, a tale in which the author seems to enjoy the way in which the king's curiosity reveals a certain ambiguity in this 'hermit' of Sherwood.[6]

Jesu that is hevyn kyng,
Yiff° them all god endyng,   *give*
    Yf it be thy wyll,
And yif them parte of hevyn gam,°   *heaven's joy*
That well can calle gestes same,°   *guests together*
    With mete and drinke to fylle.
When that men be glad and blyth,
Than were solas god to lyth,°   *it would be a pleasure to hear*
    He that wold be style°   *quiet*
Of a kyng I wyll yow telle.
What aventour hym befelle,
    He that wyll herke theretylle.

It felle be god Edwerd deys,
For soth so this romans seys.

---

5   A reference to the Five (or other number) Joys of Mary, formulae used to aid meditation and prayer.

6   In *Ten Bourdes*, ed. Furrow.

Herkyns — I will you telle.

The kyng to Scherwod gan wend ...

[... to hunt the great hart. He asks his foresters where in the forest is the best hunting, and an old forester describes a very large deer: 'so grete a hed as he bare Sych one saw I never are'.]

Upon the morne thei ryden fast

With hundes and with hornes blast;

 To wodde than are thei wente.

Nettes and gynnes° than leyd he,   *traps*

Every archer to hys tre

 With bowys redy bent ...

[The king pursues a deer through the forest all day, until the light begins to fade. He is alone and does not know where he is, nor how to get out of the forest. He recalls that he has heard poor men call on Saint Julian to give them lodging, so he too calls on him ...]

... as he rode whyll he had lyght,

And at the last he hade syght

 Of an hermyte hym besyde

Of that syght he was full feyn,

For he wold gladly be in the pleyn,°   *open*

 And theder he gan to ryde.

An hermitage he found ther,

He trowyd° a chapel that it wer.   *thought*

 Then seyd the kyng that tyde,

'Now, seynt Julyan a bonne hostel,[7]

As pylgrymes trow full wele,

 Yonder I wyll abyde.'

A lytell yate° he fond ne[y],°   *gate*   *near*

Thereon he gan to call and cry,

 That within myght here.

That herd an hermyte ther within,

Unto the yate he gan to wyn,

 Bedyng° his prayer.   *praying*

---

7 Julian was the patron saint of travellers (and of their good lodging).

And when the hermyt saw the kyng,
He seyd, 'Sir, gode evyn[yng].'
'Wele worth thee, sir frere,º   *friar*
I prey thee I myght be thy gest,
For I have ryden wyllº in this forest,   *astray*
    And nyght neyghesº me nere.'   *approaches*

The hermyte seyd, 'So mote I the,
For sych a lord as ye be,
    Y have non herbour tyll,º   *lodging ready*
Bot if it wer for pore a wyght,
I ne der not herbour hym a nyght,
    But he for faute schuld spyll.º   *die of hunger*
I won here in wylde[r]nes,
With rotys and ryndesº among wyld bests,   *roots and bark*
    As it is my Lordes wylle.'

[So the king asks for directions to the town. But, hearing that it is five miles, and 'a wyld wey', he announces, 'Ermyte, I schall harborow with ye this nyght'. 'Sych gode as thou fynde here, take', says the hermit — and there is little food on offer. With the remark 'a nyght wyll sone be gon' the king busies himself, hewing the wood and attending to the stable. When he relaxes in front of the fire, he begins to muse …]

…The kyng seyd, 'Be Gods are,º   *grace*
Andº I sych an hermyte were,   *if*
    And wonyd in this forest,
When forsters were gon to slep[e],
Than I wold cast off my cope,º   *cape*
    And wake both est and weste,
Wyth a bow of hueº full strong   *yew*
And arowys knyte in a thong,
    That wold me lyke best.
The kyng of venyson hath non nede,
Yit might me hape to have a brede.º   *loaf*
    To glad me and my gest.'

[Ignoring this, the hermit asks him where he dwells: 'in the kyngs courte …
many a dey' says the king, and he describes the long and tiring chase of the
deer. He asks for food: 'thou take sych gode as we have,' says the hermit,
and brings out bread and cheese and thin drink. 'Hermit,' says the king,
'You live in a merry place. And you should learn to shoot.' But the hermit
is worried about being imprisoned and in fear of being hanged. The king
says he would keep it secret, and makes a direct request: 'Now, hermyte,
for thy profession, Yiff thou have any venison, Thou yiff me of the best.'
The hermit still demurs: 'I eat no meat, and drink milk.' But he seems to
recognise something in his guest.]

'Thou semys a felow,'° seyd the frere.	*a good chap*	
'It is long gon seth any was here,		
Bot thou thyselve tonyght.'		
Unto a cofyr he gan go.		
And toke forth candylles two,		
And sone thei were ilyght.°	*lit*	
A cloth he brought, and bred full whyte,		
And venyson ibake tyte.°	*quickly*	
Ayen° he yede ful ryght,°	*back*	*directly*
Venyson isalt° and fresch he brought,	*salted*	
And bade him chese;° wheroff hym thought	*choose*	
Colopys° for to dyght.°	*slices*	*prepare*
Well may ye wyte inow° they had,	*enough*	
The kyng ete, and made hym glad,		
And grete laughtur he lowghe,		
'Nere I had spoke of archery		
I myght have ete my bred full dryghe!'°	*dry*	
The kyng made it full towghe,°	*gave him a hard time about it*	
'Now Crystes blyssing have sych a frere,		
That thus cane ordeyn our soper,		
And stalke under the wode bowe.°	*bough*	
The kyng hymselve, so mote I the,°	*prosper*	
Ys not better at es than we,		
And° we have drinke inowghe.'	*if*	

[The hermit produces a good supply, and teaches the king some 'play' appropriate to a 'felow', exchanging the drinkers' cries of 'fusty bandias' and 'stryke pantere' as the cup goes round.[8] The king is delighted, and promises to repay the hermit. 'But', says the hermit, 'I will be forgotten when you come to your lord's hall, or perhaps, if you think upon this play, it may amuse gentyll men.' 'No,' says his guest, 'the king's gate will be opened.' 'But do you expect me', says the hermit, 'to stand in the mire at the king's gate?']

'... I have neyghbors here nyghhand;

I send them of my presente

   [S]ydes° of the wyld dere,   *sides*

Of my presantes they are feyn,

Bred and ale thei send me ageyn;°   *in exchange*

   Thusgates° lyve I here.'   *in this way*

The kyng seyd, 'So mote I the,

Hermyte, me pays wele° with thee,   *I am well pleased*

   Thou arte a horpyd° frere.'   *bold*

The kyng seyd, 'Yit myght ye com sum dey

Unto the courte for to pley,

   Aventourys° for to sene;°   *adventures*   *see*

Thou wote not what thee betyde may

Or that thou gon awey' ...

[And he assures him that no one there will 'missay' him. The hermit assents to this, since his guest seems to be a 'trew man'. 'I schall aventore the gate' [risk the journey]; but who is he to ask for? 'Jake Flecher'[9] is the answer; 'all men knowys me at home'. The hermit begins to confide ...]

'Aryse up, Jake, and go with me,

And more off my privyte°   *secrets*

   Thou schall se somthyng.'

Into a chambyr he hym lede.

The kyng saughe aboute the hermytes bed

   Brod arowis hynge.

The frere gaff hym bow in hond,

'Jake,' he seyd, 'draw up the bond.'°   *string*

---

8   These nonsense phrases may or may not mean something like 'This is good stuff!' 'Drink up!'

9   Jack Fletcher, that is a maker of arrows.

He myght oneth styre° the streng.   *scarcely move*
'Sir,' he seyd, 'so have I blys,
There is no archer that may schot in this,
    That is with my lord the kyng ...'

... 'Jake, seth thou can of flecher crafte,
Thou may me es° with a schafte.'   *help*
    Then seyd Jake, 'I schall ...'

'Jake, and I wyst that thow were trew,
Or and I thee better knew,
    Mour thou schuldes se.'
The kyng to hym grete othys swer,
'The covenand we made whyle are°   *previously*
    I wyll that it hold be.'
Till two trowys° he gan him lede.   *troughs*
Off venyson there was many a brede°   *piece*
    'Jake, how thinkes thee?
Whyle there is dere in this forest,
Somtyme I may have of the best ...'

[They return to their 'pley', and sit with 'fusty bandyas' and 'stryke pantere' until it is almost day. In the morning they leave. The hermit accompanies the king for 'a myle or two'. When they part, the hermit repeats his promise to come to the court before the following night, and the king rides homewards. His men are searching for him ...]

... They cryghed and blew with hydoys bere,°   *clamour*
Yiff thei myght of ther lord here.°   *hear*
    Wher that ever he were.
When the kyng his bugyll blew,
Knyghtes and fosters wele it knew,
    And lystind to him there.
Many men, that wer masyd and made,°   *amazed and disturbed*
The blast of that horn made them glad,
    To the town than gan they fare.

[Here the copy breaks off, without revealing what happened to the hermit at court.]

iii) Rauf Coilyear[10]

This Scottish tale of the same type, a cross between rhymed and alliterative verse, is placed here, although it is often classified as a 'Charlemagne romance', a kind with which the author was clearly familiar. It was perhaps conceived as a burlesque Charlemagne romance. Whatever category we place it in, it is a fascinating and delightful work, contrasting the two main characters with some delicate irony and giving each a distinctive 'voice' and attitude.

King Charles and his splendid retinue ride out from Paris, but on the moor they encounter a fierce tempest, and the company is scattered. The king finds himself alone in the mountains. Night is falling, and he can see no sign of any shelter. Then 'ane cant carl' comes riding along, 'with ane capill [horse] and twa creillis [baskets] cuplit [coupled] abufe'. He is Rauf Coilyear, so-called because he sells coal and charcoal. The king, who is not recognised by Rauf, asks him to bring him to some 'harbery'. However, the nearest seems to be Rauf's own house. The king gratefully accepts his offer of 'harbery', however simple, and they set off together. But Rauf prophetically remarks, 'Thank me not over airlie [early], for dreid that we threip [quarrel]'. Rauf's manner of speaking is direct and sometimes abrupt, and it turns out that he has a short temper to match. There is a small contretemps when they come to Rauf's dwelling, and they each insist that the other should enter first. This is resolved by Rauf grabbing the king by the neck 'twa part in tene' [half in anger], and reading him a brief, tough lesson in 'courtesy': 'gif thow of courtasie couth, yhow hes foryet it clene.' 'Now is anis [the first time]' he says ominously, as they go in — Rauf confidently and overbearingly, like an 'imperious host' of legend, the king uneasily and cautiously. Supper is made ready [vv. 144–234]

Sone was the supper dicht° and the fyre bet°	*prepared*	*kindled*
And thay had weschin,° iwis, the worthiest was their.		*washed*
'Tak my wyfe be the hand in feir,° withoutin let,°	*together*	*delay*
And gang begin the buird,'° said the coilyear.	*go take the place of honour*	
'That war unsemand,° for suith, and thy self unset,'°	*unbecoming*	*not seated*

10　ed. Herrtage.

The king profferit⁰ him to gang and maid ane strange   *urged*
    fair,⁰   *countenance*
'Now is twyse,' said the carl, 'me think thow hes foryet.'⁰   *forgotten*
   He leit gyrd to⁰ the king, withoutin ony mair,   *let fly at*
And hit him under the eir⁰ with his richt hand,   *ear*
     Quhill he stakkerit⁰ thairwithall   *until he staggered*
     Half the breid⁰ of the hall,   *breadth*
     He faind⁰ never of ane fall,   *pretended*
     Quhill⁰ he the eird fand.⁰   *until*   *fell to the floor*

He⁰ start up stoutly agane, uneis⁰ micht he stand,   *(Charles)*   *scarcely*
   For anger of that outray⁰ that he had their tane.⁰   *insult*   *taken*
He⁰ callit on Gyliane his wyfe, 'Ga, tak him be the hand   *(Rauf)*
   And gang agane to the buird⁰ quhair ye suld eir have gane.   *table*
Schir, thow art unskilfull,⁰ and that sall I warrand;⁰   *uncouth*   *warrant*
   Thow byrd⁰ to have nurtour⁰ aneuch and thow   *ought*   *good manners*
     hes nane.
Thow hes walkit, iwis, in mony wyld land,
   The mair vertew thow suld have to keip the fra blame,
Thow suld be courtes of kind⁰ and ane cunnand   *courteous by nature*
    courtier
     Thocht⁰ that I simpill be,   *though*
     Do as I bid the.
     The hous is myne, pardie.
     And all that is heir.'

The king said to him self, 'This is ane evill lyfe,
   Yit was I never in my lyfe thusgait⁰ leird,⁰   *in this way*   *taught*
And I have oftymes bene quhair gude hes bene ryfe,⁰   *frequent*
   That maist couth⁰ of courtasie in this Cristin eird.⁰   *knew*   *earth*
Is nane⁰ sa gude as leif of⁰ and mak na mair stryfe,   *nothing*   *leave off*
   For I am stonischit at this straik⁰ that hes me thus   *blow*
     steird.'⁰   *perturbed*
In feir fairlie he foundis,⁰ with the gude wyfe,   *together courteously he goes*
   Quhair⁰ the colyear bad, so braithlie he beird.⁰   *where*   *loudly he shouted*
Quhen⁰ he had done his bidding, as him gude thocht,⁰   *when*   *seemed*

Doun he sat the king near
And maid him glaid and gude cheir
And said, 'Ye ar welcum heir,°   *here*
Be him that me bocht.'°   *redeemed*

Quhen thay war servit and set to the suppar,
   Gyll and the gentill king, Charlis of micht,
Syne° on the tother syde sat the coilyear;   *then*
    Thus war thay marschellit but mair° and matchit°   *without more ado   set*
      that nicht.
Thay brocht breid to the buird° and braun of ane   *table   brawn of a boar*
    bair,°
   And the worthiest wyne went upon hicht,°   *on high*
Thay beirnes° as I wene, thay had aneuch° their   *people   plenty*
    Within that burelie bigging,° byrnand° full bricht.   *rough building   glowing*
Syne enteris their daynteis° on deis° dicht dayntelie.   *delicacies   high table*
    Within that worthy wane°   *dwelling*
    Forsuith° wantit thay nane.°   *in truth   lacked nothing*
    With blyith° cheir sayis Gyliane,   *glad*
    'Schir, dois glaidlie.'°   *set to merrily*

The Carll carpit° to the king cumlie and cleir,°   *spoke   handsome and illustrious*

   'Schir, the forestaris, for suith, of this forest,
Thay have me all at invy° for dreid of° the deir.°   *envy   because of fear for   deer*
   Thay threip° that I thring doun° of the fattest,   *complain   bring down*
Thay say I sall to Paris their to compeer°   *appear*
   Befoir our cumlie king, in dule to be drest.°   *treated painfully*
Sic manassing thay me mak° for suith ilk year,°   *thus they threaten me   each year*
   And yit aneuch° sall I have for me and ane gest.   *yet sufficient*
Thairfoir sic as thow seis, spend on° and not spair.'°   *set to   spare*
Thus said the gentill Charles the Mane°   *Great*
    To the colyear agane,
    'The king himself hes bene fane°   *would have been glad*
    Sum tyme of sic fair.'°   *such fare*

Of capounis and cunningis° thay had plenty, — *rabbits*

    With wyne at their will and eik° vennysoun, — *also*

Byrdis° bakin in breid,° the best that may be; — *birds*   *bread*

    Thus full freschlie thay fure into fusioun.° — *fared in abundance*

The carll with ane cleir voce carpit on he,° — *spoke loudly*

    Said, 'Gyll, lat the cop raik° for my bennysoun° — *cup go round*   *blessing*

And gar our gaist° begin and syne° drink thow to me; — *make our guest*   *then*

    Sen he is ane stranger, me think it ressoun.'° — *it seems to me proper*

Thay drank dreichlie° about, thay wosche° and thay rais.° — *copiously*   *washed*   *rose*

    The king with ane blyith cheir° — *demeanour*

    Thankit the coilyear,

    Syne° all the thre into feir° — *then*   *together*

    To the fyre gais.° — *go*

Quhen thay had maid thame eis° the coilyear tald — *settled comfortably*

    Mony sindrie taillis° efter suppair. — *various tales*

Ane bricht byrnand fyre was byrnand full bald,° — *fiercely*

    The king held gude countenance and company bair° — *behaved companionably*

And ever to his asking ane answer he yald,° — *gave*

    Quhill° at the last he began to frane farther mair,° — *until*   *question further*

'In faith, friend, I wald wit, tell gif° ye wald, — *if*

    Quhair is thy maist wynning?'° said the coilyear. — *habitual dwelling*

'Out of weir,'° said the king, 'I wayndit° never to tell. — *without doubt*   *hesitated*

    With my lady the queen

    In office maist° have I bene, — *mostly*

    All thir yeiris fyftene,° — *these fifteen years*

    In the court for to dwell.'

Further questioning leads to the king giving his name as 'Wymond of the Wardrop', in the queen's chamber, and inviting Rauf to come to the court, remarking that he will find it a profitable market for his fuel. Rauf says that he does not know where the court is, and that he is reluctant to go to a place where he is unknown. The king attempts to reassure him, and in the morning when they part Rauf announces that he will indeed try to sell his coal at court. The king goes his way, and is reunited with his retinue and his knights. They return to Paris with great ceremony and festivity. Rauf fills two baskets and, rejecting a warning from his wife about the stranger's 'gentrise' ('Lat me wirk as I will, the weird [fate] is mine awin'), also sets out in search of 'Wymond'. On the way he has an encounter with the knight Sir Roland, and finally forces his way into court. In a brief 'recognition scene' he glimpses Wymond: 'Yone is wymond, I wait … I ken him weill thocht he be cled in uther clothing.' He is very alarmed, especially when the king tells his nobles how he was treated in Rauf's house. They laugh, but say he deserves to be hanged. The king, however, will not allow such treatment to the man who 'succourit my lyfe in sa evil ane nicht … that carll for his courtasie salbe maid knicht.' And so he is and, after a further battle with a Saracen, Magog, he becomes Marshal of France.

iv) The Freiris of Berwik[11]

A Scottish fabliau, formerly attributed (without solid evidence) to William Dunbar. The anonymous author has produced a literary gem. It is one of the most enjoyable fabliaux in the English language: the action moves swiftly in its rather complicated route to a comic conclusion, with characters being nicely differentiated. The author obviously delights both in the everyday setting, and in the traditionally exaggerated turns of the plot. The comedy is sharp and satirical, but not overly dark and destructive.

In Berwick, 'a nobill toun', are two Jacobin friars, Allane and Robert. 'Rycht wondir weill plesit thai all wyffis And tawld thame tailis of haly sanctis'. Friar Allan was old and tired, but Friar Robert is young and hot of blood. Returning to the town when night is falling they are worried that they will find the gates closed, and decide to find lodging outside the town. They come to the house of one Symon, who had a fair wife — 'bot scho wes sumthing dynk and dengerous' [dressy and haughty]. Alesone receives them, tells them that her husband is away in the countryside, and gives them drink. As they are telling their merry tales, they hear

---

11   Also in *Ten Bourdes*, ed. Furrow (a revised version of her *Fifteenth-Century Comic Poems*). I have made sparing use of Furrow's notes, only where Gray left a question-mark, because it is not certain he used this edition.

the prayer bell of their own abbey and know that they cannot return. They ask for lodging for the night. The wife, at first reluctant, finally agrees that they can stay up in the loft. In fact, the wife is pleased 'that thay wer closet ther', because she has a tryst with her lover, a rich and powerful grey friar, and she dresses up for the occasion, 'als prowd as ony papingo'. Up in the loft friar Robert makes a little hole with his bodkin so that he can see what is going on. The grey friar is sitting in his chair like a prelate, and the wife is whispering in his ear. Then there is a sudden commotion, a knocking on the gate and a cry: Simon the husband has returned unexpectedly. The wife is annoyed that her plans for the evening have been brought to nothing, and the grey friar is filled with alarm … [vv. 204 to end]

… 'Quhat sall I do, allace?' the freir can say,		
'Hyd yow', scho said, 'quhill he be brocht to rest,		
Into yon troich,° I think it for the best —	*trough*	
It lyis mekle° and huge in all yone nuke,°	*big*	*corner*
It held a boll° of meill quhen that we buke.'°	*boll (6 bushels)*	*bake*
Than undir it scho gart him creip in hy,°	*quickly*	
And bad him lurk their verry quyetly;		
Scho closit him and syne went on hir way.		
'Quhat sall I do, allace?' the freir can say.		
Syne to hir madin spedyly scho spak,		
'Go to the fyre, and the meitis fra it tak.		
Be bissy als, and slokkin out° the fyre,	*put out*	
Ga clois yn burd,° and tak away the chyre,°	*board*	*chair*
And lok up all into yone almery,°	*locker*	
Baith meit and drink with wyne and aill put by,°	*aside*	
The mayne° breid als° thow hyd it with the wyne,	*finest*	*also*
That being done, thow sowp° the hous clene syne,	*sweep*	
That na appearance of feist° be heir sene,	*feasting*	
Bot sobirly our selffis dois sustene.'		
And syne, withowttin ony mair delay,		
Scho castis of hail° hir fresch array.	*off completely*	
Than went scho to hir bed annone,		
And tholit° him to knok his fill, Symone.	*suffered*	
Quhen he for knoking tyrit° wes and cryid,	*tired*	

Abowt he went unto the udir° syd,   *other*

And on Alesone fast cold° he cry,   *did*

And at the last scho anserit crabitly°   *crossly*

'Ach, quha be this that knawis sa weill my name?

Go hens,' scho sayis, 'for Symon is fra hame,

And I will herbry no gaistis° heir parfey.   *shelter no guests*

Thairfoir I pray yow to wend on your way,

For at this tyme ye may nocht lugit° be.'   *lodged*

Than Symone said, 'Fair dame, ken ye nocht me?

I am your Symone and husband° of this place.'   *owner*

'Ar ye my spous Symone?' scho sayis, 'allace!

Be misknawlege I had almaist misgane,°   *made a mistake*

Quha wenit° that ye sa lait wald haif cum hame?'   *expected*

Scho stertis° up and gettis licht in hy,°   *jumps*   *quickly*

And oppinit than the yet° full haistely,   *gate*

Scho tuk fra him his geir at all devyis,°   *completely*

Syne welcomit him on maist hairtly wyis.°   *manner*

He bad the maddin kindill° on the fyre,   *kindle*

'Syne graith me meit,° and tak ye all thy   *prepare me food*
    hyre.'°   *recompense*

The gudwyf said schortly, 'Ye may trow

Heir is no meir that ganand° is for yow.'   *suitable*

'How sa, fair deme,° ga gait° me cheis and breid,   *lady*   *get*

Ga fill the stowp,° hald me no mair in pleid,°   *flagon*   *argument*

For I am very tyrit, wett, and cauld.'

Than up scho rais, and durst nocht mair be bauld,

Cuverit the burde,° thairon sett meit in hy,°   *table*   *quickly*

Ane sowsit nolt-fute° ane scheipheid°   *soused cow's foot*   *sheep's head*
    haistely;

And sum cauld meit scho brocht to him believe,°   *at once*

And fillit the stowp. The gudman than wes blyth,°   *happy*

Than satt he doun, and swoir, 'Be all hallow°   *saints*

I fair richt weill, and° I had ane gud fallow;°   *if*   *companion*

Dame, eit with me and drink, gif° that ye may.'   *if*

Said the gudwyf, 'Devill in the tim° may I,   *not at this ungodly hour*

It wer mair meit° into your bed to be,   *fitting*

Than now to sit desyrand company.'
Freir Robert said, 'Allace, gud bruder deir,
I wald° the gudman wist that we wer heir,   *would*
Quha wait° perchance sum bettir wald he fair —   *knows*
For sickerly° my hairt will ay be sair°   *certainly*   *ever sorrowful*
Gif yone scheipheid with° Symon birneist° be,   *by*   *burnished*
Sa mekill gud cheir being in the almerie.'°   *locker*
And with that word he gaif ane hoist° anone.   *cough*
The gudman hard, and speirit,° 'Quha is yone?'   *asked*
The gudwyf said, 'Yone ar freiris tway.'°   *two*
Symone said, 'Tell me quhat freiris be thay.'
'Yone is freir Robert and silly° freir Allane,   *good, poor*
That all this day hes travellit with grit pane.
Be° thay come heir it wes so very lait,   *when*
Curfiw° wes rung and closit wes thair yait,°   *curfew*   *gate*
And in yond loft I gaif thame harbrye.'
The gudman said, 'Sa God haif part of me,
Tha° freiris twa ar hairtly welcome hidder,   *those*
Ga call thame doun, that we ma drink togidder.'
The gudwyf said, 'I reid° yow lat thame be,   *advise*
Thay had levir° sleip nor° sit in cumpanye.'   *rather*   *than*
The gudman said unto the maid thone,°   *then*
'Go, pray thame baith to cum till me annone,'
And sone the trop° the madin oppinit then,   *trapdoor*
And bad thame baith cum doun to the gudman.
Freir Robert said, 'Now be sweit sanct Jame,
The gudman is very welcome hame,
And for his weilfair dalie do we pray;
We sall annone cum doun to him ye say.'
Than with that word thay start up baith attone,°   *together*
And doun the trop° delyverly° thay come,   *ladder*   *quickly*
Halsit° Symone als sone as thay him se,   *greeted*
And he agane thame welcomit hairtfullie.
And said, 'Cum heir, myne awin bredir° deir,   *brothers*
And sett yow doun sone besyd me heir,

For I am now allone, as ye may se;
Thairfore sitt doun and beir me cumpanye,
And tak yow pairt of sic gud as we haif.'
Freir Allane said, 'Ser, I pray God yow saif,
For heir is now annuch° of Godis gud.'   *sufficient*
Than Symon anserit, 'Now be the rud,°   *rood*
Yit wald I gif° ane croun of gold for me,   *give*
For sum gud meit and drink amangis us thre.'
Freir Robert said, 'Quhat drinkis wald ye craif,°   *crave*
Or quhat meitis desyre ye for to haif?
For I haif mony sindry° practikis seir,   *sundry*
Beyond the sey° in Pareis did I leir,°   *sea*   *learn*
That I wald preve° glaidly for your saik,   *prove*
And for your demys,° that harbry cowd us maik.°   *lady's*   *provide*
I tak on hand,° and ye will counsale keip.°   *undertake*   *keep it quiet*
That I sall gar° yow se, or° ever I sleip,   *cause*   *before*
Of the best meit that is in this cuntre,
Of Gascone wyne, gif ony° in it be,   *if any*
Or, be thair ony within ane hundredth myle,
It salbe heir within a bony quhyle.'
The gudman had grit mervell of this taill,
And said, 'My hairt [will] neir be hail°   *never be whole*
Bot gif ye preve that practik or ye pairte,°   *leave*
To mak ane sport.' And than the freir upstart;
He tuk his buk and to the flure° he gais,°   *floor*   *goes*
He turnis it our,° and reidis it a littill space,   *over*
And to the eist direct he turnis his face,
Syne to the west he turnit and lukit doun,
And tuk his buk and red ane orisoun —
And ay his eyne° wer on the almery,   *eyes*
And on the troch° quhair° that freir Johine did ly.   *trough* *where*
Than sat he doun and kest abak his hude,
He granit,° and he glowrit,° as he wer woid,°   *groaned* *glowered*   *mad*
And quhylis° still he satt in studeing,°   *sometimes*   *studying*
And uthir quhylis upoun his buk reding;

And quhylis with baith his handis he wald clap,

And uthir quhylis wald he glour and gaip;

Syne in the sowth he turnit him abowt

Weill thryis° and mair, than lawly° cowd he lowt,° *thrice* *lowly* *bow*

Quhen that he come near the almery.

Thairat our dame had woundir grit invy,° *displeasure*

For in her hairt scho had ane persaving° *perception*

That he had knawin all hir govirning.° *arrangements*

Scho saw him gif the almery sic a straik,° *such a blow*

Unto hir self scho said, 'Full weill I wait° *know*

I am bot schent,° he knawis full weill my thocht; *ruined*

Quhat sall I do? Allace, that I wes wrocht!° *created*

Get Symon wit,° it wilbe deir doing.'° *gets to know* *a fine mess*

Be that° the freir had left his studeing, *by then*

And on his feit he startis up full sture,° *sternly*

And come agane, and seyit all his cure

'Now is it done, and ye sall haif playntie

Of breid and wyne, the best in this cuntre;

Thairfoir, fair dame, get up deliverlie,° *smartly*

And ga belyfe° unto yone almerie, *quickly*

And oppin it and se ye bring us syne

Ane pair of boissis° full of Gascone wyne, *leather bottles*

Thay had ane galloun and mair, that wait° I weill; *know*

And bring us als the mayne breid° in a creill,° *fine bread* *(wicker) basket*

Ane pair of cunyngis,° fat and het pypand,° *rabbits* *piping hot*

The caponis als ye sall us bring fra hand,

Twa pair of pertrikis,° I wait there is no ma;° *partridges* *more*

And eik° of pluveris° se that ye bring us twa.' *also* *plovers*

The gudwyf wist it wes no variance,° *alternative*

Scho knew the freir had sene hir govirnance,

Scho saw it wes no bute° for to deny *use*

With that scho went unto the almery

And oppinit it, and than scho fand their

All that the freir had spokin of befoir.

Scho stert abak, as scho wer in afray°   *alarmed*
And sanyt hir,° and smyland° cowd scho say,   *crossed herself   smiling*
'Ha, banadicite, quhat may this bene?°   *be*
Quha evir afoir° hes sic a fairly° sene?   *before   wonder*
Sa grit a mervell as now hes apnit° heir,   *happened*
Quhat sall I say? He is ane haly freir;
He said full suth° of all that he did say.'   *truth*
Scho brocht all furth,° and on the burd cowd lay   *out*
Baith breid and wyne, and uthir thingis moir,
Cunyngis and caponis, as ye haif hard befoir,
Pertrikis and pluveris befoir thame hes scho brocht.
The freir knew well and saw thair wantit nocht,
Bot all wes furth brocht evin at his devyis,°   *according to his wish*
And Symone saw it appinnit° on this wyis.°   *happened   manner*
He had grit wondir, and sweris be the mone°   *moon*
That freir Robert weill his dett had done,
'He may be callit ane man of grit science,°   *learning*
Sa suddanly that all this purviance°   *provision*
Hes brocht us heir, throw his grit subteltie
And throw his knawlege in filosophie —
In ane gud tyme it wes quhen he come hidder;
Now fill the cop that we ma drink togidder.
And mak gud cheir eftir this langsum° day,   *tedious*
For I haif riddin ane wonder wilsome° way.   *wandering*
Now God be lovit,° heir is suffisance°   *praised   sufficiency*
Unto us all throw your gud govirnance.'
And than annone thay drank evin° round abowt   *equally*
Of Gascone wyne; the freiris playit cop owt.°   *(= drained the cup)*
Thay sportit thame, and makis mirry cheir
With sangis lowd, baith Symone and the freir.
And on this wyis the lang nicht thay ourdraf;°   *drove away*
Nothing thay want that thay desyrd to haif.
Than Symon said to the gudwyf in hy,
'Cum heir, fair dame, and sett yow doun me by,
And tak parte of sic gud as we haif heir,

And hairtly I yow pray to thank this freir
Off his bening° grit besines and cure,   *benign*
That he hes done to us upoun this flure,°   *floor*
And brocht us meit and drink haboundantlie,
Quhairfoir of richt we aucht° mirry to be.'   *ought*
Bot all their sport, quhen thay wer maist at eis,°   *ease*
Unto our deme it was bot littill pleis°   *pleasure*
For uther thing thair wes into° hir thocht;°   *in*   *mind*
Scho wes so red,° hir hairt wes ay on flocht°   *fearful*   *flutter*
That throw the freir scho sowld° discoverit be,   *should*
To him scho lukit ofttymes effeiritlie°   *fearfully*
And ay disparit° in hart wes scho,   *despairing*
That he had witt° of all hir purveance° to.°   *known*   *provision*   *too*
Thus satt scho still, and wist no udir wane;°   *other alternative*
Quhatevir thay say, scho lute° him all allane,°   *let*   *alone*
Bot scho drank with thame into company
With fenyeit° cheir and hert full wo and hevy.   *pretended*
Bot thay wer blyth annuche,° God watt, and sang,   *happy enough*
For ay the wyne was rakand° thame amang,   *going*
Quhill at the last thay woix° richt blyth ilkone.°   *grew*   *each one*
Than Symone said unto the freir annone,
'I marvell mikill° how that this may be,   *greatly*
Intill° schort tyme that ye sa° suddanlye   *in*   *so*
Hes brocht to us sa mony denteis deir.'°   *exquisite dainties*
'Thairof haif ye no marvell,' quod the freir.
'I haif ane pege° full prevy° of my awin,°   *page*   *confidential*   *own*
Quhenevir I list, will cum to me unknawin.°   *unknown, secretly*
And bring to me sic° thing as I will haif;   *such*
Quhatevir I list it neidis° me nocht to craif.°   *is necessary*   *desire*
Thairfoir be blyth and tak° in pacience,   *accept*
And trest ye weill I sall do diligence.°   *exert myself*
Gif that ye list or thinkis to haif moir,°   *more*
It salbe had and I sall stand thairfoir,
Incontinent° that samyn° sall ye se.   *immediately*   *same (= just that)*
Bot I protest° that ye keip it previe,°   *insist*   *secret*

Latt no man wit that I can do sic thing.'
Than Symone swoir and said, 'Be hevynnis king,
It salbe kepit prevy as for me,º   *as far as I am concerned*
Bot, bruder deir, your servand waldº I se,   *would*
Gif it yow pleis, that we may drynk togidder,
For I wait nocht gifº ye ma ay cum hidderº   *know not if   may always*
                                                                                  come hither

Quhen that we want our neidis sic as this.'
The freir said, 'Nay, so motº I haif hevynis blis,   *may*
Yow to haif the sichtº of my serwand   *sight*
It canº nocht be — ye sall weill understand,   *must*
That ye may se him graithlyº in his awin kynd,º   *readily   own form*
Bot ye anone sowldº go owt of your mynd.   *immediately should*
He is so fowll and ugly for to se.
I dar nocht awnterº for to tak onº me   *venture   undertake*
To bring him hidder heir into our sicht,
And namelyº now so lait into the nicht,   *especially*
Bot gif it wer on sic a maner wyisº   *in such a kind of way*
Him to translaitº or ellis disagyisº   *transform   disguise*
Fra his awin kind into ane uder stait.'º   *other form*
Than Symone said, 'I mak no moir debait,º   *argument*
As pleisisº yow so likis it to me,   *pleases*
As evir ye list,º bot faneº wald I him se,'   *wish   gladly*
Freyr Robert said, 'Sen that your will is so,
Tell onto me withouttin wourdis mo,
Intill quhat kyndº sall I him garº appeir?'   *form   cause*
Than Symone said, 'In liknes of a freir,
In quhytº cullour, right as your self it war,º   *white   were*
For quhyt cullour will na body deir.'º   *harm*
Freir Robert said that swa it cowld nocht be,
For sic causis as he may weill foirse,º   *foresee*
That he compeirº into our habeitº quhyt: *appear   monastic dress*
'Untillº our ordour it wer a grit dispyte,º   *unto   insult*
That ony sic unworthy wichtº as he   *creature*
Intillº our habeit men sowld behald or se.   *in*
Bot sen it pleissis yow that ar heir,

Ye sall him se in liknes of a freir,
In habeit blak it was his kind to weir,
Into sic wyis that he sall no man deir.º   *harm*
Gif ye so do, and rewll yow at all wyis
To hald yow clois and stillº at my devyis,º   *hidden and quiet*   *according to my wish*

Quhatevir it be ye owdirº se or heir,   *either*
Ye speik no word nor mak no kynd of steir,º   *stir*
Bot hald yow clois, quhillº I haif done my cure.'   *until*
Than said he, 'Semon, ye moneº be on the flure,º   *must*   *floor*
Neirhandº besyd, with staff intoº your hand;   *close*   *in*
Haif ye no dreid, I sall yow ay warrand,'º   *protect, be surety for*
Than Symone said, 'I assent that it be swa.'
And up he start, and gat a libberlaº   *cudgel*
Into his hand, and on the flure he stert,
Sumthing effrayit,º thocht stalwart was his hart.   *somewhat afraid*
Than to the freir said Symone verry sone,º   *quickly*
'Now tell me, maister, quhat ye will haif done.'
'Nothing,' he said, 'bot hald yow clois and still.
Quhatevir I do, tak ye gud tent thairtill,º   *heed therto*
And near the durº ye hyd yow prevely,º   *door*   *secretly*
And quhen I bid yow stryk, strek hardely,º   *strike boldly*
Into the nek se that ye hit him richt.'º   *directly*
'That sall I warrand,' quod he, 'with all my micht.'
Thus on the flure I leifº him standand still,   *leave*
Bydand his tyme, and turne agane I will,
Howº that the freir did take his buke in hy,º   *[to tell] how*   *quickly*
And turnit ourº the levis full besely,   *over*
Ane full lang space,º and quhen he had done swa,   *very long time*
Towart the trochº withowttin wordis ma   *trough*
He gois belyfe,º and on this wyisº sayis he,   *quickly*   *manner*
'Ha, how! Hurlybas,º now I conjure the,   *(the fiend's name)*
That thow uprysº and sone to me appear   *rise up*
In habeitº blak in liknes of a freir;   *habit*
Owt of this troch, quhair that thou dois ly

Thow rax the° sone, and mak no dyn nor cry.   *rouse yourself*
Thow tumbill our° the troch that we may se,   *tumble over*
And unto us thow schaw the° oppinlie,   *show yourself*
And in this place se that thow no man greif,°   *harm*
Bot draw thy handis boith into thy sleif,°   *sleeve*
And pull thy cowll doun owttour° thy face.   *over*
Thow may thank God that thow gettis° sic a grace   *get*
Thairfoir thow turs° the to thyne awin ressett,°   *make off*   *own abode*
Se this be done and mak no moir debait;°   *argument*
In thy depairting se thow mak no deray°   *disturbance*
Unto no wicht,° bot frely pas thy way;   *person*
And in this place se that thow cum no moir,
Bot I command the, or ellis the charge befoir,
And our the stair° se that thow ga gud speid;°   *across the stairs   quickly*
Gif thow dois nocht, on thy awin perrell beid.'°   *be it*
With that the freir, that under the troch lay,
Raxit him sone, bot he wes in afray,°   *state of alarm*
And up he rais, and wist na bettir wayn,
Bot of the troch he tumlit our° the stane   *stumbled over*
Syne fra the samyn° quhairin he thocht him lang   *same (trough)*
Unto the dur he preisit° him to gang,   *hurried*
With hevy cheir and drery countenamce,
For nevir befoir him hapnit sic a chance.°   *event*
And quhen freir Robert saw him gangand° by,   *going*
Unto the gudman full lowdly cowd° he cry,   *did*
'Stryk, stryk herdely, for now is tyme to the.'°   *now is your time*
With that Symone a felloun flap° lait fle.°   *fierce blow   let fly*
With his burdoun° he hit him on the nek;   *staff*
He wes sa ferce° he fell owttour the sek,°   *fierce   over the sack (of corn)*
And brak° his heid upoun ane mustard stane.°   *broke   stone (for grinding mustard)*

Be this freir Johine attour° the stair is gane   *over*
In sic wyis° that mist he hes the trap,°   *such a way   missed the ladder*
And in ane myr° he fell — sic wes his hap° —   *mire   fortune*
Wes fourty futis of breid° undir the stair,   *forty feet in breadth*

Yeit gat° he up with clething° nothing fair, *yet got* *clothes*

Full drerelie° upoun his feit he stude, *miserably*

And throw the myre full smertly° than he yude,° *quickly* *went*

And our the wall he clam° richt haistely, *climbed*

Quhilk° round abowt wes laid with stanis dry. *which*

Of his eschaping° in hairt he wes full fane,° *escape* *glad*

I trow° he salbe laith° to cum agane. *believe* *will be loath*

With that freir Robert stert abak and saw

Quhair the gudman lay sa woundir law° *wondrously low*

Upoun the flure, and bleidand° wes his heid;° *bleeding* *head*

He stert° to him, and went° he had bene deid, *hurried* *thought*

And clawcht° him up withowttin wordis moir, *caught*

And to the dur delyverly° him bure;° *quickly* *carried*

And fra° the wind wes blawin twyis° in his face, *when* *blown twice*

Than he ourcome° within a lytill space, *came to*

And than freir Robert franyt at him fast,° *asked him earnestly*

Quhat ailit° him to be so soir agast. *what ailed*

He said, 'Yone [feynd had maid° me in effray]' *made*

'Latt be,' quod he, 'the werst is all away —

Mak mirry, man, and se ye morne na mair° — *sorrow no more*

Ye haif him strikin° quyt owttour° the stair. *knocked* *quite over*

I saw him slip, gif I the suth° can tell, *truth*

Doun our the stair. Intill a myr he fell.

Bot lat him go, he wes a graceles gaist,° *spirit*

And boun° yow to your bed, for it is best,' *go*

Thus Symonis heid upoun the stane wes brokin,

And our the stair the freir in myre hes loppin,° *leapt*

And tap our tail;° he fyld° wes *top over tail* *defile*
 woundir ill,° *wondrously badly*

And Alesone on na wayis gat° hir will. *no ways got*

This is the story that hapnit of that freir,

No moir there is, bot Chryst us help most deir.° *dear*

v) Kynd Kittok[12]

Scotland produced a remarkable tradition of popular comic tales:
Colkrelbie Sow, Sym and his Bruder, and some which find comic
entertainment of a weird 'eldritch' kind, as in Lichtoun's Dreme or The
Gyre Carling (the 'mother witch' of Scotland).[13] Sadly, there is no space
to celebrate this varied tradition here in the manner it deserves. We must
be content with the lively *Freiris of Berwik* (above) and the following little
tale of how Kitty found an alehouse close to the gate of heaven.

My gudame° wes a gay wif, bot scho wes right gend.° *grandmother simple*
Scho duelt furth fer into France upon Falkland Fell;
Thay callit her Kynd Kittok, quhasa° hir weill kend.° *whoever   well*
                                                                    knew

Scho wes like a caldron cruke° cler° under   *hook   beautiful*
   kell,°   *headdress*
Thay threpit° that scho deit of thrist,° and *alleged*
   maid a gud end.
Efter hir dede,° scho dredit° nought in hevin for to *death   feared*
   duell,
And sa to hevin the hie way dreidles scho wend.
Yit scho wanderit and yeid° by to ane elriche° well. *went   fairy*
   Scho met thar, as I wene,
   Ane ask° rydand° on a snail,   *newt   riding*
   And cryit, 'Ourtane° fallow, hail!' *overtaken*
   And raid° ane inche behind the tail, *rode*
   Till it wes near evin.

Sa scho had hap to be horsit to hir herbry° *shelter*
Att ane ailhous near hevin, it nyghttit thaim° thare; *night fell on them*
Scho deit of thrist in this warld, that gert° hir be so dry, *made*
Scho never eit, bot drank our° mesur and mair. *over*
Scho sleipit quhill° the morn at none, and rais airly;° *until   rose early*

---

12   For Kynd Kittok (Kittie), as well as The Freiris of Berwick, see *The Poems of William
       Dunbar*, ed. MacKenzie.
13   See Gray's *Later Medieval English Literature* (on Scottish writing, headed Robert
       Henryson), pp. 509 ff (book-list pp. 531–2).

And to the yettis° of hevin fast can° the wif   *gates*   *did*
   fair,°   *go*
And by sanct Petir, in at the yet scho stall prevely,°   *stole secretly*
God lukit° and saw hir lattin° in and lewch° his hert   *looked* *let* *laughed*
   sair.
     And thar yeris sevin
     Scho levit a gud life,
     And wes our Ladyis hen wif,
     And held sanct Petir at strif,
     Ay quhill° scho wes in hevin.   *ever while*

Sche lukit out on a day and thought right lang
To se the ailhous beside, intill ane evill hour;
And out of hevin the hie gait cought° the wif gaing°   *did*   *go*
For to get hir ane fresche drink — the aill of hevin wes sour.
Scho come againe to hevinnis yet, quhen the bell rang,
Saint Petir hat° hir with a club, quhill a gret clour°   *hit*   *bump*
Rais° in hie heid,° because the wif yeid wrang.   *rose*   *head*
Than to the ailhous agane scho ran the pycharis to pour.
     And for to brew and baik.
     Frendis, I pray yow hertfully
   Gif° ye be thirsty or dry,   *if*
   Drink with my guddame, as ye ga by,
   Anys° for my saik.   *just once*

vi) The Wright's Chaste Wife[14]

An example of how a comic tale can also be a moral tale. Similarly, stories which appear in the pages of moralists and preachers, like that of the poor man and his cow, which illustrates how mercy increases temporal goods, can also appear in fabliaux — like the French 'Brunain'.[15]

Allmyghty God, maker of alle,

---

14   *Adam of Cobsham*: *The Wright's Chaste Wife*, ed. Furnivall.

15   'Brunain, la vache au prêtre' is one of Jean Bodel's fabliaux. This Old French poet wrote chansons de geste as well as fabliaux; he lived c. 1165–c. 1210, in Arras.

Save you my sovereynns in towre and halle,

    And send you good grace!

If ye wyll a stounde blynne,

Of a story I wyll begynne,

    And telle you all the cas.

Meny farleyes that I have herde,

Ye would have wondyr how yt ferde —

    Lystyn, and ye schall here …

[An honest, hard-working wright is slow to enter marriage, but finally chooses the fair daughter of a widow in the area. The widow says that the only marriage portion she can give him is a garland of roses. However, it has a marvellous property: if his wife is faithful the roses will retain their colour, but if she is fickle the colour will change. They are married and return home after the festivities. Then the wright is struck by the thought that his wife is so beautiful that other men will desire to have her 'and that hastly and sone'. And so he plans and builds a crafty room from which no one can escape, 'wyth wallys stronge as eny stele And dorres sotylly made and wele'. It has a cunningly-made trapdoor with a 'pit' beneath it: 'whoso touchyd yt ony thing, Into the pytt he schuld flyng.' The wright is summoned by the lord of the town to work on the construction of a wooden hall which will take two or three months …]

The lord seyd, 'woult thou have thi wyfe?

I wyll send after her blyve°   *quickly*

    That sche may come to the.'

The wryght hys garlond hadde take wyth hym.

That was bryght and no thing dimme,

    Yt was feyre on to see.

The lord axyd hym as he satt,

'Felowe, where hadyst thou this hatte

    That ys so feyre and newe?'

[And when he hears of its marvellous nature …]

The lord thought 'By Godys myght,

That wyll I wete thys same nyght

    Whether thys tale be trewe.'

To the wryghtes howse anon he went,

He fonde the wyfe therin presente

    That was so bryght and schene,

Sone he hayled her trewly,
And so dyd sche the lord curtesly,
 Sche seyd, 'Welcome ye be!'
Thus seyd the wyfe of the hows,
'Syr, howe faryth my swete spowse
 That hewyth upon your tre?'

'Sertes, dame,' he seyd, 'wele,
And I am come, so have I hele,
 To wete the wylle of the.
My love ys so upon the cast
That ne thynketh my hert wolle brest,º   *break*
 It wolle none otherwise be!

Good dame, graunt me thy grace
To pley with the in some prevy place
 For gold and eke for fee.'º   *reward*
'Good syr, lett be your fare,
And of such words speke no mare
 For hys love that dyed on tre —

Hadde we onys begonne that gle,
My husbond by his garlond myght see,
 For sorowe he would wexe woode.'º   *go mad*
'Certes, dame,' he seyd, 'naye.
Love me, I pray you, in that ye maye —
 For Godys love change thy mode,

Forty marke schall be youre mede
Of sylver and of gold[e] rede,
 And thay schall do the good.'
['Syr, that deede schall be done', she says, and asks for the money. She takes it and says …]
'… into the chambyr wyll we,
That no man schall us see;
 No lenger wyll we spare.'

Up the steyer they gan hye;
The stepes were made so queyntly°   *cunningly*
    That farther myght he nott fare.

The lord stumbyllyd as he went in hast,
He fell doune into that chaste°   *pit*
    Forty fote and somedele more.
The lord began to crye,
The wyfe seyd to hym in hye,°   *quickly*
    'Syr, what do ye there?'

'Dame, I cannot seye howe
That I am come hydder nowe
    To thys hows that ys so newe;
I am so depe in thys sure flore
That I ne can come owte att no dore —
    Good dame, on me thou rewe!'
[But she refuses, until her husband will return ...]
... The lord arose and lokyd abowte
If he myght enywhere gete owte,
    Butt yt holpe hym ryght noght,
The wallys were so thycke wythyn,
That he nowhere myght owte wynne
    But helpe to hym were brought ...
[Angrily he threatens the wife, but she says she does not care: 'I recke nere
While I am here and thou art there, I schrewe here that the doth drede.' Putting
him out of her mind, she retires to her loft and carries on with her own tasks.
On the next day he asks for some food, but that will not be forthcoming unless
he is willing to 'swete or swynke.']
'... I have both hempe and lyne,°   *flax*
And a betyngstocke° full fyne,   *beating-stock*
    And a swyngyll° good and grete.   *board*
If thou wylt worke, tell me sone.'
'Dame, bring yt forthe, yt schall be done,
    Full gladly would I ete.'

[She throws the tools down to him in the pit 'wyth a grete hete'. 'Syr lord …
have thou that And lerne for to swete', and he begins to beat. So he carries on
working, and the wife gives him food if his work is satisfactory, but 'hys men
knewe nott of hys woo Nor of ther lordes pyne.' But his steward notices his
absence.]

The stuard to the wryght gan saye,

'Sawe thou owte of my lord todaye,

    Whether that he ys wen[t]?'

The wryght answerde and seyd 'Naye —

I sawe hym nott syth yesterday;

    I trowe that he be schent.'

The stuard stode the wryght by,

And of hys garlond had ferly

    What that yt bemente …

[When he learns of its power …]

The stuard thought, 'By Godes myght,

That schal I preve thys same nyght

    Whether thou blys or banne.'

And into hys chambyr he gan gone,

And toke treasure full good wone,

    And forth he spedde hem⁰ than.   *him*

Butt he ne stynt att no stone

Tyll he unto the wryghtes hows come

    That ylke same nyght.

He met the wyfe amydde the gate,

About the necke he gan her take.

    And seyd, 'My dere wyght,

All the gode that ys myne

I wyll the geve to be thyne

    To lye by the all nyght.'

[As with the lord, she demurs, but the steward presses twenty marks on her.
She remarks …]

'Syr, and⁰ I graunt that to you,   *if*

Lett no man wete butt we two nowe.'
    He seyd, 'Nay, wythowtyn drede.'
The stuard thought, 'Sykerly
Women beth both queynte and slye …'

… Up the sterys sche hym le[d]de
Tyll he saw the wrightes bedde —
    Of tresoure thought he none;

He went and stumblyd att a stone,
Into the seller he fylle sone,
    Downe to the bare flore.
The lord seyd, 'What devyll art thou?
And thou hadest falle on me nowe,
    Thou hadest hurt me full sore!'

The stuard stert and staryd abowte
If he might ower° gete owte   *anywhere*
    Att hole lesse or mare.
The lord seyd, 'Welcome, and sytt be tyme,
For thou schalt helpe to dyght this lyne°   *flax*
    For all thy fers[e] fare.'

The stuard lokyd on the knyght.
He seyd, 'Syr, For Godes myght,
    My lord, what do you here?'
[The steward, who seems to have a high opinion of himself, is very reluctant to
work: 'rather would I dy for hungyr Wythowte hosull or shryfte'. The lord's
rejoinder, 'Thowe wylt worke, yf thou hungyr welle. What worke that the be
brought', is soon proved true: 'The lord satt and dyd hys werke, The stuard
drewe into the derke, Gret sorowe was in hys thought'. When the lord is given
his dinner, he will not share it with the steward.]
The stuard satt all in a stody,
His lord had forgote curtesy.
    Tho seyd the stuard, 'Geve me some.'
The lord seyd, 'Sorowe have the morsel or sope°   *bread soaked in liquid*

That schall come in thy throte!
    Nott si much as o crome!º   *crumb*

Buttº thou wylt helpe to dyght this lyne,   *unless*
Much hungyr yt schall be thyne
    Though thou make much mone.'

[The steward capitulates. Meanwhile, back in the town, the lord's people are increasingly worried about his fate. The proctor of the parish church approaches the wright, hears of the power of his garland, and immediately reacts in the same way as the lord and the steward: 'in good faye That schall I wete thys same daye Whether yt may so be'. He goes to the wife and makes his proposition, which is received in the same manner as those of his predecessors. He offers twenty marks, and this is accepted.]

Nowe hath sche the treasure tane,º   *taken*
And up the steyre be they gane,
    (What helpyth yt to lye?)
The wyfe went the steyre beside.
The proctoure went a lytyll to wyde —
    He fell downe by and by.

Whan he into the seller felle
He wenteº to have sonke into helle,   *thought*
    He was in hert full sory.
The stuard lokyd on the knyght,
And seyd, 'Proctoure, for Godes myght,
    Come and sytt us by.'

The proctoure began to stare,
For he was he wyst never whare,
    Butt wele he knewe the knyght
And the stuard tht swyngelyd the lyne.
He seyd, 'Syres, for Godes pyne,
    What do ye here this nyght?'

The stuard seyd, 'God geve the care,

Thowe camyst to loke howe we fare,

    Nowe helpe this lyne were dyght.'

[The proctor pleads lack of training: 'I lernyd never in lond For to have a swyngell in hond By day nor be nyght'. But the need for food begins to make itself felt: 'the proctoure stode in a stody Whether he might worke hem by'. Finally ...]

The proctoure began to knocke,

The good wyfe rawte° hym a rocke,°   *gave*   *distaff*

    For therto hadde sche nede,

Sche seyd, 'Whan I was mayde at home,

Other werke cowed I do none

    My lyfe therwyth to lede.'

Sche gave hym in hande a rocke hynde,°   *well-made*

And bade hem fast for to wynde

    Or ellys to lett be hys dede.

'Yes, dame,' he seyd, 'so have I hele,

I schall yt worke bothe feyre and welle

    As ye have taute me ...'

[The lord criticises his workmanship, but the three of them sit and toil away 'tyll the wekedayes were past'.]

    Then the wright, home came he,

And as he cam by hys hows syde

He herd noyse that was nott ryde°   *small*

    Of persons two or thre ...

['What ys thys dynne?' he asks, and his wife tells him it is workmen who have come to help them. When the wright sees his lord there he is very alarmed, but the knight apologises and asks for mercy ...]

The wryght bade hys wyfe lett hym owte.

'Naye, then sorowe come on my snowte

    If they passe hens todaye

Tyll that my lady coome and see

Howe they would have done with me ...'

[So the lady is brought, 'for to fett home her lord and knight ... therto sche seyd noght.' She is glad that her lord is alive, and ...]

Whan sche came unto the steyre aboven,

Sche lokyd unto the seller downe,
    And seyd — this is nott to leyne —

'Good syres, what doo you here?'
'Dame, we by owre mete full dere,
    Wyth gret travayle and peyne;
I pray you helpe that we were owte,
And I wyll swere wythowtyn dowte
    Never to come here agayne.'

The lady spake the wyfe untylle,
And seyd, 'Dame, yf yt be youre wylle,
    What doo thes meyny here?'
The carpentarys wyfe her anserd sykerly,
'All they would have leyne me by,
    Everych, in ther manere.

Gold and sylver they me brought,
And forsoke yt, and would yt noght,
    The ryche gyftes so clere.
Wyllyng they were to do me schame —
I toke ther gyftes wythowtyn blame,
    And ther they be all thre!'

The lady answerd her anon,
'I have thynges to do att home
    Mo than two or thre —
I wyst my lord never do right noght
Of no thing that schuld be wrought,
    Such as fallyth to me.'

The lady lawghed and made good game
Whan they came owte all insame
    From the swyngyll tre ...
... And when they cam up aboven

They turnyd abowte and lokyd downe,

    The lord seyd, 'so God save me,

Yet hadde I never such a fytte

As I have hadde in that lowe pytte —

    So Mary so mutt me spede!'

[The lord and the lady return home, and the steward and the proctor ride off, vowing not to return. All the treasure that the suitors brought is given by the lady to the wright's wife. And the wright's garland remains 'feyre of hewe.']

I take wytnes att gret and small,

Thus trewe bene good women all

    That nowe bene on lyve ....

vii) 'Noodle' Stories[16]

This little sub-category of the comic tale, in which a fool demonstrates his own folly, was obviously popular. In the fifteenth and sixteenth centuries this kind of folly was attributed especially to the inhabitants of Gotham in Nottinghamshire.

The Man who had a Goose

... Som tyme ther was a man that had a guse. And sho warpyd everilk day ane egg. And on a tyme he umthoght that he wold hafe all thies eggis at ons, and he slew his guse and oppend hur, and he fand bod one egg in hur. And so for grete haste that he had of that at was for to com, he loste all.

Penning the Cuckoo

On a tyme the men of Gotam wold have pynned the Cockow that she should sing all the yeare and in the myddest of the towne they dyd make a hedge (round in compass), and they had got a cocow, and put her in it

---

16   *Simple Forms*, pp. 146–7 (where he calls them Numskull stories). Three of these four are in *The Book of Noodles*, ed. Clouston; I have not so far identified the first. Its analogues are, of course, the story of the goose that laid the golden eggs; and another about the wife who overfed her hen to get more eggs but ended up with only a fat hen.

and sayde, 'Singe here all the yeare, and thou shalte lacke neyther meate nor drincke.' The Cocow, as soone as shee was set within the hedge, flew her waye. 'A vengeaunce on her!' sayde they, 'We made not our hedge high ynough.'

Runaway Cheese

There was a man of Gotam the which went to the market to Nottingham to sell cheese. And as he was goynge downe the hyll to Nottingham bridge, one of his cheeses dyd fall out of his poake, and did runne downe the hyll. 'A horsons,' said the fellow, 'Can you runne to the market alone I will sende the one after the other of you.' He layde downe hys poake, and tooke the cheeses, and dyd trundle them downe the hyll one after another; and some ran into one busshe, and some into another. And at the laste he sayde, 'I charge you all meete me in the market place.' When the fellowe dyd come into the market place to meete hys cheeses, hee dyd tarie tyll the market was almoste done. Then he went about, and dyd enquire of hys neighboures, and other men if they did see his cheeses come to the market. 'Who shoulde bringe them?' sayd one of the market men. 'Marye! themselves,' sayd the fellow, 'They knew the way well ynoughe.' He taryed still tyll it was nyght. At nyghte he said, 'A vengeaunce on them al! I dyd feare to see that my cheeses dyd runne so faste, that they runne beyond the market. I am sure that they be almoste now at Yorke.' He hyred a horse to ryde after to Yorke to seeke hys cheeses wheare they were not. But to thys daye, no man coulde tell hym of hys cheeses.

A Demonic Grasshopper

On a tyme theare was one of Gotam mowynge in the meads, and found a great gras-hopper. He dyd caste downe hys sythe and dyd runne home to his neighbours and sayde that there was a devill in the fyelde that hopped in the grasse. Then there was everye man readye wythe clubbes and staves, wythe holbardes [halberds] and other weapons, to go to kill the grasshopper. Whan they did come to the place where that the Grashopper shoulde bee, sayde the one to the other, 'Lette everye man crosse hymselfe from this devill, for we wyll not meddle wyth hym.' And so they returned home againe and sayde, 'Wee weare well bleste thys daye that we went no further.' 'A! cowardes!' sayd he that had the sythe in the mead, 'Helpe me to fetch my sithe.' 'No,' saide they, 'It is good to sleap in a whole skynne. Better it is to leese [lose] thy sithe, than to mar all.'

German Merry Tales Translated

viii) How that Howleglas would fly from the Town House of Maybrough[17]

After that, came Howleglass to Maybrough where he did many marvellous things that his name was there well known. Then bade the principal of the town that he should do something that was never seen before. Then said he that he would go to the highest of the Council House and fly from it. And anon that was known through all the town that Howleglass would fly from the top of the Council House in such that all the town was there assembled and gathered in the market place to see him. Upon the top of the House stood Howleglass with his hands waving as though he would have flown. Whereat he laughed and said to the people, 'I thought there had been no more fools than myself. But I see well that here is a whole town full. For had ye altogether said that ye would have flown, yet I would not have believed you. And now ye believe one afore that saith he will fly, which thing is impossible, for I have no wings, and no man can fly without wings.' And then went he his way from the top of the Council House, and left the folk there standing. And then departed the folk from thence, some blaming him and some laughing, saying, 'He is a shrewd fool, for he telleth us the truth.'

ix) The Parson and the Bishop's Lady Paramour[18]

The parson of Kalenborowe perceyvynge that the bysshope wolde have hym with hym to every church-holowynge [hallowing], he sought a wile to byde at home and kepe howse with his servant or wenche, for it was moste his ease. And incontinent he went to the byssopes soverayne lady and prayed her that she wolde help hym that he might byde at

---

17   This anti-hero is also known as Till Eulenspiegel, a German folk hero or anti-hero. In *A Hundred Merry Tales* (ed. Zall), the first story is on p. 167.

18   In Gray's *Later Medieval English Literature*, see pp. 223–4, where this story is described (the English version is probably from a Dutch prose version of a Low German text; references on p. 228).

home and nat go to no churche-halowynge, 'And I wyll gyve you a gode rewarde'. She answered agayne and sayd, 'That is nat in my power.' The parson sayd, 'Yes,' and sayd, 'Holde here a purse with money for your labour, for I knowe well the bysshope wyll lay with you tonight; thus I pray you to shewe me the hour of his commyng that I may lay under the bed.' She answered and saide, 'Than come at seven of the clocke, for eight of the clocke is his houre.' And in the meane season she prepared the chamber lyke an erthely paradyse and sett rownde about the wallis of it candellis burnynge bright against the bisshopes commyng, and at the houre assigned the parson came and crepte under the bedde in her chamber. Whan the bisshope com, he merveyled sore to se this sight and asked her what it ment. 'My lorde,' she saide, 'this is for the honoure of you, for this nyght I hope ye wyll halowe my lytell chapel standing benethe my navyll in Venus valaye and that by and by, or ellys from hens forth I wyll shewe you no point of love whilst I leve.'

The bysshope went to bedde with his soverayn lady and he fulfilled all her desire and began to holowe her chapel to the best of his power. The parson laynge under the bedde herd this right well and began fore to singe with a hye voice lyke as they do at every church-holowynge in this maner, '*Terribilis est locus iste*',[19] wherof the bishop marvayled and was abashed and blessed hym with the signe of the holy crosse, and wenynge to hym that the devyll had bene in the chamber, and wolde have conjured hym. Than spake the parson laynge under the bedde with grete haste, saynge thus (and with that he crepte out), 'Reverende fader, I fere so sore to breke your commaundement that I had lever crepe on hande and fote to fulfyll your mynde and wyll than to be absent at any of all your churche-holowinges, and for that cause I wolde be at this chapel also.' The bysshope sayde, 'I had nat called the to be at the holownge herof! I trowe the devyll brought the hether! Get the hens out of my sight and come nomore to me!' 'My lorde, I thanke you and also your lady paramours.' Thus wente the preste on his way and thanked God that he was so rydde from the bysshope, and so come home and kepte house with his fayr wenche as he was wont to do, the whiche was glad of his commynge home, for she had great disease of suche thynges as he was wonte to helpe her of. And some that envied the preste shewed the

---

19   This is a dreadful place!

bysshop that he had suche a fayre wenche. And because he had layde under the bysshops bedde and played hym that false touche, the bisshope sent a commission ento hym, that upon payne of curssinge he shold put awaye frome hym his yonge lusty wenche, and to kepe his house that he shold take an olde woman of xl yere of age, or ellys he sholde be put in pryson. The parson, hering this, made a gret mournynge complaint to his wenche and said, 'Now must I wasshe and plasshe, wringe and singe and do al my besines myself', wherof she gave hym gode comforte and said, 'The whele of fortune shall turne ones againe', and so departed for a seson. And than he toke gode hert a grece, and said to himself, 'No force, yet shall I begyle hym, for I wyll kepe ii wenches of xx yere of age, and twise xx maketh xl! Holde thyne owne, parson!'

Early Sixteenth-Century Jests

x) Wedded Men at the Gates of Heaven[20]

A certain wedded man there was, which when he was dead came to heaven-gates to saint Peter, and said he came to claim his heritage which he had deserved. Saint Peter asked him what he was, and he said, 'A wedded man.' Anon Saint Peter opened the gate and bade him come in, and sayd he was worthy to have his heritage because he had had much trouble, and was worthy to have a crown of glory. Anon after that there came another man that claimed heaven, and said to Saint Peter that he had had two wives; to whom Saint Peter answered and said, 'Come in, for thou art worthy to have a double crown of glory, for thou hast had double trouble.' At the last there came a third claiming heaven, and said to Saint Peter that he had had three wives and desired to come in. 'What!' quod Saint Peter, 'Thou hast been once in trouble and thereof delivered, and then willingly wouldst be troubled again, and yet again therof delivered; and for all that couldst not beware the third time, but entered'st willingly in trouble again! Therefore go thy way to hell, for thou shalt never come in heaven, for thou art not worthy.'

This tale is a warning to them that have been twice in peril to beware how they come therein the third time.

---

20   In *A Hundred Merry Tales* (ed. Zall), pp. 85–6.

xi) No Welshmen in Heaven[21]

I find written among old jests how God made Saint Peter porter of heaven, and that God of his goodness, soon after his Passion, suffered many men to come to the kingdom of heaven with small deserving; at which time there was in heaven a great company of Welshmen which with their cracking [bragging] and babbling troubled all the others. Wherefore God said to Saint Peter that he was weary of them and that he would fain have them out of heaven. To whom Saint Peter said, 'Good Lord, I warrant you, that shall be done.' Wherefore Saint Peter went out of heaven-gates and cried with a loud voice, 'Caws pob!' that is as much as to say 'roasted cheese' — which thing the Welshmen hearing, ran out of heaven a great pace. And when Saint Peter saw them all out, he suddenly went into heaven and locked the door, and so sparred all the Welshmen out.

By this ye may see that it is no wisdom for a man to love or to set his mind too much upon any delicate or worldly pleasure whereby he shall lose the celestial and eternal joy.

---

21 *Ibid.* (p. 132), though judging by its spelling of (for example) 'Cause Bob!' Gray probably used a different edition.

Chapter 6

Animal Tales

There is a long and extensive medieval tradition of animal tale, which has its roots in antiquity, and also looks forward to the modern world. It is a tradition in which learned, popular, and folk elements are intertwined. In it the animals have a variety of functions: they offer moral examples, practical instruction, and entertainment. The idea that man can learn from the animals is a venerable one; a very early English example is Bede's story of the sparrow, offered as advice to a Northumbrian king: 'It seems to me that the life of man on earth is like the swift flight of a single sparrow through the banqueting hall …'.[1] Later in the Middle Ages we find disapproving clerics recording popular superstitions concerning the possibility of learning the future from the behaviour of birds, as well as evidence in sophisticated writers like Chaucer, a knowledge that sometimes seems to come from observation. As in modern traditional societies, animals were not only 'good to eat' but also 'good to think'.

Again, as in modern traditional societies, people were very close to animals. This is evident from many references in the works of literary authors. Chaucer remarks that the cock is the orloge [clock] of small villages (*Parliament of Fowls*, v. 350), and in the *House of Fame* (v. 1516) observes that there are as many writers of old tales 'as ben on trees rokes nestes'. He gives names to common animals in and around the house: a sheep called Malle (Molly); dogs called Colle, Talbot, and

---

1   See Bede, *Ecclesiastical History of the English People*, trans. Sherley-Price, in Ch. 13 (pp. 129–30).

    https://doi.org/10.11647/OBP.0170.06

Gerland; horses Brok and Scot. He uses proverbial and colloquial locutions, 'stynken as a goot', etc, and refers to the behaviour of household animals: the hole 'there as the cat was wont to crepe' in the Miller's Tale (another household cat is swept from its resting-place by a visiting friar, III. 1775). There is even an allusion to 'pets' or proto-pets: the lap dogs that the Prioress fed (vv. 146–9). In Langland we find an allusion to a less attractive household creature, in the description of Covytise's tattered tabard (V 188 ff.), 'al totorne ... and ful of lys crepynge ... But if that [unless] a lous couthe have lopen [jumped] the bette, She sholde nought have walked on that welche [Welsh flannel], so it was thredbare ...'.[2] Household animals like the cat appear in carved misericords, and there is a ring with a figure of a cat devouring a mouse, with the legend 'gret wel Gibbe oure cat'. This closeness could lead to knowledge and to some acute observation, reflected in some manuscript illustrations, although usually mingled with popular lore (as in proverbs, see below). Similarly, some 'scientific' material and observation has become embedded in traditional lore, as for instance in the guileful and treacherous nature of the fox, so firmly established that it can be symbolic; Criseyde can address Pandarus (Tr. 3, v. 1565) as 'fox that ye ben'.

Medieval English proverbial lore is full of references to animals. Whiting's collection of proverbs contains references to well over a hundred animals, birds, fish, and insects; some are exotic (chameleon, crocodile) but the majority are more local and familiar.[3] And they include one or two which would have been more prominent in medieval town life than in modern, notably bears and apes. One proverb [Whiting B 102] alludes to bear-baiting, another [B 101] to the differing thoughts of the bear and its leader, which Chaucer uses in Tr. 4, vv. 1453–4: 'for thus men seyth, "That on thenketh the bere, But al another thenketh his leder." ' Elsewhere, bears are traditionally black, fierce, and 'boistous'; and rough and slow. Captive apes were obviously a source of interest

---

2   Langland, Piers Plowman, ed. Schmidt, p. 48, and see editor's footnote for the extra line cited.
3   There is no online version of Whiting, but it is widely available in libraries and very easy to use. Therefore I am not listing every single proverb or proverb-like sentence that Gray cites, and I have simplified the references; he often gives not only the Whiting number but also the source used by Whiting.

and entertainment. Among the characteristics alluded to are their imitative behaviour ('men sein commonly that the ape doth as he other seeth' [Whiting A 136]), their grimacing and their foolishness. Ape seems sometimes almost synonymous with 'fool'; see Chaucer's 'he made the person and the peple his apes' (*Tales*, I, v. 706). People may be 'drunken as an ape' or 'ape-drunk'.

The mixture of 'scientific' and 'popular' lore is an important element in the background of the very rich medieval literary tradition of animal tales, in which, in Britain, the achievements of Chaucer and Henryson are pre-eminent. Here we are in a wonderful fictional time when, as Chaucer says, 'bestes and brides koude speke and synge' (*Tales*, VII. v. 2881). Here beasts and birds engage in formal debate on matters significant to humans, or appear as actors in moral tales for their instruction and entertainment. The animal fable is a very ancient literary form, traceable back to the mysterious figure of Aesop and beyond, to the 'wisdom literature' of the ancient near East and the fables of the Old Testament. Animal fables, both Aesopic and non-Aesopic, lived on in the Middle Ages in versions in Latin and in the vernaculars. The 'moralities' which they engender are sometimes religious and high-minded, but not always. Sometimes the 'morality' seems rather to be advice on how to survive in a hostile world; and the fable, while not quite a 'slave' fable, often seems to be an expression of the views and attitudes of the lower classes of society. Here, cleverness, ingenuity, and cunning seem to be prized. An excellent (and extreme) example is to be found in the nefarious activities of Reynard the Fox, stories which moved through literary sources, but almost certainly against a background of popular storytelling, into a kind of beast epic, the French *Roman de Renart*. Reynard the Fox comes from a widespread folk interest in small animals who can by cleverness and cunning defeat the stronger and larger, but rather stupid, creatures; but he seems to have developed into a rather sinister and amoral comic Trickster figure, similar to Coyote in some North American Indian mythologies.

'The overlapping of the human and animal worlds provides a powerful stimulus for the imagination' says D. D. R. Owen in the Introduction to his translation of the *Roman de Renart*. It certainly does — and the creators of animal tales seem to have discovered (before literary theory) the 'elasticity of mind' and the capacity to find 'equivalences in the most disparate phenomena, and for substituting one for another which lies at the mysterious heart of metaphor'.[4]

While it is clear that both popular and learned elements coexist in the developed tradition of the written medieval animal story, we must not forget that at the same time animal tales were being told by oral story tellers. For example, Thomas More, speaking as Anthony in the *Dialogue of Comfort against Tribulation*, recalls a 'Mother Maud' who used to tell the children stories as she sat by the fire. One of her 'fond childish tales' was the story of how 'the Ass and the Wolf came on a time to confession to the Fox'.[5] And Wyatt's 'mothers maydes sang a song of the field mouse'.[6] There was probably a large body of such tales, which have vanished, almost without trace, but if we have lost the exact words that Mother Maud and other mothers' maids used in telling their tales, we sometimes feel close to the presence of an oral teller in the fables in exemplary stories. A realisation of this has led me, rather boldly, not to illustrate the animal tale in the sophisticated form given to it by Chaucer or Henryson, but in Caxton's version, where in spite of the apparent 'literary' background of his Aesop and Renard (the first translated from Macho's version of Steinhowel, the second from a Dutch version), and in spite of his own occasional verbosity, there is a striking simplicity of narrative.

A. Man and Animal

Animals in histories, Cats and adages

Spectacular scenes involving animals are occasionally recorded in chronicles, sometimes associated with other 'portents'. The *Brut* chronicle records (in the thirteenth century) 'there fill so mich rayne in hay-tyme yhat it wasted and distroyed bothe corn and hey; and ther was suche a debate and fighting of sparows, by divers places in thes dayes, that men founden unnumerable multitudes of hem ded in feldes as they

---

4   Cited in Gray, *Robert Henryson*, p. 57 in the chapter 'Beasts and Wisdom (i)'.
5   See 'Tales of Mother Maud', in *A Thomas More Source Book*, eds Wegemer and Smith.
6   Wyatt, Of the Mean and Sure Estate, in *Poetical Works*, ed. Clarke. The poem is available online (see Bibliography, below).

wenten …'.[7] There was also a very severe pestilence, and a sickness called 'the pockes'. A little later eagles fought 'oppon the sonde of the Scottyssh see, that meny a man hyt sye the iii dayes togedir there were ii egles, of the which the tone come out of the southe. And the tother out of the north, and cruelly and strongly they foughten togider and warstled togider; and the suth egle ferst overcome the northe egle, and al torent and tare hym with his bille and his clowes, that he shold not reste ne take no brethe; and aftir, the suth egle flye home to his owne costs'. This was followed by a cosmic disturbance.

The Middle Ages had developed quite an impressive learned tradition of natural history, but it is very difficult to know how far this impinged upon popular lore. We give two possible examples: a passage on the fox from the Middle English *Physiologus*, and one on the cat from Trevisa's fourteenth-century translation of the encyclopedia of Bartholomew the Englishman.

i) The Fox[8]

A wilde der° is that is ful of fele° wiles —	*creature*	*many*
Fox is hire to name for hire qwethsipe.°	*her*	*wickedness*
Husebondes° hire haten for hire harmdedes:°	*householders*	*harmful deeds*
The coc and te capon she feccheth° ofte in the tun,°	*steals*	*yard*
And te gander and te gos, bi the necke and bi the nos.°		*beak*
Haleth is° to hire hole — forthi° man hire hatieth,	*drags them*	*therefore*
Hatien and hulen° bothe men and fules.°	*drive off with shouts*	*birds*
Listneth nu° a wunder that tis der doth for hunger —		*hear now*
Goth o felde to a furgh° and falleth tharinne,		*furrow*
In eried° lond er in erth-chine,° for to bilirten° fuyeles.	*ploughed*	*crack* *deceive*
Ne stereth she noght of the stede a god stund deies°	*good while in the day*	

---

7   In Brie ed, vol. 2 p. 316. The story continues (with the eagles) on p. 319.
8   The *Physiologus* is in *Selections from Early Middle English*, ed. Hall (text in vol. 1, notes in vol. 2). See also *The Middle English Physiologus*, ed. Wirtjes, p. 11 (*Natura wulpis*). There is only one manuscript, dated around 1300; the Early Middle English is not easy to read (commentary and glossary may be consulted).

Oc dareth°, so she ded were, ne dragheth she non onde.°	*but lies*	*nor draws breath*
The raven is swathe° redi, weneth that she rotieth,°	*very*	*is rotting*
And other fules hire fallen bi° for to winnen fode.°	*alight beside her*	*get food*
Derflike° withuten dred° he wenen that she ded beth,	*boldly*	*fear*
He wullen° on this foxes fel° and she it wel feleth;°	*wish (to come) skin*	*feels*
Lightlike she lepeth up and letteth hem sone,°	*quickly stops them*	
Yelt hem here billing rathe° with illing,°	*repays their pecking quickly injury*	
Tetoggeth° and tetireth° hem mid hire teth sarpe,	*tears apart*	*tears in pieces*
Fret° hire fulle and goth than ther° she wille.	*devours*	*where*

[It is followed by its *Significacio*: it is the devil, and the wicked man.]

ii) The Cat[9]

The catte … is a beste of uncerteyn here and colour. For som catte is whyte, som reed, and som blak, and som scowed and splenked [spotted and dappled] in the feet and the face and in the eeren, and is most yliche to the lepard. And hath a gret mouth and sawe teeth and scharpe, and longe tonge and pliaunt, thynne, and sotile. And lapeth therwith whanne he drynketh, as othere bestes doon that haven the nether lippe schorter than the over, for bycause of unevenesse of lippes suche bestes souken nought in drynkynge but lapeth and likketh, as Aristotil seith and Plinius also. And he is a ful leccherous beste in youthe, swyfte, plyaunt, and mery. And lepeth and reseth [pounces] on alle thing that is tofore him and is yladde by a strawe and pleyeth therwith. And is a wel hevy beste in eelde [old age] and ful slepy. And lith sliliche [lies slyly] in awayte for mys and is ware where they ben more by smelle than by sight. And hunteth and reseth on hem in privey place. And whanne he taketh a mous he pleyeth therwith and eteth him after the pleye. And is as it were wylde and goth aboute in tyme of generacioun. Among cattes in tyme of love is hard fightynge for wyves, and oon craccheth [scratches] and rendeth the other grevousliche with bytyng

---

9   In *Batman uppon Bartholome his booke* [1582], Bk. 18, Ch. 76, *De Murilego*.

and with clawes. And he maketh a reweliche noyse and horrible whan oon profreth to fighte with another. And is a cruel beste whanne he is wilde and wonyeth in wodes and hunteth thanne smale wilde bestes, as conynges [rabbits] and hares. And falleth on his owne feet whanne he falleth out of highe place and is unnethe [scarcely] yhurte whanne he is ythrowe doun of an high place. His drytte [droppings] stynketh ful foule and therefore he hydeeth it under erthe and gadereth thereupon coverynge with feet and clawes. And whanne he hath a fayre skynne he is as it were prowde therof and goth faste aboute; and whanne his skynne is ybrende [burnt] he abydeth at home. And is ofte for his fayre skynne ytake of the skynnere and yslayne and yhulde [skinned].

iii) Animals in Adages

We give a very small selection from a large mass of material (quotations and references are from Whiting).[10] The long and complicated background to medieval animal lore produced traditional similitudes and common proverbial comparisons (a good many of which have survived), and a great range of traditional animal attributes and behaviour, and of human attitudes to them. Some animals seem to have become especially significant or almost symbolic: the lamb is gentle, chaste and humble, meek and mild (as is the dove, which has no gall).[11] At the other extreme are hostile, dangerous or wicked animals like the serpent. There are foolish animals, like the ass (variously described as dull, ignorant, rude, slow), and animals which are traditionally mad or crazed, like the March hare. Some are unpleasant, like the stinking brock (badger), the 'rammish' goat, or the foul pig wallowing in its sty. Occasionally we can glimpse the hierarchies of the animal world: the cowardly kite may not fly with the royal eagle, whose eye pierces the sun. Some creatures are more ambiguous. In animal tales and fables the fox is the supreme example of wiliness and cunning, but one sometimes senses a barely-hidden admiration for its ingenuity. Can we perhaps catch a hint of this even in the fox proverbs, with their apparently 'objective' accounts of its behaviour: 'the fox feigns dead

---

10 Keywords in Whiting can easily be found, for example C for Cat.
11 See below in chapter 8, our footnote to Henryson on medicine identifies a reference to this belief.

till the birds come to his tongue', 'when the fox preaches keep well the geese'? The cat, in its nature an even more ambiguous creature, associated with the house but also with the world outside it, is found in many adages, but is not confined to them: 'a cat falls on its feet', 'the cat would eat fish but would not wet its feet', 'see like a cat in the night', 'who shall find a cat true in keeping milk?', and so on. We have already met two Chaucerian cats. Of a third (an example of its often noticed passionate hunting of its 'contrary' the mouse) it is said that even if given milk and exquisite food, 'Lat hym seen a mous go by the wal, Anon he weyveth [refuses] milk and flesh and al ... Swich appetite hath he to ete a mous' (*Tales*, IX. 176–80). But for all its ambiguity, the cat could have a moral function.

The most obvious result of this proverbial animal lore was the development of a large number of proverbial similitudes of an almost formulaic kind: 'busy as a bee', black as any crow / raven', 'swift as the hind / doe / falcon / swallow', 'proud as a peacock', grey as a goose', etc., or expressions of the worthlessness of something: 'not worth a bee / fly / flea / gnat / haddock / plucked hen', and so on. Some seem clearly observed: 'as tattered [shaggy] as a foal' or 'be cocksure' [C 358], even if sometimes unexpected: 'yt ys as clen as a byrdis ars'. And sometimes the proverbs give a miniature picture of animal behaviour ready-made for a poet or a moralist: 'a cony covers her head and weens all is well' [C 416], 'the cuckoo sings only of himself' [C 601], 'where asses get lordships there is seldom good rule' [A 230], 'it is a foul bird that fouls its own nest' [B 306], 'the crow thinks her own young are white' [C 568].

iiia) Animal Proverbs

And summe other elder [children] whanne thei desiren and asken to be leid in bed to slepe, thei seie, 'lete the cat wynke,' or sum othere inpertynent resound [C 96]

Wele wotith [knows] the cat whos berde she likkith [C 108]

Grete fyssches are takyn in the net and slayn, smale fyssches scapen through the net into the watyr, and liven [F231; and the very common 'the great fishes eat the small', F 232]

Now find I weill this proverb trew ... 'Ay rinnis the foxe als lang as he fute hais' [F 592]

Gaillard he was as goldfinch in the shawe [G 319, Chaucer][12]

As wytles as a wylde goos [G 377]

Masid [crazed] as a Marche hare [H 113, H 110, H 116]

A man maie well bring a horse to the water, but he can not make him drinke without he will [H 541]

It is nought good a slepyng hound to wake [H 569, Chaucer][13]

Thai al fled from hym as schep from the wolfe [S 215]

One swallow maketh not somer [S 924]

He hath ... as many braynes as a wodcok [W 565]

B. Fables, and Stories of Reynard

Aesopic fables produced large and interesting literary tradition in the Middle Ages in both Latin and the vernacular. Caxton's version (1483–4) is based on the French translation by Macho of Steinhowel's extensive collection. Beside the various literary versions there was almost certainly a body of oral versions, known to the likes of 'Mother Maud'. Caxton follows Macho fairly closely. Sometimes he tries to heighten his style, but many of his fables are simple and unsophisticated in form. It is in these, and in the many retellings of fables in moral tales, that we come probably as close as we can to the style of the oral taletellers. We begin with an Anglo-Norman example in Bozon (who quotes a couple of English proverbs), followed by examples from Caxton, and finally (nos xiii ff.), by examples in moral tales.

iv) Bozon: the Goshawk and the Owl[14]

The owl asked the goshawk to bring up her son; the other agreed, and said that she should bring him and put him with her own nestlings. As soon as the little bird arrived among the others, the hawk told him to

---

12 *Tales*, I. 4367, Perkyn 'the reveller' at the start of the Cook's Tale.

13 *Tr.* 3. 764.

14 In the *Contes Moralisés*, no. 17 (le Huan et le Ostur): *Quod ignobiles, licet educati, gestus habent ignobiles.* This means you can educate them as much as you like but you won't change their nature.

behave like her young and learn their ways. When the goshawk flew off to seek their food, she returned to find her nest disgustingly soiled. 'What is this,' she said, 'which I find contrary to good upbringing? Who has done this?' 'Your nursling,' said her children. 'Indeed!' said she, 'it is true what is said in English: "Stroke oule [owl] and schrape [scratch] oule, and evere is oule oule." '

So it is with many people who are born of low lineage. Although they have risen high, often instructed and informed in religion or in the ways of the world or in noble positions, they always revert to their estate or to the ways to which they were born. For this reason it is said in English: 'trendle the appel never so fer [no matter how far the apple rolls], he conyes [makes known] fro what tre he cam.'[15]

Examples from Caxton[16]

v) The Rat and the Frog

Now it be so that as the rat wente in pylgremage he came by a river, and demaunded helpe of a frogge for to passe and goo over the water. And thenne the frogge bound the rats foote to her foote, and thus swymed unto the myddes over the river. And as they were there the frogge stood stylle, to th'ende that the rat shold be drowned. And in the meane whyle came a kite upon them, and bothe bare them with hym. This fable made Esope for a symylytude whiche is prouffitable to many folks, for he that thynketh evylle ageynst good, the evylle whiche he thynketh shall ones [one day] falle upon hymself.

vi) The Eagle and the Fox

How the puyssaunt and myghty must doubte the feble Esope reherceth to us suche a fable. Ther was an egle whiche came theras yong foxes were, and took awey one of them and gaf hit to his yonge egles to fede them with. The fox wente after hym and praid hym to restore and

---

15   Whiting A 169.
16   In Caxton's *Fables*. The first section is the 'Fable Collection Romulus': Rat and Frog
       (1.3), Eagle and Fox (1.13), Lion and Rat (1.18). Finally, the Cat and the Rat is in a
       later section, 'Fables of Esope not found in the books of Romulus', no. 8.

gyve hym ageyne his yong foxe. And the egle sayd that he wold not, for he was over hym lord and maister. And thenne the foxe fulle of shrewdness and of malice beganne to put togider grete habondaunce of strawe round aboute the tree whereupon the egle and his yonge were in theyr nest, and kyndeled it with fyre. And whan the smoke and the flambe began to ryse upward, the egle ferdfulle and doubting the dethe of her lytylle egles restored ageyne the yonge foxe to his moder. This fable sheweth us how the mighty men oughte not to lette [harm] in ony thynge the smale folke, for the lytyll ryght ofte may lette and trouble the grete.

vii) The Lion and the Rat

The mighty and puyssaunt must pardonne and forgyve to the lytyll and feble, and ought to kepe hym fro al evylle, for oftyme the lytyll may wel gyve ayde and help to the grete — wherof Esope reherceth to us suche a fable of a lyon whiche slepte in a forest and the rats disported and playd aboute hym. It happed that the rat wente upon the lyon, wherfore the lyon awoke, and within his clawes or ongles he tooke the rat. And whanne the rat saw hym thus taken and hold sayd thus to the lyon, 'My lord, pardonne me, for of my deth nought ye shalle wynne, for I supposed not to have done to yow ony harme ne displaysyre.' Thenne thought the lyon in himself that no worship ne glorye it were to put it to dethe, wherfor he graunted his pardone and lete hym goo within a lytell whyle. After this it happed so that the same lyon was take at a grete trappe. And as he sawe hym thus caught and taken, he beganne to crye and make sorowe. And thenne whan the rat herd hym crye he approached hym and demaunded of hym wherefore he cryed. And the lyon ansuerd to hym, 'Seest thow not how I am take and bound with this gynne?' Thenne sayd the ratte to hym, 'My lorde, I wylle not be unkynde, but ever I shal remembre the grace whiche thou hast done to me, and yf I can I shall now helpe the.' The ratte beganne thenne to byte the lace or cord, and so long he knawed it that the lace brake, and thus the lyon escaped. Therfore this fable techeth us how that a man myghty and puyssaunt ought not to dispraise the lytyll, for somtyme he that can nobody hurte ne lette [hinder] may at a nede gyve help and ayde to the grete.

viii) The Cat and the Rat

He which is wyse, and hath ones hath ben begyled, ought not to truste more hym that hath begyled hym, as reherceth this fable of a catte whiche wente into a hows where as many rats were, the whiche he dyd ete one after other. And whanne the rats perceyved the grete fyersnes and crudelyte of the catte, held a counceylle togyder where as they determined of one comyn wylle that they shold no more hold them ne come nor goo on the lowe floore. Wherfore one of them moost auncyent proffered and sayd to al the other suche words, 'My bretheren and my frendes, ye knowe wel that we have a grete enemye, whiche is a grete persecutour over us alle, to whom we may not resyste, wherfore of nede we must hold our self upon the hyghe balkes [beams] to th'ende that he may not take us.' Of the whiche proposycion or wordes the other rats were wel content and apayd, and bylevyd this counceylle. And whanne the kat knewe the counceylle of the rats, he hynge hymself by his two feet behind at a pynne of yron whiche was styked at a balke, feynynge hymself to be dede. And whanne one of the rats lokynge dounward sawe the katte, beganne to lawhe and sayd to the cat, 'O my frend, yf I supposed that thow were dede, I shold goo doune, but wel I knowe the so fals and pervers that thow mayst wel have hanged thyself, faynynge to be dede — wherfore I shall not go doune.' And therfore he that hath ben ones begyled by somme other ought to kepe hym wel fro the same.

Fox Tales

ix) Tybert the Cat is tempted by Reynard[17]

... 'O dere Reyner, lede me thyder for alle that I may doo for yow!' 'Ye, Tybert, saye ye me truth? Love ye wel myes?' 'Yf I love hem wel?' said the catte, 'I love myes better than ony thyng that men gyve me! Knowe ye not that myes savoure better than venison — ye, than flawnes or pasteyes? Wil ye wel doo, so lede me theder where the myes ben, and thenne shal ye wynne my love, ye, al had ye slayn my fader, moder, and alle my kun.' Reynart sayd, 'Ye moke and jape therwith!' The catte saide, 'So helpe me God, I doo not!' 'Tybert,' said the fox, 'wiste Y that verily, I wolde yet this nyght make that ye shuld be ful of myes.' 'Reynart!' quod he, 'Ful? That were many.' 'Tyberte, ye jape!' 'Reynart,' quod

---

17   Caxton, *The History of Reynard the Fox*, ed. Blake, p. 21.

he, 'in trouth I doo not. Yf I hadde a fat mows, I wold not gyve it for a golden noble.' 'Late us goo thenne, Tybert,' quod the foxe, 'I wyl brynge yow to the place er I goo fro you' …

[Unsurprisingly, disaster ensues, much to the gleeful delight of Reynard]

x) The Fox and the Wolf in the Well[18]

An example of a Reynard narrative from the Early Middle English: *The Vox and the Wolf*

A hungry fox finds a building with hens in it, but is driven off by the cock. He sees a pit filled with water, with two buckets, one going up, the other down. Jumping into one he finds himself at the bottom, to his great distress …

… The fox wep and reuliche bigan.°	*lamented piteously*
Ther com a wolf gon,° after than,	*came walking*
Out of the depe wode blive,°	*quickly*
For he wes afingret swathe.°	*really starving*
Nothing he ne founde, in al the nighte,	
Wermide° his honger aquenche° mightte.	*by which* *quench*
He com to the putte,° thene fox iherde;°	*pit* *heard*
He him kneu wel bi his rerde.°	*voice*
For hit was his neighebore	
And his gossip,° of children bore.	*friend*
Adoun bi the putte he sat;	
Quod the wulf, 'Wat may ben that°	*what can that be?*
That ich in the putte ihere?°	*hear*
Ertou Cristine other mi fere?°	*are you a Christian or my friend*
Say me soth° — ne gabbe° thou me nout,	*truly* *deceive*
Wo haveth the in the putte ibrout?'°	*brought you*
The fox hine ikneu wel for his kun,°	*kinsman*
And tho eroust° com wiit° to him;	*then first* *idea*
For he thoute mid sommne ginne,°	*trick*

---

18   This is printed in *Early Middle English Verse and Prose* (Bennett and Smithers, pp. 70–5); if Gray used this version, he normalized the spelling.

Himself oupbringe,° thene wolf therinne.°　　*bring up*　　*put in it*
Quod the fox, 'Wo° is nou there?　　*who*
Ich wene° hit is Sigrim that ich here.'　　*think*
'That is soth,' the wolf sede.
'Ac wat° art thou, so God the rede?'°　　*but what*　　*help*
'A!' quod the fox, 'Iche wille the telle —
On alpi word° ich lie nelle.　　*one single word*
Ich am Reneuard,° thi friend;　　*Reynard*
And yif ich thine come° hevede iwend,°　　*coming*　　*had expected*
Ich hedde so ibede° for the　　*would have prayed*
That thou sholdest comen to me.'
'Mid° the?' quod the wolf, 'warto?'°　　*with*　　*wherefore*
Wat shulde ich ine the putte do?'
Quod the fox, 'Thou art ounwis!°　　*unwise*
Her is the blisse of Paradiis —
Her ich mai evere wel fare,
Withouten pine, withouten kare.
Her is mete, here is drinke;
Her is blisse withouten swinke.°　　*toil*
Her nis hounger nevermo,
Ne non other kunnes° wo —　　*of any other kind*
Of alle gode her is inou!'°　　*sufficient*
Mid° thilke words the wolf lou.°　　*at*　　*laughed*
'Art thou ded, so God the rede.
Other° of the worlde?'° the wolf sede.　　*or*　　*alive*
Quod the wolf, 'Wenne storve thou?°　　*when did you die?*
And wat dest thou° there nou?　　*are you doing?*
Ne beth nout° yet thre daies ago　　*it is not*
That thou, and thi wif also,
And thine children, smale and grete,
Alle togedere mid me ete!'
'That is soth,'° quod the fox,　　*true*
Gode thonk° nou hit is thus　　*thanks be to God*
That I am to Criste wend!°　　*gone*
Not hit° non of mine frend;　　*knows it not*

I nolde,° for al the worldes gode,	would not
Ben ine the worlde, ther° ich hem fond.°	where met them
Wat shuld ich ine the worlde go	
Ther nis bote kare and wo,	
And livie in fulthe° and in sunne?°	filth sin
Ac her beth° joies fele cunne° —	are of many kinds
Her beth bothe shep and get.'°	goats
The wolf haveth hounger swithe gret,°	very great
For he nedde yare i-ete;	
And tho he herde speken of mete,	
He wolde bletheliche° ben thare.	gladly
'A!' quod the wolf, 'gode ifere,°	good friend
Moni gode mel° thou havest me binome°	meal deprived
Let me adoun to the kome,	
And al ich wole the foryeve.'°	forgive
'Ye!' quod the fox, 'Were thou ishrive,°	shriven
And sunnen° hevedest° al forsake,	sins had you
And to klene° lif itake,°	pure committed yourself
Ich wolde so bidde° for the	pray
That thou sholdest comen to me.'	
'To wom° shuld ich,' the wolf seide,	whom
Be iknowe° of mine misdeed?	be confessed
Ther nis nothing alive	
That me kouthe° her nou shrive.	could
Thou havest ben ofte min ifere —	
Woltu nou mi shrift ihere,°	hear
And al mi liif I shal the telle?'	
'Nay!' quod the fox, 'I nelle.'°	will not
'Neltou?' quod the wolf, 'thin ore!°	thy mercy!
Ich am afingret° swathe sore —	hungry
Ich wot, tonight iche worthe° ded.	I shall be
Bote° thou do me somne reed.°	unless help
For Cristes love, be mi prest!'	
The wolf bey° adoun his brest	bent
And gon to siken° harde and stronge.	sighed

'Woltou', quod the fox, 'shrift ounderfonge?°   receive
Tel thi sunnen,° on and on,°   sins   one by one
That° ther bileve° never on.'   so that   remains
'Sone,'° quad the wolf, 'wel ifaie!°   at once   gladly
Ich habbe ben qued° al mi lif-daie;   wicked
Ich habbe widewene kors° —   widows' curse
Therfore ich fare the wors.
A thousent shep ich habbe abiten°   slaughtered
And mo, yef hy° weren written;°   they   written down
Ac me ofthinketh sore,°   I regret it bitterly
Maister, shal I tellen more?'
'Ye!' quod the fox, 'al thou most sugge,°   tell
Other elleswer° thou most abugge.'°   or elsewhere   pay for it
'Gossip!' quod the wolf, 'foryef hit me,
Ich habbe ofte seid qued bi the.°   evil things about you
Men seide that thou on thine live
Misferdest° mid mine wive.   misbehaved
Ich the aperseivede one stounde,°   saw you once
And in bedde togedere you founde:
Ich wes ofte you ful ney°   near
And in bedde togedere you sey.°   saw
Ich wende, also other doth,°   thought as others do
That° ich iseie° were soth,°   what   saw   true
And therefore thou were me loth° —   hateful
Gode gossip, ne be thou nout wroth!'
'Wolf!' quad the fox him tho,
'Al that ihou havest herbifore° ido,°   before   done
In thout, in speche, and in dede,
In euch otheres kunnes quede,°   every other kind of wickedness
Ich the foryeve° at thisse nede.'°   forgive   necessity
'Crist the foryelde!'° the wolf seide,   repay
'Nou° ich am in clene live,   now that
Ne recche° ich of childe ne of wive!   care
Ac sei me wat I shal do
And hou ich mai comen the to.'

Tho quod the fox, 'Ich wille the lere.º   *instruct*

Isiist º thou a boket hongi ther?   *seest thou*

Ther is a bruche º of hevene blisse!   *opening*

Lep therinne, mid iwisse,º   *indeed*

And thou shalt comen to me sone.'

Quod the wolf, 'That is light º to done!'   *easy*

He lep in — and way sumdel º —   *weighed a certain amount*

(That weste º the fox ful wel)   *knew*

The wolf gon sinke, the fox arise —

Tho gon the wolf sore agrise!º   *was afraid*

Tho he com amide º the putte,   *in the middle of*

The wolf thene fox opward º mette.   *the fox going up*

'Gossip,' quod the wolf, 'wat nou?

Wat havest thou imunt?º Weder wolt thou?'º   *in mind*   *where are you going?*

'Weder ich wille?' the fox sede,

'Ich wille oup,º so God me rede!º   *up*   *help*

And nou go doun with thi meel º —   *for your food*

Thi biyete worth º wel small!   *profit will be*

Ac ich am therof glad and blithe

That thou art nomen º in clene live.   *taken*

Thi soule-cnul º ich wile do ringe.'º   *death-knell*   *cause to be rung*

The wrecche binethe º nothing ne find,   *at the bottom*

Bote cold water and hounger º him bind.º   *hunger*   *makes helpless*

To colde gistninge º he wes ibede:º   *banquet*   *invited*

Froggen º haveth his dou iknede!º   *frogs*   *kneaded his dough*

[The wolf's tribulations are not yet over. When he is rescued by a friar, the other friars come and beat him severely.]

Foxes in Songs

xi) A Fox Carol[19]

This carol, or the idea behind it, seems to survive in a modern folksong,
The Fox and the Goose,[20] though the exact route of its transmission
remains uncertain.

'*Pax vobis*,'° quod the fox.   *Peace be with you*
'For I am comyn to toowne.'

It fell ageyns° the next nyght   *happened on*
The fox yede to with all hys myghte,
Withoouten cole or candelight,
Whan that he cam unto the toowne.
Pax vobis ...

Whan he cam all in° the y[e]rde,   *right into*
Soore te geys wer ill aferde;°   *terrified*
'I shall macke some of yo[w] lerde°   *better instructed*
Or that° I goo from the toowne.   *before*
Pax vobis ...

Whan he cam all in the croofte,°   *croft, enclosed ground*
There he stalkyd wundirfull soofte —
'For here have I be frayed° full ofte   *frightened*
Whan that I have come to toowne.
Pax vobis ...

He hente a goose all be the heye,°   *eye*
Faste the goos began to creye;°   *cry out*
Oowte yede° men as they might heye°   *went*   *as fast as they could*
And seyde, 'Fals fox, ley it doowne!'
Pax vobis ...

---

19   In *The Oxford Book of Medieval Verse*, no. 240.
20   See Green, 'The Ballad and the Middle Ages', in Cooper and Mapstone eds, *The
     Long Fifteenth Century*.

'Nay,' he saide, 'soo mote I the,º   *may I thrive*
Sche shall goo unto the wode with me;
Sche and I wntherº a tre.   *under*
Emange the beryis browne.
Pax vobis ...

'I have a wyf, and sche lyeth seke;
Many smale whelppis sche have to eke
Many bones they muste pike
Willº they ley adowne!   *while*
Pax vobis ...'

xii) The False Fox[21]

The fals fox came unto our croft,
And so our gese ful fast he sought.
    With how fox, how! with hey fox, hey!
    Come no more unto our howse to bere our gese aweye!

The fals fox came unto our stye,º   *pen*
And toke our gese ther by and by.º   *one by one*
    With how, fox ...

The fals fox cam into our yerde,
And ther he made the gese aferde,º   *afraid*
    With how, fox ...

The fals fox came unto our gate,
And toke our gese ther wher they sate,
    With how, fox ...

The fals fox came to our halle dore,

---

21   *Ibid.* no. 239.

And shrove° our gese ther in the flore.   *heard confession*
    With how, fox ...

The fals foxe came into our halle,
And assoiled° our gese both grete and small.   *absolved*
    With how, fox ...

The fals fox came unto our cowpe,°   *coop*
And ther he made our gese to stowpe,°   *bow down*
    With how, fox ...

He tok a gose fast by the nek,
And the goose tho° began to quek.°   *then*   *quack*
    With how, fox ...

The goodwife came out in her smok.
And at the fox she threw her rok.°   *distaff*
    With how, fox ...

The goodman came out with his flayle,
And smote the fox upon the tayle.
    With how, fox ...

He threw a gose upon his back,
And furth he went thoo with his pak.°   *burden*
    With how, fox ...

The goodman swore yf that he myght,
He wolde hym slee or° it wer nyght.   *before*
    With how, fox ...

The fals fox went into his denne,
And ther he was full mery thenne.
    With how, fox ...

He came ayene yet the next weke,
And toke awey both henne and cheke.º   *chick*
    With how, fox …

The goodman saide unto his wyfe,
'This fals fox lyveth a mery lyfe.'
    With how, fox …

The fals fox came upon a day,
And with our gese he made affray.º   *disturbance*
    With how, fox …

He tok a gose fast by the nek,
And made her to sey 'wheccumquek!'
    With how, fox …

'I pray the, fox,' seid the goose thoo,
'Take of my federsº but not of my to.'º   *feathers*   *toe*
    With how, fox …

C. Animals in Exempla or Moral Stories

Aesopic tales and others; examples mainly from the *Alphabet of Tales*

xiii) Adulators rewarded, Truth Tellers condemned[22]

Esopus tellis in his fables how ther was ii men, ane a trew man and a noder a lyer. And thai come togedur into the region of apis [apes]. And emang thaim was a chiefe ape, that satt in a hye sete that was ordand for hym emang all the toder apis. And he askid thaim many questions; emangis all other he said unto thaim, '*Quis sum ego*? Who am I?' And this lyer ansswerd agayn and sayd, 'Sur, thou erte ane emperour, and thies abowte the er [these around you are] thi dukis and thine erlis and

---

22   Tale number XXXIII, *Adulator*.

thi barons.' And onone as he had thus said, this ape commandid hym to hafe a grete reward. And than this trew man saw how this lyer was rewarded, and said privalie unto hym selfe, 'Now, sen he this at [that] did bod [but] ma[k]e a lye hase had suche a grete reward, I mon hafe a grete reward for my suth saying.' And than this ape askid this trew man and said, 'Who am I?' And he ansswerd ageyn and said, 'Thow ert bod ane ape, and all thies other apis er like the.' And onone as he had thus said, he commandid all the toder apis for to bite hym and skratt hym with ther tethe and ther naylis; and so thai did, to [until] he unnethis [scarcely] gatt away with his life. This tale is gude to tell agayn flaterers, and agayns thaim that wull here no thing bod at is to ther plesur.

xiv) The World's Glory[23]

Esopus in *Fabulis* tellis how ther was a hors that was arrayed with a brydyll of gold, and a gay saddyll, and he met ane ass that was ladyn; and this ass made hym no reverens, bod held evyn furth his way. So this prowde hors was wrothe therwith, and said, 'Bod at I will not vex my selfe, els I sulde sla the with my hinder fete, becauce thou wolde not voyde the way, and giff me rowm to pass by the.' And when this ass hard hym, sho made mekyll sorrow. So within a little while after, this hors, that was so gaylie cled, was wayke and lene, and had a sare gallid bakk; and the ass met hym undernethe a carte, ledand muke unto the felde — and the ass was fayr and fatt. And the ass said unto hym, 'Whar is now thi gay aray at thou was so prowde of? Now blissid be God, thou erte put to the same occupacion at I use, and yit my bak is haler [more whole] than thyne. And therfor now thi gay gere helpis the nott.'

xv) Saint Jerome's Lion and the Ass[24]

On a day when Sant Jerom satt with his brethir, sodanlie ther come a haltand [limping] lion and went into the abbay. And onone as the brethir saw hym thai fled all, and Saynt Jerom rase and met [him] as he had bene a geste. And this lyon lifte up his sare fute and lete hym se it, and he callid his brethir and garte [made] one of thaim wash it, and layd salvis and

---

23   Tale number CCCXLII, *Gloria mundi parum durat*.
24   Tale number CCCCXXXVIII, *Leo custodiebat asinum*.

medcyns therto, made of herbys, and onone this lion was hale [restored] and was als meke as a hors. And Saynt Jerom chargid hym that he sulde evure day take charge of and kepe ane ass that broght hym and his brethir fewell [fuel] fro the wud, and he wolde everilk day at dew tyme hafe this ass of [from] the felde and bring it hame, and kepid hur surelie. So on a day as this ass was pasturand, this lyon liste wele slepe, and layde hym down and fell apon a sad [deep] slepe; and ther come merchandes with camels be this ass away, and saw at no bodie was stirrand, and thai tuke this ass with thaim. And when thai war gone, this lyon wakend and myssyd his fellow, and soght here and ther romyand [wandering] and couthe not fynde hit. And when he saw he cuthe not fynd it, he went home all hevylie unto the abbay, and stude at the yate oferrom [at a distance] and durste com no ner becauce he broght not hame the ass; and he durste not com in as he was wunt to do. And the monkis, when thai say [saw] hym at he come home and broght not the ass with hym as he was wunt to do, and thai trowed he had etyn hur, and herefor withdrew his meate fro hym at thai war wunte to giff hym and wold not giff hym it, bod bad hym go and ete the hynder-end of the ass as he had etyn the for-end. And than Saynt Jerom charged this lyon to do the ass offes, and to bring home wod [wood] on his bak daylie to the kychyn as it was wunt to do; and mekelie he did it as he was commandid and gruchid nothing therwith. So on a day as this lyon was walkand be his one [alone], he was war of thies merchandis com of ferrom [afar] with ther camels ladyn, and this lyon ass at he kepid emang thaim. And with a grete romyng [sc. rounyng = roaring] he ran opon thaim, and all the men fled and war passand ferd, and all thies camels and this ass bothe with merchandis as thai war ladyn, he broght unto the abbay. And when Saynt Jerom saw, he commawndid his brethir to giff thies catell meate, and than to abyde the will of God. And than this lyon come into the abbay as he was wunte to do, and wente to Saynt Jerom and syne [then] fro monk to monke, and fawnyd thaim and lowtid [bowed] unto the erth, evyn as he had askid thaim forgyfnes. And than the merchandis come and knew [acknowledged] ther fawte and askid Saynt Jerom forgyfnes; and he forgaff thaim when thai confessed how thai did, and lete thaim hafe all ther gudis agayn. And thai gaff the abbay to amendis a messur of oyle, and band thaim and ther successurs for evurmore yerelie to giff unto that abbay the same messur, and so thai do yerelie unto this day.

xvi) Silent Bribes: the Cow and the Ox[25]

Som tyme ther was a ballay [bailiff] of a grete lordshup, that made a feste grete and costios unto the weddyng of a son of his. So ther was a tenand in the lordship, that had a grete cauce ther in the cowrte to be determynd befor the Stewerd. And agayn this baillay son sulde be wed, he com unto the baillay and said, 'Sur, I pray you stand for me befor the stewerd in the courte, at I may hafe right, and I sall giff yow a fatt cow to your son weddyng.' And he tuke the cow and sayd that he suld. So this mans adversarie harde tell hereoff, and he come unto this baillay wyfe and gaff hur a fatt ox, and besoght hur at sho wold labur unto hur husband that he wold answer for hym agayns his adversarie in the courte. And sho tuke the cow and laburd unto hur husband, and he promysid hur at he suld fulfil hur entent. So bothe the parties come into the courte afor the stewerd, and put furth ther cawsis, and the baillay stude still and spak not a wurd for nowdur of thaim, unto so mekyll at he that gaff the ox was like to be castyn [defeated]. And the man that gaff hym the ox said unto the baillay, 'Sur, whi spekis nott the ox?' and the baillay answerd hym agayn and said, 'For suthe! The ox may nott speke, for the cow is so fayr and so gude that sho will nott latt hym speke.'

xvii) Swallows[26]

… somtyme ther was a husbandman, that had bygand [dwelling] in his howse everilk yere many swallows. So at tyme of the yere when thai wer bown [ready] att [to] goo, he tuke ane of the old swallows, and he wrate a bill with thir wurdis therin, 'O Irund[o], ubi habitas in yeme?'[27] and he band it unto the fute therof, and lete hur goo, for he knew be experiens that sho wold come agayn the next yere. And so sho flow hur wais with other into the lande of Asie; and ther sho biggid in a howse all wynter. And so this gude man of the howse on a tyme beheld hur. And he tuke this burd, and lowsid the bill, and lukid whatt was therin; and he tuke it away, and wrate anoder, of thies wurdis, 'In Asia, in domo Petri.'[28] And he knytt [fastened] it unto hur fute, and lete hur go. And sho come agayn

---

25   Tale number XCIX, *Balliui frequenter munera recipiunt.*
26   Tale number CCCLV, *Hirundo singulis annis eadem loca repetit.*
27   O swallow, where do you live in winter?
28   In Asia, in Peter's house.

att sommer unto this husband howse, whar sho had bred befor; and he tuke hur and lowsid this bill, and redd it. And he told the storie therof unto many men, evyn as it had bene a miracle.

xviii) Malevolent Mice[29]

… a riche man on a day satt at his meate. And sodanlie he was umlappid with a grete flok of myce, and sodanly thai lefte all at was in the howse, and pursewid uppon hym. And men tuke hym and had hym unto a ship on the water at he mot so [might thus] esskape the myce, and void thaim fro hym. And thai lepid after hym into the watyr, and come to the shupp and gnew [gnawed] it thurgh. And so he mott on no wyse kepe hym fro thaim, unto so muche [until such time] att he was had to land agayn; and ther the myce fell on hym and kyllid hym, and ete hym up evere morsell unto the bare bonys.

xix) A Mouse and a Cat[30]

A mowse on a tyme felle into a barell of newe ale, that spourgid [was fermenting], and myght not come oute. The cate come beside, and herde the mouse crie in the barme [froth], 'Pepe! pepe!' for she myght not come oute. The cat seide, 'Why cries thou?' The mouse seide, 'For I may not come oute.' The catte saide, 'If I delyver the this tyme, thou shalte come to me when I calle the.' The mouse seide, 'I graunte the, to come when thou wilte.' The catte seide, 'Thou moste swere to me', and the mouse sware to kepe covenaunte. Then the catte with his fote drew oute the mouse, and lete hym go. Afterward, the catte was hungry, and come to the hole of the mouse, and called and bade hire come to hym. The mouse was aferde, and saide, 'I shall not come.' The catte saide, 'Thou hast made an othe to me, for to come.' The mouse saide, 'Brother, I was dronkyne when I sware, and therfore I am not holdyn to kepe myn othe.'

---

29   Tale number DXLV, *Mures eciam homines aliquando inuadunt.*
30   In *Gesta Romanorum*, tale XLV (fable of a cat and a mouse). Very well known, it also appears among Spanish tales in Brewer's *Medieval Comic Tales.*

xx) A Theft cannot be Hidden[31]

… Som tyme ther was a man at [that] stale his neghbur shepe, and ete it; and this man that aght [owned] this shepe come unto saynt Patryk, and told hym how a shepe was stollen from hym, and he chargid oft sithis that who somevur had it sulde bryng it agayn, and no man wolde grawnte it. So on a haly day, when all the peple was in the kurk, saynt Patryk spirrid and commaundid, in the vertue of Jesu at this shepe sulde blete in his belie that had etyn itt, at all men might here. And so it did, and thus the thefe was knowen, and made amendis for his trispas. And all other that hard ever after was ferd to stele.

xxi) Animals Know that Theft is Sinful[32]

… Som tyme ther was ane hermett that dwelt in wyldernes, and everilk day at meate tyme ther com unto his yate a sho-wulfe [she-wolf], and sho wulde never away or [before] he gaff hur somewhat at [to] eate. So on a day this hermett was with anoder bruther of his in occupacion, and come not home att meate-tyme of the day. And this wulfe come and fand hym not ther, and was war of a little bread in a wyndow, and sho brak in and tuke it, and eete it and went away. And when the hermett come home, he fand the crombis of the bread at the wyndow, and he demyd who had takyn it. And this wulfe knew hur deffaute, and wolde not com at this hermett a sennett [week] afterwerd. And when this hermet myssid this wulfe, at used to com daylie unto hym, he made his prayer unto God; and this wulfe com agayn upon the sennet day, bod sho stude of ferrom [far away], and durste not com nere hym. And sho layd hur down and held down hur head, as sho suld aske hym forgyfnes; and he tuke it for a confession, and bad hur com ner hym boldly, and he suld forgiff hur. And fro thensfurth evur after sho come at tyme of the day, and did hur offes as sho was wunt.

D. Some further Middle English Literary examples

These are not easy to find. One problem is that of all the types of Middle English popular literature, animal tales and poems are the result of

---

31   In *Alphabet of Tales*, number CCCXXXV, *Furtum non potest celari.*
32   *Ibid.* number CCCXXXVI, *Furtum commitendo eciam bruta se peccasse cognoscunt.*

a very intimate interrelation between the 'learned' and the popular tradition. Birds make brief but significant appearances in lyrics. The high points, especially the elaborate bird debates, are to be found in poets like Chaucer, Henryson, and Holland. I have preferred examples which seem to come from the popular end of the spectrum (of which but few have survived), in contrast to the merry tales.

xxii) Bird on Briar[33]

A love song, with music, apparently addressed to a bird, perhaps a confidant and the representative of Love.

Bryd on brere, brid, brid one brere,		
Kynd⁰ is come of Love, love to crave⁰	*nature*	*desire*
Blithful⁰ biryd, on me thu rewe,⁰	*joyous*	*have pity*
Or greith,⁰ lef,⁰ grei[th] thu me my grave.	*make ready*	*dear one*

[I]c am so blithe so⁰ bryhit brid on brere	*as happy as*	
Quan I se that hende⁰ in halle —	*gracious one*	
Yhe⁰ is quit of lime,⁰ loveli, trewe,	*she*	*white of limb*
Yhe is fayr and flur⁰ of alle.	*flower*	

Mikte [i]c⁰ hire at wille haven,	*if I could*
Stedefast of love, loveli, trewe,	
Of mi sorwe yhe may me saven,	
Joye and blisse were me newe.⁰	*renewed*

xxiii) Foweles in the Frith[34]

Foweles in the frith,⁰	*wood*	
The fisses in the flod,⁰	*water*	
And I mon⁰ waxe wod;⁰	*must*	*grow mad*
For beste⁰ of bon and blod.⁰	*the best (lady)*	*bone and blood (= alive)*

---

33 In *The Oxford Book of Medieval English Verse*, no. 64 (this well-known poem appears in numerous anthologies).

34 In *Medieval English Lyrics*, no. 4 (another well-known poem).

xxiv) I have Twelve Oxen[35]

This poem seems close to folksong — perhaps a nursery rhyme

I have xii oxen that be fare and brown.
And they go agraysynge down by the town,
With hay, with howe, with hay!
Sawyste thow not myn oxen, thou litill prety boy?

I have xii oxen, and they be fayre and whight,
And they go agrasyng down by the dyke,º   *ditch*
With hay, with howe, with hay!
Sawyste thou not myn oxen, thou lytyll prety boy?

I have xii oxen and they be fayre and blak,
And they go a grasyng down by the lak.º   *pond, lake*
With hay, with howe, with hay!
Sawyste not thou myn oxen, thou lytyll prety boy?

I have xii oxen, and thei be fayre and rede,
And they go a grasyng down by the mede.º   *meadow*
With hay, with howe, with hay!
Sawiste not thou my oxen, thou litill prety boy?

Debates between animals, and especially between birds, were a favourite form of the sophisticated literary authors: like Chaucer's *Parliament of Foules*; or Holland's *Buke of the Howlat*, a Scottish poem in alliterative verse. One or two, however, seem possibly closer to the popular tradition. I give extracts from two thirteenth-century poems: firstly, from the Thrush and the Nightingale (in MS Digby 86), a somewhat stiff and uninspired debate on the nature of women.

---

35   In *The Oxford Book of Medieval English Verse*, no. 250.

xxv) The Thrush and the Nightingale[36]

Somer is comen with love to toune,°	*the dwellings of men*	
With blostme, and with brides roune,°	*song of little birds*	
The note° of hasel springeth,	*nut*	
The dewes darkneth° in the dale;	*grow dark or misty*	
For longing of the nighttegale,		
This foweles° murie° singeth.	*these birds*	*merrily*

Hic herde° a strif° bitweies two —	*I heard*	*dispute*
That on° of wele,° that other of wo,	*one*	*happiness*
Bitwene two ifere,°	*together*	
That on hereth° wimmen that hoe beth	*praises*	
hende,°		*pleasant, kind*
That other hem wole with mighte shende.°	*forcefully revile*	
That strif ye mowen ihere° …	*hear*	

[the Thrush speaks]

'… I ne may° wimen herein° nout,	*cannot*	*praise*
For hy beth swikele° and false of thohut.°	*treacherous*	*mind*
Also ich am ounderstonde.°	*am informed*	
Hy beth feire and bright on hewe,°	*complexion*	
Here thout° is fals, and ountrewe°	*their thought*	*untrue*
Ful yare° ich have hem fonde'° …	*certainly*	*found*

The nightingale hoe° wes wroth:°	*she*	*angry*
'Fowel, me thinketh° thou art me loth°	*it seems to me*	*hateful*
Swiche tales for to showe;		
Among a thousent levedies° itolde°	*ladies*	*enumerated*
Ther nis non° wickede I holde	*is not one*	
Ther hy sitteth on rowe.		

Hy beth of herte° meke and milde.	*heart*	
Hemself hy cunne° from shome° shilde°	*are able*	*shame* *guard*

36   In *English Lyrics of the XIIIth Century*, ed. Brown, no. 52.

Withinne bowres wowe,°	*a bower's wall*
And swettoust thing in armes to wre°	*embrace*
The mon that holdeth hem in gle.°	*pleasure*
Fowel, wi ne art thou hit icnowe?'°	*why not acknowledge it*

'Gentil fowel, seist° thou hit me?	*sayest*	
Ich habbe° with hem in boure ibe,°	*have*	*been*
I haved al mine wille.		
Hy willeth for a luitel mede°	*small reward*	
Don a sunfoiul° derne dede,°	*sinful*	*secret deed*
Here° soule forto spille.°	*their*	*destroy*

Foel, me thinketh thou art les;°	*false*	
They° thou be milde and softe of pes,	*though*	
Thou seyst thine wille.		
I take witnesse of Adam,		
That wes oure furste man,		
That fonde° hem wycke and ille.'°	*found*	*wicked and evil*

'Threstelcok,° thou art wod,°	*thrush*	*mad*	
Other° thou const° to luitel goed,°	*or* *know*	*little good*	
This° wimmen for to shende.°	*these*	*shame*	
Hit is the swetteste driwerie,°	*love*		
And mest° hoe counnen° of curteisie.	*most*	*they know*	
Nis° nothing al so hende° ...'	*there is*	*gracious*	

[And so the argument continues, with the thrush citing further examples of the wickedness of women, and traditional examples of men (like Samson) brought down by them, until the Nightingale produces the Virgin Mary]

'O fowel, thi mouth the haveth ishend!°	*shamed*	
Thoru wam° wes al this world iwend?°	*through whom*	*transformed*
Of a maide meke and milde,		
Of hire sprong that holi bern°	*child*	
That boren wes in Bedlehem,		
And temeth al that is wilde ...'		

[Whereupon the thrush admits defeat, apologetically says that she will no longer speak ill of women, and that she will fly away out of this land.]

xxvi) From *The Owl and the Nightingale* [vv. 91–138][37]

The Nightingale Attacks the Owl

Our second debate is a much more lively affair, done with genuine wit and vivacity. The protagonists in their exchanges use exempla, fables, and proverbs, as well as rhetorical techniques of a less honourable kind. The poem's editor says of the anonymous author that he was 'a man of wide sympathies, a man who has seen something of the world and yet was not without the kind of learning valued among the religious.'[38] He seems to have been well read in the literature of his day, but he was also deeply responsive to the popular tradition, as we can see in the way he uses traditional and proverbial animal lore.

The poem's protagonists are introduced at the beginning. The Nightingale, sitting on a bough, looks down on the old stump which is the dwelling-place of the owl. She has a very low opinion of the Owl's singing: 'Me luste bet [better] speten [spit] thane singe Of thine fule yogelinge [wailing, hooting]'. Later, in the evening, the Owl does sing, and remarks triumphantly 'Hu thincthe [do you think] nu bi mine songe? Wenst thu that ic ne cunne singe, Thegh ich ne kunne of writelinge [warbling]', and ends with a threat: if I held you in my foot you would sing 'in other wise'. The Nightingale replies that she will remain secure in her cover because she knows that the Owl is hostile to small birds, and in consequence is hated by them all; and they try to drive the Owl away. The Owl is ugly, unclean, and unnatural. And the altercation gets off to a fine start with a mixture of comedy, satire, deep-seated incompatibility, and outright hostility …

… Thu art lodlich° and unclene,	*loathsome*
Bi thine neste ich hit mene,	
And ek bi thine fule brode:°	*foul brood*
Thu fedest on hom a wel ful fode.[39]	

---

37 *The Owl and the Nightingale*, ed. Stanley (extracts from this poem are added to chapter 7, below).

38 p. 32.

39 'When you feed them, you feed very foul offspring' (Stanley's note to line 94, p. 107).

[W]el wostu that° hi doth tharinne:			*you know what*
Hi fuleth hit up to the chinne;			
Ho° sitteth thar so° hi bo bisne.°	*she*	*as if*	*be blind*
Tharbi men segget a vorbisne:°	*proverb*[40]		
'Dahet habbe that ilke best°	*bad luck may that creature have*		
That fuleth° his owe nest,'	*fouls*		
That other yer° a faukun bredde;°	*year*		*falcon bred*
His nest noght wel he ne bihedde.°			*did not watch over*
Tharto thu stele° in o° dai,	*stole*		*one*
And leidest° tharon thi fole ey.°	*placed*		*foul egg*
Tho° hit bicom° that he haghte°	*then*	*happened*	*hatched*
And of his eyre° brides° wraghte,°	*eggs*	*chicks*	*were brought to life*
Ho broghte his brides mete°	*food*		
Bihold° his nest, isey hi ete;°	*looked at*		*saw them eat*
He isey bi one halve°	*at one side*		
His nest ifuled uthalve.°	*soiled on the outside*		
The faukun was wroth wit his bride,°			*chicks*
And lude yal,° and sterne chidde,°	*loudly screamed*		*chided*
'Segget° me, wo havet this ido?	*tell*		
Ou° nas never icunde° tharto.	*to you*		*natural*
Hit was idon ou a loth custe.°	*loathsome way*		
Segge[t] me, yif ye hit wiste!'			
Tho quath that on,° and quad that other,			*then said one*
'Iwis, hit was ure oghe° brother.	*our own*		
The yond,° that haved that grete heved;			*that one there*
Wai that he nis tharof bireved!°	*what a pity he is not deprived of it*		
Worp hit ut° mid the alre wrste,°	*throw it out* *with the worst rubbish of all*		
That his necke him toberste!'°	*that he breaks*		
The faucun ilefde° his bride°	*left*		*chicks*
And nom that fule brid a midde,°	*in the middle*		
And warp hit of than wilde bowe,°			*branch*
Thar pie° and crowe hit todrowe.°	*magpie*		*tore to pieces*
Herbi men segget° a bispel° —	*say*	*parable, tale*	
Thegh hit ne bo fuliche spel° —	*though it is not a full narrative*		

---

40   Whiting B 306.

'Also hit is bi° than ungode°   *with*   *wicked churl*

That is icumen of fule brode

And is meind° wit fro° monne,   *is brought together*   *noble*

Ever he cuth° that he com thonne,°   *shows*   *from there*

That he com of than adel eye°   *the addled egg*

Thegh he a fro nest leie:°   *in noble nest lay*

Thegh appel trendli fron thon trowe°   *may roll from the tree*[41]

Thar° he, and other mid,° growe,   *where*   *with him*

Thegh° he bo tharfrom bicume°   *though*   *be escaped from there*

He cuth° wel whonene° he is icume.'   *shows*   *whence*

xxvii) The Hare's Lament[42]

It is rare to find any expression of sympathy, however brief, in Middle English animal tales, for hunted animals like the fox or the hare.

Bi a forrest as I gan fare,°   *went*

    Walkyng al myselven alone,

I hard° a morning° of an haare,   *heard*   *lament*

    Rouffully schew° mad here mone.°   *piteously she*   *complaint*

'Dereworth° God, how schal I leve°   *beloved*   *live*

    And leyd my lyve° in lond?   *lead my life*

Frou° dale to doune° I am idrevfe° —   *from*   *down*   *driven*

    I not° where I may syte or stond.   *know not*

I may nother° rest nor slepe   *neither*

    By no wallay° that is so derne,°   *valley*   *secret*

Nor no covert° may me kepe,°   *thicket*   *protect*

    But ever I rene° fro herne° to herne.   *run*   *hiding place*

Hontteris° wyll not heyre ther mase°   *hunters*   *hear Mass*

    In hope° of hunttyng for to wend;°   *anticipation*   *go*

---

41   Whiting A 169.
42   In *The Oxford Book of Medieval English Verse*, no. 178.

They cowpullyth° ther howndes more and lase,°   *couple*   *large and small*

And bryngyth theme to feldys° ende.   *field's*

Rochis° rennyn on every syde   *hounds*

    In furrous that hoppe° me to fynd;   *hope*

Honteris takythe ther hors and ryde,

    And cast° the conttray° to the wynd,°   *search*   *country*   *up wind*

Anone as° they commyth me behynde,   *as soon as*

    I loke and syt ful style° and lo[w]e —   *still*

The furst mane that me doth fynde

    Anon° he cryit, 'so howe! so hoowe!   *at once*

'Lo,' he sayth, 'where syttyt an haare —

    Aryse upe, Watte,° and go forth blyve!'°   *Wat*[43]   *quickly*

With sorroe and with mych care°   *great grief*

I schape° away with my lyve,   *escape*

Att wyntter in the depe sno[w]e

    Men wyl me seche for to trace,°   *track*

And by my steyppes° I ame iknowe;°   *footprints*   *recognised*

    And followyth me fro place to place.

And yf I to the toune° come or torne,°   *town*   *turn*

    Be hit in worttes or in leyke,°   *whether for vegetables or leek(s)*

Then wyl the wyffys° also yeorne°   *women*   *as eagerly*

    Flec[h]e° me with here dogis heyke.°   *drive out*   *also*

And yf I syt and crope the koule,°   *nibble the kale*

    And the wyfe be in the waye,°   *road*

Anone schowe° wyll swere, 'By cokes° soule!   *she*   *God's*

    There is an haare in my haye!'°   *hedge*

---

43   Wat is a country name for a hare, cf. Tod for fox (it is called Coward, or Couart, in
      the Reynard stories, and the German word 'Hase' means both hare and poltroon).

Anone sche wyle clepe forth° hure knave°   *call out*   *boy*
    And loke right we[l] wer° I syte;   *where*
Behynd sche wyl with a stave
    Ful wel porpos° me to hette.°   *intend*   *hit*

'Go forthe, Wat, wit° Crystus curse,   *with*
    And yf I leve,° thou schalt be take;°   *live*   *caught*
I have an hare-pype° in my purce,°   *hare-trap*   *bag*
    Hit schal be set al for thi s[a]ke!'

Then hath this wyffe .ii. dogges grete,
    On me sche byddyt heme° goe;   *them*
And as a schrowe° sche wyll me thret,°   *shrew*   *threaten*
    And ever sche cryit, 'Go, do[g]ge, gooe!'

But allway this° most I goo,   *thus*
    By no banke I may abyde —
Lord God, that me is woo!
    Many a hape° hath me bytyde.°   *mishap*   *befallen*

There is no best° in the word° I wene° —   *beast*   *world*   *think*
Hert, hynd, buke ne dowe° —   *buck nor doe*
That suffuris halfe so myche tene°   *misery*
    As doth the sylly Wat° — go where° he go.   *poor hare*   *wherever*

Yeyfe° a genttyllmane wyl have any game,   *if*
    And fynd me in forme° where I syte,   *lair*
For dred° of lossynge of his name°   *fear*   *losing his honour*
    I wot° wel he wyle not me hyte.°   *know*   *strike*

For an acuris bred° he wyll me leve,°   *acre's breadth*   *allow*
    Or° he wyll let his hondes rene;°   *before*   *hounds run*
Of all the men that beth alive
    I am most behold to genttylmen!

As sone as I can ren to the laye,°   *open ground*
    Anon the greyhondys wyl me have;
My bowels beth ithrowe° awaye,   *are thrown*
    And I ame bore home on a stavfe.°   *stave*

Als sone as I am come home,
    I ame ihonge hye upon a pyne,°   *hook*
With leke-worttes° I am eete° anone,   *leeks*   *eaten*
    And whelpes play with my skyne!

Chapter 7

Proverbs and Riddles

The proverb and the riddle are two very ancient forms of 'wisdom literature', found in the ancient near East (there are examples of both forms in the Bible) and in pre-Conquest Britain (Old English gnomic verses and maxims, and riddles). And both are found throughout the world. The forms of the two seem to be related. It has been suggested that they have the same 'deep structure': the proverb is, as it were, an 'answer' to the riddle's unspoken enigmatic and covert question. Certainly they sometimes share the same image or topic: a French riddle asks 'which of all the household utensils is always readily available?' [a candlestick], and a proverb remarks 'a candlestick is always ready for any candle.' Neither proverbs nor riddles are well-known or frequently used in modern Western societies (at least outside the world of children), but in the Middle Ages they were esteemed and commonly used.

The proverb, 'a short pithy saying in common recognised use … some homely truth expressed in a concise and terse manner' (*OED*), is constantly used by medieval authors, and often appears in manuscript collections. Proverbs are sometimes attributed to wise sages like Solomon or 'Alfred',[1] sometimes said to be in common use, ancient, the property of peasants and rustics. They seem to have existed in both an oral and a written tradition, and to have moved easily from one

---

1   Gray writes 'Alfred' in quotation marks; one might as well put such quotes around other names such as Solomon. Once a figure has acquired a reputation for wisdom, many sayings are ascribed to him (rarely, her) whether he wrote them or not. Gray explains this further, below.

    https://doi.org/10.11647/OBP.0170.07

to the other. Some seem to have had their origin in the 'folk', others apparently have a 'literary' origin (often from the Bible or Aesop). As in modern 'traditional' societies, they seem to have had a variety of social and rhetorical uses: in argument and oratory, as a means of making generalisations, as 'normative' vehicles of satire, as expressions of social discontent. Some characteristics of the proverb probably appealed to sophisticated authors. For all its firmness in generalising, the proverb's 'truth' does not always prove to be absolute. It often seems to need, or invite, some contextualisation or interpretation. Quite often we find proverbs which express opposing views: dreams are true / dreams are false, for example. This fluidity and flexibility was exploited by writers such as Chaucer. There was a body of 'proverbial similitudes' (warm as wool, etc); these as well as common (and perhaps overused) proverbs could be enlivened or revivified by writers, thus in Chaucer's *Troilus and Criseyde* (2. v. 1276) Pandarus 'felte iren hot, and he bigan to smite'.[2]

The examples in this section have been chosen to illustrate briefly some of the characteristics and literary potential of proverbs. We begin with some Early Middle English examples, attributed to figures of wisdom, like King Alfred, then further examples from the fourteenth and fifteenth centuries. The use of proverbs in literary texts is illustrated by the *Owl and the Nightingale*. There was obviously an interest in poems of general wisdom and instruction: moral proverbial verses were sometimes painted as *tituli* in secular buildings like the Percy castles at Leconfield and Wressel, and the sixteenth-century 'Painted Room' in Oxford contained a set of the 'precepts in –ly' (for example, 'in the mornynge earlye serve God devoutlye').[3] I have illustrated this briefly with a couple of moral carols. The vividness of some proverbs seems to call for visual depiction. England cannot rival the achievement of the Netherlandish artists, but there is a nice depiction of 'shoeing the goose' (that is, performing useless and nonsensical tasks).[4] We continue with proverbs in epitaphs and end with an extract from the proverb contest

---

2   Whiting I 160.
3   At no. 3, Cornmarket St; there are other similarly inscribed walls in the vicinity, for example in what is now a Pizza Express in the adjoining Golden Cross.
4   A reference to English carvings (there is a similar proverb in French): one is among the choir stalls at Beverley Minster, another at Whaley (Lancs). The latter is captioned: 'who so melles hym of yat al men dos, let hym cum heir and shoe the gos.' The feet of geese being driven to market might be dipped in tar to protect them from damage on the road, since they could not be shod. Whiting G 389.

between *Solomon and Marcolfus*, which illustrates many of the qualities of the proverb tradition: its oppositions, and its combination of high-minded wisdom with a crude and vulgar realism.

The Riddle, 'a question or statement intentionally couched in a dark or puzzling manner, and propounded in order that it may be guessed or answered, especially in pastime; an enigma or dark saying' (*OED*), seems to imply a kind of contest: an audience is challenged by a questioner. It is not surprising to find that riddle contests are common throughout the world's traditional societies, and in the history of literature. A riddle will usually have only one answer, though some are ambiguous, encouraging the audience to think of a possible obscene solution (see no. xiv), and perhaps sometimes 'doubly ambiguous' with the more literal solution returning to shame the obscene thoughts of the audience? In some of the early riddle-contests 'pastime' gives way to a very grim context: the forfeit for failure is death, as in the story of the princess Turandot, who tested her suitors with riddles.[5] There is a vestige of this remaining in our nos xv & xvi (although, in xv, the threatening fiend is seen off by the maid with some briskness). However, in most, 'pastime' seems ever present: the riddles are genuinely 'demandes joyous' (see D, below). And there is some delight in the artful and playful strategies which mislead the audience, making a riddle the verbal equivalent of those trick pictures in which a duck may be a rabbit, depending on how we interpret the 'signs'. Lurking behind the riddle is the rhetorical figure of 'enigma' which seems to have fascinated some writers — and some preachers and theologians — presenting the 'paradoxes of the faith' or reflecting, like Nicholas of Cusa, on 'learned ignorance'.[6]

Our selection illustrates something of the nature of the riddle. We begin with examples from manuscripts and early prints, some of them demonstrating that riddles, like proverbs, can have an amazing longevity. In manuscripts, riddles are not recorded in the very large numbers that proverbs are, but they are obviously 'there', as is a liking for puzzles (see nos xiii & xiv). Examples of riddle-contests

---

5   The story of Turandot, famous because of Puccini's opera, was based on part of a twelfth-century Persian epic.

6   Nicholas of Cusa (1401–64) contributed to European history and culture notably by his writings on 'learned ignorance'.

are followed by a number of 'riddling' poems, one of which (no. xvii) sounds rather like a nursery rhyme — but has an 'adult' conclusion. The religious examples are especially interesting: they include a witty riddling poem on 'earth' (no. xxi; compare 'Remember O man that thou art dust ...', and the proverbial 'Earth must to Earth'),[7] and a very interesting example (no. xxii) of an enigmatic presentation of a traditional devotional image, the significance of which is gradually revealed by the central figure. We end with a brief example of the way in which enigma was used in narrative.

A. Proverbs recorded in Manuscripts and Prints

i) *Proverbs of Alfred*[8]

'Maxims' were used and collected in pre-Conquest times, and are found in Early Middle English versions. The Anglo-Saxon king was remembered as a wise and learned sage, but there is no evidence that the historical ruler ever produced a collection of proverbs. His name seems to be used rather to confer a certain authority. Alfred's name is sometimes attached to individual proverbs. The collection (not absolutely fixed), known as the *Proverbs of Alfred*, is early (perhaps from the twelfth century).

Thus queth° Alvred,	*said*	
'Wythute wysdome		
Is weole° wel unwurth;°	*wealth*	*worthless*
For thei o mon ahte°	*though a man possessed*	
Huntseventi° acres,	*seventy*[9]	
And he hi hadde sowen°	*had sown them*	
Alle mid reade° golde,	*red*	
And that gold greowe		
So gres° doth on eorthe,	*as grass*	
Nere he° for his weole°	*he would not be*	*for his wealth*

---

7   Whiting E 22.
8   These are in Hall's *Selections* (vol. 1, pp. 20 & 23; notes in vol. 2).
9   *MED* gives 'seventy', citing this text among six other quotations.

Never the [w]urther,º	*better off*
Buteº he him of frumtheº	*unless* *from the beginning*
Freond iwrche,º	*he makes friends*
For what is gold bute stonº	*but stone*
Bute if hit haveth wis mon?'º	*unless a wise man possesses it*

… Thus queth Alvred,	
'Ne schal tuº nevere thi wif	*thou must not*
By hire wlyteº cheose,º	*beauty* *choose*
For nevere none thinge	
That heo to the bryngeth,º	*which she brings to you (= a dowry)*
Ac leorne hire custe,º	*but learn her qualities*
Heo cutheth hi wel sone'º ….	*she makes them known very quickly*

ii) From *The Book of St Albans*[10]

Too wyves in oon hous, Too cattys and oon mous,
Too doggis and oon boon: Theis shall never accorde in oon.

iii) From MS Balliol 354, the early-sixteenth century book of Richard Hill[11]

4. It is a sotill mowse, that slepith in the cattis ere
6. A bird in hond is better than thre in the wode
24. Mani hondis makith light werke
23. When the stede is stolen shit [shut] the stable dore
31. Between two stolis [stools] the ars goth to ground

---

10 In *The Oxford Book of Medieval English Verse*, no. 309. This and the next (iii) are cited in *Simple Forms* (see the whole chapter, entitled Proverb); at p. 169, where Gray remarks 'There is no need to catalogue all the Middle English examples'.

11 EETS ES 101, in section VI Proverbs — a long treasury of proverbs in English and Latin, pp. 128–41. Numbers above are those on Richard Hill's page 128.

iv) Miscellaneous Proverbs

To trust myche in dremes is ful gret abusion[12]

And alle be hit that sum folkis say To truste on dremys nys but triffle play, Yet oon may mete the dreme wel yn his s[w]evyn As afterward that shalle bifalle him evyn[13]

For al is noght trewe that faire spekyt[14]

Hunger makth hard beanes sweete[15]

Tharfor men seye, and wel ys trowed, 'The nere [nearer] the cherche, the fyrther fro God'[16]

As it is seide in olde proverb — 'pore be hangid be the necke, a riche man bi the purs'[17]

Wo [who] wyll have law, must have monye[18]

He that in yowthe no vertu wyll yowes [use] In aege al honor shall hym refuse[19]

B. Proverbs in Literary Texts

v) *The Owl and the Nightingale*

The Owl's answer to the Nightingale's criticisms (see above, ch. 6, xxvi); vv. 625–38

... Yet thu me telst° of other thinge,	*accuse*	
Of mine brides° seist gabbinge,°	*chicks*	*you speak falsehood*
That hore° nest nis noght clene:	*their*	

---

12   Whiting D 387, 388.
13   Charles of Orleans, *Poems*, EETS OS 215 (EETS OS 220 contains the notes). The verse appears in a poem entitled (on the Contents page) The Dream of Venus and Fortune, p. 159 (v. 4739 ff).
14   Whiting S 583.
15   A well-known proverb that appears in a number of collections. See Richard Hill's book, p. 133.
16   *Ibid.* p. 130. Whiting C 251.
17   Cited (*inter al.*) in Owst, *Literature and Pulpit*, p. 43.
18   Spoken by Understanding in an early English morality (*Mind, Will and Understanding*, aka *Wisdom*) among the Macro Plays published *inter al.* by EETS.
19   A common proverb (Whiting Y 30), 1151 in the *Index of Middle English Verse*.

Hit is fale other wighte° imene,°	*to many other creatures common*
Vor° hors a° stable and oxe a stalle	*for in*
Doth al that hom wule thar falle,°	*that will fall from them there*
An lutle° children in the cradele	*little*
(bothe chorles an ek athele°)	*churls and also nobles*
Doth al that in hore yoethe°	*their youth*
That hi vorleteth in hore dugethe.°	*give up when they are adults*
Wat° can that yongling° hit bihede?°	*how child prevent*
Yif hit misdeth,° hit mod nede.°	*does wrong it is forced to by necessity*
A vorbisne° is olde ivurne,°	*proverb from long ago*
That node° maketh old wif urne° ...	*need run²⁰*
[vv. 679–700]	
Ac° notheles, yut upe thon,°	*but as against that*
Her° is to red wo hine kon,°	*here counsel to him that knows*
Vor never nis wit so kene°	*is wit so keen*
So thane° red him is a wene;°	*as when counsel is in doubt*
Thanne erest° kumed° his yephede°	*only then comes cunning*
Thone° hit is alre mest on drede.°	*when most of all in jeopardy*
For Alvered° seide of olde quide° —	*Alfred a saying*
And yut° hit nis of horte islide:°	*still it is not forgotten*
'Wone the bale° is alre hecst°	*distress highest of all*
Thane is the bote° alre necst'°	*remedy nearest of all²¹*
Vor wit° west° among his sore,°	*wisdom grows sorrows*
An vor his sore hit is the more.°	*greater*
Vorthi° nis nevere a mon redles°	*therefore helpless*
Ar° his horte bo witles,°	*before without reason*
Ac yif° he forlost° his wit	*but if loses*
Thonne is his redpurs° al toslit:°	*counsel-bag cut open*
Yif he ne kon his wit atholde°	*preserve*
Ne vint he red° in one volde.°	*does not find counsel fold (of the bag)²²*

---

20 See Stanley's note to this line: the proverb is well known not only in English. His Appendix gives a table of Proverb Literature (pp. 160–3).

21 Gray cites this proverb in his introduction to *Sir Aldingar*, above; Whiting B 18, 22.

22 See Stanley's notes to vv. 694 & 696: the 'bag of tricks' idea is found in several versions of The Fox and the Cat.

Vor Alv[er]id seide, that wel kuthe° —	*knew*	
Evre° he spac mid sothe muthe:°	*ever*	*true mouth*
'Wone the bale is alre hecst°	*highest*	
Thanne is the bote alre nest'° ...	*nearest*	
[vv. 751–70]		
... Wi atuitestu° me mine unstrengthen°	*why do you reproach*	*lack of strength*
An mine ungrete and mine unlengthe,		
An seist that ich nam noght strong		
Vor° ich nam nother° gret ne long?	*because*	*neither*
Ac thu nost° never wat thu menst,°	*do not know*	*mean*
Bute lese° words thu me lenst:°	*false*	*give*
For ich kan° craft, and ich kan liste,°	*know*	*cunning*
An tharevore ich am thus thriste.°	*bold*	
Ich kan wit and song mani eine,°	*one*	
Ne triste° ich to non other maine;°	*trust*	*strength*
Vor soth° hit is that seide Alvred,	*true*	
'Ne mai° no strengthe ayen red.'	*can (do)*[23]	
Oft spet° wel a lute° liste	*succeeds*	*little*
Thar muche strengthe sholde miste:°	*fail*	
Mid lutle strengthe thurgh ginne°	*through cunning*	
Castel and burg me° mai iwinne;	*one*	
Mid liste me mai walles felle		
An worpe of° horse knightes snelle.°	*cast from*	*strong*
Uvel strengthe° is lutel wurth,	*brute strength*	
Ac wisdom [ne wrth never unwrth°] ...	*is never worthless*	

---

23   See Stanley's note to v. 762 (and to vv. 769–72): this is also the subject of much proverbial wisdom.

C. Proverbs in Verses, or Adages

vi) A Balade attributed to Squire Halsham[24]

The worlde so wide, th'aire so remuable,°	*changeable*	
The sely° man so litel of stature,	*helpless*	
The grove and grounde° and clothinge so mutable.		*earth*
The fire so hoote and subtil° of nature,	*ethereal*	
The water never in oon° — what creature	*the same*	
That made is of these foure, thus flyttyng,°	*shifting*	
May stedfast be as° here in his lyving?°	*in respect of*	*life*

The more I goo the ferther I am behinde,		
The ferther behind the ner° my ways° ende,	*nearer*	*journey's*
The more I seche the worse kan I fynde,		
The lighter leve° the lother for to wende,°	*easier to leave*	*more loath to go*
The bet° y serve the more al out of mynde.°	*better*	*forgotten*
Is thys fortune, not I,° or infortune?	*I know not*	
Though I go lowse,° tyed am I with a lune.°	*free*	*leash (for a hawk)*

vii) Keep Thy Tongue[25]

Kep° thi tunge, thi tunge, thi tunge;	*guard, watch*	
Thi wykyd tunge werkit me wo.		

Ther is non gres that growit on ground,		
Satenas° ne peny-round,°	*satin-flower*	*penny-flower, sheep's bane[26]*

Wersse then is a wykkyd tunge

---

24 In *The Oxford Book of Medieval English Verse* (p. 385, no. 156); a whole poem made from proverbs and proverbial matter. The note (p. 591) says it may be by Lydgate.

25 This is printed in *The Oxford Book of Medieval English Verse* (no. 198).

26 It is not clear from flower-books what these are. Satin-flower (glossed in the anthology as 'a poisonous plant') may be honesty, or chickweed; Peny-round is perhaps pennywort, a plant with rounded leaves (*OED*). An online search finds only a South American 'satin-flower'; penny-flower may be honesty, and sheep's bane a species of pennywort.

That spekit bethe° evyl of frynd and fo.   *both*
    Kep thi tunge …

Wykkyd tunge makit° ofte stryf   *makes*
Betwyxe a good man and his wyf;
Quan° he shulde lede a merie lyf,   *when*
Here qwyte° sydys waxin ful blo.°   *white*   *livid*
    Kep thi tunge …

Wykkyd tunge makit ofte stauns,°   *dissension*
Bothe in Engelond and in Frauns;
Many a man wyt spere and launs
Throw wykkyd tunge to ded° is do.   *death*
    Kep thi tunge …

Wykkyd tunge brekit bon,
Thow the self° have non;   *itself*
Of his frynd° he makit his fon°   *friend*   *foes*
In every place qwer that he go.
    Kep thi tunge …

Good men that stondyn and syttyn in this halle,
I prey you, bothe on and alle
That wykkyd tunges fro you falle,
That ye mowun to hefne go.
    Kep thi tunge …

viii) Proverbs appear in epitaphs …[27]

Farewell, my frendis! The tide abidith no man:
I moste departe hens, and so shall ye.
But in this passage, the best song that I can

---

27   The first of these is in *Index of Middle English Verse*, no. 765; and see Gray, 'A Middle
     English Epitaph'. They include 'Time and tide wait for no man', and 'End comes to
     the longest day'.

Is *Requiem Eternum*[28] — I pray God grant it me!

Whan I have endid all myn adversite,

Graunte me in Paradise to have a mancyon.

That shede his blode for my redempcion.

ix) Most eloquently in the fictional epitaph of Graunde Amour,[29]
in Hawes's *Pastime of Pleasure*

O mortall folke, you may beholde and se

How I lye here, somtyme a mighty kyght.

The ende of joye and all prosperyte

Is dethe at last, through his course and might.

For though the day be never so longe

At last the belles ryngeth to evensonge.

x) Adages as embodiments of ancient wisdom[30]

In the *Adagia* of Erasmus adages (like later emblems) took on the nature of gnomic utterances, darkly and deeply meaningful, 'often having inner senses far more moral than it would ever occur to a modern reader to give them'.

Know Time[31]

Nosce Tempus: know time. Opportunitie is of such force that of honest it maketh unhonest, of damage avauntage, of pleasure grevaunce, of a good turne a shrewd turne, and contraryewyse of unhonest honest, of avauntage damage, and brefly to conclude it cleane chaungeth the nature of thynges.

---

28 Rest Eternal, a phrase from the burial service. Medieval Latin is often incorrect (it would normally read *eternam*).

29 Stephen Hawes, *The Pastime of Pleasure* (there are a number of editions), in Chapter XLII.

30 Erasmus, *Adages*, trans. Phillips *et al*. Other editions, of selected Adages, may be consulted.

31 From Taverner's *Proverbs and Adages*, cited in *Simple Forms*, p. 170.

xi) *Solomon and Marcolfus*

In the Old English period the dialogues of the rival sages Solomon and Saturn present a debate. In the late Middle Ages Solomon's opponent was his parodist, the ugly, churlish Marcolphus, whose earthy proverbs are modelled on the proverbial lore of the peasants, and present a world view quite opposed to that of the king.[32] The Latin version appeared in vernacular form; the English version of Leeu was printed at Antwerp in 1492.[33]

Upon a season heretofore as king Salomon, full of wisdom and richesse, sate upon the kings sete or stole [throne] that was his fadres Davyd, sawe coming a man out of th'Este that was named Marcolphus, of visage greatly myshapen and fowle; nevyrethe lesse he was right talkatyf, elloquend, and wyse. His wif had he wyth hym, whiche was more ferefull and rude to beholde. This Marcolf was of short stature and thykke. The head had he great; a brode forhede rede and full of wrinkelys or frouncys [creases]; his erys hery [hairy] and to the myddys of chekys hangyng; great yes [eyes] and rennyng; his nether lyppe hangyng lyke an horse; a berde harde and fowle lyke unto a gote; the hands short and blockyssh [gross]; his fyngres great and thycke; rounde feet and the nose thycke and croked; a face lyke an asse, and the here of hys heed lyke the heer of a gote. His shoes on his fete were ovyrmoche chorlyssh and rude, and his clothys fowle and dirty; a short cote to the buttockys; his hosyn hinge [hung] full of wrynkelys, and alle his clothes were of the moost fowle coloure ...

... Salomon sayde, 'I have herd of the that thou kanst right wele clatre [chatter] and speke, and that thou art subtyle of wyt, although that thou be mysshapyn and chorlyssh. Lete us have betwene us altercacion. I shal make questyons to the, and thou shalt therto answere.' Marcolfus answeryd, 'He that singyth worste begynne furste.' Salomon: 'If thou kanst answere to alle my questyons I shall make the ryche, and be named above all other withyn my reaume.' Marcolphus: 'The physician promysyth the seeke folke helthe whan he hath no power.' Salomon: 'I have juged betwixt two light women whiche dwellyd in oon house and forlaye [smothered] a chylde.' Marcolphus: 'Were erys [ears] are, there are causes; where women be, there are wordys.' Salomon: 'God yave wysdam in my mouth; for me lyke is none in all partys of the worlde.' Marcolphus: 'He that hath evyll neighborys praysyth himself.' Salomon: 'The wykkyd man fleyth, no man folwyng.' Marcolphus: 'Whan the kydde rennyth, men may se his ars.' Salomon: 'A good wyf and a fayre is to hir husbonde a pleasure.' Marcolphus: 'A potfull of mylke muste be kepte wele from the katte ...'

---

32 Brewer tells us that characters such as the Parson of Kalenborowe, and Owlglass, developed from the Marcolf figure (*Medieval Comic Tales*, p. xxvi).

33 For this text, see *The Dialogue of Solomon and Marcolf*, eds Bradbury and Bradbury.

[Because of the king's hostility, Marcolphus flees and hides in an old oven, having made footprints in the snow with the foot of a bear. When these are discovered the king sets out hunting and is led to the oven …]

… The king Salomon discended from hys hors, and began to loke into the oven. Marcolphus laye all crokyd, hys visage from hymwarde; had put downe hys breche into hys hammes that he might se hys arshole and alle hys other fowle gere. As the king Salomon, that seyng, demawnded what laye there, Marcolphus answeryd, 'I am here.' Salomon: 'Wherefore lyest thou thus?' Marcolphus: 'For ye have commanded me that ye shulde nomore se me betwixt myn yes. Now and ye woll not se me betwixt myn yes, ye may se me between my buttockys in the myddes of myn arsehole.' Than was the king sore movyd [provoked]; commanded his servauntys to take him and hange hym upon a tre. Marcolphus so takyn sayde to the kyng: 'My lord, well it please you to yeve me leve to chose the tre whereupon that I shall hange.' Salomon sayde, 'Be it as thou hast desired, for it forcyth not on what tre that thou be hangyd.' Than the kynges servauntes token and leddyn Marcolph wythoute the citie and through the vale of Josaphath, and ovyr the hyghte of the hylle of Olyete from thens to Jericho, and cowde fynde no tre that Marcolf wolde chese to be hanged on. From thens went they ovyr the flome Jordane, and all Arabye through, and so forth all the grete wyldernesse unto the Rede See, and nevyrmore cowed Marcolph fynde a tre that he wolde chese to hange on. And thus he askapyd out of the dawnger and hands of King Salomon, and turnyd ayen unto hys house and levyd in pease and joye.

D. Riddles

xii) From the *Demaundes Joyous* (1511)[34]

3) Who was Adams moder? (the earth)

4) What space is from the hyest space of the se to the deepest? (but a stone's cast)

6) How many calves tayles behoveth to reche from the erthe to the skye? (one, if it's long enough)

9) Whiche parte of a sergeaunte love ye best towarde you? (his heels)

11) Which is the moost profitable beest, and that men eteth leest of? (bees)

12) Which is the broadest water and leest jeopardye to passe over? (dew)

---

34   These are printed in [Solomon] *The Dialogue of Salomon and Saturnus*, ed. Kemble, pp. 287–92; there are fifty-four Demaundes (including these thirteen), with answers. See also *The Demaundes Joyous*, ed. Wardroper.

15) Why dryve men dogges out of the chyrche? (because they make no offering)

16) Why come dogges so often to the churche? (because they think the altar-cloth is a table-cloth, for dinner)

19) What beest is it that hath her tayle bytweene her eyen? (a cat washing its bottom)

25) Wherfore set they upon chyrche steples more a cocke than a henne? (if a hen laid eggs up there, they would fall)

41) Which was first, the henne or the egge? (the hen, when God made her)

42) Why doth an ox or a cowe lye? (because it cannot sit)

45) What tyme in ther yere bereth a gose moost feders? (when the gander is on her back)

xiii) A Puzzle

Water frosen, Caines brother; So hight my leman, and no other.[35]

xiv) A Riddle with ambiguous solution[36]

I have a hole above my knee And pricked yt was and pricked shal be
And yet yt is not sore And yet yt shal be pricked more.

E. Riddle Challenges

xv) *The Devil and the Maid*[37]

Wol ye here° a wonder thynge   *do you want to hear*
Betwyxt a mayd and the foule fende?

Thys spake the fend to the mayd:
'Beleve on me, mayd, today.

---

35   That is, Yssabel: Ice and Abel; in *The Oxford Book of Medieval English Verse*, no. 332 ii.
36   Cited, with references and solution (a sheath) in *Simple Forms*, p. 185.
37   *Inter diabolus et virgo*, Child no. 1. Gray follows the version in Oxford, Bodleian Library, Rawlinson MS. D. 328, fol. 174 b, which he may have edited himself.

Mayd, mote yᵒ thi lemanᵒ be,   *if I might*   *lover*
Wyssedom y wolle teche the:

All the wyssedom off the world,
Hyf thou wolt be true and forwardᵒ holde,   *agreement*

What ys hyer than ys [the] tre?
What ys dypperᵒ than ys the see?   *deeper*

What ys scharpper than the thorne?
What is loderᵒ than the horne?   *louder*

What [ys] longger than ys the way?
What ys raderᵒ than ys the day?ᵒ   *redder*   *dawn (of day)*

What [ys] betherᵒ than is the bred?   *better*
What ys scharpper than ys the dede?ᵒ   *death*

What ys grenner than ys the wode?
What ys sweeter than ys the note?ᵒ   *nut*

What ys swifter than ys the wynd?
What ys richer than ys the kynge?

What ys yeluerᵒ than ys the wex?ᵒ   *yellower*   *wax*
What [ys] softer than ys the flex?ᵒ   *flax*

Butᵒ thou now answer me,   *unless*
Thou schalt for sotheᵒ my leman be.'   *you must in truth*

'Jesu, for thy myld[e]ᵒ myghth,   *gentle*
As thu art kynge and knight,

Leneᵒ me wisdom to answere here ryghth,   *grant*
And schylde me fram the foule wyghth.ᵒ   *creature*

Hewene° ys heyer than ys the tre,   *heaven*
Helle ys dypper than ys the see.

Hongyr ys scharpper than [ys] the thorne.
Thonder ys lodder than ys the horne.

Loukynge° ys longer than ys the way,   *expectation*
Syn° ys rader than ys the day,   *sun*

Godys flesse° ys betur than ys the brede,   *flesh*
Payne ys strenger than ys the dede.°   *death*

Gras ys grenner than ys the wode,
Love ys swetter than ys the note.

Thowt° ys swifter than ys the wynde,   *thought*
Jesus ys richer than ys the kynge.

Safer° ys yeluer than ys the wexs,   *saffron*
Selke ys softer than ys the flex.

Now, thu fende, styl° thu be;   *silent*
Nelle ich° speke no more with the!'   *I will not*

xvi) *King John and the Bishop*[38]

Off an ancient story Ile tell you anon,
Of a notable prince that was called King John,
In England was borne, with maine and with might;
Hee did much wrong and maintained litle right.
This noble prince was vexed in veretye,°   *truth*
For he was angry with the Bishopp of Canterbury;
For his house-keeping and his good cheere,
The° rode post for him, as you shall heare.   *they*

---

38   *PFMS*, vol i p. 508. Gray gives vv. 1–78 & 87–142.

They rode post for him very hastilye;
The king sayd the bishopp kept a better house than hee:
A hundred men even, as I [heard] say,
And fifty gold chaines, without any doubt,
In velvet coates waited the bishop about.
The bishopp, he came to the court anon,
Before his prince that was called King John.
As soone as the bishopp the king did see,
'O,' quoth the king, 'Bishopp, thow art welcome to mee.
There is noe man soe welcome to towne
As thou that workes treason against my crowne.'
'My leege,' quoth the bishop, 'I wold it were knowne
I spend, your grace, nothing but that that's° my owne;   *what is*
I trust your grace will doe me noe deare°   *harm*
For spending my owne trew gotten geere.'°   *property*
'Yes,' quoth the king, 'Bishopp, thou must needs dye,
Eccept thou can answere mee questions three,
Thy head shalbe smitten quite from thy bodye,
And all thy living remayne unto mee.
First,' quoth the king, 'tell me in this steade,°   *place*
With this crowne of gold here upon my head,
Amongst my nobilitye, with joy and much mirth,
Lett me know within one pennye what I am worth.
Secondlye, tell me without any dowbt
How soone° I may goe the whole world about;   *quickly*
And thirdly, tell mee or° ever I stinte,° *before* *stop*
What is the thing, bishop, that I doe thinke.
Twenty dayes pardon thoust° have trulye,   *you shall*
And come againe and answere mee.'
The bishop bade the king god night att° a word; *with*
He rode betwixt Cambridge and Oxenford,
But never a doctor there was soe wise
Cold shew him these questions or enterprise.
Wherewith the bishopp was nothing gladd,
But in his hart was heavy and sadd.

And hyed him home to a house in the countrye,
To ease some part of his melanchollye.
His halfe-brother dwelt there, was fierce and fell,
Noe better but a shepard to the bishoppe himsell;
The shepard came to the bishopp anon,
Saying, 'My lord, you are welcome home!
What ayles you,' quoth the shepard, 'that you are soe sadd,
And had wonte to have beene soe merry and gladd?'
'Nothing,' quoth the bishopp, 'I ayle att this time;
Will not thee availe to know, brother mine.'
'Brother,' quoth the shepheard, 'you have heard itt,
That a foole may teach a wisemane witt;
Say me therefore whatsoever you will,
And if I doe you noe good, Ile doe you noe ill.'
Quoth the bishop, 'I have beene att the court anon,
Before my prince is called King John.
And there he hath charged mee
Against his crowne with traitorye.
If I cannott answer his misterye,
Three questions hee hath propounded to mee,
He will have my land soe faire and free.
And alsoe the head from my bodye.
The first question was to tell him in that stead,
With the crowne of golde upon his head,
Amongst his nobilitye, with joy and much mirth,
To lett him know within one penye what hee is worth.
And secondlye to tell him without any doubt
How soone he may goe the whole world about,
And thirdlye to tell him, or ere I stint,
What is the thinge that he does thinke.'
'Brother,' quoth the shepard, 'you are a man of learninge;
What neede you stand in doubt of soe small a thinge?
Lend me,' quoth the shepard, 'your ministers° apparel,   *clerical*
Ile ryde to the court and answere your quarrel.'°   *dispute*
…

The shepard hee came to the court anon
Before [his] prince that was called King John.
As soone as the king the shepard did see,
'O,' quoth the king, 'Bishopp, thou art welcome to me.'
The shepard was soe like the bishopp his brother,
The king cold not know the one from the other.
Quoth the king, 'Bishopp, thou art welcome to me
If thou can answer me my questions three.'
Said the shepeard, 'If it please your grace,
Show me what the first quest[i]on was.'
'First,' quoth the king, 'tell mee in this stead,
With the crowne of gold upon my head,
Amongst my nobilitye, with joy and much mirth,
Within one pennye what I am worth.'
Quoth the shepard, 'To make your grace noe offence,
I thinke you are worth nine and twenty pence,
For our lord Jesus, that bought us all,
For thirty pence was sold into thrall
Amongst the cursed Jewes, as I to you doe showe —
But I know Christ was one penye better then you.'
Then the king laught, and swore by St Andrew
He was not thought to bee of such a small value.
'Secondlye, tell mee without any doubt
How soone I may goe the world round about?'
Saies the shepard, 'It is noe time with your grace to scorne,
But rise betime with the sun in the morne,
And follow his course till his oprising,
And then you may know without any leasing,º   *falsehood*
And this [to] your grace shall prove the same,
You are come to the same place from whence you came
[In] twenty-four houres, without any doubt.
Your grace may the world goe round about,
The world round about, even as I doe say,
If with the sun you can goe the nextº way.'   *most direct*
'And thirdlye tell me or ever I stint,

What is the thing, bishoppe, that I doe thinke?'
'That shall I doe,' quoth the shepeard, 'for veretye,
You thinke I am the bishopp of Canterburye.'
'Why, art not thou? The truth tell to me,
For I doe thinke soe,' quoth the king, 'by St Marye.'
'Not soe,' quoth the shepeard, 'the truth shalbe knowne:
I am his poore shepeard, my brother is att home.'
'Why,' quoth the king, 'if itt soe bee,
Ile make thee bishopp here to mee.'
'Noe, sir,' quoth the shepard, 'I pray you be still,
For Ile not bee bishopp but against my will,
For I am not fit for any such deede,
For I can neither write nor reede.'
'Why then' quoth the king, 'Ile give thee cleere
A patent° of three hundred pound a yeere: *licenced privilege*
That I will give thee franke and free;°   *unconditionally*
Take thee that, shepard, for coming to me,
Free pardon Ile give,' the kings grace said,
'To save the bishopp, his land and his head;
With him nor thee Ile be nothing wrath;
Here is the pardon for him and thee both.'

[He takes it back to the bishop, whose heart is 'of a merry cheere'; the shepherd announces that he will no longer 'crouch nor creep' before him, nor keep his sheep.]

F. Poetic Uses of Enigma

xvii) I have a yong suster[39]

I have a yong suster
Fer beyondyn the se,
Many be the drowryis°   *love tokens*
That che° sente me.   *she*

---

39   In *The Oxford Book of Medieval English Verse*, no. 192.

Che sente me the cherye
Withoutyn ony ston,
And so che ded° the dowe°   *did*   *dove*
Withoutyn ony bon.

Sche sente me the brer°   *briar*
Withoutyn ony rynde°   *bark*
Sche bad me love my lemman° *beloved*
Withoute longgyng.

How shuld ony cherye
Be withoute ston?
And how shuld ony dowe
Be withoute bon?

How shuld ony brer
Ben withoute rynde?
How shuld [y] love myn lemman
Without longyng?

Quan the cherye was a flour,
Than hadde it non ston.
Quan the dowe was an ey°   *egg*
Than hadde it non bon.

Quan the brer was onbred,°   *unbred (= still in seed)*
Than hadde it non rynd.
Quan the maydyn hath that che lovit,
Che is without longing

Religious writings sometimes make use of 'enigma'.

xviii)[40]

Byhalde merveylis: a mayde ys moder.
Her sone her fader ys and broder;
Lyfe faught with dethe and dethe is slayne;
Most high was lowe — he stygheº agayne.   *rose up*

xix)[41]

A God, and yet a man?
A mayde, and yet a mother?
Witt wonders what witt can
Conceave this or the other.

A God, and can he die?
A dead man, can he live?
What witt can well replie?
What reason reason give?

God, Truth itselfe doth teache it;
Mans witt sinkes too farr under,
By reasons power to reach it —
Believe, and leave to wonder.

xx)[42]

Mirabile misterium;[43]
In forme of bred ys Godes Son.

---

40   In *A Selection of Religious Lyrics*, no. 71.
41   *Ibid.* no. 72.
42   In the *Digital Index of Middle English Verse*, no. 3379, A Song of the Host.
43   Miraculous mystery.

Man, that in erth abydys here,
Thou must beleve withouten d[e]re°   *without difficulty*
In the sacrement of the auter
That God made hymself at hys soper.
    Mirabile …

Thowgh yt seme whit, yt ys rede,
Yt ys flesshe, yt semeyth° bred,   *appears to be*
Yt ys God in his manhed,
As he hong upon a tre.
    Mirabile …

Thys bred ys brokyn for you and me
Which priestes consecrate, as ye may se,
Which, flesshely man in Deite,
Dyed for us upon a tre.
    Mirabile …

xxi)[44]

Erthe toc of erthe erthe wyth woh,
Erthe other erthe to the erthe droh,°   *drew*
Erthe leyde erthe in erthene throh,°   *pit*
Tho hevede° erthe of erthe erthe ynoh.°   *had*   *sufficient*

xxii) The first sixty lines of a religious visionary poem.[45]

The meaning of the enigmatic images gradually becomes clear. This poem also provides an introduction to our following section.

In the vaile of restles mynd
    I sowght in mownteyn and in mede,°   *meadow*
Trustyng a treulofe° for to fynd.   *truelove*

---

44   In *A Selection of Religious Lyrics*, ed. Gray, no. 86a; Whiting E 22.
45   *Ibid.* no. 43 (pp. 41–5).

Upon an hyll than toke I hede,°   *took I heed*
   A voyse I herd (and nere I yede°)   *nearer I went*
In gret dolour° complaynyng tho,°   *grief*   *then*
   'See, dere soule, my sydes blede.
Quia amore langueo.'°   *because I languish for love*

Upon this mownt I fand° a tree,   *found*
   Under thys tree a man sittyng;
From hede to fote wowndyd° was he,   *wounded*
   His hert blode I saw bledyng,
   A semely man to be a kyng
A graciose face to loke unto.
   I askyd hym how he had paynyng,°   *suffering*
He said, '*Quia amore langueo.*

I am treulove, that fals was never.
   My sister, mannys soule, I loved hyr thus;
Bycause I wold on no wyse dissevere°   *part*
   I left my kyngdome gloriouse.
   I purveyd° hyr a paleis preciouse,   *prepared*
She flytt,° I folowyd, I luffed° her soo   *fled*   *loved*
   That I suffred thes paynes piteuouse
Quia amore langueo.

My faire love, and my spouse bryght.
   I saved hyr fro betyng, and she hath me bett;°   *beaten*
I clothed hyr in grace and hevenly lyght,
   This blody surcote° she hath on me sett.   *surcoat*
   For langyng love° I will not let° —   *love-longing* *give up*
Swete strokys be thes, loo!
   I haf loved ever als I hett,°   *as I promised*
Quia amore langueo.

I crownyd hyr with blysse, and she me with thorne,
   I led hyr to chamber, and she me to dye;

I browght hyr to worship,° and she me to skorne,   *honour*

    I dyd hyr reverence, and she me velanye.°   *shame*

    To love that loveth is no maystrye,°   *is no hard thing*

Hyr hate made never my love hyr foo° —   *foe*

    Ask than no moo° questions whye,   *more*

Quia amore langueo.

Loke unto myn handys, man!

    Thes gloves were geven° me whan I hyr sowght;   *given*

They be nat white, but rede and wan,°   *leaden-coloured*

    Embrodred° with blode (my spouse them bowght!);   *embroidered*

    They wyll not of° — I lefe them nowght!°   *off*   *I do not take them off*

I wowe° hyr with them where ever she goo.°   *woo*   *goes*

Thes hands full friendly for hyr fowght,

Quia amore langueo.

Marvell not, man, thof° I sitt styll —   *though*

    My love hath shod me wondyr strayte,°   *wondrously tight*

She boklyd° my fete, as was hyr wyll,   *buckled*

    With sharp nailes (well thow maist waite!)°   *may observe*

    In my love was never dissaite,°   *deceit*

For all my membres I haf opynd hyr to;°   *opened to her*

    My body I made hyr hertys baite,°   *bait for her heart*

Quia amore langueo.

In my syde I haf made hur nest —

    Loke° in me, how wyde a wound is here! —   *look*

This is hyr chamber, here shall she rest,

    That she and I may slepe in fere° …'   *together*

G. Enigma in Narrative

Middle English literature provides numerous examples, but it is difficult to illustrate this briefly. In romances, protagonists are sometimes confronted with 'hard questions' (like 'what is it that women most desire?') which determine the movement of the plot. Romances often have mysterious figures, sometimes with enigmatic names; sometimes nameless, or apparently visitants from the Otherworld or shape-shifters (like the Green Knight);[46] they contain enigmatic scenes or events (as in *Huon of Bordeux* when the ship approaches a mysterious 'high rock' surmounted by a thick wood and a high castle with towers of alabaster — which turns out to be the rock of Adamant with the masts of wrecked ships and the bones of their crews).[47] We end therefore with a shorter 'narrative', in the famous Corpus Christi Carol, where there has been considerable argument over the interpretation.[48]

xxiii) The 'Corpus Christi Carol'[49]

Lully, lulley; lully, lulley,
The fawcon° hath born my mak° away.   *falcon*   *mate*

He bare hym up, he bare hym down,
He bare hym into an orchard brown,
  Lulley ...

In that orchard ther was an hall,
That was hangid with purpill and pall°   *rich purple fabric*
  Lulley ...

And in that hall ther was a bede;
Hit was hangid with gold so rede.
  Lulley ...

And yn that bed ther lythe a knyght,

---

46 In *Sir Gawain and the Green Knight*.
47 In *Huon of Burdeux*, ed. Lee, p. 370 ff.
48 It is difficult to decide whether we are dealing with a self-conscious use of enigma involving a fusion of 'religious' and 'secular', or whether it is the result of changes or attempts at clarification which occurred during the transmission of a mysterious poem about the body of a dead knight. Compare the modern variants in our chapter Ballads (ix), Three Ravens, and the Scottish carol in the Appendix (xii).
49 In *The Oxford Book of Medieval Verse*, p. 524 (no. 247). *Corpus Christi* means Body of Christ.

His wowndes bledyng day and nyght.
    Lulley ...

And by that bedes side ther kneleth a may,º   *maid*
And she wepeth both nyght and day.
    Lulley ...

And by that beddes side ther stondith a ston,
'*Corpus Christi*' wretyn theron,
    Lulley ...

Chapter 8

Satire

Satire is a protean term.[1] Together with its derivatives, it is one of the most heavily-worked literary designations and one of the most imprecise. The great English lexicographer Samuel Johnson defined satire as 'a poem in which wickedness or folly is censured', and more elaborate definitions are rarely more satisfactory. No strict definition can encompass the complexity of a word that signifies, on the one hand, a kind of literature … and, on the other, a mocking spirit or tone that manifests itself in many literary genres but can also enter into almost any kind of human communication. Whenever wit is employed to expose something foolish or vicious to criticism, there satire exists, whether it be in song or sermon, in painting or in political debate, on television or in the movies. In this sense satire is everywhere.[2]

It certainly seems to be almost everywhere in medieval England. From this period, although much has been lost — or was never written down — there survives a mass of satirical writing, in both verse and prose. Alongside a tradition of popular satire there was of course a 'learned' one, rooted (remotely) in ancient classical satire and (more obviously) in that of the Old Testament prophets, their successors among

---

1   See Brewer, *Medieval Comic Tales* (2nd edn), p. xix: 'Derision is a general attitude of humorous, superior contempt, very characteristic of medieval humour'; therefore it is a better concept than 'satire' in this context. See also Gray's chapter Satire in *Simple Forms*.
2   R. C. Elliott, in *Encyclopedia Britannica*.

   https://doi.org/10.11647/OBP.0170.08

the early fathers of the church, and the extensive and often brilliant satirical works in medieval Latin. This learned tradition in England includes writers like Chaucer, Gower, Lydgate, and Dunbar and Skelton. The popular tradition, which overlaps and interacts with it, rarely has the wit or the precision shown by such writers: it prefers a direct, heavy blow, sometimes delivered 'below the belt'. We seem to be in a world of homely taunts and stereotypes, mockery and invective. In its attempts to expose folly and vice it will employ ridicule and simple abuse. But it is a tradition not only vehement and aggressive, but also varied. The attitudes behind our examples show a remarkable range, from outright venom — sometimes close to the feared *nith* of earlier satire to a more relaxed and almost urbane attitude (as in *The Land of Cokaygne*),[3] or in the high-spirited burlesque of the *Tournament of Tottenham*.[4] Modern readers quickly become impatient with the general 'complaints' on the wickedness of the age, but we need to remember that such complaints could be telling and pointed if quoted in a particular context to an audience of receptive listeners. And if context is important, so is performance, whether in song or recitation or, visually, in the satirical 'bills' posted in public places. The simple, direct style of some pieces seems to bring us close to the style of the now lost satirical songs of the oral tradition, as we find it in the few fragments quoted by chroniclers. The popular flyting, an exchange of taunts, is known to us mainly through its appearance as a kind of courtly game in the writings of Dunbar and Skelton. But its oral antecedents could still be heard in medieval streets: Dunbar, addressing the merchants of Edinburgh, remarks that no one can pass through the city's streets 'for stink of haddockis and of scattis [skates], For cryis of carlingis [old women] and debbaittis [quarrels], For feusum [foul] flyttingis of defame'.[5] It seems that Keats's remark, that it was hateful to see quarrelling in the streets, but 'the energies displayed are fine', may have been as true of this period as it was of the eighteenth century.[6]

In this chapter I have attempted to present examples which have something of the strange energy of satire, both destructive and creative.

---

3   In *Early Middle English Verse and Prose* (number IX, commentary pp. 336–41). For 'nith', see *Simple Forms* pp. 195–6.

4   In *Middle English Verse Romances*, ed. Sands.

5   In *Selected Poems of Henryson and Dunbar*, Bawcutt and Riddy, 'Quhy Will Ye, Merchantys of Renoun', pp. 161–4.

6   A letter from John Keats to George and Georgiana Keats, March 1819.

We begin with an introductory group of 'snatches': poems referred to or quoted by chroniclers (the words of these are the nearest we can come to the actual words of the oral song). These songs seem to have been common. Our no. (ii) is a poem attributed to John Ball at the time of the Peasants' Revolt, a poem related to the general laments on the wickedness of the contemporary world, like the common 'Abuses of the Age', and which also shows how these 'general' poems may be given a pointedness in a particular political context. No. (iii) introduces us to the writing of satirical or threatening bills which could be displayed on doors or gates. Sadly, the verses in question — 'englische billes rymed in partie' (perhaps a reference to the doggerel verse sometimes used) — have not survived. A well-known example, 'The Cat, the Rat, and Lovel our Dog Rule all England under a Hog', was fixed to the doors of St Pauls.[7] There follows a group of poems on various wickednesses, culminating in *London Lickpenny*, a satirical journey around the streets and institutions of London by one who lacks money; and brief examples of medical and religious satire. Poems against Scots and Flemings bring us to verses directed at individuals, like the hated Suffolk. We end with examples of parody and burlesque, where high spirits rather than satirical venom seem to rule. If Chaucer's *Sir Thopas* is a witty and elegant literary burlesque of popular romance, *The Tournament of Tottenham* gives us a more forthright and boisterous example.

A. Snatches: Popular Satire in Action

i)[8]

Maydenes of Engelande, sare may ye morne,		
For tynt° ye have uoure lemmans at	*lost*	
Bannokes born°		*Bannockburn*
With hevalogh.		
What wende° the kyng of Engeland have	*thought*	
ygete° Scotlande		*taken*
With rombylogh.		

7　In *The Oxford Book of Medieval English Verse*, no. 329 (and see note): Catesby, Ratcliffe, and Lovell were among Richard III's supporters.

8　In *The Oxford Book of Medieval English Verse*, no. 282; and *Simple Forms*, p. 202.

ii)[9]

Now raygneth pride in price,°	*high esteem*
Covetise is holden wise	
Lechery without shame,	
Gluttonie without blame,	
Envye raygneth with reason,	
And sloath° is taken in gret season.	*sloth*
God doe boote° for nowe is time.	*bring remedy*

(iii) Scottish Derision[10]

Longe beerdys hartles,
Paynted hoodys wytles,
Gay cotis graceles,
Makyth Englande thryfteles.

B. The Wickedness of the World

iv) Now the Bisson Leads the Blind [vv. 1–24][11]

Fulfyllyd ys the profesy for ay	
That Merlyn sayd and many on mo°	*more*
Wysdam ys wel ny away,	
No man may knowe hys frend fro fo°	*foe*
Now gyllorys° don gode men gye,°	*deceivers*　　*guide*
Ryght° gos redles° all behynde,	*justice*　　*without counsel*
Truthe ys turnyd to trechery,	
For now the bysom° ledys the blynde.	*purblind*

9　Part of a letter attributed to John Ball; see *Historical Poems*, ed. Robbins, no. 17 (John Ball's Letters, I; 1381), p. 54. See also *Fourteenth Century Verse and Prose*, pp. 160–1 (and notes) for another part of the letter.

10　See *Simple Forms*, p. 207.

11　This verse, from London, BL MS Harley 5396, is printed in *Reliquiae Antiquae* eds Wright and Halliwell-Phillipps (vol. II), p. 238 ff.

Now gloserys° full gayly they go.	*flatterers*
Pore men be perus° of this land —	*peers*
Sertes sum tyme° hyt was not so,	*once*
But sekyr° all this is synnys sonde° —	*surely* *dispensation*
Now maynttenerys°	*those who interfere in litigation*
be made justys°	*justices*
And lewde° men rewle the lawe of kynde,°	*ignorant* *as by right*
Nobull men be holdyn wyse,	
For now the bysom ledys the blynde ….	

v) Where is Truth?[12]

God be with trewthe qwer° he be —	*wherever*
I wold he were in this cuntre!	
A man that shuld° of trewthe telle,	*would*
With grete lordys he may not dwelle —	
In trewe story, as klerkes telle,	
Trewthe is put in low degree.°	*station*
God be with trewthe …	
In ladyis chaumberys comit he not —	
Ther dare trewthe settyn non fot;°	*foot*
Thow he wolde, he may not	
Comyn among the heye mene.°	*noble company*
God be with trewthe …	
With men of lawe he haght non spas° —	*hath no room*
They loven trewthe in no plas,°	*place*
Me thinkit they han a rewly grace,°	*have sorry manners*
That trewrthe is put° at swych degree.°	*placed* *level, esteem*
God be with trewthe …	

---

12   In *The Oxford Book of Medieval English Verse*, pp. 430–1, no. 186.

In holy cherche he may not sytte —	
Fro man to man they shuln hym flytte;°	*drive, pass on*
It rewit me sore,° in myn wytte —	*it grieves me sorely*
Of° trewthe I have grete pete,	*for*
God be with trewthe …	
Relygius° that shulde be good —	*those in religious orders*
If trewthe cum ther I holde hym wood!°	*mad*
They shuldyn hym rynde° cote and hood,	*tear from him*
And make hym bare for to fle.°	*flee*
God be with trewthe …	
A man that shulde of trewthe aspyre,°	*long for*
He must sekyn esylie°	*quietly*
In the bosom of Marye.	
For there he is forsothe.°	*truly*
God be with trewthe ….	

vi) Abuses of the Age[13]

Bissop lorles,°	*without learning*
Kyng redeles,°	*lacking counsel*
Yung man rechles,°	*heedless*
Old man witles,	
Womman ssamles.°	*shameless*
I swer bi heven kyng	
Thos beth five lither° thing,	*evil*

vii) Sir Penny is a Bold Knight[14]

Go bet,° Peny, go bet, go	*better*[15]
For thou mat° makyn bothe frynd and fo.	*may*

---

13   *Ibid.* no. 283.
14   *Ibid.* pp. 441–2, no. 196.
15   In this anthology, 'go bet' is glossed as 'get on'.

Peny is an hardy knyght,
Peny is mekyl of myght,
Peny, of wrong he makyt right
    In every cuntre qwer he goo.
    Go bet, Peny …

Thow I have a man islawe°   *killed*
And forfetyd the kynges lawe,
I shal fyndyn a man of lawe
    Wil takyn myn peny and let me goo.
    Go bet, Peny …

And if I have to don° fer or ner   *things to do*
And Peny be my massanger,
Than am I no thing in dwer° —   *doubt*
    My cause shal be wel idoo,°   *done*
    Go bet, Peny …

And if I have pens bothe good and fyn,
Men wyl byddyn me to the wyn —
'That I have shal be thi[n]!'
    Sekyrly° thei wyl seyn so.   *certainly*
    Go bet, Peny …

And quan I have non in myn purs,
Peny bet° ne peny wers,°   *better*   *worse*
Of me thei holdyn but lytil fors° —   *take little account*
    'He was a man; let hym goo.'
    Go bet, Peny …

viii) *London Lickpenny*[16]

To London once my stepps I bent,
   Where trouth in no wyse should be faynt,
To Westmynster-ward I forthwith went,
   To a man of law to make compleynt.
   I sayd, 'For Marys love, that holy saynt,
   Pyty the poore that wolde proceede!'°   *go to law*
   But for lack of mony I cold not spede.°   *prosper*

And as I thrust the prese° amonge,   *crowd*
   By froward° chaunce my hood was gone,   *evil*
Yet for all that I stayd not longe,
   Tyll at the Kynges Benche I was come,
   Before the Judge I kneled anon,°   *at once*
   And prayd hym for Gods sake to take heede —
   But for lack of mony I myght not spede.

Beneth them sat clarkes a gret rout,°   *crowd*
   Which fast dyd wryte by one assent;
There stoode up one and cryed about,
   'Rychard, Robert, and John of Kent!'
   I wyst° not well what this man ment;   *knew*
   He cryed so thycke° there in dede —   *quickly (indistinctly)*
   But he that lackt mony myght not spede.

Unto the Common Place° I yode thoo,°   *Common Pleas*   *went then*
   Where sat one with a sylken hoode;
Dyd hym reverence for I ought to do so,
   And told my case as well as I coolde.
   How my goodes were defrauded me by falsehood.
   I gat not a mum° of his mouth for my meed° —   *word*   *reward*
   And for lack of mony I myght not spede.

---

16   A shorter version is in *The Oxford Book of Medieval English Verse*, pp. 446–50, no. 200
(note p. 595).

Unto the Rolls I gat me from thence,
Before thee clarkes of the Chauncerye
Where many I found earning of pence,
    But none at all once regarded mee.
    I gave them my playnt uppon my knee.
    They liked it well, when they had it reade —
    But lackyng mony I could not be sped.

In Westmynster Hall I found out one,
    Which went in a long gown of raye,°   *striped cloth*
I crowched and kneled before hym anon —
    For Maryes love, of helpe I hym praye.
    'I wot not what thou meanest,' gan he say;
    To get me thence he dyd me bede° —   *order*
    For lack of mony I cold not speede.

Within this hall nether rych nor yett poor
    Wold do for me ought, although I shold dye;
Which seing, I gat me out of the doore,
    Where Flemynges began on me for to cry,
    'Master, what will you copen° or by?   *purchase*
    Fyne felt hates, or spectacles to reede?°   *read*
    Lay down your sylver, and here you may speede!'

Then to Westmynster gate I presently went,
    When the sonn was at hyghe pryme;°   *Prime*[17]
Cookes to me they tooke good entent,°   *attention*
    And proffered me bread with ale and wyne,
    Rybbs of befe, both fat and ful fine°   *thin*
    A fayre cloth they gan for to sprede —
    But wantyng mony I might not speede.

---

17   The first of the daytime hours, about 6 am, and the second of the canonical hours
    (*OED*).

Then unto London I dyd me hye,
    Of all the land it beareth the pryse.°   *is pre-eminent*
'Hot pescodes!'° one began to crye.   *pea pods*
    'Strabery rype!' and 'cherryes in the ryse!'°   *on the branch*
    One bad me come nere and by some spyce;
    Peper and safforne they gan me bede° —   *offer*
    But for lack of mony I might not spede.

Then to the Chepe° I gan me drawne,   *Cheapside*
    Where mutch people I saw for to stand;
One ofred me velvet, sylke, and lawne;°   *fine linen*
    Another he taketh me by the hande,
    'Here is Parys thred, the finest in the land!'
    I never was used to such thynges in dede,
    And wanting mony I myght not spede.

Then went I forth by London stone,[18]
    Throughout all Canwyke° Streete;   *Candlewick*
Drapers mutch cloth me offred anone;
    Then comes one, cryed, 'hot shepes feete!'
One cryde, 'makerell!'; 'ryshes° grene!' another gan   *rushes[19]*
    greete.°   *shouted*
    On bad me by a hood to cover my head —
    But for want of mony I myght not be sped.

Then I hyed ne into Estchepe,°   *Eastcheap*
    One cryes, 'rybbs of befe, and many a pye!'
Pewter pottes they clattered on a heape;
    There was harpe, pype, and mynstrelsye.
    'Yea, by cock!'° 'Nay, by cock!' some began crye;   *by God*
    Some songe of Jenken and Julyan for there mede —
    But for lack of mony I might not spede.

---

18   London Stone stood in the middle of Cannon Street.
19   Rushes were used as floor-covering.

Then into Cornhyll° anon I yode,   *Cornhill*[20]
    Where was mutch stolen gere amonge;
I saw where honge° myne owne hoode,   *was hanging*
    That I had lost amonge the thronge.
    To by my own hood I thought it wronge —
    I knew it well as I dyd my crede;
    But for lack of mony I could not spede.

The taverner tooke me by the sleve,
    'Sir,' sayth he, 'wyll you our wyne assay?'°   *try*
I answerd, 'that can not mutch me greve;
    A peny can do no more than it may.'
    I drank a pynt, and for it dyd paye,
    Yet sore ahungerd fron thence I yede,
    And wanting mony I not spede.

Then hyed I me to Belyngsgate,°   *Billingsgate*
    And one cryed, 'Hoo! Go we hence!'
I prayd a bargeman, for Gods sake,
    That he wold spare me my expence.
    'Thou scapst° not here,' quod he, 'under .ii. pence;   *escape*
    I lyst° not yet bestow my almes-dede!'   *wish*
    Thus, lackyng mony, I could not spede,

Then I conveyed me into Kent,
    For of° the law wold Y meddle no more,   *with*
Because no man to me tooke enten.°   *paid attention*
    I dyght me to do as I dyd before.
    Now Jesus that in Bethlem was bore,
    Save London, and send trew lawyers there mede!
    For whoso wants mony, with them shall not spede.

---

20   Cornhill was noted for drapers and vendors of old clothing.

C. Particular Abuses and Wicked Deeds

Medical and religious satire: although quack doctors and their remedies figure in popular drama, both medieval and later, English satirical poems on them have not survived in great numbers. We include one simple burlesque example. Here the more learned tradition produced one little masterpiece in Henryson's *Sum Practysis of Medecyne*, a dazzling performance which unites the style of 'flyting' with a wonderfully wild sense of fantasy: the 'remedies' include 'sevin sobbis of ane selche' [seal] and 'the lug of ane lempet'.[21] The much more extensive surviving corpus of religious satire — Lollard attacks on the church, orthodox attacks on Lollards — also presents problems for an anthologist of popular literature, since many examples seem more learned and 'literary'. We simply present two poems against friars.

ix) A Good Medicine for Sore Eyes[22]

For a man that is almost blynd:	
La hym go barhed° all day ageyn the wynd	*bare-headed*
Tyll the soyne° be sette;	*sun*
At evyn wrap hym in a cloke	
And put hym in a hows full of smoke,	
And loke that every hol be well shet.°	*shut*
And whan hys eyen begyne to rope,°	*water*
Fyl hem full of brynston and sope.	
And hyll° hym well and warme;	*cover*
And yf he se not by the next mone°	*moon*
As well at mydnyght as at none	
I schall lese° my ryght arme.	*lose*

---

21 In *The Middle Scots Poets*, ed. Kinghorn; a note mentions the medieval belief that doves had no gall (see Animal Tales, above).
22 In *The Oxford Book of Medieval English Verse*, p. 474, no. 213.

x) These Friars[23]

This poem is more lively than many anti-fraternal attacks, but it is sometimes obscure. The author seems to be thinking of wall-paintings in a church, such as are found in the large churches of the preaching friars.

Of thes frer mynors° me thenkes noch wonder,	*Minorites*
That waxen are° thus hauteyn,° that som tyme were under,	*are grown haughty*
Among men of holy chirch thai maken mochel blonder°	*confusion*
Nou He that sytes us above, make ham° sone to sonder!°	*them scatter*
With an O and an I, thai praysen not seynt Poule,	
Thai lyen° seyn Fraunceys, by my fader soule!	*tell lies about*

First thai gabben° on God that all men may se,	*mock*
When thai hangen him on high on a grene tre,	
With leves and with blossemes that bright are of ble,°	*colour*
That was never Goddes son by my leute.°	*faith*
With an O and an I, men wenen° that thai wede,°	*think go mad*
To carpe° so of clergy° that can not thair crede.[24]	*prate learning*

Thai have done him on a croys° fer up in the skye,	*cross*
And festned in hym wyenges,° as he shuld flie.	*wings*
This fals, feyned byleve shal thai soure bye,°	*pay for dearly*
On that lovelych lord, so for to lye.	
With an O and an I, one sayd ful still,°	*quietly*
Armachan° distroy ham, if it is Goddes will.	*Archbishop of Armagh*[25]

Ther comes one out of the skye in a grey goun	
As it were a hog-hyerd° hyand° to toun;	*shepherd hurrying*
Thai have mo° goddess then we, I say, by Mahoun,[26]	*more*

---

23 A short version of this is in *Medieval English Lyrics* (ed. Davis), pp. 141–2, no. 59; the note (p. 331) says it is frankly rather puzzling. See also *Historical Poems*, ed. Robbins (no. 66, on the Minorites).

24 Who do not know their Creed; this, and the Lord's Prayer, were the two prayers that everybody was expected to know by heart.

25 This was Richard Fitzralph, who preached against mendicant abuses.

26 'Saracens' and other 'pagans' were thought to swear by Mahomet.

All men under ham that ever beres croun,º   *tonsure*
    With an O and an I, why shuld thai not be shent?º   *destroyed*
    Ther wants noght bot a fyre that thai nereº all brent!   *were not*

Went I forther on my way in that same tyde,º   *time*
Ther I sawe a frere bled in myddes of his syde,
Bothe in hondes and in fete he had woundes wyde;
To serve to that same frer, the pope mot abyde.º   *must wait*
    With an O and an I, I wonder of thes dedes,
    To se a pope holde a dische whyl the frer bledes.

A cart was made al of fyre, as it shuld be,
A gray frer I sawe therinne, that best liked me
Wele I wute thai shal be brent, by my leaute —
God graunt me that grace that I may it se.
    With an O and an I, brent be thai all,
    And all that helpes therto faire mot befall.º   *may it prosper*

Thai preche all of povert,º but that love thai noght —   *poverty*
For gode meteº to thair mouthe the toun is thurghsoght;º   *food*   *searched*
Wyde are thair wonnyngesº and wonderfully wroght —   *dwellings*
Murdre and horedome ful dere has it boght.º   *paid for*
With an O and an I, for sixe pens, erº thai fayle,   *before*
Sleº thi fadre and japeº thi modre, and thai wyl the   *kill*   *seduce*
    assoille!º   *absolve*

xi) Thou that Sellest the Word of God[27]

Thou that sellest the worde of God
Be thou berfot,º be thou shod,   *bare-foot*
    Cum nevere here;
In principio erat verbum[28]
Is the worde of God, all and sum,º   *the whole of it*

---

27   In *The Oxford Book of Medieval Verse*, pp. 410–11, no. 171.
28   In the Beginning was the Word, the opening of John's Gospel.

That thou sellest, lewed° frere,   *ignorant*

Hit is cursed symonie
Ether to selle or to bye
 Any gostly° thinge;   *spiritual*
Therfore, frere, go as thou come,
And hold the in thi hows at home
 Tyl we the almis° brynge.   *alms*

Goddes lawe ye reverson,°   *overthrow*
And mennes howsis ye persen,°   *get into*
 As Poul berith wittnes,[29]
As mydday develis goynge abowte,
For money lowle° ye lowte,°   *lowly*   *bow*
 Flatteringe boythe more and lesse.°   *great and small*

D. Against Particular Groups or Individuals

Satirical verses against foreigners: a number have survived, mostly against Flemings and Scots. Those against the Scots are more numerous, and also more eloquent; and there are some sharp Scottish ripostes: Scots and English seem to have exchanged 'males chansons'.

xii) Against the Rebellious Scots [1296][30]

Tprut° Scot rivelling°   *(exclamation of contempt)*   *rascal (lit. a rough boot)*
With mikel mistiming
Crop thu° ut of kage.   *you crept*

---

29 This may be I Peter 5:8–9 (not an epistle of Paul). The Bible was well known in the Middle Ages, but Bible books and authors were often confused. The 'noonday devil' was the sin of sloth, 'the destruction that wasteth at noonday' (Ps. 91:6 in the Authorized Version, Ps. 90 in the Latin and Douay bibles).

30 In Pierre de Langtoft's *Chronicle*, see note (on p. 391) to v. 156 (on p. 283); *The Political Songs of England*, ed. Wright.

xiii) A Scottish song against Edward I when he besieged Berwick[31]

Wenes kyng Edward, with his longe shankes	
Forto wyn Berwik, al oure unthankes?°	*against our wishes*
Gas pikes° him!	*go pierce*
And when he hath hit,	
Gas diche° him!	*dig*

xiv) Black Agnes at the siege of Dunbar [1388][32]

An English soldiers' song recorded by a Scottish chronicler

… Off this ilk sege° in hething°	*siege*	*derision*
The Ingllismen maid oft carping:°	*complaint*	
'I wow° to God, scho° beris hir weill,	*vow*	*she*
The Scottis wenche with her ploddeill;°	*band of ruffians*	
For cum I airly,° cum I lait,	*early*	
I fynde ay Annes at the gate!'		

xv) The Execution of Sir Simon Fraser[33]

Sir Simon Fraser (or Frisell) was captured by the English at the battle of Methven or Kirkencliff (1306). He was taken to London and executed in that year. Perhaps the poem was written shortly after the execution, by a professional ballad-maker; it seems generally similar to the 'news ballads' found in later popular literature. [vv. 169–208]

For al is grete poer,° yet he wes ylaht:°	*power*	*caught*
Falsnesse and swykedom° al hit geth to naht.°	*treachery*	*nought*

---

31 In *The Oxford Book of Medieval English Verse*, p. 58, no. 32 a.
32 From Andrew of Wyntoun's *Chronicle*, viii, 4993 (ed. Amours; Laing's edn. may also be consulted). Several versions of vv. 3–6 in the present extract are cited in *DIMEV*, no. 2298 (*IMEV* 1377); none matches this extract exactly. See also Wilson, 'More Lost Literature', p. 44; and Flood, *Prophecy, Politics and Place*, p. 129; *DIMEV*'s reference to Wilson's (1952) book incorrectly gives p. 231; it is in fact p. 213. Agnes successfully defended her castle against the English in the absence of her husband.
33 This poem is found in London, BL MS Harley 2253; see *The Complete Harley 2253 Manuscript*, vol. 2, ed. and trans. Fein *et al*, article 25.

Tho° he wes in Scotland, lutel wes ys thoht	*when*
Of the harde jugement that hym wes bysoht°	*sought, demanded*
In stounde,°	*time*
He wes foure sithe° forswore°	*times* · *perjured*
To the kyng ther bifore,	
And that him brohte to grounde.°	*brought down*
With feteres and with gyves ichot° he wes todrowe,°	*I know* · *drawn*
From the Tour of Londone, that monie myhte	
knowe,°	*so that many be aware*
In a curtel of burel° a selkethe° wyse.	*tunic of sackcloth* · *strange*
Ant a garland on ys heved of the newe guyse,	
Thurh Cheepe.°	*through Cheapside*
Moni mon of Engelond	
For to se Symond	
Thideward° con lepe.°	*thither* · *did run*
Tho° he com to galewes, furst he wes anhonge,	*when*
Al quic° byheveded, thah him thohte° longe.	*living* · *though it seemed to him*
Seththe° he wes yopened, is° bowels ybrend;°	*then* · *his* · *burnt*
The heved to Londone Brugge wes send	
To shonde.°	*shame*
So ich ever mote the:°	*may prosper*
Sum while° wende° he	*once* · *expected*
Ther lutel to stonde —	
He° rideth thourh the site,° as I telle may,	*they* · *city*
With gomen and wyth solas,° that wes here pay	*games and fun*
To Londone Brugge hee nome° the way —	*they took*
Mony wes the wyves chil° that theron loketh a° day,	*child* · *by*
And seide alas,	
That he was bore°	*born*
And sovilliche forlore°	*vilely undone*
So feir mon° as he was.	*man*

Nou stont the heved above the tubrugge,º   *drawbridge*
Faste bi Waleis,º soth forte sugge;º   *Wallace*   *say*
After socour of Scotlond longe he mowe prye.º   *gaze*
And after help of Fraunce wet halt it to lye,º   *what profits it to lie*
    Ich wene.º   *I think*
    Betere him were in Scotlond
    With is ax in ys hond,
    To pleyen oº the grene.   *on*

xvi) Revenge for Bannockburn[34]

The Englishman Laurence Minot wrote a series of poems celebrating the deeds of Edward III against the Scots and his other enemies. This vigorous example is occasioned by the English victory at Halidon Hill (1333), which he sees as a triumphant revenge for the Scots' defeat of the English by Robert the Bruce at Bannockburn (1314). Minot sees the Scots as rough and boastful — and untrustworthy.

Skottes out of Berwik and of Abirdene,
At the Bannok burn war ye to kene;º   *bold*
Thare sloghº ye many sakles,º als it wes sene,   *slew*   *innocent*
And now has king Edward wrokenº it, I wene,   *avenged*
It is wroken, I wene, wele wurth the while,º   *happy the day!*
War yit withº the Skottes, for thai er ful of gile.   *still watch out for*

Whare er ye, Skottes of saint Johnes toune?º   *Perth*
The bosteº of yowre baner es betin al doune;   *pride*
When ye bosting wll bede,º sir Edward es bouneº   *offer*   *ready*
For to kindle yow care and crak yowre crowne.
He has cracked yowre croune, wele wurth the while!
Schame bitydeº the Skottes, for thai er ful of gile.   *befall*

Skottes of Striflinº war steren and stout,º   *Stirling*   *fierce and strong*
Of God ne of gude men had thai no dout;º   *fear*

---

34   This is printed in *Fourteenth Century Verse and Prose*, ed. Sisam, pp. 152–3 (notes pp. 253–4).

Nou have thai, the pelers,º prikedº obout,	*robbers*	*galloped*
Bot at the last sir Edward rifildº thaire rout.º	*stripped*	*host*
He has rifild thaire rout, wel wurth the while!		
Bot ever er thai underº bot gaudesº and gile.	*underneath*	*tricks*

Rughfute riveling,º now kindels thi care,	*rough-footed rascal (with brogues)*
Berebagº with thi boste, thi bigingº es bare;	*bag-carrier* *dwelling*
Fals wretche and forsworn, whider wiltou fare?	
Buskº the into Brig,º and abide thare.	*hurry* *Bruges*
Thare, wretche, saltou wonº and weryº the while;	*live* *curse*
Thi dwelling in Dondeº es doneº for thi gile.	*Dundee* *finished*

The Skotte gase in Burghesº and betesº the stretes,	*Bruges*	*frequents*
All thise Inglis men harmes he hetes,º	*promises*	
Fast makes he his moneº to men that he metes,	*complaint*	
But foneº frendes he finds that his bale betes.º	*few*	*misery assuages*
Funeº betes his bale, wele wurth the while,	*few*	
He uses all threting with gaudes and gile.		

Bot many man thretes and spekes ful ill.	
That sum tyme war better to be stane-still,º	*silent as stone*
The Skot in his wordes has wind for to spill,º	*waste*
For at the kast Edward sall have al his will.	
He had his will at Berwik, wele wurth the while,	
Skottes broght him the kayesº — bot getº for thaire gile.	*keys* *watch out*

xvii) The Fall of Suffolk [1450][35]

Popular resentment at events in England and France had become centred on William de la Pole, Duke of Suffolk, 'the Fox of the South': he was blamed for the unpopular marriage of Henry VI to Margaret of Anjou, for recent defeats and losses in France, and for his suspected role

---

35 Cited in Gray's *Later Medieval English Literature*, p. 337; see *Historical Poems*, ed. Robbins, no. 75.

in the death of Humphrey Duke of Gloucester (1447). He was indicted and held in the Tower prior to banishment. The poem was written at this point, probably in February 1450. Later in 1450 he set out for France, but was intercepted and murdered. Another satirical poem 'celebrates' his death. The 'fox' poem makes some play with animal names and heraldic imagery: Talbot 'our dog', the Earl of Shrewsbury, one of the great English generals (a talbot is a kind of hound); Jack Napes, a tame ape, suggested by Suffolk's badge of clog and chain; John Beaumont, Constable of England, is 'that gentill rache' (hunting dog), and 'beaumont' was the name of a hound; 'oure grete gandere' is Duke Humphrey, whose badge was a swan.

Now is the fox drevin° to hole! Hoo to hym, hoo, hoo!	*driven*
For and° he crepe out, he will yow alle undo,	*if*
Now ye han founde° parfite, love well your game;	*have discovered game*
For and ye ren countre,° then be ye to blame.	*in the opposite direction*
Sum of yow holdith with the fox and rennyth hare;	
But he that tied Talbot our doge, evyll mote he fare!	
For now we mys the black dog with the wide mouth,	
For he wold have ronnen well at the fox of the south.	
And all gooth backward, and don is° in the myre,	*is put, or stuck*[36]
As they han deserved, so pay they ther hire.	
Now is tyme of Lent; the fox is in the towre;	
Therfore send hym Salesbury° to be his confessoure.	*Bishop Ayscough of Salisbury*

Many mo ther ben, and we kowd hem knowe,°		*make known*
But won° most begyn the daunce, and all com arowe,°	*one*	*in a line*
Loke that your hunte° blowe well thy chase;°	*huntsman*	*pursuit*
But° he do well is part, I beshrewe° is face!	*unless*	*curse*
This fox at Bury slowe oure grete gandere;		
Therfore at Tyborn mony mon on hym wondere.		
Jack Napes, with his clogge		
Hath tied Talbot, oure gentill dogge,		
Wherfore Beaumownt, that gentill rache,		

---

36   *MED* 'don', a dun horse; it cites a similar line to this one, meaning 'horse and cart are in the mire', but neither is likely in this context (this poem is not cited). It may refer to a game which involved pulling on a log.

Hath brought Jack Napiis in an evill cache.º	*pursuit*
Be ware, al men, of that blame,	
And namlyº ye of grete fame,	*especially*
Spirituall and temperall, be ware of this,	
Or els hit will not be well, iwis.	
God save the kyng, and God forbade	
That he suche apes any mo fede,	
And of the perille that may befall	
Be ware, dukes, erles, and barouns alle.	

E. Parody and Burlesque

Two examples of verse satire which make good use of the extensive and deep-rooted tradition.

xviii) *The Land of Cokaygne*[37]

This Early Middle English poem, with its witty combination of anti-monastic satire and parody of the delights of the Eathly Paradise, manages to create a glorious vision of a comic utopia; and the (monastic) world upside down. [vv. 51–166]

… Ther is a wel fair abbei		
Of white monkes and of grei;		
Ther beth bowrisº and halles —	*chambers*	
Al of pasteisº beth the walles,	*pasties*	
Of fleis,º of fisse, and rich met,º	*meat*	*food*
The likfullistº that man mai et,	*most delightful*	
Flurenº cakes beth the schinglesº alle	*of flour*	*shingles*
Of cherche, cloister, boure, and halle;		
The pinnesº beth fat podingesº —	*fastening pegs*	*sausages*
Rich met to princes and kings.		
Manº mai therof et inoghº	*one*	*enough*

---

37 In *Early Middle English Verse and Prose*; see also Gray's *From the Norman Conquest* pp. 352–5. Bennett describes it as the first fully comic poem in our literature (*Middle English Literature*, pp. 14–17).

Al with right and noght with wogh;° *wrong*

Al is commune to yung and old,

To stoute and sterne, mek and bold.

Ther is a cloister, fair and light,

Brod and lang, of sembli sight;° *handsome appearance*

The pilers of that cloister alle

Beth iturned of° cristale, *shaped from*

With har bas° and capitale *their base*

Of grene jaspe° and rede corale. *jasper*

In the praer° is a tre, *meadow*

Swithe likful° for to se — *very pleasant*

The rote° is gingevir° and galingale,[38] *root* *ginger*

The siouns° beth al sedwale° *shoots* *zedoary*

Trie maces° beth the flure, *excellent mace*

The rind canel° of swet odur, *bark cinnamon*

The frute gilofre° of gode smakke;° *clove* *taste*

Of cucubes° ther is no lakke. *cubebs*

Ther beth rosis of rede ble,° *colour*

And the lilie likful° forto se *delightful*

That faloweth° never dai no night *withers*

This aght° be a swet sight, *ought*

Ther beth .iiii. willis° in the abbey, *wells*

Of treacle° and halwei,° *medicine* *healing water*

Of baum° and ek piement° ... *balm* *also spiced wine*

[There are precious stones, and many birds.]

... Ther beth briddes mani and fale° ... *numerous*

The gees irostid° on the spitte *roasted*

Flees° to that abbey, God hit wot,° *fly* *knows it*

And gredith,° 'Gees, al hote! al hot!' *call out*

Hi° bringeth garlek, grete plente, *they*

The best idight° that man mai se. *prepared*

The leverokes,° that beth cuth,° *larks* *esteemed*

Lightith adun° to manis muth, *down*

Idight in stu,° ful swathe° wel, *cooked in a pot* *very*

---

38   An aromatic root (see *OED*).

Pudrid° with gilofre and canel.	*powdered*
Nis no spech° of no drink;	*nothing is said of*
Ak take° inogh withute swink° …	*but taken* *labour*
… The yung monkes euch° dai	*each*
Aftiir met° goth to plai;	*food*
Nis ther hauk no fule° so swifte	*hawk nor bird*
Bettir fleing° be the lifte,°	*flying* *through the air*
Than the monkes heigh of mode°	*in high spirits*
With har° slevis and har hode.	*their*
Whan the abbot seeth ham flee,°	*sees them fly*
That he holt for° moch glee;°	*regards as* *amusement*
Ak natheles,° al ther amang,°	*but nevertheless* *in the midst of it all*
He biddith ham light to evesang.°	*come down to evensong*
The monkes lightith noght adun,	
Ac furre° fleeth in o randun.°	*but further* *headlong*
Whan the abbot him iseeth	
That is monkes fram him fleeth,	
He takith a maidin of the route°	*crowd*
And turnith up har white toute,°	*bottom*
And betith the taburs° with is hond	*as a drum*
To make is monkes light to lond.	
Whan is monkes that iseeth,	
To the maid dun hi fleeth.	
And goth the wench al abute	
And thakketh° al hir white toute.	*pat*
And sith aftir her swinke°	*their toil*
Wendith meklich hom to drink,	
And goth to har collacione	
A wel fair processione.	
Another abbei is therbi —	
Forsoth, a gret fair nunnerie,	
Up° a river of swet milke,	*upon*
Whar is gret plente of silk.°	*such*
Whan the someris dai is hote,	
The yung nunnes takith a bote	

And doth ham forthin that river,

Both with oris and with stere.º   *oars and rudder*

Whan hi beth furº fram the abbei   *far*

Hi makith ham naked forto plei.

And lepith dune into the brimmeº   *water*

And doth ham sleilichº forto swimme.   *skilfully*

The yung monkes that hi seeth,º   *see them*

Hi doth ham upº and forth hi fleeth,   *get up*

And cummith to the nunnes anon,º   *quickly*

And euch monke him taketh on,º   *one*

And snellichº berith forth har prei   *quickly*

To the mochil greiº abbei,   *large grey*

And techith the nunnes an oreisunº   *prayer*

With jambleveº up and doun ....   *legs raised*

xix) *The Tournament of Tottenham*[39]

A merry burlesque of a chivalric event, played out by humble locals
rather than by armed knights. [vv. 1–90]

Of alle these kene conqueroures to carpe it were kynde,

Off feleº feghtyng folk ferlyº we fynde.   *fierce*   *wondrously*

The tournament of Totenham have we in mynde —

It were harme sich hardynesse were holdyn behynde.

    In story as we rede

    Of Hawkyn, of Harry,

    Off Tymkyn, of Tyrry.

    Off theym that were dughtyº   *valiant*

    And hardy in dede.

Hit befell in Totenham on a dere day,

Ther was made a schartyngº be the hy way —   *festival*

Thider com alle the men of tho contray.

---

39 In *Middle English Verse Romances*. Sands has modernized the spelling slightly,
    compared with the version presented here.

Of Hyssylton, of Hygate, and of Hakenay.
    And alle the swete swynkers.º   *toilers*
Ther heppedº Hawkyn,   *hopped*
Ther dawnsed Dawkyn.
Ther trumpedº Tomkyn,   *trumpeted*
    And alle were trewe drynkers.

Tyl the day was gon and evesong past,
That thay shuld rekyn ther skot and ther counts caste
Perkyn the potter into the pressº past   *crowd*
And seid, 'Rondol the refe,º a doghter thou hast,   *reeve*
Tyb thi dere,
Therfor wytº wold I,   *know*
Whych of all this bachelery
Were best worthy
To wed her to his fere.'º   *consort*

Upsterte thos gadelyngysº with ther lang staves   *fellows*
And sayd, 'Rondol the refe, Lo, this lad raves!
Baldely amang us thy doghter he craves,
And we er richer men than he, and more godº haves   *property*
Of catel and corn.'
Then sayd Perkyn to Tybbe, 'I have hyghtº   *promised*
That I schal be always redy in my right
If that it schulkd be thys dat sevenyght
Or ellis yet to morn.'

Then seid Randolfe the refe, 'Ever be he waryd,º   *cursed*
That about thys carping lenger wold be taryed,
I wold not my doghter that sche were myscaryed,
But at her most worschypº I wold she were maryed,   *honour*
Therfor a tournament schal begyn
Thys day sevenyght.
With a flayle for to fight.
And he that ys of most myght
Schal broukeº hur with wynne.º   *enjoy*   *pleasure*

Whoso berys hym best in the tournament,

Hym shal be granted the gre° be the common assent,   *prize*

For to wynne my doghter with dughtyness of dent,°   *blows*

And Coppeld my brode° henne, was broght out of Kent,   *brood*

And my donnyd° cow.   *dun*

For no spens wyl I spare,

For no catell wyl I care,

He schal have my gray mare,

And my spottyd sowe.'

Ther was many a bold lad ther bodyes to bede;

Than thay toke thayre leve, and hamward thei yede,°   *went*

And alle the woke afterward thay graythed ther wede,°   *prepared their equipment*

Tyll it come to the day that thay suld do ther dede.

Thay armed ham in mattes;

Thay set on ther nollys,°   *heads*

For to kepe ther pollys,°   *guard their heads*

Gode blake bollys°   *bowls*

For batryng° of battes;   *against battering*

They sewed tham in schepe skynnes, for they suld not brest,

And ilkon toke a black hatte instead of a crest.

A harrow brod° as a fanne aboune° on ther brest,   *broad*   *above*

And a flayle in ther hande, for to fight prest.°   *ready*

Furth gone thay fare.

Ther was kyd mekyl° fors,   *shown great*

Who schuld best fend his cors.°   *defend his body*

He that had no gode hors,

He gat hym a mare.

Sych another gadryng have I not sene oft,

When all the gret company come rydand to the croft:

Tyb on a gray mare was set upon loft

On a sek° full of feerys° for she shuld syt soft,   *sack*   *feathers*

And led hur to the gap —

Forther wold not Tyb then
For crying of al the men,
Tyl scho had hur gode brode hen
Set in hur lap.

A gay gyrdyl Tyb had on, borwed for the monys,º   *for the occasion*
And a garland on hur hed ful of rounde bones.
And a broche on hur brest, ful of saferº stones,   *sapphire*
Wyth the haly rude tokening was wrethyn for tho nonys.[40]
No catel was ther spared.
When joly Gyb saw hure hare,
He gyrd so hus gray mere
That she lete a faucon-fareº   *fart*
At the rerewarde.º   *at the back end*
[The company proceeds to make vows, one after the other in the manner of
Charlemagne's knights in *Voeux du Paon*.[41] vv. 145–71]
When thay had ther othes made, furth gan they hyeº   *hasten*
With flayles and hornes and trumpes mad of tre.º   *wood*
Ther were all the bachelerys of that contre,
Thay were dyght in aray as thamselfe wold be —
     Thayr baner was full bright
Of an pled raton fell,º   *rat skin*
The cheveroneº of a ploo mellº   *chevron*   *plough mallet*[42]
And the schadow of a bell,
     Quartered with the mone light.

I wot it ys no childer game whan thay togedyr met,
When ich freke in the feld on his felayº bet,   *fellow*
And layd on styfly — for nothyng wold thay let,
And faght ferly fast, tyl ther horses swet.
     And fewe wordys spoken.

---

40   The Holy Rood was worked in, as well.
41   This was an immensely popular chanson de geste (c. 1312) by Jacques de Longuyon
     of Lorraine.
42   For breaking up clods.

Ther were flayles al to-slatred,
Ther were scheldys al to-flatred,
Bollys and dyschis al to-schatred,
And many hedys brokyn.

Ther was clynkyng of cart sadellys and clattiryng of connes,º   *canes*
Of fele frekis in the feld brokyn were ther fannesº   *winnowing shovels*[43]
Of sum were the hedys brokyn, of sum the brayn panes.
And yll ware thay beseyn orº they went thens,   *before*
Wuth swyppyng of swepyllys.º   *striking of flail-ends*
The boyes were so wery for-fught,º   *fought to a standstill*
That thay might not fight mare oloft.
But creped then about in the croft,
As thay were crokid crypils.

[vv. 190–214] Perkyn turnyd hym about in that ych thrange,
Among thos wery boyes he wrest and he wrang,
When he saw Tirry away with Tyb fang,
And wold have lad hir away with a luf song,
And after hym ran
And of hys hors he hym droghº   *pulled*
And gaf hym of hys flayle inogh.
'We, te-he,' quod Tyb, and lughº   *laughed*
'Ye ar a dughty man!'

Thus thay tugged and rugged tyl yt was nere nyght,
Alle the wyves of Totenham come to se that syght,
With wyspys and kexis and ryschys ther light,[44]
To fech hom ther husbandes, that were tham trouth-plight,
And sum broght gret harwesº   *sledges*
Ther husbandes hom for to fech;
Sum on dores and sum on hech,º   *gratings*
Sum on hyrdyllys and sum on crech,º   *crutch*
And sum on welebaraws.

---

43   Probably here being used as shields.
44   With lit straw, flax, and rush-lights.

They gaderyd Perkyn about everych syde

And grant hym ther the gre,° the more° was his pride.   *prize*   *greater*

Tyb and he with gret myrthe homward can they ride,

And were al nyght togedyr tyl the morn tide,

And thay in fere° assent: *together*

So wele his nedys he has sped,

That dere Tyb he had wed ...

[And there is a rich feast ...][45]

---

45   Gray presents most of this text, breaking off at v. 214 (it ends at v. 234).

Chapter 9

Songs

In spite of considerable losses of material in manuscripts and early prints, a surprisingly large number of early songs and lyrics have survived. The corpus must have been a very substantial one. And behind and beside it lay another: an equally large mass of oral songs, now almost totally lost to us, but which lived in the memories of contemporary literate poets. The heads of some clerks were probably filled with snatches of old songs, remembered from younger days or still heard in the communities in which they lived. They will sometimes refer to such songs in their sophisticated works: Chaucer makes his Pardoner sing 'Come hider, love, to me';[1] Gavin Douglas quotes (among other examples) 'the schip salis our the salt fame, Will bring thir merchandis and my lemman hame'.[2] And, as we have already seen in the pages of this anthology, other 'snatches' are sometimes quoted by (usually hostile) preachers and moralists. A number are quoted below. Such snatches are probably the closest we can come to the lost corpus of early oral song. But many of the lyrics printed below are the work of clerks related in various degrees to the tradition of oral song. Some of these 'popular lyrics' are (as Greene described them, see below) popular 'by destination', intended for the use of an illiterate or partly-literate audience. The literary skill of the clerks and the quality of their imitations of the simple styles and forms of oral songs often make it very difficult to decide whether a lyric should

---

1   *Tales*, 1A (Prologue), v. 672.
2   In the Prologue to the 12th book of his translation of Virgil's *Aeneid*.

© 2019 Douglas Gray and Jane Bliss, CC BY-NC 4.0   https://doi.org/10.11647/OBP.0170.09

be described as 'popular' or 'learned' and, if we decide to place it in
the category of popular lyric (a category whose boundaries are not
absolutely fixed), how closely it approximates to the oral song from
which it came. Thus Greene,[3] discussing the plough song (xiii), records
numerous parallels in later folksong, but points out that the carol is
'intended for more sophisticated performance, probably by choir-
boys', and concludes cautiously that 'it is conceivable that a carol on
this theme may be the result of a learned clerical composer's interest in
an air heard in the fields.' Similarly, in the fine drinking song 'Bryng
us in good ale' (xvi) he notes the 'repeated formula with a portion
changed with each repetition, an old device used by very elementary
folk-poetry' — and which allows improvisation.[4] However, the
repetition is quite artful, with the rejected items of food becoming
a splendidly bizarre ensemble, and the accompanying (apparently
explanatory) 'asides' are sometimes wonderfully fantastic. Could it
be a clever imitation, and transformation, of the techniques of oral
folk-poetry? 'Performance' seems to lie behind almost all the popular
lyrics. Some of them are clearly dance songs; in nearly all of them we
seem to hear the voice of the singer. They survive in a variety of forms.
Perhaps the most distinctive is the 'carol', not yet limited to Christmas
songs. The name derives from the French 'carole', a ring-dance, and
the ideas of performance and entertainment continue to lurk even in
the more sophisticated and literary examples. Characteristically the
Middle English carol is a stanzaic poem, secular or religious, marked
by a recurring 'burden' or refrain. Other forms of song are also found,
and we see brief glimpses of sharp satire, and examples of popular
talk (like the ducks that 'slobber in the mere', in xvi below), double
entendre, and some entertaining rascals. But in general the popular
lyric presents us with a rich and varied array of merry entertainment.
Our selection attempts to give a sense of this. After a 'welcome song'
delivered by a minstrel or a master of ceremonies, we move to a series
of snatches of oral songs, then to the merriment of the festal season
and throughout the year, and to various contemporary figures, pedlars
'light of foot', roving bachelors and an amorous priest, encounters

---

3   *Early English Carols*, 1977 (revised) edition. The Plough Song is no. 418.2 (pp. 248–9),
     notes pp. 464–5.
4   Gray cites this in *Simple Forms* (p. 223), giving a reference to *Early English Carols* p.
     cxx; the comment is not in Greene's notes to the song.

between men and women; to some songs which seem to hover between children's songs and erotic lyric, and to merry nonsense verse. We end with some religious popular lyrics, some of which show the same zest and merriment as their secular counterparts.

Snatches of Oral Songs

i)[5]

Bon jowre, bon jowre a vous!°	*good day to you*
I am cum unto this hows	
With 'par la pompe',° I say.	*with ceremony*
Is ther any good man here	
That will make me any chere?°	*entertainment*
And if ther were, I wold cum nere	
To wit° what he wold° say.	*know* *would*
A, will ye be wild?°	*hard to catch*
By Mary myld,	
And her swete child,	
I trow ye will synge gay.°	*merrily*
Bon jowre …	
Be gladly,° masters everychon!	*joyful*
I am cum myself alone	
To appose° you on° by on;	*question* *one*
Let se who dare say nay	
Sir, what say ye?	
Syng on, let us see.	
Now will it be	
Thys or another day?	
Bon jowre …	

---

5   In *The Oxford Book of Medieval Verse*, no. 259. Normally, only one reference is given for each poem.

Loo, this is he that will do the dede!

He tempereth° his mowth° — therefore take hede.   *tunes*   *voice*

Syng softe, I say, lest yowr nose blede,

For hurt yowrself ye may.

  But, by God that me bowght,°   *redeemed*

   Your brest is so towght,°   *congested*

Tyll ye have well cowght°   *coughed*

Ye may not therwith away.°   *do away with it*

Bon jowre …

Sir, what say ye with your face so lene?

Ye syng nother good tenowre, treble, ne mene.°   *nor mean*[6]

Utter not your voice without° your brest be clene,°   *unless*   *clear*

Hartely I you pray.

I hold you excused,

  Ye shall be refused,

For ye have not be° used   *been*

To no good sport nor play.

Bon jowre …

Sir, what say ye with your fat face?

Me thynkith ye shuld bere a very good bace.°   *maintain bass*

To a pot of good ale or ipocras,°   *sweet spiced wine*

Truly as I you say.

  Hold up your hede,

   Ye loke lyke lede,°   *lead*

  Ye wast myche° bred   *waste much*

Evermore from day to day.

Bon jowre …

Now will ye see wher he stondith behynde?

Iwis,° brother, ye be unkind;   *indeed*

Stond forth, and wast with me som wynd°   *breath*

---

6 Mean would be a middle line in the part-song.

For ye have ben called a synger ay.º   *always*
    Nay, be not ashamed —
    Ye shall not be blamed,
For ye have ben famed
The worst in this contrey.
Bon jowre …

ii)[7]

Of every kuneº tre,   *kind (of)*
Of every kune tre,
The hawethorn blowet suotes[t]º   *blossoms most sweetly*
Of every kune tre

My lemmonº she shal boe,º   *lover*   *be*
My lemmon she shal boe,
The fairest of e[very] kinne,
My lemmon she shal boe.

iii)[8]

Al nistº by the rose, rose   *night*
Al nist bi the rose I lay,
Dar[st]º ich noust the rose stele,   *dared*
Ant yet ich bar the flourº away.   *I took the flower (= maidenhood)*

iv)[9]

Mayden in the mor lay,
In the mor lay,

---

7   *Ibid.* no. 66.
8   In *Medieval English Lyrics*, ed. Silverstein, no. 61.
9   *Ibid.* no. 62.

Sevenyst° fulle, sevenist fulle.   *seven nights*
Maiden in the mor lay,
In the mor lay,
Sevenistes fulle ant a day.

Welle° was hire mete,°   *excellent*   *food*
Wat was hire mete?
The primerole° ant the,   *primrose*
The primerole ant the,
Welle was hire mete,
Wat was hire mete?
The primerole
Ant the violet.

Welle was hire dryng,°   *drink*
Wat was hire dryng?
The chelde° water of the,   *cold*
The chelde water of the,
Welle was hire dryng,
Wat was hire dryng?
The chelde water of the,
Of the welle-spring.

Welle was hire bour,°   *dwelling*
Wat was hire bour?
The rede rose an te,°   *the*
The rede rose an te,
Welle was hire bour,
Wat was hire bour?
The rede rose an te,
The rede rose an te
An te lilie flour.

v)[10]

Ich am of Irlaunde
And of the holy londe
Of Irlande.
Gode sire, pray ich the,
For of saynte charite,°   *holy charity*
Come and daunce wyt me
In Irlaunde.

vi)[11]

Me thingkit° thou art so lovely,   *seems*
So fair and so swete,
That sikirli° it were mi det°   *certainly*   *death*
Thi companie to lete.°   *give up*

vii)[12]

Westron wynde when wyll thow blow?
The smalle° rayne downe can° rayne.   *fine*   *does*
Cryst, yf my love wer in my armes
And I in my bed agayne!

viii)[13]

Sing, cuccu nu! Sing cuccu!
Sing, cuccu! Sing, cuccu nu!

Somer is ycumen in,
Lhude° sing, cuccu!   *loudly*

---

10 *Ibid.* no. 60.
11 *Ibid.* no. 63.
12 *Medieval English Lyrics*, ed. Davies, no. 181.
13 *Ibid.* no. 3.

Groweth sed and bloweth° med°   *blossoms*   *meadow*
And springth the wode° nu.   *wood*
Sing, cuccu!

Awe° bleteth after lomb,   *ewe*
Lhouth° after calve° cu,   *lows*   *calf*
Bulluc sterteth,° bucke verteth°   *leaps*   *farts*
Murye sing, cuccu!
Cuccu, cuccu,
Wel singes thu, cuccu,
Ne swik thu naver° nu!   *do not ever cease*

Christmas and New Year

ix)[14]

Make we mery both more and lasse°   *high and low*
For now ys the tyme of Crystymas.

Lett no man cum into this hall —
Grome,° page, nor yet marshall,°   *servant*   *steward*
But that sum sport he bring with all,
For now ys the tyme of Crystmas.
Make we mery …

Yff that he say he can not syng,
Sum oder sport then lett hym bring,
That yt may please at thys festyng,
For now ys the tyme of Crystmas.
Make we mery …

Yff he say he can nowght do,
Then for my love aske hym no mo —
But to the stokes° then let hym go,   *stocks*

---

14   *Ibid.* no. 168.

For now ys the tyme of Crystmas.

Make we mery …

x) The Boar's Head[15]

Po, po, po, po,°	*(a barnyard call for pigs)*
Love brane° and so do mo.°	*brawn* *more*

At the begynnyng of the mete

Of a borys hed ye schal hete,°   *eat*

And in the mustard ye shal wete,°   *dip*

And ye shal syngyn or ye gon.

Po, po …

Wolcum be ye that ben here,

And ye shal have ryth gud chere,

And also a ryth gud fare,

And ye shal syngyn or ye gon.

Po, po …

Welcum be ye everychon,

For ye shal syngyn ryth anon;

Hey yow fast, that ye had don,

And ye shal syngyn or ye gon.

Po, po …

xi) The Holly and the Ivy[16]

Nay, nay, Ive,

It may not be, iwis,

For Holy must have the mastry,

As the maner is.

---

15 *IMEV* 436, from Wright, *Songs and Carols* (song 38, pp. 42–3); also in *Early English Carols*, ed. Greene, no. 134.

16 *In Medieval English Lyrics*, ed. Davies, no. 171.

Holy berith beris, beris rede ynowgh;°   *very*

The thristilcok,° the popyngay,° daunce in every   *cock thrush*   *parrot*
   bow,

Welaway, sory Ivy, what fowles hast thow

But the sory howlet,° that syngith, 'How, how.'   *owl*

Nay, nay ...

Ivy berith beris as black as any slo;

Ther commeth the woode-colver° and fedith her of   *wood-pigeon*
   tho,°   *those*

She liftith up her tayll and she cakes° or° she go —   *craps*   *before*

She wold not for hundred poundes serve Holy soo.

Nay, nay ...

Holy and his mery men, they can daunce in hall,

Ivy and her jentyll women can not daunce at all,

But lyke a meyny of bullokkes in a waterfall,

Or on a whot° somers day, whan they be mad all.   *hot*

Nay, nay ...

Holy and his mery men sytt in cheyres of gold;

Ivy and her jentyll women sytt withowt° in fold,°   *outside*   *on the ground*

With a payre of kybid° helis cawght with cold —   *chilblained*

So wold I that every man had that with Yvy will hold.

Nay, nay ...

xii)[17]

What cher? Gud cher, gud cher, gud cher!

Be mery and glad this gud New Yere.

'Lyft up your hartes and be glad

In Crystes byrth', the angell bad;

---

17   *Ibid.* no. 177.

Say eche to oder for hys sake,
    'What cher?' What cher …

I tell you all with hart so fre,
Ryght welcum ye be to me,
Be glad and mery, for charite —
    What cher? What cher …

The gudman of this place in fere°   *in company, together*
You to be mery he prayth you here,
And with gud hert he doth to you say,
    What cher? What cher …

Merriment, of various kinds, throughout the Year

xiii) God speed the Plough[18]

The merthe of alle this londe
Maketh the gode husbonde°   *farmer*
With erynge° of his plowe.   *ploughing*

Iblessyd be Cristes sonde°   *grace*
That hath us sent in honde
    Merthe and joye ynowe.°   *in plenty, much*
The merthe …

The plowe goth mony a gate°   *path*
Both erly and late,
In winter in the clay.
The merthe …

Abowte barley and whete,
That maketh men to swete,°   *sweat*

18   In *The Oxford Book of Medieval English Verse*, no. 152.

God spede the plowe al° day.   *every*
The merthe …

Browne Morel and Gore°   *names of the horses (or oxen)*
Drawen the plowe ful sore°   *laboriously*
Al in the morwenynge.
The merthe …

Rewarde hem therefore
With a shefe° or more   *sheaf*
   Alle in the evenynge.
The merthe …

Whan men bygynne to sowe,
Ful wel here corne they knowe°   *judge*
In the mounthe of May.
The merthe …

Howe ever Janyver° blowe,   *January*
Whether hye or lowe,
   God spede the plowe allway!
The merthe …

Whan men begynneth to wede°   *weed*
The thystle fro the sede,
   In somer whan they may.
The merthe …

God lete° hem wel to spede°   *grant*   *prosper*
And longe gode lyfe to lede,
   All that for plowemen pray.
The merthe …

xiv)[19]

We ben chapmen° light of fote,   *pedlars*
The fowle weyis for to fle,

We beryn° abowtyn non cattes skynnys,   *carry*
Pursis, perlis,° sylver pynnis   *pearls*
Smale wympeles° for ladyis chynnys;   *elegant head-dress*
Damsele, bey° sum ware of me.   *buy*
We ben …

I have a poket for the nonys,°   *for the occasion*
Therine ben tweyne° precious stonys;   *two*
Damsele, hadde ye asayid hem onys;
Ye shuld the rathere° gon with me.   *sooner*
We ben …

I have a jelyf° of Godes sonde,°   *jelly*   *grace*
Withoutyn fyt° it can stonde;   *feet*
It can smytyn and haght non honde;°   *hath no hand*
Ryd° yourself quat it may be.   *guess*
We ben …

I have a powder for to selle,
Quat it is can I not telle —
It makit maydenys wombys to swelle;
Therof I have a quantyte.
We ben …

_____

19   *IMEV* 3864; also in Greene's *Early English Carols*, no. 416.

Drinking Songs

xv)[20]

How,° butler, how! Bevis a towt!°	*hey!*	*drink to all!*
Fill the boll, jentill butler, and let the cup rowght!°		*go round*

Jentill butler, bell amy,°   *fine friend*
Fyll the boll by the eye,°   *to the brim*
That we may drink by and by.°   *one and all*
With how, butler, how! Bevis a towt!
Fill the boll, butler, and let the cup rowght!

Here is mete° for us all,   *food*
Both for gret and for small —
I trow° we must the butler call,   *believe*
With how, butler, how! Bevis a towt!
Fill the boll, butler, and let the cupe rowght!

I am so dry I cannot spek,°   *speak*
I am nere choked with my mete° —   *food*
I trow the butler be aslepe.
With how, butler, how! Bevis a towght!
Fill the boll, butler, and let the cup rowght!

Butler, butler, fill the boll,		
Or elles I beshrewe° thy noll!°	*curse*	*head*
I trow we must the bell toll.°	*ring*	
With how, butler, how! Bevis a towght!		
Fill the boll, butler, and let the cup rowght!		

Iff the butlers name be Water,°   *Walter (apparently so pronounced)*
I wold he were a galow-claper,°   *gallows-bird*

---

20   In *The Oxford Book of Medieval English Verse*, no. 260.

But if° he bryng us drynk the rather.°　　　　*unless*　　　*sooner*

With how, butler, how! Bevis a towght!

Fill the boll, butler, and let the cup rowght!

xvi)[21]

　Bryng us in good ale, and bryng us in good ale,
　Fore owr blyssyd lady sak, bryng us in good ale.

Bryng us in no browne bred, fore that is mad of brane,°　　*bran*

Nor bring us in no whyt bred, fore therin is no game,°　　*pleasure*

But bryng us in good ale.

Bryng us …

Bryng us in no befe,° for ther is many bonys,　　　　　*beef*

But bryng us in good ale, for that goth downe at onys,

And bryng us in good ale.

Bryng us …

Bryng us in no bacon, for that is passing fate,°　　　　*fat*

But brynge us in god ale, and gyfe us inought° of that,　　*plenty*

And bryng us in good ale.

Bryng us …

Bryng us in no mutton, for that is often lene,

Nor bryng us in no trypys, for thei be syldom clene,

But bryng us in good ale.

Bryng us …

Bryng us in no eggys, for ther ar many schelles,

But bryng us in good ale, and gyfe us nothyng ellys,

And bryng us in good ale.

Bryng us …

21　In *Medieval English Lyrics*, ed. Davies, no. 119.

Bryng us in no butter, for therin ar many herys,°   *hairs*
Nor bryng us in no pygges flesch, for that wyl mak us borys,
But bryng us in good ale.
Bryng us ...

Bryng us in no podynges,° for therin is al   *black pudding*
    gotes° blod.   *goats'*
Nor bring us in no veneson, for that is not for our gode,
But bring us in good ale.
Bryng us ...

Bryng us in no capons flesch, for that is often der,
Nor bring us in no dokes° flesch, for thei   *ducks'*
    slober in the mer,°   *pond*
But bring us in good ale.
Bryng us ...

Amorous Encounters; Men and Women

xvii)[22]

    Hey, noyney!
    I wyll love our Ser John
    And° I love eny.   *if*

O Lord, so swett° Ser John dothe kys   *sweetly*
At every tyme when he wolde pley;
Off hymselfe so plesant he ys,
I have no powre to say hym nay.
Hey, noyney ...

Ser John love[s] me and I love hym,
The more I love hym the more I maye,

---

22   In *Medieval English Lyrics*, ed. Silverstein, no. 113.

He says, 'swett hart, cum kys me trym.'º   *nicely*
I have no powre to say hym nay.
Hey, noyney ...

Ser John to me is proferyng
For hys pleasure right well to pay,
And in my box he puttes hys offryng —
I have no powre to say hym nay.
Hey, noyney ...

Ser John ys taken in my mousetrappe;
Fayne wold I have hemº bothe nyght and day;   *him*
He gropith so nyslye abought my lape,
I have no po[w]re to say hym nay.
Hey, noyney ...

Ser John gevyth me relyusº rynges   *glittering*
With pratyº pleasure for to assay,º   *sweet*   *try*
Furres off the finest with othyr thynges —
I have no powre to say hym nay.
Hey, noyney ...

xviii)[23]

How, hey! It is non les:º   *lie*
I dar not seyn quan che seygh 'Pes!'º   *speak when she says peace! (be quiet!)*

Yyngº men, I warne you everychon,   *young*
Eldeº wy[v]ys tak ye non,   *old*
For I myself [at hom have on] —
I dar not seyn quan che seyght, 'Pes!'
How, hey ...

---

23   In *The Oxford Book of Medieval English Verse*, no. 195.

Quan I cum fro the plow at non,º	*noon*
In a reven dychº myn mete is don,º	*cracked dish* *put*
I dar not askyn our dame a sponº —	*spoon*
I dar not seyn quan che seyght, 'Pes!'	
How, hey ...	

If I aske our dame bred,	
Che takyt a staf and brekitº myn hed	*breaks*
And doth me rennynº under the ledº —	*run* *cauldron*
I dar not seyn quan che seyght 'Pes!'	
How, hey ...	

If I aske our dame fleych,º	*meat*
Che brekit myn hed with a dych,	
'Boy, thou art not worght a reych!'º	*worth a rush (= a thing of no value)*
I dar not seyn quan che seyght 'Pes!'	
How, hey ...	

Yf I aske our dame chese,	
'Boy,' che seyght, al at ese,º	*quite unmoved*
'Thou art not worght half a pese!'º —	*pea*
I dar not seyn quan che seyght 'Pes!'	
How, hey ...	

xix)²⁴

Hogyn cam to bowersº dore,	*chamber*
Hogyn cam to bowers dore,	
He tryld upon the pynº for love,	*rattled at the latch*
Hum, ha, trill go bell,	
He tryld upon the pyn for love,	
Hum, ha, trill go bell.	

---

24 From Richard Hill's commonplace-book; *IMEV* 1222 (*NIMEV* TM 601, *DIMEV* 2035).

Up she rose and let hym yn,
Up she rose and let hym yn,
She had a-went° she had worshipped° all   *thought*   *honoured*
  he[r] kyn,
Hum, ha, trill go bell,
She had a-went she had worshipped all her kyn,
Hum, ha, trill go bell.

When thei were to bed browght,
When thei were to bed browght,
The old chorle he cowld do nowght,°   *nothing*
Hum, ha, trill go bell,
The old chorle he cowld do nowght,
Hum, ha, trill go bell.

'Go ye furth to yonder wyndow,
Go ye furth to yonder wyndow,
And I will cum to you withyn a throw',°   *while*
Hum, ha, trill go bell,
'And I will cum to you withyn a throw.'
Hum, ha, trill go bell.

Whan she hym at the wyndow wyst,°   *knew*
Whan she hym at the wyndow wyst,
She torned° owt her ars and that he kyst,   *put*
Hum, ha, trill go bell,
She torned owt her ars and that he kyst,
Hum, ha, trill go bell.

'Ywys,° leman,° ye do me wrong,   *indeed*   *sweetheart*
Ywys, leman, ye do me wrong,
Or elles your breth ys wonder strong',
Hum, ha, trill go bell,
'Or ells your breth ys wonder strong',
Hum, ha, trill go bell.

xx)[25]

'Say me, viit° in the brom,°		creature	broom
Teche ne wou° I sule don°		how	must act
That min hosebonde°		husband	
Me lovien wolde.'°		should	

'Holde thine tunke° stille	tongue
And hawe° al thine wille.'	have

Miscellaneous Songs

xxi)[26]

I have a gentil co[k],°	cock
Crowyt me [the] day°	daybreak
He doth° me rysyn erly,	causes
My matyins for to say.	

I have a gentil co[k],	
Comyn he is of gret;°	distinguished family
His comb is of red [c]orel,°	coral
His tayil js of get.°	jet

I have a gentil co[k],	
Comyn he is of kynde;°	high lineage
His comb is of red corel,	
His tayl is of inde.°	indigo

His legges ben of asor,°	azure	
So geintil and so smale;°	slender	
His spores° arn of sylver qwyt°	spurs	shining silver
Into the wortewale.°	roots	

---

25   In *The Oxford Book of Medieval English Verse*, no. 28.
26   *Ibid.* no. 189.

His ey[e]n° arn of cristal,   *eyes*
Lokyn° al in aumbyr;°   *set*   *amber*
And every nyght he perchit° hym   *perches*
In myn ladyis chaumbyr.

xxii)[27]

I have a newe gardyn,
And newe° is begunne;   *newly*
Swych° another gardyn   *such*
Know I not under sunne.

In the myddis of my gardyn
Is a peryr° set,   *pear-tree*
And it wele non per bern°   *bear*
But a per jenet.°   *early-ripening pear*[28]

The fairest mayde of this toun
Preyid me
For to gryffyn her a gryf°   *insert a shoot, graft*
Of myn pery tre.

Quan I hadde hem gryffid°   *planted*
Alle at her wille,°   *as she wished*
The wyn and the ale
Che dede in fille.°   *she poured out*

And I gryffid her
Ryght up in her home;
And be that day xx wowkes°   *weeks*
It was qwyk in her womb.

---

27 In *Medieval English Lyrics*, ed. Silverstein, no. 106. Its introduction explains the use of nursery rhyme for double meanings.
28 By St John's Day (24th June), hence a 'John pear'.

That day twelfus month
That mayde I mette,
Che seyd it was a per Robert,°   '*Robert*' *pear*
But non per Jonet.

Nonsense Verse, sometimes used for satire, sometimes simply for enjoyment

xxiii)[29]

Whan netilles in winter bere rosis rede,
And thornys bere figges naturally,
And bromes° bere appylles in every mede,°   *brooms*   *meadow*
And lorelles° bere cheris in the croppis° so hie, *laurels*   *top branches*
And okys° bere dates so plentuosly,   *oaks*
And lekes° geve hony in ther superfluens,°   *leeks*   *superabundance*
Than put in a woman your trust and confidens.

Whan whiting walk in forestes hartes° for to chase,   *harts*
And herynges° in parkys hornys boldly blowe,   *herrings*
And flownders° morehennes° in fennes embrace.   *flounders*   *moor-hens*
And gornardes° shote grengese° owt of a   *gurnards*   *goslings*
    crossebowe,
And rolyons° ride in hunting the wolf to overthrowe,   *fish*
And sperlynges° rone with speris in harness to   *smelts*
    defence°   *for protection.*
Than put in a woman your trust and confidence.

Whan sparowys bild chirches and stepulles hie,
And wrennes cary sakkes to the mylle,
And curlews cary clothes° horsis for to drye,   *cloths*
And se-mewes bryng butter to the market to sell,
And wod-dowes° were wod-knyffes° theves to kyll, *wood-pigeons hunting knives*

---

29   In *Medieval English Lyrics*, ed. Davies, no. 125.

And griffons° to goslynges don obedience —   *vultures*
Than put in a woman your trust and confidence.

Whan crabbis tak wodcokes° in forestes and parkes,   *woodcocks*
And haris ben taken with swetnes of snaylis,
And [cammels in the ayer tak swalows and larkes],
And myse mowe corn with wafeyyng° of ther taylis,   *waving*
Whan dukkes of the dunghill sek° the Blod of Hayles,[30]   *seek*
Whan shrewd° wyffes to ther husbondes do non offens —   *shrewish*
Than put in a woman your trust and confidence.

xxiv)[31]

Hay, hey, hey, hey!
I wyll have the whetston and I may.°   *if I can*

I sawe a doge sethyng° sowse°   *boiling*   *pork for pickling*
And an ape thechyng° an howse   *thatching*
And a podyng° etyng a mowse;   *sausage*
I will have the whetston and I may.
Hey, hey …

I sawe an urchin° shape° and sewe   *hedgehog*   *cut out cloth*
And another bake and brewe,
Scowre the pottes as they were newe;
I will have the whetston and I may.
Hey, hey …

I sawe a codfysshe corn sowe
And a worm a whystyll blowe

---

30   It was alleged that some of the Blood of Christ was preserved at Hailes Abbey, in Gloucestershire.

31   In *Early English Carols* (ed. Greene), no. 471; *DIMEV* 2256. The whetstone, a token of falseness, was hung about the nect of a convicted liar (*MED*); he means 'I shall prove the best liar'.

And a pye° tredyng a crow;   *magpie*
I will have the whetston and I may.
Hey, hey …

I sawe a stokfysshe° drawing a harrow   *dried fish*
And another dryveyng a barrow
And a saltfysshe shotyng an arrow;
I will have the whetston and I may.
Hey, hey …

I sawe a bore burdeyns bynd
And a froge clewens° wynd   *balls of yarn*
And a tode mustard grynd;
I will have the whetston and I may.
Hey, hey …

I sawe a sowe bere kyrchers to wasshe,
The second sowe had an hege to plasshe,°   *weave*
The thirde sowe went to the barn to thr[a]sshe;
I will have the whetston and I may.
Hey, hey …

I sawe an ege etyng a pye —
Geve me drynke, my mowth ys drye,
Ytt ys not long syth° I made a lye;   *since*
I will have the whetston and I may.
Hey, hey …

Religious Songs (a brief selection)

xxv)[32]

Nou goth° sonne under wod,°   *goes*   *wood*
Me reweth,° Marie, thi faire rode.°   *I pity*   *face*

---

32   In *The Oxford Book of Medieval English Verse*, no. 269.

Nou goth sonne under tre,
Me reweth, Marie, thi sone and the.

xxvi)[33]

Adam lay ibowndyn, bowndyn in a bond,
Fowre thousand winter thowt he not to long.

And al was for an appil, An appil that he tok,
As clerkes fyndyn wretyn, wretyn in here bok

Ne hadde the appil take ben, the appil take ben,
Ne hadde never our Lady a° ben hevene qwen.   *have*

Blyssid be the tyme that appil take was,
Therfore we mown° syngyn '*Deo gratias!*'°   *may*   *thanks be to God*

xxvii)[34]

Levedie, I thonke the
Wid° herte suithe° milde   *with*   *very*
That god° that thou havest idon me   *good*
Wid thine suete childe,

Thou ard god and suete and briht,
Of° alle otheir icoren;°   *above*   *chosen*
Of the was that suete with°   *sweet creature*
That was Jesus iboren.°   *born*

Maide milde, biddi° the   *I pray*
Wid thine suete childe
That thou er[e]ndie° me   *intercede for*

---

33 *Ibid*. no. 191.
34 *Ibid*. no. 29.

To habben Godis milce.°   *mercy*

Moder, [thou] loke one me
Wid thine suete eye;
Rest and blisse [gef] thou me,
Mi levedi, then° ic deye.   *when*

xxviii)³⁵

    Can I not syng but 'hoy',
    Whan the joly shepherd made so mych joy.

The sheperd upon a hill he satt,
He had on hym his tabard° and his hat,   *cloak*
Hys tarbox, hys pype, and hys flagat;°   *flask*
Hys name was called Joly, Joly Wat,
For he was a gud herdes° boy.   *shepherds'*
    [W]ith hoy!
For in hys pype he made so mych joy.
Can I not syng …

The sheperd upon a hill was layd,
Hys doge° to hys gyrdyll was tayd,°   *dog*   *tied*
He had not slept but a lytill br[a]yd°   *while*
But 'Gloria in excelsis'° was to hym sayd.   *Glory in the Highest*
For he was a gud herdes boy,
With hoy!
For in his pype he mad so mych joy.
Can I not syng …

The sheperd on a hill he stode;
Rownd abowt hym his shepe they yode;°   *went*
He put hys hond under hys hode;°   *hood*

---

35 *Ibid.* no. 252.

He saw a star as rede as blod.
For he was a gud herdes boy,
    With hoy!
For in his pype he mad so mych joy.
Can I not syng …

'Now farwell Mall, and also Will;
For my love go ye all styll°   *quietly*
Unto° I cum agayn you till,°   *until*   *back to you*
And evermore, Will, ryng well thy bell.'
For he was a gud herdes boy,
    With hoy!
For in his pipe he made so mych joy.
Can I not syng …

'Now must I go ther° Cryst was borne;   *where*
Farwell, I cum agayn tomorn;
Dog, kepe well my shepe fro the corn,
And warn well, Warroke,° when I blow my horn.'   *Wat's dog, or his 'boy'*[36]
For he was a gud herdes boy,
    With hoy!
For in his pype he made so mych joy.
Can I not syng …

The sheperd sayd anon right,°   *immediately*
'I will go se yon farly° syght,   *wondrous*
Wheras the angell syngith on hight,°   *loudly*
And the star that shynyth so bright,'
For he was a gud herdes boy,
    With hoy!
For in his pipe he made so mych joy.
Can I not syng …

---

36   The editor (Sisam) marks this name as 'obscure'.

Whan Wat to Bedlem° cum was,   *Bethlehem*
He swet° — he had gon faster than a pace.°   *was sweating   walking-pace*
He fownd Jesu in a sympill place
Between an ox and an asse.
For he was a gud herdes boy,
    With hoy!
For in his pipe he mad so mych joy.
Can I not syng …

'Jesu, I offer to the here my pype,
My skyrte,° my tarbox, and my scrype;°   *kilt   bag*
Home to my felowes now will I skype,°   *hasten*
And also loke unto° my shepe.'   *see to*
For he was a gud herdes boy,
    With hoy!
For in his pipe he mad so mych joy.
Can I not syng …

'Now, farewell, myne own herdsman Wat,'
'Ye, for God, lady, even so I hat.°   *am called*
Lull well Jesu in thy lape
And farewell, Joseph, wyth thy rownd cape.'°   *round cap*
For he was a gud herdes boy,
    With hoy!
For in hys pipe he mad so mych joy.
Can I not syng …

'Now may I well both hope° and syng,   *dance*
For I have bene a Crystes beryng.°   *birth*
Home to my felowes now wyll I flyng.°   *hurry*
Cryst of hevyn to his blis us bryng!'
For he was a gud herdes boy,
    With hoy!
For in his pipe he mad so myche joy.
Can I not syng …

xxix)[37]

'Lullay, myn lykyng,° my dere sone, myn swetyng,   *beloved*
Lullay, my dere herte, myn owyn dere derlyng.'

I saw a fayr maydyn syttyn and synge;
Sche lullyd a lytyl chyld, a swete lording.°   *lord*
Lulllay myn lykyng ...

That eche° Lord is that that made alle thinge;   *same*
Of alle lordis he is Lord, of all kynges Kyng.
Lullay, myn lykyng ...

Ther was mekyl° melody at that chyldes berthe;   *great*
Alle tho° that wern in hevene blys, they made mekyl merth.   *those*
Lullay, myn lykyng ...

Aungele[s] bright, thei song that nyght and seydyn to that chyld,
'Blyssid be thou, and so be sche that is bothe mek and myld.'
Lullay, myn lykyng ...

Prey we now to that chyld, and to his moder dere,
Grawnt hem his blyssyng that now makyn chere,°   *joy*
Lullay, myn lykyng ....

xxx)[38]

Mery hyt ys in May morning
Mery wayys for to gone,

And by a chapel as y came,
Mett y wythe Jesu to chyrcheward° gone,   *towards church*
Petur and Pawle, Thomas and Jhon,

---

37   In *Medieval English Lyrics*, ed. Davies, no. 77.
38   In *The Oxford Book of Medieval English Verse*, no. 180.

And hys desyplys° everychone.°   *disciples*   *every one*
Mery hyt ys ….

Sente Thomas the bellys gane° ryng,   *did*
And Sent Collas° the Mas gane syng;   *Nicholas*
Sente Jhon toke that swete offering,
And by a chapell as y came.
Mery hyt ys …

Owre Lorde offeryd whate he wollde,°   *wished*
A challes° off ryche rede gollde,   *chalice*
Owre Lady the crowne off hyr mowlde° —   *from her head*
The son° owte off hyr bosom schone.   *sun*
Mery hyt ys …

Sent Jorge, that ys owre Lady knyghte,
He tende the tapyrys° fayre and bryte,   *lit the tapers*
To myn yghe° a semley syghte —   *eyes*
And by a chapell as y came.
Mery hyt ys …

Chapter 10

Drama

The surviving texts of early English drama have preserved for us a large number of plays, but these probably represent only a very small portion of what once existed. The question of 'lost literature' has figured throughout this anthology, but is especially important in the case of songs and drama. The loss of so much of the early drama is undoubtedly very regrettable, and at first dispiriting. But it need not be. What has survived is often of very high quality and a remarkable variety, even giving us a few surviving examples of folk drama in the Robin Hood plays (two are included here). And the surviving records give a further impression of a once very large and varied body of work: more saints' plays (a form which obviously lost favour after the Reformation), and even a couple of plays seemingly based on romance stories, and a glimpse of the many dramatic or semi-dramatic plays and performances associated with seasonal festivals. The surviving texts and the records sometimes present us with unanswerable questions: for example, whether the impression given by the surviving texts that England (at least before the 'morality' plays, interludes, and comedies of the early sixteenth century) had fewer secular plays than France is in fact the truth. There seem to be some early secular plays, like the *Interludium de clerico et puella* or (possibly) Dame Sirith, and later plays seem to have 'secular' elements — the ending of the Woman Taken in Adultery, with the lover fleeing, suggests a scene from a merry tale or fabliau.

 https://doi.org/10.11647/OBP.0170.10

More often the records excite our curiosity to discover more about the dramatic or semi-dramatic pieces in May games — the processions, 'ridings', and so on. Processions were common, associated with Saint George, Robin Hood; there was even a ship procession at Hull associated with a Noah play (the ship or Ark was carried in procession and then kept in the church), and the seasonal festivals and pastimes, with their summer kings and queens, abbots of unreason and others. These are noted by disapproving moralists, but we are not given any precise details.[1] And we know very little about the 'folk plays' which once existed. However, the surviving dramatic texts do give us hints of possible scenes, topics, or practices in folk plays: the use of masks, players making entrances and exits through the audience and introducing themselves, combats and mock deaths and revivals, comic doctors and blustering tyrants — as in the later mummers' plays, with their doctors who can revive the 'dead', their swaggering blusterers, and giants like Blunderbore. It would be very rash to assume that lost medieval folk plays were identical with these mummers' plays, but it is quite possible that some were similar to them. A couple of relevant points may be cited in support of this view: similar plays are found throughout Europe, and although texts of the English mummers' plays are recorded only from the eighteenth century on, it is likely that they go back further. They were 'exported' to early British colonies such as Newfoundland. There, although the first precise account appears in a work of 1819, it is possible that they were part of the 'Morris dancers, Hobby Horses and Maylike conceits' brought there by Gilbert in his voyage of 1583.[2]

Some of these points suggestive of folk-drama are illustrated here in extracts from early morality plays and interludes, and from plays forming part of the 'mystery cycles'. The mystery cycles are of special significance; presenting the epic story of man's Creation, Fall, and Redemption, they remained popular for centuries. They were mostly, it seems, written by clerics, but these clerics were obviously very close to their lay folk. They use colloquial speech, and exploit the forms of

---

1 Chambers *Mediaeval Stage* remains valuable for the history of drama. Another Chambers (R. W.) refers to what has been lost, citing his namesake, on p. 319 of his article 'Lost Literature', but without indicating where among the two volumes this information is detailed.

2 See Sponsler, *Ritual Imports*.

popular literature seen in this anthology: proverbs, flytings (Mak and Gyll, the mothers of the Innocents and Herod's soldiers), and so on. They offered instruction together with entertainment, but instruction in the manner of late medieval devotion — so close to 'popular religion' with its simplicity and homeliness, as in the shepherds' gifts to the Christ Child, or Noah talking familiarly to God. Two final points may be made briefly, and confidently. First, the high quality of much of the writing arguably makes the mystery plays one of the supreme achievements of Middle English popular literature; and second, the insight they give us into the world of the 'folk' brings us very close indeed to the ordinary men and women of medieval England with their faith and devotion, their fears and their courage. And it is a clear-sighted view: we are also made to see the less admirable qualities of humankind, such as violence and cruelty, the deviousness of Mak the sheep-stealer and trickster, the grumpiness and bleak scepticism of the shepherds.

i) The Entrance of Cain in the Wakefield *Mactatio Abel*

The 'Wakefield' (a town near York) or 'Towneley' (the name of a former owner of the manuscript) Cycle contains thirty-two plays, some apparently taken from the York cycle, others showing the bold and original technique of a very talented dramatist, now known as the 'Wakefield Master'. The *Mactatio Abel* (The Killing of Abel), with the fascinating, brutal figure of Cain, almost certainly owes something to his imagination. The Biblical story of strife between brothers is already a dramatic one, and this is intensified by the dramatist's use of colloquial, earthy speech and his skill in characterisation. Cain is at once a short-tempered and violent husbandman, and an eerily sinister and mysterious figure doomed to wander in exile in the land of monsters (early legends already show a fascination with him). It is not hard to see 'popular' elements at work here: in language, behaviour (the angry cursing of the ploughing team) or theatrical technique (as when Garcio introduces himself, in the manner of the later mummers' plays: 'All hayll. All hayll. Bothe blithe and glad, For here com I, a mery lad').[3]

3　This and the next, from Noah, are in *The Towneley Plays*, eds England and Pollard. See also *Towneley Plays*, ed. Epp (Kalamazoo, 2017), although Gray is unlikely to have known this edition. For dating the Towneley plays, see also King, 'Manuscripts, Antiquarians, Editors, and Critics' (2016).

After a brief prologue by Garcio, Cain's 'boy' (called Pykeharnes later in the play), Cain comes in with his ploughing team.[4]

Cain. Io furth, Greyn-horne! and war oute, Gryme!

Drawes on! God gif you ill to tyme!°   *befall*

Ye stand as ye were fallen in swyme,°   *swoon*

    What! will ye no forther, mare?

War! Let me se how Down will draw.

Yit, shrew, yit! pull on a thraw!

What! it semys for me ye stand none aw!

    I say, Donnyng, go fare!

A, ha! God gif the soro and care!

Lo! now hard° she what I saide.   *heard*

    Now yit art thou the warst mare

In plogh that ever I haide.

How! Pike-harnes, how! Com heder belief!°   *hither quickly*

(Enter Garcio)

Garcio. I fend, Godis forbot,° that ever thou thrife!   *forbid*

What, boy, shal I both hold and drife?

    Heris thou not how I cry?

(Garcio drives the team)

Garcio. Say, Mall and Stott, will ye not go?

Lemyng, Morell, White-horne, Io!

    Now will ye not se how thay hy?

Cain. Gog gif° the sorrow, boy. Want of mete it   *God give*

    gars.°   *causes it*

Garcio. Thare provand,° sir, for-thi, I lay behind thare ars,   *provender*

And tyes them fast bi the nekis,

With many stanys° in thare hekis.°   *stones*   *hay-racks*

Cain. That shall bi° thi fals chekis.   *pay for*

(hits him)

Garcio. And have agane as right.

(hits back)

Cain. I am thi master — wilt thou fight?

---

4   I have reinstated a phrase or two omitted by Gray (or by the edition he used) perhaps out of delicacy.

Garcio. Yai, with the same mesure and weght

That boro will I qwite,º   *requite*

Cain. We! now, no thing, bot call on tyte,º   *quickly shout to the team*

That we had ployde º this land.   *ploughed*

Garcio. Harrer, Morell, iofurth, hyte!

And let the plogh stand.

(Enter Abel)

Abel. God, as he both may and can,

Spede the, brother, and thi man.

Cain. Com kis myne ars, me list not banº   *curse*

   As welcome standis the route.

Thou shuld have bide til thou were cald.

Com nar,º and other drife or hald,   *nearer*

   And kys the dwillis toute.º   *Devil's bum*

Go grese thi shepe under the toute,

For that is the moste lefe.º   *dearest to you*

Abel. Broder, ther is none here aboute

That wold the any grefe.

ii) *A Flyting between Noah and his Wife*

Another Towneley play deals with a moment of crisis in the story of redemption when God decides to destroy sinful mankind — except his true servant Noah and his family — by a great Flood.[5] The dramatist's treatment is both awesome and familiar. The reaction of the carpenter in Chaucer's Miller's Tale, when the Flood is threatened to come again, shows even in comic context the terror associated with the event. Noah, the agent of God's salvation, is a simple and very ordinary person, obedient and practical, but he is extremely old (he laments the consequent aches and pains); and he has a domestic problem in the form of his very vocal wife. Again, the range of colloquial language is impressive, from the simple (as when Noah speaks to God when he has finally recognised him and they converse) to the wild and violent (in the

---

5   The Bible story seems to have been influenced by a Middle Eastern myth (Gray is probably thinking of the *Epic of Gilgamesh*).

flyting itself). The quarrel quickly turns to domestic violence, but there is a nice moment when the participants pause and address the men and the women in their audience.

God has been speaking to Noah, telling him of the coming flood, and giving him instructions on the building of the Ark. He ascends to heaven …

Noah. Lord, homeward will I hast as fast as that I may;

My [wife] will I frast° what she will say,   *ask*

And I am agast° that we get som fray°   *afraid*   *strife*

    Betwixt us both,

For she is full tethee,°   *touchy*

For litill oft angre;

If any thing wrang be

    Soyne° is she wroth.   *at once*

[Then he goes to his wife]

God spede, dere wife, how fayre ye?

Wife. Now, as ever myght I thryfe,° the   *prosper*

    wars° I thee see.   *worse*

Do tell me belief° where has thou thus long be?   *quickly*

To dede° may we dryfe,° or lif, for the,°   *death*   *hasten*   *for all you care*

    For want.°   *lack of food*

When we swete or swynk,°   *toil*

Thou dos what thou think,°   *seems good to you*

Yit of mete and of drynk

    Have we veray skant.°   *truly little*

Noah. Wife, we ar hard sted° with   *put to it*

    tythyngis° new.   *happenings*

Wife. Bot thou were worthi be cled in

    Stafford blew;°   *blue (= you deserve a beating)*

For thou art alway adred,° be it fals or trew,   *frightened*

Bot God knows I am led,° and that may I   *treated*

    rew,°   *regret*

    Full ill;

For I dar be thi borrow,°   *surety*

From even unto morrow°   *morning*

Thou spekis ever of sorow;

 God send the onys° thi fill!   *once*

We women may wary° all ill husbandis;   *curse*

I have oone, bi Mary that lowsyd me

 of my bandis!°   *loosed my bonds (of pregnancy)*

If he teyn,° I must tary,° how so ever it *feels grief*   *stand by*

 standis,

With seymland° full sory, wryngand both my handis   *expression*

 For drede.°   *in fear*

Bot yit other while,°   *times*

What with gam and with gyle,°   *merriment and trickery*

I shall smyte and smyle,

 And qwite hym his mede.°   *give him his deserts*

Noah. We!° hold thi tong, ram-skyt,° or I *ah!* *sheep-shit*

 shall the still.°   *quieten*

Wife. By my thrift,° if thou smyte, I shal *may I prosper*

 turne the until.°   *turn on you*

Noah. We shall assay as tyte.° Have at the, Gill! *put it to the test at once*

Apon the bone shal it byte.

Wife. A, so, Mary! Thou smytis ill!

 But I suppose°   *imagine*

I shal not in thi det°   *debt*

Flyt of this flett!°   *leave this place*

Take the there a langett°   *thong*

To tye up thi hose!°   *stockings*

Noah. A! wilt thou so? Mary! that is myne.° *there's one from me*

Wife. Thou shal thre for two, I swere bi Godis pyne!°   *torment*

Noah. And I shall qwyte the tho,° in faith, *those*

 or syne.°   *before long*

Wife. Out apon the, ho!

Noah. Thou can both byte and whyne

With a rerd;°   *loud noise*

For all if° she stryke,   *although*

Yit fast will she skryke;°   *screech*

In faith, I hold none slyke°   *reckon none like her*

 In all meddill-erd.°   *the world*

Bot I will kepe charyte,° for I have at do° *keep my temper* *work to do*

Wife. Here shal no man tary° the, I pray the *delay*

 go to!°   *get on with it*

Full well may we mys the,° as ever have I ro;° *do without you* *peace*

To spyn will I dres° me ....   *set about*

[Noah builds the Ark, and looks at it admiringly. But the Flood approaches. When he and his sons manage to persuade his wife to enter, her reaction is far from admiring: 'I was never bard ere [penned in before], as ever might I the, In sich an oostre [lodging] as this. In fath, I can not fynd Which is before, which is behind', and she promptly goes to continue with her spinning. However, after another exchange, she finally comes back in.]

Wife. Yei, water nyghys so nere that I sit not dry,

Into ship with a byr° therfor will I hy° *rush*   *hurry*

For drede that I drone° here.   *drown*

Noah. Dame, securely°   *certainly*

It bees boght ful dere° ye abode so long by° *it will be paid for dearly* *alongside*

 Out of ship.

Wife. I wyll not, for thi bydyng,

Go from doore to mydyng.°   *rubbish heap*

Noah. In faith, and for youre long tarrying° *delay*

 Ye shal lik on° the whyp.   *taste of*

Wife. Spare me not, I pray the, bot even as thou think,° *seems good to you*

Thise grete wordis shall not flay° me. *frighten*

Noah. Abide, dame, and drynk.

For betyn shall thou be with this staf to° thou stynk, *until*

Ar strokis good? say me.

Wife. What say ye, Wat Wynk?[6]

Noah. Speke!

Cry me mercy, I say!

Wife. Therto say I nay.

Noah. Bot thou do, bi this day!

 Thi hede shall I breke.

Wife. Lord, I were at ese, and hertely° full *in heart*

 hoylle,°   *healthy*

---

6 An alliterative nickname; compare Nicholl Nedy, below.

Might I onys have a measse of wedows coyll;[7]

For thi saull, without lese,° shuld I dele peny doyll,[8] *lie*

So wold mo,° no frees,° that I se on this sole° *more* *doubtless* *place*

  Of wifis that ar here,

For the life that thay leyd,

Wold thare husbandis ere dede.

For, as ever ete I brede,° *bread*

  So wold I oure syre° were. *master*

Noah. Yee men that has wifis, whyls they ar yong,

If ye luf youre lifis, chastice thare tong:° *tongue*

Me thynk my hert ryfis,° both levyr and long,° *is torn* *liver and lung*

To se sich stryfis wedmen emong,° *among wedded folk*

  Bot I,

As have I blys.

Shall chastise this.

Wife. Yit may ye mys,

  Nicholl Nedy!

Noah. I shall make the still° as stone, *silent*
  begynnar of blunder!° *trouble-maker*

I shall bete the bak and bone, and breke all in sunder.

  [They fight]

Wife. Out, alas, I am gone! Oute apon the, mans wonder!° *monster*

Noah. Se how she can grone,° and I lig° *lament* *lie*
  under;

  Bot, wife,

In this hast° let us ho,° *violence* *cease*

For my bak is nere in two.

Wife. And I am bet so blo° *beaten so black and blue*

  That I may not thryfe.° *recover*

[After some reproving words from their children, their thoughts turn to the Flood.]

---

7 If I could have a taste of widows' cabbage soup.

8 Pay a mass-penny (for the souls of the dead).

iii) A dangerous blustering tyrant: *Herod* in a Coventry play[9]

The Coventry cycle originally consisted of ten plays, but only two have survived; the manuscript was destroyed by fire in the nineteenth century. The last recorded performance of the plays was in 1579: it is possible that the young Shakespeare may perhaps have seen them. The pageant of the Shearmen and Taylors presented the Annunciation, the Nativity, and the Massacre of the Innocents. The story of the latter is an inherently powerful one: part of a cosmic struggle beween God and Satan, and with a folktale pattern perhaps lurking beneath it.[10] A boy is born to be king, but the actual king tries to destroy him by murdering all the children of the same age. The fearsome figure of Herod was long remembered in the phrase 'out-herods Herod'. See, for example, Shakespeare's allusion to 'Herod's bloody-hunting slaughtermen' in Henry V's threatening speech to the citizens of Harfleur.

Herod comes in and brags of his omnipotence (brandishing his 'bryght bronde')

… For I am evyn he that made bothe hevin and hell,		
And of my myghte powar holdith up this world rownd.		
Magog and Madroke, bothe them did I confownde,		
And with this bryght bronde° there bonis I brak on-sunder,		*sword*
Thatt all the wyde worlde on those rappis did wonder.		
I am the cawse of this grett lyght and thunder —		
Ytt ys through my fure that they soche noyse dothe make.		
My feyrefull contenance the clowdis so doth incumbur		
That oftymis for drede therof the verre yerth° doth quake.		*very earth*
Loke! When I with males° this bryght brond doth schake,		*malice*
All the whole world, from the north to the sowthe,		
I ma° them dystroie with won° worde of my mowthe! ….	*can*	*one*

[Later in the play the decision of the Three Kings to depart 'another way' causes a furious outburst]

Herod. Anothur wey? owt! owt! owtt!

---

9   Pageant of the Shearmen and Taylors, in *Two Coventry Corpus Christi Plays*, ed. Craig, pp. 17–18 & 27.

10   King Arthur destroys young children in an attempt to kill his son Mordred.

Hath those fawls trayturs done me this ded?

I stampe! I stare! I loke all abowtt!

    Myght I them take, I schuld them bren at a glede!º   *fire*

I rent!º I rawe! And now run I wode!º   *tear (my hair)*   *mad*

A! that these velenº trayturs hath mard thisº my mode!   *villainous*   *thus*

    They schalbe hangid, yf I ma cum them to!

[Here Erode ragis in the pagondº and in the strete also.]   *pageant wagon*

iv) The N-Town play of *The Trial of Joseph and Mary*[11]

[Den the summoner's introductory speech]

Avoyd, serys,º And lete mylorde the buschop come   *make way, sirs*

    And syt in the courte, the laws for to doo.

And I shal gon in this place, them for to somowne,

    Tho that ben in my book — the court ye must com too!

I warne yow here all abowte

That I somown yow, all the rowte!

Loke ye fayl for no dowte

    At the court to pere.

    Both Johan Jurdon and Geffrey Gyle,

    Malkyn Mylkedoke and fayr Mabyle,

    Stephen Sturdy and Jak-at-the-Style,

    And Sawdyr Sadlere.

Thom Tynkere and Betrys Belle,

Peyrs Pottere and What-at-the-Welle,

Symme Smalfeyth and Kate Kelle,

    And Bertylmew the bochere.

    Kytt Cakelere and Colet Crane,

    Gylle Fetyse and fayr Jane,

    Powle Pewterere and Pernel Prane,

And Phelypp the good flecchere.º   *fletcher*

Cok Crane abd Davy Drydust,

---

11   In *The N-Town Plays*, eds Sugano and Scherb.

Luce Lyere and Letyce Lytyltrust,

Miles the myllere and Colle Crakecrust,

    Bothe Bette the bakere and Robyn Rede.

    And like ye rynge wele in° youre purs.   *dig well into*

    For ellys youre cause may spede the wurs,

    Thow that ye slynge Goddys curs

Evyn at myn hede!

Fast com away,

    Bothe Boutyng the browstere° and Sybyly Slynge,   *brewer*

    Megge Merywedyr and Sabyn Sprynge,

    Tyffany Twynklere, fayle for nothynge.

The courte shal be this day!

v) *The Play of the Sacrament*[12]

An unusual 'miracle play', which treats a rather extraordinary late-medieval legend of a Jewish attempt to destroy a consecrated Host in the manner of folk drama; readers will recognise the motif of 'all sticking together' in the *Tale of the Basyn* (above), as well as a comic doctor. It is often called the 'Croxton Play of the Sacrament' because of a mention in the introductory 'Banns': 'at Croxton on Monday yt shall be sen' — but this sounds like a kind of advertisement for a travelling company.[13]

The Jew Jonathas (who prays to 'almyghty Machomet') buys a Host from a rich Christian merchant, Aristorius; Jonathas and his friends attack it violently. However, their attempts to destroy or dispose of it run into difficulties. [vv. 493 ff]

Malcus. Loo, here ys fowre° galons off oyle clere!   *four*

Have doon fast! Blowe up the fere!°   *fire*

Syr, bryng that ylke° cake nere,   *same*

Manly,° with all yowre mygthe.°   *bravely*   *strength*

Jonathas. And I shall bryng that ilke cak[e]

---

12   *The Croxton Play of the Sacrament*, ed. Sebastian.

13   The Introduction to the edition discusses this, and other aspects of this dramatized legend.

And throw yt in, I undertake.

[He grabs the Sacrament, which sticks to his hand]

Out! out! Yt werketh me wrake!º   *injury*

    I may not awoyd yt owt of my hond!

I wylle goo drencheº me in a lake,   *drown*

And in woodnesse I gynne to wake!º   *I begin to go mad*

    I renne! I lepe over this land!

— Her he renneth wood, wuth the Ost in hys hond

Jason. Renne, felawes, renne, for Cokkysº peyn!   *God's*

Fastº we had owr mayster ageyne!   *quickly*

[They catch Jonathas]

Hold prestlyº on this pleyn,º   *strongly*   *ground*

    And faste bynd hyme to a poste.

Jason. Here is an hamer and naylys thre, I s[e]ye.

Lyffte up hys armys, felawe, on hey,º   *high*

Whyll I dryve thes nayles, I yow praye,

    With strong strokys fast.

[They nail the Sacrament to the post]

Masphat. Now set on, felouse, wyth mayne and myght,

And plukeº hys armes awey in fyght!   *pull*

Wat ife he twycche, felouse, aright!º   *properly*

    Alas, balys brewethº ryght badde!   *disasters are at hand*

— Here shall thay pluke the seme, and the hond shall hang styll with the
    Sacrament

Malcus. Alas! alas! what devyll ys thys?

Now hat[h] he but oon hand, iwyse!º   *in truth*

For sothe, mayster, ryght woo me is

    That ye this harme have hadde.

Jonathas. Ther ys no more; I must enduer!

    Now hastely to owr chamber lete us gon,

Tyll I mat get me sum recuer;º   *relief*

    And therfor charge yow everychoonº   *everyone*

That yt be counsell that we have doon.

— Here shall the lechys man come into the place.

[This is Colle, the irreverent 'boy' of the quack doctor Master Brundyche, 'the most famous phesycyan That ever sawe uryne'. Colle introduces himself and is ordered to make a 'proclamation'. vv. 608 ff].

Colle. All manar of men that have any syknes,

To Master Brentberecly loke that yow redresse,º   *address yourselves*

What dysease or syknesse that ever ye have,

He wyll never leve yow tyll ye be in yowr grave.

Who hat[h the canker, the collyke, or the laxe,º   *diarrhoea*

The tercyan, the quartan,[14] or the brynnyng axs,º   *pains*

For wormys, for gnawyng, gryndyng in the wombe or in the boldyro,[15]

Alle maner red-eyn, bleryd-eyn, and the myegrymº also,   *migraine*

For hedache, bonache, and therto the tothache,

The colt-evyll, and the brostyn men he wyll undertak,[16]

Alle tho that [have] the poose, the sneke, or the tyseke;º   *catarrh, cold,*
                                                                phthisis

Thowh a man were right heyle,º he cowd soone   *healthy*
    make hym seke.º   *sick*

Inquyre to the Colkote,º for ther ys hys loggyng,   *coal-shed*

A lytyll beside Babwell Myll, yf ye wyll have understanding.

Morality plays and interludes also contain popular figures and scenes. Often apparently meant to be presented in halls or inn-yards, their characters make entrances and exits through the audience: in *Mankind*,[17] Nowadays cries 'make rom, sers, for we have be longe! We wyll cum gyf yow a Crystemes songe', and 'all the yemandry hat ys here' is asked to join in the singing. Actors collect money from the audience. The Vices are similar to the 'gallants' of satire ('nyse in ther aray, in langage they be large'), and they indulge in much shouting and huffing. There is a comic devil, Titivillus, with a big devil mask, who announces as he enters 'I com with my leggis under me': becoming 'invisible', he sabotages Mankind's work by placing a plank under the ground where he is digging. Our next example is the entry

---

14 Tertian fever, and quartan fever, were named for their usual duration (attacks every three, or four, days).

15 A note in the edition says this bodily organ might be the penis, but it is not clear.

16 A swelling of the penis, men suffering from hernia.

17 In *Three Late Medieval Morality Plays*, ed. Lester.

of another giant, Tedyousnes, in a later interlude, Redford's *Wyt and Science*. This play, probably written for the singing boys of St Paul's, has an appropriately educational subject, the proposed marriage of Wyt the student to the lady Science, the daughter of Reason, and it requires some skilled musicians. It has some nice moments — as when Wyt transformed into a fool, Ignorance, sees his new appearance in a mirror — some of them clearly 'popular', as when Wyt is 'slain' by Tedyousnes and later 'revived', as in a folk play.

vi) *Wyt and Science*[18]

Tedyousnes cumth in with a vyser overe hys hed [and with a club in his hand]
Oh the body of me!
What kaytives be those
That wyll not once flee
From Tediousnes nose …
… [swinging his club]
Stand back, ye wrechys!
Beware the fechys°   *blows*
Of Tediousnes,
Thes kaytyves to bles!
Make roome, I say!
Rownd evry way!
Thys way! That way!
What care I what way?
Before me, behind me,
Rownd abowt wynd me!
Now I begyn
To swete in my skin.
Now am I nemble
To make them tremble.
Pash° hed! Pash brayne!   *smash*
The knaves are slayne,
All that I hyt!

---

18   *The moral play of Wit and Science, and early poetical miscellanies*, ed. Halliwell, pp. 7–9.

Where art thow, Wyt?

Thow art but deade!

Of goth thy hed

At the first blow!

Ho, ho! ho, ho!

[Swearing 'by Mahoundes bones' and 'by Mahounes nose', he drives off Study and Diligence 'In twenty gobbets [lumps] I showld have squatted [smashed] them, To teche the knaves to cum neere the snowte Of Tediousnes.']

vii) *Youth*: A Gallant[19]

Youth is delighted when Charity leaves, and looks for entertainment

… I wold I had some company here.

Iwis, my brother Riot wold helpe me

For to beate Charitye,

And his brother to.

[enter Riot]

Huffa, huffa, who calleth after me?

I am Riot, ful of jolyte.

My heart is light as the wynde.

And all on Riot is my mynde,

Where so ever I go.

But wote ye what I do here?

To seke Youth my compere.º   *companion*

Fayne of hym I wolde have a sight,

But my lippes hange in my light.º   *[the blindness of folly]*

God spede, master Youth, by my faie.º   *faith*

Youth. Welcom, Ryot, in the devels waye —

Who brought the hither today?

Riot. That dyd my legges, I tell the.

Me thought thou dyd call me,

And I am come now here

To make roiall chere,

---

19   In *Two Tudor Interludes*, ed. Lancashire, vv. 205–67.

And tell the how I have done.
Youth. What, I wende° thou hadst been henged,   *thought*
But I se thou arte escaped;
For it was tolde me here
You toke° a man on the eare,   *hit*
That his purse in your bosome did flye,
And so in Newgate ye dyd lye.
Riot. So it was, I beshrewe your pate.
I come lately from Newgate.
But I am as readye to make chere
As he that never came there.
For and° I have spending,   *if*
I wyll make as mery as a kynge,
And care not what I do.
For I wyll not lye longe in prison,
But wyll get forthe soone.
For I have learned a pollycie
That wyll lose me lyghtlye°   *easily*
And sone let me go.
Youth. I love well thy discretion,
For thou arte all of one condicion.
Thou arte stable and stedfast of mynde
And not chaungable as the wynde.
But sir, I praye you, at the leaste,
Tell me more of that jeste
That thou tolde me right nowe.
Riot. Moreover I shall tell the:
The mayre of London sent for me,
Forth of Newgate for to come,
For to preche at Tyborne.
Youth. By our Lady, he dyd promote the
To make the preche at the galowe tre.
But syr, how diddest thou scape?°   *escape*
Riot. Verely, syr, the rope brake,
And so I fell to the ground.

And ran away safe and sound.

By the way I met with a courtyers° lad.   *courtier's*

And twenty nobles of gold in hys purs he had.

I toke° the ladde on the eare —   *hit*

Besyde his horse I felled him there.

I toke his purs in my hande,

And twenty nobles therin I fande.

Lorde, howe I was mery!

Robin Hood Plays

The preceding extracts have given us many possible glimpses of the techniques and practices of 'folk drama', but no complete dramatic text. The nearest we can come to this is in the surviving Robin Hood plays, which were obviously numerous and popular throughout the fifteenth and sixteenth centuries,[20] but of which only a handful survive. We give two examples: *Robyn Hod and the Shryff of Notyngham* and *Robin Hood and the Friar*. Robin Hood plays are 'performance-based versions of the same myth presented in the ballads'.[21] Like the ballads they have dramatic scenes, minimal dialogue, and much energetic and often violent mimed action; interestingly, the combats of the ballads and plays reappear in modern film versions of Robin's adventures. The Robin Hood plays are certainly not dramatic masterpieces, but they provide us with an invaluable glimpse of the folk's entertainment. No doubt Robin Hood plays were used or adapted in the widespread 'summer games' and 'church-ales', which were clearly the source of much pleasure, as we see from the experience of Latimer, mentioned earlier.[22] Sometimes the Robin Hood festivities seem to have consisted of processions or 'ridings'. In Scotland there survives a comic monologue, 'the droichis [dwarf's] pairt of the play', in which a dwarf (and shape-shifter) of an extraordinary age announces his arrival in a whirlwind to bring 'plesans, disport and play', and urges the noble merchants to 'follow furth on Robyn Hude ... in lusty grene lufraye [livery]'.

---

20   Gray notes the earliest surviving reference is from Exeter in 1426–7 (*Simple Forms*, pp. 235–6).

21   In *Robin Hood*, eds Knight and Ohlgren.

22   The anecdote appears towards the end of the Introduction, above.

viii) *Robin Hood and the Sheriff of Nottingham*[23]

The earliest surviving Robin Hood play is a dramatic fragment consisting of a single page of text (c. 1475), with no formal stage directions, although in the manner of early drama actions are indicated in the speakers' texts (for example: 'off I smyte this sory swyre'). It has been associated with East Anglia, and with John Paston's lament that his horse-keeper Woode, who used to play 'Seynt Jorge and Robyn Hod and the Shryff of Notyngham' has gone into Barnsdale, a locality often favoured by Robin Hood in the ballads. The story is probably based on one or more ballads, now lost. Friar Tuck makes his first appearance in recorded English literature here. A connection with the ballad of Robin Hood and Guy of Gisborne (surviving in *PFMS*) has been made, but although there are similarities, that ballad does not seem to be the source. The text presented here attempts to indicate a possible plot, making use of suggestions from earlier editors and commentators, but much is open to debate. The first part is reasonably clear. There is a dialogue between the Sheriff and a knight, who promises to capture Robin Hood. Robin appears, is accosted by the knight, and the two engage in combats: archery, stone-casting, and wrestling. What follows is less clear …

Scene 1

Knight. Syr Sheryffe for thy sake
Robyn Hode wull y take;
Sheriff. I wyll the gyffe golde and fee°   *reward*
This behest° thou holde me.°   *promise*   *if you fulfil*
[Exit Sheriff; enter Robin Hood, for an archery contest]
Knight. Robyn Hode, fayre and fre,
Undre this lynde° shote we.   *linden tree*
Robin. With the shote y wyll
Alle thy lustes° to fullfyll.   *desires*
Knight. Have at the pryke!°   *target*
Robin. And y cleve the styke.°   *split the wand*
[They continue with a competition in stone-casting and tossing the beam]
Robin. Late us caste the stone.
Knight. I graunte well, be seynt John.

---

23   In *Rymes*, pp. 203–7.

Robin. Late us caste the exaltre.°   *axle-beam*

[They do so]

Robin. Have a foote before the!   *(invitation to wrestling)*

[They wrestle]

Robin. Syr knight ye have a falle!

Knight. And I the, Robyn, qwyte° shall;   *requite*

Owte on the! I blowe myn horne.

Robin. Hit ware better be unborne.

Lat us fight at ottraunce,°   *to the death*

He that fleth, God gyfe hym myschaunce!

[They fight]

Robin. Now I have the maystry here,

Off I smyte this sory swyre!°   *neck*

[Beheads him]

Robin. This knyghtys clothis wolle I were

And in my hode his hede woll bere.

Scene 2

Robin Hood and his companions seem to have been captured by the Sheriff,
but help is on the way (the two outlaws may be Little John and Scarlet).

Outlaw 1. Welle mete, felowe myn,

What herest thou of gode Robyn?

Outlaw 2. Robyn Hode and his menye°   *company*

With the Sheryffe takyn be.

Outlaw 1. Sette on foote with gode wyll,

And the Sheryffe wull we kyll.

Outlaw 2. Beholde wele Frere Tuke

Howe he doth his bowe pluke.°   *pull the string*

[Enter the Sheriff and his men][24]

Sheriff. Yeld° yow, syrs, to the sheryffe,   *yield*

Or elles° shall your bowes clyffe,°   *else*   *crack*

[All three are now captured]

---

24 There are some questions about what is actually happening, whether Friar Tuke
    is attacking the Sheriff single-handed, or whether he is fighting with the other
    outlaws against him; the Sheriff may be leading two, or three, of them (see notes in
    the edition, and in Knight and Ohlgren).

Little John. Now we be bownden alle in same.º   *bound all together*

Sheriff. Come thou forth, thou fals outlawe,

Thou shall be hangyde and ydrawe.º   *drawn*

Friar Tuck. Nowe, allas, what shall we doo?

We moste to the prysone goo.

Sheriff. Opyn the gatis faste anon,

And late.º theis thevys ynne gon.   *let*

It is not clear what happens then: 'as the gates are opened, Robin and the other outlaws presumably attack the Sheriff and escape' (Knight and Ohlgren). Dobson and Taylor think of a sequel in which the disguised Robin enters and rescues his men; earlier editors added a few lines in which Robin, disguised as Guy of Gisborne comes in, and rescues his men.

ix) *Robin Hood and the Friar*[25]

This is one of two short plays (the other is *Robin Hood and the Potter*) printed by William Copland at the end of his Mery Geste of Robyn Hoode, between 1549–69, perhaps in the year 1560, when he entered a Robin Hood play in the Stationers' Register. He calls them 'the Playe of Robyn Hoode, verye proper to be played in Maye Games', in which perhaps Robin Hood was a kind of Summer Lord with 'a lady' who may or may not be the Maid Marion of the May Games (probably played by young man) and a comic muscular Friar Tuck with his dogs. It might well have been given an outdoor performance: costumes were probably important but 'props' are not numerous; perhaps including a body of water, if available — otherwise that episode would have been mimed. The plays are related to ballads: quite closely to *Robin Hood and the Potter* [Child 121], and less closely to the *PFMS Robin Hood and the Curtal Friar* [Child 123].[26]

Robin Hood. Now stand ye forth my mery men all,

And harke what I shall say:

Of an adventure I shal you tell,

---

25   In *Rymes*, pp. 208–14.

26   Both are printed in *Rymes*.

The which befell this other day,
As I went by the high way,
    With a stoute frere° I met,   *friar*
And a quarter staffe° in his hande.   *thick pole*
    Lyghtely° to me he lept,   *quickly*
And styll he bade me stande.
    There were strypes° two or three,   *blows*
But I cannot tell who had the worse —
    But well I wote° the horeson° lepte within me,   *know*   *rascal*
And fro me he toke my purse.
Is there any of my mery men all
    That to that frere wyll go
And bryng him to me forth withall,
    Whether he wyll or no?
Lytell John. Yes, mayster, I make God avowe,
    To that frere wyll I go,
And bryng him to you,
    Whether he wyll or no.
[Exeunt; enter Friar Tuck with his dogs]
Friar. *Deus hic*! *Deus hic*! God be here!
Is not this a holy worde for a frere?
    God save al this company!
But am not I a jolly fryer?
For I can shote both farre and nere,
And handle the sworde and buckler,
    And this quarter staffe also,
If I mete with a gentyman or yeman,°   *yeoman*
I am not afrayde to loke hym upon,
    Nor boldly with him to carpe;°   *talk*
If he speake any words to me,
He shall have strypes° two or thre,   *blows*
    That shal make his body smarte.
But, maister, to shew you the matter
Wherfore and why I am come hither,
    In faith I wyl not spare:

I am come to seke a good yeman,

In Barnisdale° men sai is his habitacion. *Barnsdale (Yorks.)*

    His name is Robin Hode,

And if that he be better man than I,

His servaunt wyll I be and serve him truely;

    But if that I be better man than he,

    By my truth my knave° shall he be, *boy*

    And lead these dogges all three.

[Enter Robin Hood, disguised, and seizes the friar's throat]

Robin. Yelde° the fryer, in thy long cote!° *yield* *friar's habit*

Friar. I beshrew° thy hart, knave, thou hurtest my throt!° *curse* *throat*

Robin. I trowe,° fryer, thou beginnest to dote:° *believe* *act foolishly*

Who made the so malapert° and so bolde *impudent*

To come into this forest here

Among my falowe dere?

Friar. Go louse the,° ragged knave *de-louse yourself*

If thou make mani words,

I wil geve° the on the eare, *hit*

Though I be but a poore fryer.

To seke Robyn Hode I am com here,

And to him my hart to breke,° *open*

Robin. Thou lousy frer, what wouldest thou with hym?

He never loved fryer nor none of freiers kyn.

Friar. Avaunt, ye ragged knave!

Or ye shall have° on the skynne. *sc. a blow*

Robin. Of all the men in the morning thou art the worst,

To mete with the I have no lust;

For he that meteth a frere or a fox in the morning.

To spede ell° that day he standeth in jeopardy.° *prosper ill* *danger*

Therfore I had lever° mete with the devil of hell, *rather*

Fryer, I tell the as I thinke,

Then mete with a fryer or a fox

In a mornyng, or° I drynke. *before*

Friar. Avaunt, thou ragged knave, this is but a mock!

If you make mani words, you shal have a knock.

Robin. Harke, frere, what I say here —

Over this water thou shalt me bere;°   *carry*

The bridge is borne away.

Friar. To say naye I wyll not —

To let the of thin oth it were great pitie and sin;

But upon a fryers backe and have even in.

Robin. (climbing on to the friar's back)

Nay, have over.

Friar. Now am I, frere, within,° and thou, Robin,   *in (the water)*
    without,°   *out (of it)*

To lay the° here I have no great doubt.°   *throw you down   fear*

[He does so]

Now art thou, Robyn, [within], and I, frere, [without],

    Lye ther, knave, chose whether thou wilt sinke or swym!

Robin. Why, thou lousy frere, what hast thou doon?

Friar. Mary, set a knave over the shone,°   *shoes*

Robin. Therfore thou abye!°   *will pay for it*

Friar. Why, wylt thou fyght a plucke?°   *bout*

Robin. And God send me good lucke.

Friar. Than have a stroke for Fryer Tucke.

[They fight]

Robin. Holde thy hande, frere, and here me speke.

Friar. Saye on, ragged knave.

Me semeth° ye begyn to swete,°   *it seems to me   sweat*

Robin. In this forest I have a hounde,

I wyl not give him for a hundredth pound —

Geve me leve my horne to blowe,

That my hounde may knowe.

Friar. Blowe on, ragged knave, without any doubte,

Untyll bothe thyne eyes starte° out.   *pop*

[Robin sounds his horn; his band enters]

Here be a sorte of ragged knaves come in,

Clothed all in Kendale grene,

And to the they take their way nowe.

Robin. Peradventure they do so.

Friar. I gave the leve to blow at thy wyll,

Now give me leve to whistell my fyll.

Robin. Whystell, frere, evyl mote thou fare!

Untyl bothe thyne eyes star[e].

[The friar whistles. Enter two of his men, Cut and Bause]

Friar. Now Cut and Bause!

Breng forth the clubbes and staves,

And downe with those ragged knaves!

[Battle is joined]

Robin. How sayest thou, frere, wylt thou be my man,

To do me the best servyse thou can?

Thou shalt have both golde and fee.

And also here is a lady free

[Enter a lady]

I wyll geve her unto the,

And her chapplayn° I the make   *chaplain*

To serve her for my sake.

Friar. Here is an huckle duckle,²⁷   *(probably obscene)*

An inch above the buckle.

She is a trul° of trust,   *trollop*

To serve a frier at his lust.

A prycker,° a prauncer, a terer of she[t]es,°   *rider*   *tearer of sheets*

A wagger of ballockes when other men slepes,

Go home, ye knaves, and lay crabbes° in the fyre,   *crab-apples*

For my lady and I wil daunce in the myre,°   *mire*

For very pure joye.

[They dance]

---

27   Gray notes 'probably obscene'; it is not glossed in the edition.

Appendix

Afterlife

Medieval popular literature did not suddenly disappear at the end of the Middle Ages, but fed into the voluminous mass of a continuing popular literature. To illustrate this fully would require another anthology. What follows is simply a few examples which illustrate this. Some areas, however, have been deliberately omitted: proverbs and riddles (which continued to appear in popular prints), and satire (where we find descriptions of the charivari and flyting). The examples follow the order of the book's chapters.

1. A couple of examples which afford a glimpse of the survival of older beliefs[1]

The new reformed religion owed much to the past. Some beliefs were strictly censored (and we sometimes find cases in early books where offending 'Popish' material or images have been crossed out), but there are some striking continuities, especially with the characteristic affective devotion fostered by the medieval church. People continued to visit healing wells, for instance. Scott, who quotes another version of this Dirge in Minstrelsy of the Scottish Border, quotes a very similar Elizabethan account. The folk belief in the 'shoes for the dead' sits easily with the medieval stress on the necessity of performing bodily works of mercy.

---

1   See chapter 1, Voices from the Past, above.

     https://doi.org/10.11647/OBP.0170.11

i) *The Lykewake Dirge*[2]

John Aubrey gives an example of this dirge in his 'Remains of Gentilisme and Judaisme'. He says that in the early seventeenth century the belief in Yorkshire was that after a person's death the soul went over a 'whinny moore', covered with thorns or gorse, and the mourners led by a woman sang this song.

This ean° night, this ean night.	*very*
every night and awle;	
Fire and Fleet and Candle-light[3]	
and Christ receive thy Sawle.	
When thou from hence doest pass away	
every night and awle	
To Whinny-moor thou comest at last	
and Christ receive thy silly° poor sawle.	*unfortunate*
If ever thou gave either hosen or shun°	*shoes*
every night and awle	
Sitt thee downe and putt them on	
and Christ receive thy sawle.	
But if hosen nor shoon thou never gave nean°	*none*
every night …	
The Whinnes shall prick thee to the bare beane°	*bone*
and Christ receive thy sawle.	
From Whinny-moor that thou mayst pass	
every night …	
To Brig o' Dread thou comest at last	
and Christ …	
From Brig of Dread that thou mayest pass	
no brader° than a thread	*broader*
every night …	
To Purgatory fire thou com'st at last	
and Christ …	

---

2   In *The New Oxford Book of English Verse*, ed. Gardner, number 361 (p. 368) and note (p. 950). Gray has not used this version; there are numerous versions.

3   Similar in meaning to 'hearth and home', this phrase probably refers to the comforts of the house ('fleet' is related to 'flet', meaning 'floor').

If ever thou gave either milke or drinke
    every night ...
The fire shall never make thee shrink
    and Christ ...
But if milk nor drink thou never gave nean
    every night ...
The Fire shall burn thee to the bare bene⁰   *bone*
    and Christ receive thy sawle.

ii) A Prophecy

Like magical charms (examples in Chapter 1), prophecies can easily be underestimated by modern readers. From a literary point of view they are usually unimpressive, full of (in Shakespeare's phrase) 'skimble scamble stuff' and it is very difficult to avoid words like 'credulity'; they are highly adaptable, able to fit a number of possible historical situations. But a more sympathetic view would be to see them as attempts by simple folk to make some sense of the difficult world they lived in. And they must have been 'useful', since they survive in large numbers.

Our example gives the beginning and conclusion of *The Prophecie of Thomas Rymour*,[4] as printed in The Whole Prophecie of Scotland, England, and some parts of France and Denmark (Waldegrave, Edinburgh 1603, Andro Hart, 1615 and later editions), a work which contains prophecies of Merlin, Thomas the Rhymer, Bridlington, and others. It was apparently much consulted during the Jacobite rising in 1745 (the Stuart duke of Gordon being recognised as the 'Cock of the North'). 'The "Whole Prophecie" continued to be printed as a chap-book down to the beginning of the present century, when few farm-houses in Scotland were without a copy of the mystic predictions of the Rhymer and his associates' (Murray, p. xlii). And in England also there were local prophets, and more celebrated legendary figures like Robert Nixon 'the Cheshire prophet' and Mother Shipton.

---

4   See *Thomas of Erceldoune*, ed. Murray, beginning on p. 48.

Still on my waies as I went,

Out through a land, beside a lie,

I met a beirne upon the way.

Me thought him seemlie for to see,

I asked him holly his intent.

Good Sir, if your wil be,

Sen that ye byde upon the bent

Some uncouth° tydinges tell you me,   *unknown*

When shal al these warres be gone,

That leile men may leve° in lee,   *live*

Or when shall Falsehood goe from home

And Laughtie° blow his horne on hie ...   *Loyalty*

[he sees a series of strange events]

... When all these Ferlies was away

Then sawe I non, but I and he

Then to the birne couth I say

Where dwels thou or in what countrie:

Or who shal rule the Ile of Bretaine

From the North to the South sey:

A French wife shal beare the Son,

Shall rule all Bretaine to the sey,

That of the Bruces blood shall come

As neere as the nint degree.

I franed° fast what was his name,   *asked*

Where that he came from what countrie?

In Erslingtoun I dwell at hame

Thomas Rymour men calles me.

A boy shall be born with three thumbs on one hand,

Who shall hold three kings' horses

Wllst England is three times lost and won in one day.[5]

---

5   The last three lines appear to have crept in from *Nixon's Original Cheshire Prophecy*
     (1801). They may be appended to whatever version of the text Gray used for this
     book; we cannot be sure where he got his extracts.

2. Ballads

Some ballads recorded later are possibly of medieval origin (see Chapter 2, in which the medieval origin of the ballads is more clearly discernible), but often the process of transmission remains unknown or uncertain. One famous possible example:

iii) Sir Patrick Spens[6]

This version is less well-known (and more wordy) than the famous version in Percy's *Reliques* (1765). It is recorded in Herds MSS (18th). There are other Scottish versions; Hirsh prints a version in *Medieval Lyric*. The date of origin is uncertain. It has been suggested that it shows a dim memory of a wreck of 1281 in which the Scottish princess Margaret and her husband Eric of Norway perished.

The king he sits in Dumferling,
    Drinking the blude reid wine, O
'O where will I get a gude sailor,
    That'l sail the ships o mine?' O
Up then started a yallow-haird man,
    Just be the kings right knee:
'Sir Patrick Spence is the best sailor
    That ever saild the see.'
Then the king he wrote a lang letter,
    And sealid it with his hand,
And sent it to Sir Patrick Spence,
    That was lyand at Leith Sands.
When Patrick lookd the letter on,
    He gae loud laughters three;
But afore he wan to° the end of it   *reached*
    The teir blindit his ee.
'O wha is this has tald the king,
    Has tald the king o me?
Gif° I but wist the man it war,   *if*

---

6   Child 58 B.

Hanged should he be.
Come eat and drink, my merry men all,
　　For our ships maun° sail the morn;　　　　　*must*
Bla'd wind, bla'd weet,° bla's sna° or sleet,　　*rain*　　　*snow*
　　Our ships maun sail the morn.'
'Alake and alas now, good master,
　　For I fear a deadly storm;
For I saw the new moon late yestreen,
　　And the auld moon in her arms.'
They had not saild upon the sea
　　A league but merely three.
When ugly,° ugly were the jaws°　　　　　*fearsome*　　*waves*
　　That rowd° unto their knee.　　　　　　　*rolled*
They had not saild upon the sea
　　A league but merely nine,
When wind and weit and snaw and sleit
　　Came blowing them behind.
'Then where will I get a pretty boy
　　Will take my steer° in hand,　　　　　　*rudder*
Till I go up to my tap-mast,°　　　　　　　*topmast*
　　And see gif I see dry land?'
'Here am I, a pretty boy
　　That'l take your steir in hand,
Till you go up to your tap-mast.
　　And see an° you see the land.'　　　　　*if*
Laith,° laith were our Scottish lords　　　　*loath*
　　To weit their coal-black shoon;
But yet ere a' the play was playd.
　　They wat° their hats aboon.°　　　　　　*wet*　　　*above*
Laith, laith war our Scottish lords
　　To weit their coal-black hair;
But yet ere a' the play was playd,
　　They wat it every hair.
The water at St Johnston's wall

Was fifty fathom deep.[7]
And there ly a' our Scottish lords,
    Sir Patrick at their feet.
Lang, lang may our ladies wait
    Wi the tear blinding their ee,
Afore they see Sir Patrick's ships
    Come sailing oer the sea,
Lang, lang may our ladies wait,
    Wi their babies in their hands,
Afore they see Sir Patrick Spence
    Come sailing to Leith Sands.

iv) Tam Lin [extract][8]

Beliefs in fairies and spirits continued to flourish. In the seventeenth century Aubrey describes fairy activity at Hackpen Hill, Wiltshire.[9] *The Lore of the Land* contains many examples (for example, a story from Addy's *Household Tales*);[10] interest in them also continued.

Tam Lin tells the story of a love affair with a person in fairyland, and the recovery of a human from the fairies in their ride. This story is probably medieval — it is alluded to in the mid-sixteenth century *Complaynt of Scotland* — and possibly much older. Child found parallels with an ancient Greek tale, but we cannot be certain of the form in which it appeared. In *The Complaynt*, the shepherds tell 'the tayl of the yong Tamlene', and a dance 'Thom of Lyn' is mentioned. In the sixteenth century it is licensed as 'A ballet of Thomalyn', and it is found as the name of an 'air' in a seventeenth-century medley. Had it already assumed its characteristic ballad form? Possibly it circulated in various forms, rather like the tale of Thomas the Rhymer.

---

7   Perth, on the Tay. The ballad's geography is rather vague: other versions (while agreeing on 'fifty fathom deep') suggest Aberdour and Aberdeen.

8   Child, 39 A (Johnson's Museum, 1792, communicated by Burns). This extract is stanzas 1–2, then 13 to end.

9   See *Simple Forms*, p. 135.

10   *Household Tales, with other Traditional Remains* (London, 1895; these were collected in the counties of York, Lincoln, Derby, and Nottingham), in Westwood and Simpson. See also Kirk, *The Secret Commonwealth of elves, fauns and fairies* (Stirling, [1933]).

O I forbid you, maidens a',
    That wear gowd° on your hair,   *gold*
To come or gae° by Carterhaugh,   *go*
    For young Tam Lin is there.
There's nane that gaes by Carterhaugh
    But they leave him a wad,°   *wed (pledge or forfeit)*
Either their rings, or green mantles,
    Or else their maidenhead.

[Janet comes to Carterhaugh, a wood near Selkirk, and when she pulls a 'double rose' Tam Lin appears. (Some of the ballad is lost here.) She returns to her father's hall. 'An auld grey knight' says 'Alas, fair Janet, for thee But we'll be blamed a' ', but she angrily tells him to hold his tongue: 'Father my bairn on whom I will, I'll father nane on thee.']

… Out then spak her father dear,
    And he spak meek and mild,
'And ever alas, sweet Janet,' he says,
    'I think thou gaes wi child.'
'If that I gae wi child, father,
    Mysel maun° bear the blame.   *must*
There's neer a laird about your ha'°   *hall*
    Shall get the bairn's name.
If my love were an earthly knight,
    As he's an elfin° grey,   *elf*
I wad na gie° my ain true-love   *would not give*
    For nae° lord that ye hae.°   *any*   *have*
The steed that my true-love rides on
    Is lighter than the wind,
Wi siller° he is shod before,   *silver*
    Wi burning gowd behind.'
Janet has kilted° her green kirtle°   *tucked up*   *gown*
    A little aboon° her knee,   *above*
And she has snooded° her yellow hair   *fastened with a band*
    A little aboon her bree,°   *brow*
And she's awa° to Carterhaugh,   *away*
    As fast as she can hie.°   *hurry*
When she cam to Carterhaugh,

Tam Lin was at the well,
And there she fand° his steed standing,   *found*
 But away was himsel.
She had na pu'd° a double rose,   *pulled*
 A rose but only twa,
Till up then started young Tam Lin,
 Says, 'Lady, thou pu's nae mae°   *no more*
Why pu's thou the rose, Janet,
 Amang the groves sae° green,   *so*
And a' to kill the bonie babe
 That we gat us between?'
'O tell me, tell me, Tam Lin,' she says,
 'For 's° sake that died on tree,   *his*
If eer° ye was in holy chapel.   *ever*
 Or Christendom did see?'
'Roxbrugh he was my grandfather,
 Took me with him to bide,°   *stay*
And ance° it fell upon a day   *once*
 That wae° did me betide.   *woe*
And ance it fell upon a day,
 A cauld° day and a snell,°   *cold*   *sharp*
When we were frae° the hunting come *from*
 That frae my horse I fell —
The queen o fairies she caught me,
 In yon green hill to dwell;
And pleasant is the fairy land,
 But an eerie tale to tell.
Ay° at the end of seven years   *always*
 We pay a tiend° to hell —   *tithe*
I am sae fair and fu° o flesh,   *full*
 I'm feard° it be mysel.   *afraid*
But the night is Halloween, lady,
 The morn is Hallowday,°   *All Saints Day*
Then win me, win me, an° ye will, *if*
 For weel I wat ye may.°   *know you can*

Just at the mirk° and midnight hour   *dark*
   The fairy folk will ride,
And they that wad° their truelove win,   *would*
   At Miles Cross they maun bide.'°   *wait*
'But how shall I thee ken,° Tam Lin,   *recognise*
   Or how my truelove know,
Amang sae mony unco° knights   *strange*
   The like I never saw?'
'O first let pass the black, lady,
   And syne° let pass the brown,   *then*
But quickly run to the milk-white steed,
   Pu° ye his rider down.   *pull*
For I'll ride on the milk-white steed,
   And ay nearest the town,
Because I was an earthly knight
   They gie me that renown.°   *honour*
My right hand will be glovd, lady.
   My left hand will be bare,
Cockt up shall my bonnet be,
   And kaimd° down shall [be] my hair,   *combed*
And thae's the takens° I gie thee,   *these are the signs*
Nae doubt I will be there.
[Next, he warns her of the terrible transformations the fairy folk will work on
him in order to frighten her away]
They'll turn me in your arms, lady,
   Into an esk° and adder,   *newt*
But hold me fast and fear me not,
   I am your bairn's father.
They'll turn me to a bear sae grim,
   And then a lion bold;
But hold me fast and fear me not,
   As ye shall love your child.
Again they'll turn me in your arms
   To a red het gand of airn,°   *bar of iron*
But hold me fast and fear me not

I'll do to you nae harm.
And last they'll turn me in your arms
    Into the burning gleed,°   *brand of fire*
Then throw me into well water,
    O throw me in wi speed.
And then I'll be your ain true-love,
    I'll turn a naked knight;
Then cover me wi your green mantle,
And cover me out o sight.'
Gloomy, gloomy was the night,
    And eerie was the way
As fair Jenny in her green mantle
    To Miles Cross she did gae.
About the middle o the night
    She heard the bridles ring,
This lady was as glad at that
    As any earthly thing.
First she let the black pass by,
    And syne she let the brown,
But quickly she ran to the milk-white steed,
    And pu'd the rider down.
Sae weel she minded what he did say,
    And young Tam Lin did win,
Syne covered him wi her green mantle,
    As blithe's a bird in spring.
Out then spak the Queen o Fairies,
    Out of a bush of broom:
'Them that has gotten young Tam Lin
    Has gotten a stately groom.'
Out then spak the Queen o Fairies,
    And an angry woman was she:
'Shame betide her ill-far'd face,
    And an ill death may she die,
For she's taen awa the bonniest knight
In a' my companie.

But had I kend, Tam Lin,' she says,
    'What now this night I see,
I wad hae taen out thy twa grey een,
    And put in twa een o tree!'°   *two eyes of wood*

v) The Cherry-Tree Carol

Child 54 A, from Sandys, *Christmas Carols* (1833). Another version
(Child 54 B) is found in an eighteenth-century broadside, but the
date of the carol's composition is unknown. It is based on a legend
in the apocryphal gospel of Pseudo-Matthew, ch. XX.[11] Such legends
circulated in the Middle Ages and made their way into later tradition
(cf. The Carnal and the Crane, Child 55, also recorded in the eighteenth
century).

Joseph was an old man,
    And an old man was he,
When he married Mary,
    In the land of Galilee.
Joseph and Mary walked
    Through an orchard good,
Where was cherries and berries,
    So red as any blood.
Joseph and Mary walked
    Through an orchard green
Where was berries and cherries,
    As thick as might be seen.
O then bespoke Mary,
    So meek and so mild,
'Pluck me a cherry, Joseph.
    For I am with child.'
O then bespoke Joseph,
    With words most unkind:
'Let him pluck thee a cherry

---

11   *The Apocryphal New Testament*, trans. James, pp. 70–9 (p. 75).

That brought thee with child.'
O then bespoke the babe
    Within his mother's womb:
'Bow down then the tallest tree,
    For my mother to have some.'
Then bowed down the highest tree
    Unto his mother's hand;
Then she cried, 'See, Joseph,
    I have cherries at command!'
O then bespoke Joseph:
    'I have done Mary wrong;
But cheer up, my dearest,
    And be not cast down.'
Then Mary plucked a cherry,
    As red as the blood,
Then Mary went home
    With her heavy load.
Then Mary took her babe,
    And sat him on her knee,
Saying, 'My dear son, tell me
    What this world will be.'
'O I shall be as dead, mother,
    As the stones in the wall;
O the stones in the streets, mother,
    Shall mourn for me all.
Upon Easter-day, mother,
    My uprising shall be;
O the sun and the moon, mother,
    Shall both rise with me.'

vi) Brown Robyn's Confession

Child 57, from Buchan's 'Ancient Ballads and Songs of the North of Scotland' (Edinburgh, 1828). There are Scandinavian parallels, usually with a tragic ending for the hero. The ending of the Scottish ballad suggests the possibilty that a 'Miracle of the Virgin' story may lie behind it (cf. Hugh of Lincoln, below).

It fell upon a Wodensday
    Brown Robyn's men went to sea,
But they saw neither moon nor sun,
    Nor starlight wi their ee.
'We'll cast kevels° us amang,   *lots*
    See wha° the unhappy° man may be.'   *who*   *unfortunate*
The kevel fell on Brown Robyn,
    The master-man° was he.   *captain*
'It is nae wonder,' said Brown Robyn,
    'Altho I dinna thrive
For wi my mither I had twa bairns,
    And wi my sister five.
But tie me to a plank o wude,
    And throw me in the sea,
And if I sink, ye may bid me sink,
    But if I swim, just lat me bee.'
They've tyed him to a plank o wude,
    And thrown him in the sea;
He didna sink, tho they bade him sink;
    He swimd, and they bade lat him bee.
He hadna been into the sea
    An hour but barely three,
Till by it came our blessed Lady,
    Her dear young son her wi.
'Will ye gang to your men again,
    Or will ye gang wi me?
Will ye gang to the high heavens,
    Wi my dear son and me?'
'I winna gang to my men again,

For they should be feared at mee;
But I woud gang to the high heavens,
    Wi thy dear son and thee.'
'It's for nae honour ye did to me, Brown Robyn,
    It's for nae guid ye did to mee,
But a' for your fair confession
    You've made upon the sea.'

vii) Hugh of Lincoln

'Sir Hugh, or the Jew's Daughter', Child 155 (surviving in a number of versions, suggesting popularity), from Jamieson's Popular Ballads and Songs 1806, from the recitation of Mrs Brown of Falkland. It also appears in Percy's *Reliques*. It is ultimately based on a medieval legend, alluded to by Chaucer in his Prioress's Tale. But just how this medieval anti-Semitic legend reached the eighteenth century is still mysterious. The possibility of contemporary contact with Catholic sources, whether in Britain or in Europe, has been raised. But it is likely that the melodramatic possibilities of a legend of child murder excited a much earlier ballad singer, and that the route of transmission may have been relatively direct.

Four and twenty bonny boys
    Were playing at the ba,°   *ball*
And by it came sweet Sir Hugh,
    And he playd oer them a'.
He kicked the ba with his right foot,
    And catchd it wi hus knee,
And throuch-and-thro the Jew's window
    He gard° the bonny ba flee.   *made*
He's doen him to the Jew's castell,
    And walkd it round about,
And there he saw the Jew's daughter
    At the window looking out.
'Throw down the ba, ye Jew's daughter,
    Throw down the ba to me!'

'Never a bit,' says the Jew's daughter,
    Till up to me come ye.'
'How will I come up? How can I come up?
    How can I come to thee?
For as ye did to my auld father
    The same ye'll do to me.'
She's gane till her father's garden,
    And pu'd an apple red and green —
Twas a' to wyle him sweet Sir Hugh,
    And to entice him in.
She's led him in through ae dark door.
    And sae has she thro nine,
She's laid him on a dressing-table,
    And stickit him like a swine.
And first came out the thick, thick blood,
    And syne came out the thin,
And syne came out the bonny heart's blood,
    And there nae mair within.
She's rowd° him in a cake° o lead,   *rolled*   *mass*
    Bade him lie still and sleep,
She's thrown him in Our Lady's draw-well,
    Was fifty fathom deep.
When bells were rung and mass was sung,
    And a' the bairns came hame,
When every lady gat hame her son,
    The lady Maisry gat nane.
She's taen her mantle her about,
    Her coffer by the hand,
And she's gane out to seek her son,
    And wanderd oer the land.
She's doen her to the Jew's castell,
    Where a' were fast asleep:
'Gin° ye be there, my sweet Sir Hugh,   *if*
    I pray you to me speak.'
She's doen her to the Jew's garden,

Thought he had been gathering fruit:
'Gin ye be there, my sweet Sir Hugh.
    I pray you to me speak.'
She neard Our Lady's deep draw-well,
    Was fifty fathom deep:
'Whareer ye be, my sweet Sir Hugh,
    I pray you to me speak.'
'Gae hame, gae hame my mither dear.
    Prepare my winding sheet,
And at the back o merry Lincoln
    The morn I will you meet.'
Now Lady Maisry is gane hame,
    Made him a winding sheet,
And at the back o merry Lincoln
    The dead corpse did her meet.
And a' the bells o merry Lincoln
    Without men's hands were rung,
And a' the books o merry Lincoln
    Were read without man's tongue,
And neer was such a burial
    Sin Adam's days begun.

viii) Robin Hood and the Curtal Friar [Stanzas 9–38][12]

A popular example of the numerous Robin Hood ballads, which circulated widely. This text (Child 123 B) is from a Garland of 1663; another, earlier but incomplete, survives in the Percy Folio MS (and what remains of it seems close to the later, although Robin's request to the friar to carry him is less autocratic in *PFMS*). Both versions are available in modern editions: Knight and Ohlgren (a composite text), and Dobson and Taylor, both with useful introductions. The style is popular and emphatic, intended for oral performance rather than reading on the page.

---

12   See *Rymes*, ch. 8; pp. 163–4 for this extract.

Robin Hood has been told of a powerful friar at Fountains Abbey (in the
Middle Ages, a Cistercian abbey, not a friary), who will be more than a
match for him ...

… Robin Hood put on his harness good,
　　And on his head a cap of steel.
Broad sword and buckler by his side,
　　And they became him weel.
He took his bow into his hand,
　　It was made of a trusty tree,
With a sheaf of arrows at his belt,
　　To the Fountains Dale went he.
And coming unto Fountain[s] Dale,
　　No further would he ride;
There was he aware of a curtal[13] friar,
　　Walking by the water-side.
The fryer had on a harniss good,
　　And on his head a cap of steel,
Broad sword and buckler by his side,
　　And they became him weel.
Robin Hood lighted off his horse.
　　And tied him to a thorn:
'Carry me over the water, thou curtal frier,
　　Or else thy life's forlorn.'
The frier took Robin Hood on his back.
　　Deep water he did bestride,
And spake neither good word nor bad,
　　Till he came at the other syde.
Lightly leapt Robin Hood off the friers back;
　　The frier said to him again,
'Carry me over this water, fine fellow,
　　Or it shall bred° thy pain.'   *be the cause of*
Robin Hood took the frier on's back,
　　Deep water he did bestride,

13　This probably refers to the short (cutted) habit worn by the friar.

And spake neither good word nor bad,
    Till he came at the other side.
Lightly leapt the fryer off Robin Hoods back;
    Robin Hood said to him again,
'Carry me over this water, thou curtal frier,
    Or it shall breed thy pain.'
The frier took Robin Hood on's back again,
    And stept up to the knee;
Till he come at the middle stream,
    Neither good nor bad spake he.
And coming to the middle stream,
    There he threw Robin in:
'And chuse thee, chuse thee, fine fellow,
    Whether thou wilt sink or swim.'
Robin Hood swam to a bush of broom,
    The frier to a wicker wand;º   *willow tree*
Bold Robin Hood is gone to shore,
    And took his bow in hand.
One of his best arrows under his belt
    To the frier he let flye;
The curtal frier, with his steel buckler,
    He put that arrow by.
'Shoot on, shoot on, thou fine fellow,
    Shoot on as thou hast begun;
If thou shoot here a summers day,
    Thy mark I will not shun.'
Robin Hood shot passing well,
    Till his arrows all were gone;
They took their swords and steel bucklers,
    And fought with might and maine;
From ten oth' clock that day,
    Till four ith' afternoon;
Then Robin Hood came to his knees,
    Of the frier to beg a boon.
'A boon, a boon, thou curtal frier,

I beg it on my knee;
Give me leave to set my horn to my mouth,
   And to blow basts three,'
'That will I do,' said the curtal frier,
   'Of thy blasts I have no doubt;
I hope thou'lt blow so passing well
   Till both thy eyes fall out.'
Robin Hood set his horn to his mouth,
   He blew but blasts three;
Half a hundred yeomen, with bows bent,
   Came raking over the lee.º   *advancing over the ground*
'Whose men are these,' said the frier,
   'That come so hastily?'
'These men are mine,' said Robin Hood;
   'Frier, what is that to thee?'
'A boon, a boon,' said the curtal frier,
   'The like I gave to thee;
Give me leave to set my fist to my mouth,
   And to whuteº whutes three.'   *whistle*
'That will I do,' said Robin Hood,
   'Or else I were to blame;
Three whutes in a friers fist
   Would make me glad and fain.'
The frier he set his fist to his mouth,
   And whuted whutes three;
Half a hundred good ban-dogsº   *ferocious dogs kept chained*
   Came running the frier unto.[14]
'Here's for every man of thine a dog,
   And I my self for thee.'
'Nay, by my faith,' quoth Robin Hood,
   'Frier, that may not be.'
Two dogs at once to Robin Hood did go,
   The one behind, the other before;
Robin Hoods mantle of Lincoln green

---

14   Gray wants to emend, to 'over the lee', to restore the rhyme.

Off from his back they tore.
And whether his men shot east or west,
 Or they shot north or south,
The curtal dogs, so taught they were,
 They kept their arrows in their mouth.
'Take up thy dogs,' said Little John,
 'Frier, at my bidding be.'
'Whose man art thou,' said the curtal frier,
 'Comes here to prate with me?'
'I am Little John, Robin Hoods man,
 Frier, I will not lie;
If thou take not up thy dogs soon,º   *at once*
 I'le take up them and thee.'
Little John had a bow in his hand,
 He shot with might and main;
Soon half a score of the friers dogs
 Lay dead upon the plain.
'Hold thy hand, good fellow,' said the curtal frier,
 'Thy master and I will agree;
And we will have new orders taken
 With all the haste that may be.'
[An agreement is apparently reached]

3. Romance

Romances enjoyed a continuing popularity, in early prints and in manuscript (some texts probably representing the work of reciters), and later in Broadside sheets. The stories of Guy of Warwick and Bevis of Hampton were especial favourites.

ix) How Bevis slew a dreadful Dragon, and what after chanced[15]

Bevis being in bed, heard a knight cry, I rot, I rot, at which sad noise Bevis wondred: and the next morning he asked what was the cause of

---

15 *The Gallant History of the Life and Death of that Most Noble Knight Sir Bevis of Southampton* (London, [1691]), Ch. 8 (pp. 16–17).

that noise. He was a knight, said they, that coming through the street the Dragon met with and cast her venome upon him, whereof he rotted and dyed. Where is that Dragon? said Bevis. Not far from this place, said they. Then Bevis called Ascapart to go with him, and Ascapart was very willing. So together they went, and when they came near the place where the Dragon was, they heard the dreadfullest yell that ever was. What Devill is that, quoth Ascapart. It is the Dragon, said Bevis: we shall see him anon. Ile go no further, said Ascapart, if she roars so loud before we come to her, what will she do when we fight with her? Fear not, said Bevis, we will teach her how to hold her Tongue. Marry, teach her thy self, said Ascapart, for I will go back again. Then farewell, said Bevis, I will go my self. So forward went Bevis, and backward went Ascapart. Bevis coming near her Den, she made forth, but never was such a Dragon seen in the world as this was, from her Head to Tail was full forty foot, her Scales glistered as bright as silver, and hard as flint. Have at thy Devils face, said Bevis and out he drew his good Morglay [and] on the Dragon laid, but her scales was so hard, his Sword cry'd twang, and never entred: then the Dragon struck Bevis to the ground, and up he got again: but she came on so fiercely that Bevis went back, and by chance fell into a Well, else the Dragon had destroy'd him: it seems the Well was holy water, and no venome might come within seven foot of it: there Bevis refreshed himself, and drank of the Water: and recovering his strength, to the Dragon he went again to have the other hour; but the Dragon assailed him so sore that Bevis was afraid he should have lost his life, yet with a valiant heart he stood to her stoutly: the Dragon finding him so strong bulkt a Gallon of her Venome upon him, which fell'd him dead to the ground, and his Armour burst all to pieces: the Dragon seeing he lay so still, she turned him with her tail, that he tumbled into the Well, and the water thereof expelled the Venome, and made himself safe and sound again: then he was a joyful man, and set upon the Dragon again: and when they had fought a long time, the Dragon would have been gone, and thinking to raise herself, lifted up her wings: Have at thee now, said Bevis: and with one sound blow hitting her under the wing, pierced her to the heart: with that she gave such a cry, which made the earth tremble: she being dead, Bevis beheaded her, and put it upon his spear, and so rode home: and when the people saw him coming, they gave a great shout, as at a Kings Coronation, and all the bells in the Town did ring. And all manner of

Musick play'd before Bevis, as he rode through the Town, where with great joy his Uncle received him.

4. Tales, Anecdotes

As in the Middle Ages stories of various kinds (merry tales, animal stories, local legends, and so on) are recorded in profusion. It is impossible to illustrate this mass of material adequately here. There are many examples in Westwood and Simpson, *The Lore of the Land*: including the story of a mysterious wooer in Bridgerule, Devon, identified by the local parson as 'The Old Un' himself. I must be content with a single example of an anecdote which, although not connected with the Middle Ages,[16] has something of the anecdote's traditionally 'gossipy' quality.

x) An eighteenth-century anecdote: Dr Johnson imitates a kangaroo[17]

On Sunday 29th August 1773, in Inverness, Johnson was in high spirits. Talk turns to Banks' description of 'an extraordinary animal called the kangaroo …'

The appearance, conformation, and habits of this quadruped were of the most singular kind; and in order to render his description more vivid and graphic, Johnson rose from his chair and volunteered an imitation of the animal. The company stared; and Mr Grant said nothing could be more ludicrous than the appearance of a tall, heavy, grave-looking man, like Dr Johnson, standing up to mimic the shape and motions of a kangaroo. He stood erect, put out his hands like feelers, and gathering up the tails of his huge brown coat so as to resemble the pouch of the animal, made two or three vigorous bounds across the room.

5. Songs

As with tales, the volume of surviving folk songs presents problems. I give only three examples. The first two are clearly related to the enigmatic 'Corpus Christi Carol'. The texts are from Greene, *Early English Carols* (1935), who prints two further versions. No. xi, like most of the others,

---

16   The kangaroo was discovered in 1700 (Cook's voyage to Australia in the *Endeavour*).

17   See [Johnson] *To the Hebrides*, ed. Ronald Black, note 236 (to p. 106) on p. 485.

is clearly 'religious', with the strange details becoming signs of Christ's coming birth. No. xii, however, which seems to preserve an echo of the 'falcon' burden of the old poem (is it too fanciful to suggest that its 'heron' may derive from 'erne' or 'eren', eagle?), and it is not overtly religious, suggesting perhaps a wounded knight and his lover — a pattern which may (according to one theory) lie behind The Corpus Christi carol. Readers will probably have their own views.

xi) from *Early English Carols*: 322 C, Derbyshire, nineteenth century

Down in yon forest there stands a hall,
The bells of Paradise I heard them ring,
It's covered all over with purple and pall,
And I love my Lord Jesus above any thing.
In that hall there stands a bed,
It's covered all over with scarlet so red.
At the bed-side there lies a stone,
Which the sweet Virgin Mary knelt upon.
Under that bed there runs a flood,
The one half runs water, the other runs blood.
At the bed's foot there grows a thorn,
Which ever blows blossom since he was born.
Over that bed the moon shines bright,
Denoting our Saviour was born this night.

xii) and *Early English Carols*: 322 D, Scotland, nineteenth century

The heron flew east, the heron flew west,
The heron flew to the fair forest;
She flew o'er streams and meadows green,
And a' to see what could be seen;
And when she saw the faithful pair,
Her breast grew sick, her head grew sair;
For there she saw a lovely bower,
Was a' clad o'er wi' lilly-flower;
And in the bower there was a bed

With silken sheets, and weel down spread:
And in the bed there lay a knight,
Whose wounds did bleed both day and night;
And by the bed there stood a stane,
And there was set a leal maiden.[18]
With silver needle and silken thread,
Stemming the wounds when they did bleed.

xiii) The Seven Virgins

Collected by Cecil Sharp [1903] and R. Vaughan Williams, but almost certainly much older (*The Oxford Book of Carols* suggests seventeenth century).[19] It is apparently based on an apocryphal legend of Mary going on a journey to see her son at Calvary. One of the late medieval Marian laments (in Carleton Brown's *Religious Lyrics of the Fifteenth Century*, 1939) with the refrain *filius Regis mortuus est* (The King's Son is dead), is given a somewhat similar narrative setting. A narrator ('as reson rywlyd my rechyles mynde By wayes & wyldernes as y hadde wente A solempne cite fortunyd me to finde') and meets a lamenting maid at the city's end — the king's son is dead. She gives vivid description of the death of her child, ending with her departure from Calvary weeping and wailing that she was born. Her final prayer, to have a sight of her son once before she dies, is given a sudden supernatural answer: a voice from heaven says 'Thu schalte se thi swete sone and say, *Filius Regis* is alive et *non mortuus est*' (which is better than the rather feeble ending of Leaves).

All under the leaves, and the leaves of life
    I met with virgins seven,
And one of them was Mary mild,
    Our Lord's Mother of heaven.
'O what are you seeking, you seven fair maids,
    All under the leaves of life?

---

18   Gray notes that the rhyme fails here, and suggests emending to 'a maid allane'. But there is no note in the edition about this line.

19   This is in *The Oxford Book of English Verse*, ed. Quiller-Couch, number 382, pp. 445–6 in the 1900–12 edition.

Come tell, come tell, what seek you
 All under the leaves of life?'
'We're seeking for no leaves, Thomas,
 But for a friend of thine;
We're seeking for sweet Jesus Christ,
 To be our guide and thine.'
'Go down, go down to yonder town,
 And sit in the gallery,[20]
And there you'll see sweet Jesus Christ
 Nailed to a big yew-tree.'
So down they went to yonder town
 As fast as foot could fall,
And many a grievous bitter tear
 From the virgins' eyes did fall.
'O peace, mother, O peace, mother,
 Your weeping doth me grieve:
I must suffer this,' He said,
 'For Adam and for Eve.
O mother, take you John Evangelist,
 All for to be your son,
And he will comfort you sometimes,
 Mother, as I have done.'
'O come, thou John Evangelist,
 Thou'rt welcome unto me;
But more welcome my own dear Son,
 Whom I nursed on my knee.'
Then He laid His head on His right shoulder,
 Seeing death it struck Him nigh:
'The Holy Ghost be with your soul,
 I die, mother dear, I die.'
O the rose, the gentle rose,
 And the fennel that grows so green!
God give us grace in every place,
 To pray for our king and queen.

---

20 Gray suggests that this is a confusion of the words 'Calvary' and 'Galilee'. One of the versions found online prints 'In the city of Galilee' for this line.

Furthermore for our enemies all
    Our prayers they should be strong:
Amen, good Lord, your charity
    Is the ending of my song.

6. Drama

Medieval popular drama is often alluded to, but complete examples are rarely found — in fact, a few early Robin Hood plays — apart from the lists of seasonal festivities given by usually disapproving moralists (which often seem to have lived on in folk tradition). We mainly have to rely on features in the written 'literary' plays which seem to have come from folk plays. Fortunately, these are not so rare: characters enter through the audience, and announce who they are, characters that are killed but then revived, a comic doctor with traditional patter, and so on. From the eighteenth century on, 'mummers' plays' are frequently found. It is far from certain that these are to be connected with the older popular drama. But the fact that they (and similar forms in Europe) seem to have been widespread may suggest a greater antiquity. The mummers' play now seems (on the printed page) a rudimentary form of drama, but dramatic moments can be found. In one interesting reference, in Hardy's *Return of the Native* (1878), when Eustacia Vye persuades the mummers' boy to let her play the part of the Turkish Knight in a Saint George play, the play was 'phlegmatically played and received' but ended with a solemn moment: 'they sang the plaintive chant which follows the play, during which all the dead men rise to their feet in a silent and awful manner'.

xiv) *Oxfordshire Saint George Play*[21]

[All the mummers come in singing, and walk round the place in a circle, and then stand on one side. Enter King Alfred and his Queen, arm in arm]
I am King Alfred, and this here is my bride.

---

21   Collected verbatim by Lee, see *Notes & Queries*, series 5 no ii, pp. 503–5, December 1874. The following is a very helpful and descriptive webpage: https://reginajeffers.blog/2017/07/20/oxfordshire-st-george-play/ See also Chapter X, The Mummers' Play, in Chambers, *The Mediaeval Stage*, vol i.

I've a crown on my pate and a sword by my side. [Stands apart]

[Enter King Cole]

I am King Cole, and I carry my stump.º   *wooden leg*

Hurrah for King Charles! Down with old Noll's
    Rump!º   *Cromwell's Rump Parliament*

[Enter King William]

I am King William of blessed me-mo-ry,

Who came and pulled down the high gallows-tree,

And brought us all peace and pros-pe-ri-ty. [Stands apart]

[Enter Giant Blunderbore]

I am Giant Blunderbore, fee, fi, fum!

Ready to fight ye all — so I says, 'Come!'

[Enter Little Jack, a small boy]

And this here is my little man Jack.

A thump on his rump, and a whack on his back! [Strikes him twice]

I'll fight King Alfred, I'll fight King Cole.

I'm ready to fight any mortal soul!

So here I, Blunderbore, takes my stand,

With this little devil, Jack, at my right hand.

Ready to fight for mortal life. Fee, fi, fum!

[The Giant and Little Jack stand apart. Enter Saint George, the leader of the dance]

I am Saint George of Merry Eng-land.

Bring in the mores-men, bring in our band.

[Morrismen come forward and dance to a tune from fife and drum. The dance being ended, Saint George continues]

These are our tricks — ho! Men, ho!

[Strikes the Dragon, who roars, and comes forward; the Dragon speaks]

Stand on head, stand on feet!

Meat, meat, meat for to eat!

[Tries to bite King Alfred]

I am the Dragon — here are my jaws!

I am the Dragon — here are my claws!

Meat, meat, meat for to eat!

Stand on my head, stand on my feet!

[Turns a summersault, and stands aside. All sing, several times repeated]

Ho! ho! ho!

Whack men so!

[Enter Old Dr Ball]

I am the Doctor, and I cure all ills,

Only gullup my portions,° and swallow my pills;   *potions*

I can cure the itch, the stitch, the pox, the palsy, and the gout,

All pains within, and all pains without.

Up from the floor, Giant Blunderbore!

[Gives him a pill, and he rises at once]

Get up, King! get up, Bride!

Get up, Fool! and stand aside.

[Gives them each a pill, and they rise]

Get up, King Cole, and tell the gentlefolks all

There never was a doctor like Mr Doctor Ball.

Get up, St George, old England's knight!

[Gives him a pill]

You have wounded the Dragon and finished the fight.

[All stand aside but the Dragon, who lies in convulsions on the floor]

Now kill the Dragon, and poison old Nick;

At Yule-tyde, both o' ye, cut your stick!

[The Doctor forces a large pill down the Dragon's throat, who thereupon roars, and dies in convulsions. Then enter Father Christmas]

I am Father Christmas! Hold, men. Hold!

[Addressing the audience]

Be there loaf in your locker, and sheep in your fold,

A fire on the hearth, and good luck for your lot,

Money in your pocket, and a pudding in the pot!

[He sings]

Hold, men, hold!

Put up your sticks;

End all your tricks;

Hold, men, hold!

[Chorus all sing, while one goes round with a hat for gifts]

Hold, men, hold!

We are very cold.

Inside and outside,

We are very cold.

If you don't give us silver,

Then give us gold

From the money in your pockets …

[Some of the performers show signs of fighting again]

Hold, men, hold! [etc]

[Song and chorus]

God A'mighty bless your hearth and fold,

Shut out the wolf, and keep out the cold!

You gev' us silver, keep you the gold.

For 'tis money in your pocket … Hold, men, hold!

[Repeat in chorus]

God A'mighty bless, &c.

[*Exeunt omnes*]

Bibliography[1]

Primary Texts

(Primary texts are listed alphabetically by title, unless the author is known. Cumbersome titles are alphabetized by key-word in square brackets.)

Adam of Cobsham: *The Wright's Chaste Wife*, ed. F. J. Furnivall, EETS OS 12 (London, 1865).

Andrew of Wyntoun, *Chronicle*, 6 vols, ed. F. J. Amours, Scottish Text Society (Edinburgh, 1903–14). https://digital.nls.uk/publications-by-scottish-clubs/archive/113606171

An Alphabet of Tales, ed. Mary Macleod Banks, EETS OS 126 & 127 (London, 1904–05).https://quod.lib.umich.edu/cgi/t/text/text-idx?c=cme;cc=cme;view=toc;idno=AlphTales

The Apocryphal New Testament, trans. M. R. James (1924; repr. Oxford, 1926). https://archive.org/details/JAMESApocryphalNewTestament1924/page/n3

Batman uppon Bartholome his booke, Stephen Batman, John Trevisa, Bartholomaeus Anglicus (London [1582]). https://quod.lib.umich.edu/cgi/t/text/text-idx?c=eebo;idno=A05237.0001.001

Bede, *Ecclesiastical History of the English People*, trans. Leo Sherley-Price, with R. E. Latham and D. H. Farmer (1955; repr. London, 1990). https://pilarr.com/download.php?q=ecclesiastical-history-of-the-english-people-bede-sherley-price-leo-farmer-d

---

1 Online versions of texts are included with each entry where they are available; online versions of primary texts are not always the same edition as the one listed as available in libraries, or the one consulted for this book, and are added for readers' convenience.

[Bevis] *The Gallant History of the Life and Death of that Most Noble Knight Bevis of Southampton* (London, [1691]). https://quod.lib.umich.edu/e/eebo2/A41900.0001.001?view=toc

The Book of Noodles: Stories of Simpletons, or, Fools and their Follies, ed. W. A. Clouston (London, 1888). https://www.gutenberg.org/files/13032/13032-h/13032-h.htm

The Brut, or The Chronicles of England, ed. Friedrich W. D. Brie, EETS OS 131 & 136 (London, 1906–08). https://archive.org/details/brutorchronicles00brieuoft/page/n5

Camden, *Miscellany*, vol. IV, ed. Clarence Hopper, Camden Society (London, 1859).

Caxton, William, *The subtyl historyes and fables of Esope* (London [1483]). https://www.bl.uk/collection-items/aesops-fables-printed-by-william-caxton-1484

Caxton, William, *The History of Reynard the Fox*, ed. N. F. Blake, EETS OS 263 (London, 1970). http://bestiary.ca/etexts/morley1889/morley%20-%20history%20of%20reynard%20the%20fox.pdf

Charles of Orleans: The English Poems, 2 vols, eds R. Steele and M. Day, EETS OS 215 & 220 (1941 & 1946). https://archive.org/details/fortunesstabilne00charuoft/page/430

Chaucer: *The Riverside Chaucer*, ed. Larry D. Benson, 3rd. edition (Oxford, 1988). https://www.worldcat.org/title/riverside-chaucer/oclc/570808369

[Chevelere Assigne] *The Romance of the Chevelere Assigne*, ed. Henry H. Gibbs, EETS ES 6 (1868; repr. London, 1898).

Child, Francis James, *The English and Scottish Popular Ballads*, 5 vols (Boston MA, 1898). http://www.gutenberg.org/ebooks/44969

Codex Ashmole 61: A Compilation of Popular Middle English Verse, ed. George Shuffelton (Kalamazoo, 2008). https://d.lib.rochester.edu/teams/text/shuffelton-codex-ashmole-61-introduction

The Complaynt of Scotland, ed. Robert Wedderburn with Introduction by A. M. Stewart (Edinburgh, 1979). https://quod.lib.umich.edu/e/eebo/A11722.0001.001?view=toc

Les Contes Moralisés de Nicole Bozon, frère mineur, eds Lucy Toulmin Smith and Paul Meyer (Paris, 1889). https://archive.org/details/lescontesmoralis00bozouoft/page/n5

The Croxton Play of the Sacrament, ed. John T. Sebastian (Kalamazoo, 2012). https://d.lib.rochester.edu/teams/text/sebastian-croxton-play-of-the-sacrament-introduction

The Demaundes Joyous, ed. John Wardroper (London, 1971).

[Dunbar] *Selected Poems of Henryson and Dunbar*, eds Priscilla Bawcutt and Felicity Riddy (Edinburgh, 1992). http://www.scottishpoetrylibrary.org.uk/poet/robert-henryson/

[Dunbar] *The Poems of William Dunbar*, ed. W. M. MacKenzie (Edinburgh, 1932). https://d.lib.rochester.edu/teams/text/conlee-dunbar-complete-works-introduction

Early English Carols, ed. Richard Leighton Greene (1935; revised edn. Oxford, 1977). https://archive.org/stream/in.ernet.dli.2015.185518/2015.185518.The-Early-English-Carols_djvu.txt

Early Middle English Verse and Prose, eds J. A. W. Bennett and G. V. Smithers, glossary by Norman Davis (revised edn. Oxford, 1985).

An English Chronicle of the Reigns of Richard II, Henry IV, Henry V, and Henry VI, ed. John Silvester Davies, Camden Society 64 (London, 1856). https://archive.org/stream/anenglishchronic00camduoft/anenglishchronic00camduoft_djvu.txt

An English Chronicle, 1377–1461, A New Edition, ed. William Marx (Woodbridge 2003). https://books.google.co.uk/books?id=QcXcLhJ8HVIC

English Lyrics of the XIIIth Century, ed. Carleton Brown (1932; repr. Oxford, 1950).

Erasmus, *Adages*, 6 vols, trans. Margaret Mann Phillips *et al.* (Toronto, 1982–). https://quod.lib.umich.edu/e/eebo/A00313.0001.001?view=toc

Fourteenth Century Verse and Prose, ed. Kenneth Sisam (1921; repr. Oxford, 1975). http://www.gutenberg.org/ebooks/43736

Froissart, *Chronicles*, trans. Geoffrey Brereton (1968; repr. Harmondsworth, 1987). https://archive.org/stream/chroniclesoffroi00froi/chroniclesoffroi00froi_djvu.txt

From the Norman Conquest to the Black Death: An Anthology of Writings from England, ed. Douglas Gray (Oxford, 2011). https://bookpdf.services/downloads/from_the_norman_conquest_to_the_black_death_an_anthology_of_writings_from_england.pdf

Gaimar, Geffrei, *L'Estoire des Engleis*, ed. Alexander Bell; ANTS 14–16 (Oxford, 1960).

Sir Gawain and the Green Knight, ed. J. A. Burrow (1972; repr. Harmondsworth, 1987).

Sir Gawain: Eleven Romances and Tales, ed. Thomas Hahn (Kalamazoo, 1995). https://d.lib.rochester.edu/teams/publication/hahn-sir-gawain

Geoffrey of Monmouth, *The History of the Kings of Britain*, trans. Lewis Thorpe (1966; repr. Harmondsworth, 1973).

Gervase of Tilbury, *Otia Imperialia: Recreation for an Emperor*, ed. and trans. S. E. Banks and J. W. Binns (Oxford, 2002).

Gesta Romanorum, ed. Sidney J. H. Herrtage, EETS ES 33 (1879, repr. Oxford, 1962). https://archive.org/details/earlyenglishver03herrgoog/page/n6

Gesta Romanorum, or Entertaining Moral Stories, ed. and trans. Charles Swan and Wynnard Hooper (1876; repr. New York, 1959). https://archive.org/details/gestaromanorum02hoopgoog/page/n10

Gilte Legende (4 vols), eds Richard Hamer and Vida Russell, EETS OS 315, 327, 328, 339 (Oxford, 2000–12).

Grimms' Fairy Tales (London, c. 1896 [n.d.]) https://www.worldoftales.com/fairy_tales/Grimm_fairy_tales.html

[Harley 2253] *The Complete Harley 2253 Manuscript*, 3 vols, ed. and trans. Susanna Fein, David Raybin, and Jan Ziolkowski (Kalamazoo, 2014–15). https://d.lib.rochester.edu/teams/publication/fein-harley2253-volume-1 https://d.lib.rochester.edu/teams/publication/fein-harley2253-volume-2 https://d.lib.rochester.edu/teams/publication/fein-harley2253-volume-3

Hazlitt, William Carew, *Remains of the popular poetry of England*, 4 vols (London, 1864–66). https://archive.org/details/remainsearlypop09hazlgoog

Henry of Huntingdon, *Chronicle*, ed. and trans. Thomas Forester (1853; repr. Felinfach, 1991). https://archive.org/details/chroniclehenryh00foregoog/page/n13

Historical Poems of the XIVth and XVth Centuries, ed. Rossell Hope Robbins (New York, 1959). https://babel.hathitrust.org/cgi/pt?id=mdp.39015027254047;view=1up;seq=5

A Hundred Merry Tales, and Other Jestbooks of the Fifteenth and Sixteenth Centuries, ed. P. M. Zall (Lincoln NE, 1963).

[Huon] *The Boke of Duke Huon of Burdeux* (2 vols), ed. S. L. Lee, EETS ES 40 & 41, 43 & 50; English Charlemagne Romances I–IV (1882–87, repr. London, 1998, 2017). https://archive.org/details/bokedukehuonbur00unkngoog/page/n8

Johannes de Irlandia, *The Meroure of Wyssdome*, 3 vols; eds Charles Macpherson, F. Quinn, and Craig McDonald (Aberdeen, 1926–90).

John Mirk's Festial, 2 vols, ed. Susan Powell, EETS OS 334 & 335 (Oxford, 2009–11).

[Johnson] *To the Hebrides*: *Samuel Johnson's Journey to the western islands of Scotland; and James Boswell's Journal of a tour to the Hebrides*, ed. Ronald Black (2007; repr. Edinburgh, 2011).

Julian of Norwich, *Revelations of Divine Love*, trans. Clifton Wolters (1966; repr. Harmondsworth, 1976). https://d.lib.rochester.edu/teams/text/the-shewings-of-julian-of-norwich-part-1

The Kingis Quair of James Stewart, ed. Matthew P. McDiarmid (London, 1973). https://d.lib.rochester.edu/teams/text/mooney-and-arn-kingis-quair-and-other-prison-poems-james-i-scotland-kingis-quair

'*The Knight of Curtesy and the Fair Lady of Faguell*', ed. Elizabeth McCausland, *Smith College Studies in Modern Languages* IV.I (1922), 1–19. https://archive.org/stream/TheKnightOfCurtesyAndTheFairLadyMcCaus/The_Knight_of_Curtesy_and_the_Fair_Lady_McCaus_djvu.txt

Langland, William, *The Vision of Piers Plowman* (A Complete Edition of the B-Text), ed. A. V. C. Schmidt (1978; repr. London, 1993). http://ota.ox.ac.uk/desc/3261

Liber Eliensis: A History of the Isle of Ely from the seventh century to the twelfth, trans. Janet Fairweather (Woodbridge, 2005).

[Mannyng] *Chronicles of Robert of Brunne*, 2 vols, ed. Frederick J. Furnival, Rolls Series 87 (London, 1887).

Map, Walter, *De Nugis Curialium*, trans. Montagu R. James (London, 1923).

[Margery] *The Book of Margery Kempe*, eds Sanford B. Meech, Hope Emily Allen, and W. Butler-Bowdon, EETS OS 212 (1940). https://d.lib.rochester.edu/teams/text/staley-book-of-margery-kempe-introduction

Marie de France, *Lais*, ed. Alfred Ewert, with Glyn S. Burgess (1944, repr. London 1995).

Mary of Nemmegen, eds Margaret M. Raftery, John Norton-Smith, Douglas Gray (Leiden, 1991).

Medieval Comic Tales, ed. Derek Brewer (1996; 2nd edn. Woodbridge, 2008).

Medieval English Lyrics, ed. R. T. Davies (1963; repr. Oxford, 1978).

Medieval English Lyrics, ed. Theodore Silverstein (York, 1971).

Medieval English Political Writings, ed. James M. Dean (Kalamazoo, 1996). https://d.lib.rochester.edu/teams/publication/dean-medieval-english-political-writings

Medieval Lyric: Middle English Lyrics, Ballads, and Carols, ed. John D. Hirsh (Oxford, 2005). https://onlinelibrary.wiley.com/doi/book/10.1002/9780470756164

Middle English Verse Romances, ed. Donald B. Sands (Exeter, 1993). https://www.middleenglishromance.org.uk/

The Middle Scots Poets, ed. A. M. Kinghorn (London, 1970).

The moral play of Wit and Science (by J. Redford) and early poetical miscellanies, ed. J. O. Halliwell (London, 1848). https://archive.org/details/moralplaywitand00librgoog/page/n3

The New Oxford Book of English Verse, ed. Helen Gardner (1972; repr. Oxford, 1973).

Nixon's Original Cheshire Prophecy, in Doggrel Verse, Robert Nixon (Otley, 1801). https://archive.org/details/nixonscheshirepr00nixo/page/n17

The N-Town Plays, eds Douglas Sugano and Victor I. Scherb (Kalamazoo, 2007). https://d.lib.rochester.edu/teams/publication/sugano-the-n-town-plays

Ovid, *Metamorphoses* (2 vols), trans. F. J. Miller, Loeb Classical Library (vol. 1, 1916; 2nd edn. London, 1960).

The Owl and the Nightingale, ed. Eric Gerald Stanley (Manchester, 1972). https://archive.org/details/owlandnightinga00guilgoog/page/n14

The Oxford Book of English Verse, ed. Arthur Quiller-Couch (Oxford, 1900). https://www.bartleby.com/101/138.html

The Oxford Book of Late Medieval Verse and Prose, ed. Douglas Gray (Oxford, 1988). https://archive.org/details/oxfordbookoflate00doug

The Oxford Book of Medieval English Verse, eds Celia and Kenneth Sisam (1970; repr. Oxford, 1973).

'Oxfordshire Christmas Miracle Play', Frederick George Lee, *Notes & Queries* series 5 no. ii (December 1874), 503–5.

Paston Letters and Papers of the Fifteenth Century, vol. I, ed. Norman Davis, EETS SS 20 (London 2004). https://quod.lib.umich.edu/c/cme/paston

[*PFMS*] *Bishop Percy's Folio Manuscript, Ballads and Romances*, 3 vols, eds John W. Hales and Frederick J. Furnivall (London 1867–68). https://archive.org/details/bishoppercysfol00halegoog/page/n8

[*PFMS*] *Bishop Percy's Folio MS* (Cambridge: Chadwyck-Healey, 1992).

[Physiologus] *The Middle English Physiologus*, ed. Hanneke Wirtjes, EETS OS 299 (1991).

The Political Songs of England, Thomas Wright, Camden Society 6 (London, 1839). https://archive.org/details/politicalsongsof00wrig/page/n7

[Rauf] *The Taill of Rauf Coilyear*, ed. Sidney J. H. Herrtage; English Charlemagne Romances pt. 6, EETS ES 39 (1882). https://d.lib.rochester.edu/teams/text/lupack-three-middle-english-charlemagne-romances-tale-of-ralph-collier

[Rawlinson] *The Songs of Rawlinson MS. C 813* (Bodleian Library), eds F. M. Padelford and A. R. Benham (Seattle, 1909). https://babel.hathitrust.org/cgi/pt?id=mdp.39015036702671;view=1up;seq=3

Reliquiae Antiquae, 2 vols, Wright, Thomas and James Orchard Halliwell-Phillipps (London, 1841–43). https://archive.org/details/reliquiaeantiqua01wriguoft/page/n7

[Richard Hill] *Songs, Carols, and Other Miscellaneous Poems, from the Balliol MS 354, Richard Hill's Commonplace-Book*, ed. Roman Dyboski, EETS ES 101 (1907).

Ritson, Joseph, *Pieces of ancient popular poetry* (London, 1791). https://archive.org/details/piecesofancientp00ritsuoft/page/n5

Robin Hood and Other Outlaw Tales, eds Stephen Knight and Thomas Ohlgren (Kalamazoo, 1997). https://d.lib.rochester.edu/teams/publication/knight-and-ohlgren-robin-hood-and-other-outlaw-tales

The Romance of Reynard the Fox, trans. D. D. R. Owen (Oxford, 1994).

Rymes of Robyn Hood: *An Introduction to the English Outlaw*, R. B. Dobson and J. Taylor (London, 1976).

Secular Lyrics of the XIVth and XVth Centuries, ed. Rossell Hope Robbins (1955; repr. Oxford, 1968). https://d.lib.rochester.edu/teams/text/salisbury-trials-and-joys-secular-lyrics

A Selection of Religious Lyrics, ed. Douglas Gray (Oxford, 1975).

Selections from Early Middle English 1130–1250 (2 vols), ed. Joseph Hall (1920; repr. Oxford, 1970). http://www.gutenberg.org/ebooks/26413 http://www.gutenberg.org/ebooks/43555

Seven Sages of Rome (*Midland Version*), ed. Jill Whitelock, EETS OS 324 (Oxford, 2005).

Six Middle English Romances, ed. Maldwyn Mills (London, 1992).

[Solomon] *The Dialogue of Salomon and Saturnus*: *With an Historical Introduction*, John Mitchell Kemble (London, 1848). https://archive.org/details/dialogueofsalomo00kembuoft/page/n3

[Solomon] *The Dialogue of Solomon and Marcolf*: *A dual-language edition from Latin and Middle English printed editions*, eds Nancy Mason Bradbury and Scott Bradbury (Kalamazoo, 2012). https://d.lib.rochester.edu/teams/text/bradbury-solomon-and-marcolf-intro

Ten Bourdes, ed. Melissa M. Furrow (Kalamazoo, 2013). https://d.lib.rochester.edu/teams/publication/furrow-ten-bourdes

Ten Fifteenth-Century Comic Poems, ed. Melissa M. Furrow (New York, 1985).

A Thomas More Source Book, eds Gerard B. Wegemer and Stephen W. Smith (Washington DC, 2004).

[Thomas] *The Romance and Prophecies of Thomas of Erceldoune*, ed. James A. H. Murray, EETS OS 61 (1875). https://archive.org/details/romanceprophecie00thomuoft/page/n5

The Towneley Plays, eds G. England and A. W. Pollard, EETS ES 71 (1897; repr. New York, 1973). https://archive.org/details/townleyplays00engluoft/page/n5

Three Late Medieval Morality Plays, ed. G. A. Lester (1981; repr. London, 1997).

Two Coventry Corpus Christi Plays, ed. Hardin Craig, EETS ES 87 (1902; repr. 1966). https://archive.org/details/twocoventrycorp00craigoog/page/n8

Two English Border Ballads: *The Battle of Otterburn and The Hunting of the Cheviot*, ed. Olof Arngart (Lund, 1973).

Two Tudor Interludes: *the Interlude of Youth, Hick Scorner*, ed. Ian Lancashire (Manchester, 1980); *Youth* is also available online via internetshakespeare (ed. John D. Cox).

William of Malmesbury, *The Kings Before the Norman Conquest*, trans. Joseph Stephenson (1854; repr. Lampeter, 1989).

William of Palerne, ed. Walter W. Skeat, EETS ES 1 (London, 1867). https://archive. org/details/romancewilliamp01skeagoog/page/n8

Women's Writing in Middle English: An Annotated Anthology, ed. Alexandra Barratt (1992; 2nd edn. Harlow, 2010).

Wyatt, Sir Thomas, *The Poetical Works*, ed. Charles Cowden Clarke (Edinburgh, 1868). https://www.poetryfoundation.org/poems/45586/of-the-mean-and-sure-estate

Secondary Texts

(Some well-known reference works are listed by title.)

Baugh, A. C., 'Improvisation in the Middle English Romance', *Proceedings of the American Philosophical Society* 103.3 (June 1959), 418–54. https://www.jstor. org/stable/985475?seq=1#page_scan_tab_contents

Bennett, H. S., *The Pastons and their England, Studies in an Age of Transition* (1922; repr. Cambridge, 1975). https://archive.org/details/pastonstheirengl00 bennrich/page/n5

Bennett, J. A. W., edited and completed by Douglas Gray, *Middle English Literature* (1986; repr. Oxford, 1990).

Bliss, Jane, *Naming and Namelessness in Medieval Romance* (Cambridge, 2008).

Boklund-Lagopoulou, Karin, '*I have a yong suster*': *popular song and the Middle English lyric* (Dublin, 2002).

Burke, Peter, *Popular Culture in Early Modern Europe* (Aldershot, rev. reprint 1994). https://www.academia.edu/5649330/Peter_Burke_and_popular_culture_ in_early_modern_europe

Cawthorne, Nigel, *A Brief History of Robin Hood* (London, 2010).

Chambers, E. K., *The Mediaeval Stage*, 2 vols (Oxford, 1903). https://archive.org/ details/mediaevalstagevo030649mbp/page/n7   https://archive.org/details/ mediaevalstagevo030639mbp/page/n5

Chambers, R. W., 'The Lost Literature of Medieval England', *The Library*, Fourth Series vol. V no 4 (March 1925), 293–321.

Cooper, Helen, *The English Romance in Time: Transforming Motifs from Geoffrey of Monmouth to the Death of Shakespeare* (Oxford, 2004).

Cooper, Helen, and Sally Mapstone eds, *The Long Fifteenth Century: Essays for Douglas Gray*, (Oxford, 1997).

Davies, Norman, *The Isles: A History* (1999; repr. London, 2000).

Dictionary of Medieval Heroes, Willem P. Gerritsen and Anthony G. van Melle, trans. Tanis Guest (Woodbridge, 2000).

Flood, Victoria, *Prophecy, Politics and Place in Medieval England: from Geoffrey of Monmouth to Thomas of Erceldoune* (Cambridge, 2016).

Gerould, Gordon Hall, *The Ballad of Tradition* (Oxford, 1932). https://archive.org/details/balladoftraditio007247mbp/page/n7

Gray, Douglas, *Later Medieval English Literature* (Oxford, 2008).

Gray, Douglas, 'A Middle English Epitaph', *Notes & Queries* n.s. 8 [206] (1961), 132–5.

Gray, Douglas, *Robert Henryson* (Leiden, 1979).

Gray, Douglas, *Simple Forms*: *Essays on Medieval English Popular Literature* (Oxford, 2015).

Green, V. H. H., *Bishop Reginald Pecock*: *A Study in Ecclesiastical History and Thought* (Cambridge, 2014).

Huizinga, Johan, *Homo Ludens*: *A Study of the Play-Element in Culture* (1949; repr. London, 1980).

The Index of Middle English Verse, Carleton Brown (New York, 1943). See also *NIMEV*, and the digital version *DIMEV*. https://archive.org/details/middleeng00brow/page/n5

King, Pamela, 'Manuscripts, Antiquarians, Editors, and Critics: The Historiography of Reception', ch. 16 in *The Routledge Research Companion to Early Drama and Performance*, ed. Pamela King (London, 2016). https://www.taylorfrancis.com/books/e/9781317043669/chapters/10.4324%2F9781315612898-7

Kittredge, George Lyman, 'Sir Orfeo', *The American Journal of Philology* 7 (1886), 176–202. https://archive.org/details/jstor-287332/page/n1

Mawer, Allen, '*La Folie* in Place-names', *Romania* 247 (1936), 378–85. https://www.persee.fr/doc/roma_0035-8029_1936_num_62_247_3806

Neuberg, Victor E., *Popular literature*: *a history and guide* (London, 1977).

Oliver, Raymond, *Poems Without Names*: *The English Lyric 1200–1500* (Berkeley, 1970).

Orme, Nicholas, *Fleas, Flies, and Friars*: *Children's Poetry from the Middle Ages* (Exeter, 2011).

Owst, G. R., *Literature and Pulpit in Medieval England* (1933; revised edn. Oxford, 1961).

The Oxford Concise Companion to Classical Literature (*OCCL*), eds M. C. Howatson and Ian Chilvers (1993; repr. Oxford, 1996). https://archive.org/stream/oxfordcompaniont030316mbp/oxfordcompaniont030316mbp_djvu.txt

Oxford Dictionary of Saints, David Hugh Farmer (3rd edn. Oxford, 1992).

Sponsler, Claire, *Ritual Imports*: *Performing Medieval Drama in America* (Ithaka NY, 2004).

Stewart, Alan, *Philip Sidney: A Double Life* (London, 2000).

Westwood, Jennifer, and Jacqueline Simpson, eds, *The Lore of the Land: A Guide to England's Legends, from Spring-Heeled Jack to the Witches of Warboys* (London, 2005).

Whiting, Bartlett Jere (with Helen Westcott Whiting), *Proverbs, Sentences, and Proverbial Phrases from English writings mainly before 1500* (Cambridge MA, 1968).

Wilson, R. M., *The Lost Literature of Medieval England* (London, 1952).

Wilson, R. M., 'More Lost Literature of Medieval England', *Leeds Studies in English* 5 (1936), 1–49.

This book need not end here...

At Open Book Publishers, we are changing the nature of the traditional academic book. The title you have just read will not be left on a library shelf, but will be accessed online by hundreds of readers each month across the globe. OBP publishes only the best academic work: each title passes through a rigorous peer-review process. We make all our books free to read online so that students, researchers and members of the public who can't afford a printed edition will have access to the same ideas.

This book and additional content is available at:
https://doi.org/10.11647/OBP.0170

Customise

Personalise your copy of this book or design new books using OBP and third-party material. Take chapters or whole books from our published list and make a special edition, a new anthology or an illuminating coursepack. Each customised edition will be produced as a paperback and a downloadable PDF. Find out more at:
https://www.openbookpublishers.com/section/59/1

Donate

If you enjoyed this book, and believe that research like this should be available to all readers, regardless of their income, please become a member of OBP and support our work with a monthly pledge — it only takes a couple of clicks! We do not operate for profit so your donation will contribute directly to the creation of new Open Access publications like this one.
https://www.openbookpublishers.com/supportus

Like Open Book Publishers

Follow @OpenBookPublish

Read more at the Open Book Publishers **BLOG**

You may also be interested in:

The Anglo-Scottish Ballad and its Imaginary Contexts

David Atkinson

https://doi.org/10.11647/OBP.0041

An Anglo-Norman Reader

Jane Bliss

https://doi.org/10.11647/OBP.0110

Piety in Pieces

How Medieval Readers Customized their Manuscripts
Kathryn M. Rudy

https://doi.org/10.11647/OBP.0094